Leslie

Summary Tables:
12.3/12.4.

INFRASTRUCTURE
pp. 273-278
   74-81
Also chs. 4-11 (parts)
Appendix

Firm →
→ DC → (D)

PLACE TO SPACE

PLACE TO SPACE

Migrating to eBusiness Models

Peter Weill

Michael R. Vitale

HARVARD BUSINESS SCHOOL PRESS
BOSTON, MASSACHUSETTS

Copyright 2001 Harvard Business School Publishing Corporation

All rights reserved

Printed in the United States of America

05 04 03 02 01   5 4 3 2 1

Library of Congress Cataloging-in-Publication Data
Weill, Peter.
  Place to Space / Peter Weill, Michael R. Vitale.
    p. cm.
  Includes bibliographical references and index.
  ISBN 1-57851-245-X (alk. paper)
  1. Electronic commerce. I. Vitale, Michael. II. Title.
HF5548.32.W45 2001

658.8'4--dc21

00-053946

The paper used in this publication meets the requirements of the American National Standard for Permanence of Paper for Publications and Documents in Libraries and Archives Z39.48-1992.

*To our fathers,
smiling down at us*

Contents

		PREFACE AND ACKNOWLEDGMENTS	ix
CHAPTER	1	The E-Business Revolution	1
CHAPTER	2	E-Business Model Schematics	29
CHAPTER	3	Atomic E-Business Models and Initiatives	55
CHAPTER	4	Direct to Customer	87
CHAPTER	5	Full-Service Provider	111
CHAPTER	6	Whole of Enterprise	129
CHAPTER	7	Portals, Agents, Auctions, Aggregators, and Other Intermediaries	151
CHAPTER	8	Shared Infrastructure	183
CHAPTER	9	Virtual Community	203
CHAPTER	10	Value Net Integrator	221
CHAPTER	11	Content Provider	237
CHAPTER	12	Combining Atomic Business Models into Initiatives	257
CHAPTER	13	Choosing and Implementing an E-Business Initiative	291
		APPENDIX: IT INFRASTRUCTURE SERVICES FOR E-BUSINESS	321
		NOTES	333
		INDEX	355
		ABOUT THE AUTHORS	371

Preface and Acknowledgments

THIS BOOK FOCUSES on the key challenges facing leaders of successful established businesses migrating from their traditional marketplace business models to a combination of place and space. The rise and partial fall of the dot-com has provided a strong wake-up call to senior managers of firms all across the "old economy." These traditional firms will do much of the really hard work and make most of the profits in this revolution by migrating from place to space.[1] This migration will require executives in successful place-based firms to stop, take stock, and then lead their firms in new and often unfamiliar and uncomfortable directions. Senior managers feel the pressure to migrate from all sides—from investors, stock market analysts, employees, customers, suppliers, and new and traditional competitors. To many senior managers, this e-revolution seems like chaos—but a chaos requiring swift and decisive action. Many senior managers feel ill-equipped to confidently set new directions for their firms.

Place to Space strives to bring some order to this chaos by providing a structured approach to understanding and implementing e-business models. E-business models are being developed by pioneering firms doing business electronically today. In this process some radical new business models have emerged, including value net integrator, electronic auction, virtual community, and vortal. At the same time, some traditional business models, such as the direct-to-customer connection and full-service relationship, are undergoing radical change, taking advantage of the newly ubiquitous electronic infrastructure. We have identified a small group of atomic e-business models that can be used as building blocks for an e-business initiative. Some combinations of atomic business models are compatible and create powerful value propositions to customers. Other atomic business models are less compatible, and combining them can lead to problems such as channel conflict and competency conflict. By understanding the characteristics of each atomic model, managers can use these building blocks to compose, and decompose, e-business initiatives in firms.

To assist this migration we also provide a new charting tool to analyze electronic commerce business models. Case studies of traditional firms moving to electronic commerce are presented, illustrating the atomic models framework and the charting technique. The book is based on several years of conceptual research and fieldwork with traditional firms, classifying scores of e-business initiatives into the atomic model framework. The results from a detailed study of fifty e-business initiatives in traditional firms are used in the book to determine the synergies and conflicts between atomic models and to identify the most important information technology (IT) infrastructure services for each atomic model.

E-business is an idea whose time has come. We have both spent our entire professional lives trying to help firms gain business value from IT—whether teaching in the M.B.A. classroom, conducting research, writing, leading executive education programs, managing IT groups, or facilitating strategic planning sessions. It has been exciting, challenging, and often humbling work, and we have learned many hard lessons in the process. We have seen a number of sea changes in the use of IT, from the early days of attempting to gain competitive advantage from IT, to the Internet and the exciting e-business opportunities it presents.

The year 2000 (Y2K) "bug" and e-business have placed the issues of IT-enabled strategy and the required investment in capabilities and infrastructure on the boardroom tables of large firms around the world—perhaps for the first time. These two events neatly sum up the ambiguous role of IT in firms. On the one hand the Y2K problem was a blight on the IT industry, costing billions of dollars to repair. On the other hand, e-business epitomizes much of the best IT offers—innovative ways of doing business, often at lower cost and with added value for the customer. This book focuses on the strategic issues of e-business.

Who Should Read *Place to Space*

This book is for all senior managers charged with leading their firms from place to space. We hope senior management, including financial, strategic, marketing, and IT executives, will find this book thought-provoking and useful. Our aim is to provide a framework for discussion and dialogue supported by detailed case studies and empirical data from firms implementing e-business models. We have found the atomic e-business model framework and the e-business model schematics useful communications and analysis tools in dealing with the many opportunities enabled by e-business. To deal with the fast pace of e-business change we have included in the book detailed data analysis and speculations in almost equal weighting. People in the following roles have found the ideas useful:

- Senior managers leading firms from place to space

- Executive teams managing e-business initiatives

- Marketing managers required to understand the value propositions, segments, and channels for an e-business initiative

- IT managers charged with helping business managers understand the potential of e-business and develop e-business models

- IT managers charged with specifying and providing the IT infrastructure necessary to implement e-business initiatives

- Consultants assisting firms with strategizing about, and implementing, e-business initiatives

- Vendors and IT service providers working with firms to provide IT platforms and capabilities to implement their e-business initiatives

How the Book Is Structured

Place to Space has thirteen chapters and an appendix. Chapters 1 to 3 introduce the concepts of e-business, the atomic business models and initiatives framework, and the e-business model schematics. Each of chapters 4 to 11 describes a different atomic e-business model in detail, providing examples, e-business model schematics, and a discussion of the critical success factors, core competencies, channels, customer segments, required IT infrastructures, and the ownership of the three critical customer assets: data, relationship, and transaction. Chapter 12 summarizes all of the atomic models and addresses the issue of combining atomic models into initiatives. Finally, chapter 13 begins with a diagnostic to determine the level of threat or opportunity a firm faces and concludes with the top ten e-business leadership principles for senior management. The appendix provides detailed data of our study of fifty e-business initiatives. Detailed case studies illustrate the issues from the perspective of a firm migrating from place to space.

For convenience we use the word *firm* throughout the book to refer to any business enterprise. However, our comments relate equally to all enterprises, whether large, small, for profit, not for profit, or government. Our intention is to capture the e-business imagination of all managers in all industries.

Whom We Would Like to Thank

Many people have contributed to the ideas, case studies, empirical data, and representation of the materials in the book. First, we would like to thank and acknowledge the many senior executives we worked with, interviewed, and refined our ideas with—particularly the CEO of Lonely Planet, Steve Hibbard. The companies who participated in the study of fifty e-business initiatives are listed in the appendix. We thank them for finding the time to work with us and providing detailed answers to our questions—and sharing their insights along with many more questions! A number of people have provided insightful ideas and valuable feedback on the work including: Professor Detmar Straub at Georgia State University, Professor Cynthia Beath at University of Texas at Austin, Don St. Clair at AT Kearney, Dr. Marianne Broadbent at Gartner Group, Professor Richard Speed at the Melbourne Business School, Chris Kinsey at PricewaterhouseCoopers, Dr. Richard Tait at ANZ Bank, Dr. Margrethe Olson at Lend Lease, Susan Keyes-Pearce at Ansett, Professors Erik Brynjolfsson and Tom Malone at MIT, Tony Walter and Andrew Brand at Hewlett-Packard, and Jeff Paton at Microsoft. We particularly want to thank and acknowledge John Sviokla and Jeff Rayport for their pioneering work on marketplace and marketspace that inspired the name of this book. John Sviokla, now a partner at Diamond Cluster International, Inc., contributed to this book in many ways and we are grateful for his insights and friendship. Finally, we would like to thank Accenture (formerly Andersen Consulting) and PricewaterhouseCoopers for their ongoing support of electronic commerce research.

Andrew Brand and Peter Raisbeck, both then researchers at the Melbourne Business School, contributed in many different ways. Peter helped collect and analyze the empirical data of the fifty e-business initiatives. Andrew conducted detailed research and analyses of scores of interesting e-business models around the world, compiling comparative tables and writing descriptions. We thank them both.

We were both very fortunate to work with Debi Chetcuti at the Melbourne Business School. Debi took the concept of administrative support to a new level, contributing to this book in so many ways: data analysis and entry, proofreading and sense making, formatting and design, ensuring accuracy of the notes and diagrams, preparing educational materials, and momentous scheduling and deadline management. Above all Debi is a real colleague who was a pleasure to work with; we wish you every success in your new career and we miss you. Sue Lane joined the Melbourne Business School just in time to do the final edits of the book. Sue did a marvelous job of improving every diagram in the book as well as final formatting, collation, and keeping us on track, and we thank you.

We conducted the research and wrote the bulk of this book while we were professors at the Melbourne Business School. The Melbourne Business School (MBS) is an outstanding school and our colleagues provided a wonderfully supportive environment in which to work. We thank them all for their interest, contributions, and good humor, and most of all for creating an environment supporting scholarship and inquiry.

We hope the M.B.A. graduates from the Melbourne Business School feel a sense of ownership in this book. The many M.B.A. students who participated in the "electronic commerce" subject all contributed their insights and energy. Their discussion, projects, experience, and curiosity helped create and refine this material. But most important was their willingness to consider this the "outward bound" of M.B.A. subjects, roll up their sleeves, and work together to deal with the uncertainty and endless fascination of this emerging topic; it made this book possible. At the end of many classes, walking back to our offices we wondered who was really doing the teaching. We were certainly all learning.

We would like to thank and acknowledge Kirsten Sandberg, Jill Connor, and their colleagues at Harvard Business School Press for their support and many contributions to the book. Kirsten improved the work in many ways, from focusing us on the big ideas to effectively describing and representing them. Kirsten championed the ideas of this book from the outset. Jill helped us focus on the important words and figures, and to cut the rest.

For us, working together on this book has been a by-product of a close friendship that crosses both professional and personal realms and began when Peter was a doctoral student at New York University and Mike was at Harvard. Working together has brought about several research projects and papers, a number of case studies, many new executive education programs, and now this book. Although we are different in many ways, we work together as efficiently and effectively as in any partnership we have ever experienced. Maintaining good humor and positive outlook while both of us were changing jobs and cities just as the book neared completion could not have been possible without the support of our families.

A Personal Note from Peter

This has been a tumultuous year in many ways. I want to dedicate this book to my father; I hope he would have enjoyed it. Moving countries is quite an adventure and the new challenges and opportunities are very exciting. I want to thank all my colleagues at the MIT Sloan School for making me feel welcome in my new role, particularly Dean Don Lessard and Professor Wanda Orlikowski, the head of the IT group at Sloan. Wanda has been a long-standing colleague and friend and provided support, encouragement, and insight through good times and bad. Sloan has provided a wonderful environment to complete the book and I look forward to many more interesting projects. I would like to acknowledge and thank Professor Jack Rockart, who established the Center for Information Systems Research (CISR) twenty-five years ago at Sloan and led the way for us all. Thanks also to all the CISR family, Dr. Jeanne Ross, Chris Foglia, Dr. Chuck Gibson, Julie Coiro, David Fitzgerald III, and Deb Small for creating a wonderful working environment and being the best at what you do.

My wife Margi has been both my biggest supporter and critic. It was Margi who encouraged me in 1995 to give my inaugural professorial chair address on a risky and uncertain topic—electronic commerce—and then to develop executive and M.B.A. courses. Margi gives purpose to it all and never stops encouraging, challenging, and supporting. She is the perfect mate as well as a ferocious wielder of the red pen. Finally, I would like to thank my mother for her love and wonderful support.

A Personal Note from Mike

Moving to Australia in 1995 was the fulfillment of a long-held dream to live and work in this strong and challenging country. The reality has been even better than the dream. Among the many remarkable things that happened as a result of the move to Australia was that I met, and subsequently married, Susan Keyes-Pearce. Susan and her two sons, Robin and Simon, have accepted me as part of their family and helped me to understand the nuances of Australian culture. Susan's background in information systems led, perhaps not altogether voluntarily, to her active collaboration with me in the creation of this book. Spending Sunday afternoons together in my office working on yet another draft was not part of our marriage vows, but Susan accepted this with unfailing patience and good grace. It is a rare thing to combine personal attraction and professional regard in the same relationship, and I am grateful every day to have found this with Susan.

I would also like to thank the many managers and colleagues in Australia, America, and Singapore who have shared with me the details of their own e-business journeys and their insights into the broader issues of e-business. Any attempt at listing them all by name would risk inadvertent offense by omission, but I would like to acknowledge in particular Linda Nicholls at Australia Post, Michael Coomer at National Australia Bank, Jeanne Ross at MIT, David Feeny at Templeton College Oxford University, and Rod Laird at Accenture for their insightful, incisive, and thought-provoking comments.

PLACE TO SPACE

CHAPTER I

The E-Business Revolution

AN E-BUSINESS revolution is taking place today. Much of the focus by the media, Wall Street, and business authors has been on radical new business models being simultaneously developed and market tested by highly publicized start-up firms. However, existing businesses will do much of the really hard work and make most of the profits in this revolution. E-business will require existing businesses to migrate from *place* to *space*. Not all parts of the business will migrate—some will stay behind, continuing to make profits in the "Old World" and funding the "New World" initiatives. This migration includes making challenging leadership decisions about which e-business models will succeed and how they will integrate with current channels to the customer. Many of the assets (e.g., brand, cash, relationships, market share) of successful place-based businesses will serve equally well in space, but some liabilities are painfully apparent (e.g., lack of e-savvy leadership, corporate cultures resistant to change, reward systems incompatible with e-business, potential channel conflict, nonintegrated information technology infrastructures). This book focuses on the key challenges facing successful established businesses migrating from their traditional marketplace business models to a combination of place and space.

Hard Decisions

The look was unmistakable, combining fear, greed, and power under threat. The look appeared on the face of the chief operating officer (COO) of a large bank as we neared the end of a three-day facilitation with thirty senior managers to determine the bank's retail e-business model for the next three years. The group included both young executives, who had typically been with the bank for less than five years, and a handful of senior bank officers, including the COO and the head of retail banking. The group had recently returned from a daylong breakout session, where small groups created their vision of the future e-business model. The first group had just presented a compelling and visionary description of a *full-service provider* business model (see chapter 5) for the financial services industry. In this model the bank owns the relationship with the customer and knows more about that customer than any other player in the financial services industry. Via customers' personalized Web pages, the bank offers a full range of financial services including both the bank's own products and a wide range of products provided by other firms, including insurance, stock trading, mutual funds, financial advice, and funds management. The bank captures and keeps customer information and transaction histories in a central database used to identify product and service offerings relevant to individual customer segments. When a customer need is identified, the bank offers the customer a range of prescreened products from approved providers via a personal banker or personal Web pages.

The group brought its proposed e-business model to life with an example. A couple applying for a mortgage from the bank is offered insurance from three competing providers. The details of the three policies are compared in a table on the couple's personal bank Web page, which includes independent third-party rating agency assessments of each policy's attributes. The couple chooses an insurance policy from Delta Mutual and electronically reads and authorizes the insurance application form. Delta issues the insurance application automatically, since the couple's Web site is populated with only preapproved policies. Even though the couple chooses and clicks on Delta Mutual in the table, they complete the insurance application while still remaining within the bank's Web site. Most of the data fields in the Delta Mutual form were completed automatically from the bank's database, requiring the couple only to check and authorize the details. On completion of the application process, the couple's personal page on the bank's Web site summarizes their total financial relationship with the bank, including the new insurance policy, their investment portfolio categorized by asset class, cash position, and stock watch list.

In this business model, the bank owns the *relationship* with the customer as well as the *data* and the *transaction* related to their mortgage. The bank facilitates and then records details of the transaction to select and purchase an insurance policy. The bank stores data about this transaction and all other transactions made by the couple in the bank database, increasing the level of customer intimacy. The Delta Mutual insurance company owns the insurance transaction with the couple and the data relating only to that transaction. The insurance company does not own the relationship with the couple, and the bank provided only the minimum data necessary to complete the transaction, thus preserving the bank's ownership of the customer relationship.

Spontaneous applause erupted at the end of the presentation, followed by a highly animated discussion and question session. The small group had already thought of many of the issues raised, but some additional challenges were identified and solved by the executives, who grew increasingly excited by the business model. At this point the COO stood up and we saw "the look." The COO praised the new business model and the creativity of the group but then said the idea was not implementable. To succeed the bank would have to launch an autonomous business unit with a completely different human and technical infrastructure operating in a very different culture. The COO said that creating this new business model within the current organization was doomed to failure "since we would eat our own young." The COO said the bank's existing leadership, organizational form, skills, information technology (IT) infrastructure, and, most important, reward systems would prevent the success of the new model. The idea was killed.

The COO puzzled and disturbed us as facilitators. We thought the new business model was inspired and worth the development of a detailed business case or even a pilot. The new business model offered the bank the opportunity to evolve from its traditional high-cost "bricks-and-mortar" business model to an innovative "clicks-and-mortar" model combining physical and Internet distribution. Certainly, the new model would cannibalize parts of the existing business, but it would be the bank's own new business model, not a competitor's, that would quickly capture the bank's existing business. The new model offered a strong value proposition to particular customer segments as well as potential growth and innovation. The economics were also compelling, as the typical bricks-and-mortar models were operating at cost-to-income ratios of between 50 percent and 60 percent, whereas the group estimated 35 percent for this clicks-and-mortar model.[1]

More importantly, the new e-business model placed the bank in potentially the most powerful position in the evolving financial services industry. Owning the three customer assets highlighted in the proposed business model for the bank brings different types of leverage. Owning the customer relationship brings the leverage of *influence*. The customer looks to the relationship holder for trust, recommendations, and tailored advice. Owning the customer data brings the leverage of *insight*, as the firm has detailed information about the history and needs or likes of the customer. Owning the customer transaction generates the leverage of customer revenue from *fees* for service. The power of the proposed e-business model is profound in a future where the fees for financial transactions are steadily reducing and revenue will come from assets under management or the services implicit in owning the relationship.

The look on the face of that COO motivated us to write this book. We have seen that look on the faces of many good managers. The book is targeted at the senior managers of existing, successful businesses under threat from e-business and required to respond and lead. The book provides an analytical tool set for managers thinking through potential e-business models. Gone are the days when organizations could afford to have lengthy planning cycles resulting in large documents and detailed plans. E-business allows—indeed requires—firms to run experiments to determine quickly if a strategy is successful. If the market response is positive, firms need to seamlessly transform that strategic experiment into an integrated and industrial-strength product offering, and they must behave as if they intended the experiment as a major strategic thrust!

Defining E-Business

Defining e-business is like searching the Internet: You often don't get it all and the landscape changes day by day. For us, e-business means doing business electronically by completing business processes over open networks, thereby substituting information for physical business process.[2] This definition is broad, encompassing business-to-business (B2B), business-to-consumer (B2C), and consumer-to-consumer (C2C) interactions.[3] Our working definition of e-business is:[4]

> Marketing, buying, selling, delivering, servicing, and paying for products, services, and information across (nonproprietary) networks linking an enterprise and its prospects, customers, agents, suppliers, competitors, allies, and complementors.[5]

The essence of our definition is the conduct of business and business processes over computer networks based on nonproprietary standards. The Internet is the exemplar of a nonproprietary network used today for e-business. Given its low cost and universal access, the Internet will be the major infrastructure for the foreseeable future. However, new access technologies already on the horizon (e.g., use of wireless application protocol from mobile telephones) will supplement the Internet, and who knows what will follow. Whatever the technology, the essence of e-business is completing business processes over easily accessible computer networks that will all become nonproprietary over time. The business conducted may or may not include payment, but it is inherently commercial in its nature. We differentiate information that is not paid for from products that are paid for and may be digital (e.g., music, research). For example, e-business includes free information-seeking activities, such as "window-shopping" using an online shopping robot, that often precede a transaction that is later completed offline.

E-business will move businesses from place to space. The familiar tools of the marketplace—cash, checks, paper documents, storefronts, and face-to-face meetings—will be less important. Growing in importance will be the marketspace, where information in all its forms becomes digital and the cost of replicating and distributing this information will approach zero. The digital economy will be a knowledge economy, in which a firm's value chain is electronically interconnected. Firms will have a number of electronic allies who help to promote, sell, find, distribute, integrate, and generally increase the demand for the firm's products and services.

E-business must often integrate with traditional commerce. For example, electronic channels to the customer in the bank's full-service provider model will include proprietary automatic teller machine (ATM) networks and interactive voice response (IVR) phone-banking systems. IVR, ATMs, and the existing systems in bank branches are fundamental to the bank's business model and raise significant challenges for the bank to integrate IT applications and customer data across multiple infrastructures and channels.

In an e-business world, small companies can act like large companies, potentially able to reach many customers across geographies and time zones. Large companies can act like small companies and personalize the customer experience through better use of richer information. E-business will continue to significantly reduce the transaction costs of sellers, and thus it will increase the penetration of the seller's message into the market. At the same time e-business reduces dissemination costs by automating transactions. Conversely, customers can more easily compare prices and features from a number of sellers, challenging sellers to meaningfully differentiate their products. Trust and branding will become more important. The first industries to be fundamentally altered by e-business may be banking, education, retail, travel, and stockbroking, but no industry will remain unaffected.

Motivations for Existing Businesses to Evolve

The senior management of the bank was motivated to hold their e-business strategizing session by three trends: growth of the e-economy, rise (and perhaps fall) of the dot-coms, and a handful of exemplar success stories about existing businesses evolving to an e-business model. Assuming our readers are similarly bombarded and familiar with these three motivations, we briefly summarize the key points (with references for further reading in the notes), leading to a discussion of why the migration is so difficult. We then introduce our atomic e-business model framework to assist firms such as the bank to determine their new e-business models.

Huge Growth in E-Business

The growth of e-business has already been staggering, and this growth is just an indicator of things to come.[6] Now that half of the American population has Internet access, and access in other parts of the world is growing at exponential rates, one of the building blocks of e-business—widespread access—is becoming a reality. The rapid growth of e-business is partly due to the Internet and its open nonproprietary communications protocol (TCP/IP)[7] and partly due to the development of the World Wide Web (commonly known as "the Web"),[8] which has adopted a standard method of representing information (hypertext markup language, or HTML).[9]

How Big Is the E-Business Economy?

There are many estimates of the size of e-business. The Organization for Economic Co-operation and Development (OECD) predicts U.S.$330 billion in e-business in 2001–2, and U.S.$1 trillion in 2003–5. These estimates are speculative, but if the 2003–5 forecast is achieved, e-business will be equivalent to 15 percent of the total retail sales of the seven OECD countries.[10] Figures from the IDC (www.idc.com) put Internet commerce at $218 billion in 2000, growing to $774 billion in 2002. The IDC concludes that including both the Internet IT infrastructure and Internet business infrastructure (e.g., marketing and content management) triples the figures to over $600 billion in 2000.[11]

From this and other recent survey data, we draw some interesting and challenging conclusions:

- Approximately half of the revenues of the e-business economy are attributed to investment in Internet protocol infrastructure and applications to enable e-business, rather than actual e-business.

- The Internet economy is already significant in terms of both jobs and revenues. Large firms account for much of the activity in terms of revenue generated, investment in e-business infrastructure, and employment.[12]

- Although much attention has been paid to disintermediation—firms bypassing intermediaries or agents to go directly to the consumer—*intermediaries* (see chapter 7) account for around 20 percent of e-business revenues. Indeed, some of the most innovative business models are intermediaries such as intelligent search agents (e.g., the intelligent search agent www.jango.excite.com) and specialist agents (e.g., www.insweb.com—a free service that helps you shop for insurance).

- Most of the attention has been on B2C e-business, but most of the dollars are in B2B e-business.[13]

- Internet commerce is already significant, as it accounts for approximately one-third of the total revenue of the Internet economy. However, two-thirds of the dollars in the Internet economy are spent on technology plus the intermediary foundation to enable e-business. This large proportion of spending on infrastructure is not sustainable, but it is typical of new technology waves in which, historically, spending on infrastructure precedes revenue generation but eventually pays off handsomely.[14] In the short term this significant investment in infrastructure reduces profitability but gives the promise of a huge payoff.

- The growth of e-business is just beginning, and the major infrastructure investments are now being made. Once more of the infrastructure is in place, e-business applications will grow exponentially.[15]
- Ninety percent of Fortune 500 firms have Web sites, but only 5 percent of those sites make profits today.[16] This will change and more profits will be made as e-business infrastructures mature. Even if profits (or even sales) don't eventuate, firms will need to provide Web sites to enable customers to learn about features and to compare their products and services with those of others. Failing to have an attractive, informative, up-to-date Web site will place a firm at a disadvantage, since customers compare products either directly or via intermediaries such as shopping agents (see chapter 7).

Growth in Dot-Coms

Much of the recent media excitement, attention, and share price speculation has focused on the dot-coms, which we define as start-up companies that operate predominantly in space, often pioneering and market testing new business models. Some of these business models are new (e.g., intelligent search agents), whereas others have operated in the traditional place but are much more attractive and effective in space (e.g., online auctions). The following list is made up of some well-known examples, which we will discuss later in the book, of publicly held firms experimenting with these new e-business models. The numbers in parentheses are the market capitalization increases from the initial public offering (IPO) to valuations as of May 2000.

- E*TRADE (www.etrade.com), a direct-to-customer model (6,124 percent)
- eBay (www.ebay.com), an online auction intermediary (34,333 percent)
- Yahoo! (www.yahoo.com), a portal intermediary (228,667 percent)

- Preview Travel (www.previewtravel.com), a comparison shopping–agent intermediary (2,133 percent)
- iVillage (www.ivillage.com), a women's network and virtual community (267 percent)
- Amazon (www.amazon.com), a hybrid direct to customer, intermediary, virtual community, and content provider (35,600 percent)
- Reuters (www.reuters.com), a traditional financial information firm evolved to become an exemplar of a content provider. Reuters announced they would become an Internet company on February 8, 2000, and its share price increased by 55 percent within a month of the announcement.

There are many theories about whether these astronomical stock market valuations were justified; their descriptions range from "irrational exuberance" to "black magic." We believe that, as in any investment booms, valuations are based on expectations of growth, which will eventually translate into earnings. More modest price-to-earnings ratios now exist for most of these firms. The current rates of growth in revenues of these firms, admittedly off small bases, lead investors to expect continued revenue growth of 100 percent or more per year. The dilemma and frustration for traditional firms, some of which deliver very respectable increases in revenues and earnings each year, is that their share prices are flat or even declining. This frustration is a powerful motivating force for traditional firms to migrate their business models to e-business.

The Pioneers

A small number of existing firms operating profitably in place have evolved to e-business success stories. Here are some of our favorite motivational spectacular success stories and why they are important:

- Dell Computer Corporation's online sales increased from $7 million a day in 1997 (12 percent of revenues) to $40 million a day in early 2000 (about 50 percent of total revenues). Dell (www.dell.com) was simultaneously able to reduce the cost of sales and deliver more tailored customer service via their more than thirty thousand Premier Pages for corporate clients.[17] Dell is an exemplar of the *direct-to-customer* business model (chapter 4), which bypasses the distributor and retailer and establishes a direct relationship with the customer.

- Ernst & Young (www.ey.com), an eighty-five-thousand-person global consulting firm operating in thirty-two countries, introduced Ernie, an online business consultant. Ernie provides answers by experts to client questions electronically within two days, and it offers unlimited access to a database of previously asked questions and problem-solving tools, including the Ernie Software Selection Advisor. To deliver good answers Ernie uses a template to help users frame good questions. We don't expect products like Ernie to replace face-to-face consulting for major issues. However, for many smaller but still important questions (e.g., questions about the termination entitlements of an employee), online consulting is very convenient for the client and frees the consulting partner to focus on higher-leverage work. To succeed, leadership and investment are required to identify, codify, and digitize knowledge, as well as to change decades of consulting status quo.[18]

- Cisco (www.cisco.com), often described as the "poster child of the Internet," designs and sells the "plumbing" of the Internet, including a wide range of routers, devices that direct the flow of traffic on the Internet. Cisco has developed a very profitable and innovative e-business model, combining aspects of the direct-to-customer, *content provider,* and *value net integrator* business models (see chapters 4, 11, and 10, respectively).[19] We discuss Cisco in detail in chapter 10.

- Quicken is transforming into a financial services intermediary via their "one-stop shop" Web site www.quicken.com, which offers the more than twelve million users of Intuit's financial management software access to insurance products, share trading, mortgages, and other financial products. With

80 percent market share in the personal finance software market, Quicken has a unique opportunity to become a financial services marketplace, growing its revenue stream from fees, commissions, and advertising.[20]

- You can do your bit for the search for extraterrestrial intelligence (SETI) at home. More than 2.5 million personal computer (PC) users participate in the search by running a program that downloads and analyzes radio telescope data when they are not using the machine (http://setiathome.ssl.berkeley.edu). Although not really an e-business model, SETI at home illustrates the power and potential of *virtual communities* and the potential of distributed and real-time e-business models.

These examples describe new business models that have the potential to change the way business is conducted in a number of industries. We will explore these examples in more detail later in the book.

The Second Wave of E-Business

The powerful force of these factors has motivated existing and profitable place-based firms to marshal huge efforts to migrate to e-businesses. We are about to enter the second wave of e-business, which will have three important characteristics:

1. The difficulty to build and sustain a profitable dot-com business will be reflected in more realistic (i.e., lower) stock market valuations. We expect to see one or two dot-coms gain success in each major business sector, and the rest struggle to survive.

2. Existing firms that are evolving to an e-business model by combining the best of place and space will do much of the hard work and make most of the profits. These firms will seriously challenge dot-coms by providing their services not only more cheaply and at a higher quality but also in a manner that is integrated with their place-based channels.

3. The artificial distinctions between B2B, B2C, and C2C will disappear. Most viable e-business models will have a combination of business and household customers integrated in the same model, each representing different customer segments that require different value propositions.

The migration and evolution from place to space is a struggle for most traditional business, and the struggle will continue into the second wave.

Traditional Businesses Are Struggling to Respond

Many traditional and profitable businesses are struggling to respond to the threats and opportunities of e-business. The threats are played out not only in stock market valuations, but also in the marketspace, where dot-coms without the heavy investment in physical infrastructure can cherry pick profitable niches in which to compete. Traditional firms face a number of difficulties in responding:

- **Culture and leadership.** Most large traditional firms are successful and profitable, and they achieved their success via strong leadership and cultures suited to their industry. E-business threatens this status quo in traditional firms. The leaders are often ill-prepared to make major strategic commitments to e-business and are reluctant to take the initiative, preferring to wait and see. In firms such as the bank described earlier, the prevailing culture actively works against new initiatives that threaten the status quo. Senior management must shape the e-business vision and the employees and the culture they create must implement the models. In many places throughout the book we will refer to the importance of leadership and culture without discussing the details—that topic deserves a separate book—but in chapter 13 we provide our top ten e-business leadership principles as a starting place.

- **Channel conflict.** Potential channel conflicts exist between the new e-business channels and traditional channels, often including intermediaries. Recently one of Australia's largest retailers, Harvey Norman, announced that it would forgo A$100 million of revenue and no longer sell Compaq computers in response to Compaq's decision to sell their computers direct to the consumer via the Internet and Compaq retail outlets.[21] Harris Technologies, an online retailer owned by Australia's largest retailer, Coles Myer, also announced that it would no longer carry Compaq products.

- **Cost reduction.** Many traditional firms struggle to capitalize on the lower costs available via e-business. A recent Booz•Allen & Hamilton study found that the cost per transaction for banks by channel was (in order of decreasing cost):

    - branch: U.S.$3.00,
    - telephone: $1.50,
    - ATM: $0.78–$0.42,
    - IVR: $0.30,
    - point of sale: $0.42–$0.24, and
    - Internet: $0.12–$0.06.[22]

    While the economics of e-business are compelling for a bank, many customer segments prefer a branch or a call center with a human voice. In Australia, more than 500 bank branches have closed in the last year, with 1,131 closed in the last five years. Over the same five-year period, the number of ATMs has tripled.[23] The public and media have criticized the major Australian banks for these wholesale closures of bank branches, particularly in country towns. By contrast, in the United States, although the number of banks has steadily fallen since the 1980s, the number of branches has risen consistently at about 2 percent per year. American banks are responding to customer sentiment in some segments.[24] For customers selecting a new bank, the location and availability of branches—

regardless of the frequency of use—still are significant criteria. In response, banks are seeking more effective ways to use their branches for high-value transactions and cross-selling.

- **Skills shortage.** The skills necessary for e-business initiatives are in short supply and high demand. Traditional firms struggle to offer compensation packages that compete with the huge potential upside of stock options for employees of dot-coms. Managers of the firms that support our research and attend our executive education programs used to complain that their young people often leave potentially successful career paths in traditional firms for the learning experience, excitement, and stock options found at dot-coms.

- **Infrastructure.** The IT infrastructure requirements for e-business are stretching the capabilities of many firms' IT portfolios. Many traditional firms are struggling with B2B e-business implementation that may require integrating their recently installed and expensive enterprise resource planning systems (ERPs) with their Web sites and those of ally firms. Difficulties include incompatible technical platforms, security, data reliability, and accessibility. The compressed time frames of the e-business world compound these challenges by creating pressure to deliver IT applications in weeks rather than months or years. Firms wishing to compete via e-business must invest in IT infrastructure, which accounts for more than 50 percent of the average firm's IT budget year after year. The promise of "less infrastructure investment after this big investment" never seems to eventuate!

In summary, many traditional businesses lack the physical and IT infrastructure, skill sets, culture, and incentive schemes that are required for e-business initiatives. In addition, these businesses have customer segments that want to do business in traditional ways.

William Thiele, vice president of the General Reinsurance Corporation, sums up the challenges perceived by traditional firms as follows:

> Internally the benefits are clear: it has speeded up our business tremendously; we're now effectively open twenty-four hours a

day. People work from multiple locations in a collaborative environment.... Externally, this is both a challenge and an opportunity. We've been in business a long time; we have substantial investment in bricks and mortar. Our business model has emphasized face-to-face contact, personal relationships and direct marketing. We can easily envision someone setting up shop in Dublin or Honolulu or wherever they want to, accessing all of our customers without going through the trouble we have. And if anyone else can do that . . . we have to do it faster and better.[25]

Some firms, such as the Bank of Montreal, have responded by establishing an autonomous e-business business unit (www.bmo.com/banking) with a different brand, infrastructure, and pricing structure to appeal to the e-business-ready segment of their customers, as well as to attract new customers. The number of BMO direct-banking clients increased 48 percent in 1999 to one million.[26] Other firms have begun e-business initiatives under their existing brands, and many are still searching for a profitable business model. For example, more than twenty-seven hundred U.S. newspapers post an edition online, but they are generally struggling to find a profitable business model. Many users of the Internet expect free content, so charging a subscription fee is problematic.[27] Newspapers seek ways to migrate their successful place business models, based on subscriptions, general advertising, and classified advertising, to space. The online versions of newspapers and classified advertisements with sophisticated search capabilities provide a strong value proposition. How can they generate sustainable revenues evolving to e-business?

Traditional businesses have to respond to e-business opportunities and threats. Most businesses that operate wholly in place today will need to operate in both place and space tomorrow. The speed of the migration will be determined by the boldness of their competitors, as well as by their own vision and courage. During the process of migration, a traditional business will consider and experiment with a portfolio of potential e-business initiatives. We have developed a series of frameworks to assist this process of migration, which are illustrated by the Lonely Planet case study, the first of twelve case studies of firms evolving to e-business models.

CASE STUDY

LONELY PLANET PUBLICATIONS: Traveling from Place to Space, Part 1

Lonely Planet, one of Australia's best-known entrepreneurial firms, has pioneered the provision of travel guides for the independent traveler (www.lonelyplanet.com.au). Lonely Planet initially targeted their travel guides to cash-poor backpackers and has adapted the guides to appeal to all travelers seeking an independent travel experience. The Lonely Planet case study illustrates the dilemmas facing many successful firms, particularly those in the information business, as they migrate to e-business. How should Lonely Planet migrate its business to the marketspace? How should Lonely Planet work with its traditional channels (retail bookstores) in the future? What changes should Lonely Planet make in the way it collects information, writes travel guides, and electronically stores its vast library of text, maps, photos, and images?

Lonely Planet Publications began in the early 1970s after U.K.-born founders Tony and Maureen Wheeler completed an overland journey from London through Asia and on to Australia. Recently married, they went globetrotting to get traveling out of their systems before settling into "real-world" jobs. After arriving in Australia, so many other travelers approached the Wheelers with questions about their trip that they decided to publish a book.

Written at their kitchen table and collated, trimmed, and stapled by hand, that book, *Across Asia on the Cheap,* became the first Lonely Planet guidebook and an instant best-seller. The Wheelers' eighteen months of traveling in Southeast Asia resulted in their second book, *South-East Asia on a Shoestring,* one of the most popular guidebooks ever written.

By early 2000 nearly four hundred Lonely Planet employees work in offices in Melbourne, London, Paris, and Oakland, CA, with a crew of experienced freelance authors traveling and writing around the globe. The headquarters staff includes seventy-five cartographers who produce and maintain the numerous maps unique to the company's guidebooks. Lonely Planet publishes more than five hundred titles, including guidebooks, phrase books, walking guides, city guides, cuisine guides, and other travel-related books, and it has expanded its product line to include maps and travel videos as well. Within the travel publishing industry, Lonely Planet dominates the Australian market, leads the market in the United Kingdom, and ranks third in the United States. While its market shares in Asia and Europe are smaller, growth prospects are high. The Lonely Planet brand is well known worldwide and is viewed by the Wheelers and management as one of the company's most important assets.

To manage the many opportunities for expanding its range of books, Lonely Planet developed a process for determining the viability of a proposed new title or series. Initial ideas originated from authors, staff, senior management, publishers, or readers, and they were tested by polling marketing staff, assessing reader and author feedback, and analyzing sales history. The top forty or fifty ideas were then reviewed individually, with a benchmark of 50 percent gross profit required for a title to proceed. This benchmark was varied for projects that shared costs with other products or had strategic significance. Generally, Lonely Planet produced about twenty new titles per year.

Lonely Planet publications targeted travelers going to far-flung destinations, and they were written in a slightly irreverent style. As the company grew, Lonely Planet widened its coverage to include most parts of the globe and to cater to a wider spectrum of readers. Lonely Planet publications aimed to provide guidebook options for independent travelers of all types, including backpackers, ex-backpackers who still liked to travel to unusual places but now had more money to spend, and time-poor, cash-rich travelers who appreciated Lonely Planet's style and attention to detail. Regardless of the target market segment, Lonely Planet guides contained numerous drawings and color photographs as well as maps and text. Lonely Planet accepted no advertisements, and it stressed that its writers did not accept discounts or payment in exchange for positive coverage. As the founder and principal author of Lonely Planet Publications,

Tony Wheeler's advice was sought by independent traveler publications all over the world. The *New York Times Magazine* called him "the trailblazing patron saint of the world's backpackers and adventure travelers." *Travel & Leisure*'s twenty-fifth anniversary issue named Tony as one of the people who changed the way the world travels.

Lonely Planet products were sold primarily by bookstores and electronic retailers worldwide, and via the Lonely Planet Web site. This award-winning Web site received nearly three million hits a day, by more than two million different people a month, often from people who were already traveling. Lonely Planet's global revenues in 2000 were nearly A$65 million, maintaining a 20 percent per year growth throughout the decade. Revenues included third-party royalty payments from portals and online travel sites, such as Travelocity. The additional exposure gained from licensing arrangements with these powerful Web presences appeared to have doubled traffic to Lonely Planet's own Web site.

Privately held Lonely Planet did not disclose profit figures, but the company was doing well enough to attract a significant investment from well-known Australian advertising magnate John Singleton. Singleton, who said he paid "plenty" for the 12.8 percent stake he purchased in late July 1999, called Lonely Planet "the world's largest single influence on tourism." The remainder of the company stayed in the hands of the Wheelers and employees.

Lonely Planet generally updated its printed guidebooks every two to three years. Between editions, travelers could access instant online updates for some Lonely Planet guidebooks via the company's Web site. Containing important information and changes gathered since the most recent printed edition of a book, these upgrades were available at no charge to enhance the quality of existing Lonely Planet guidebooks. Upgrades were just one feature of the Lonely Planet Web site, the hub for a virtual community of travelers with an active bulletin board called Thorn Tree. Thorn Tree attracted around fifteen hundred postings per day from travelers sharing or requesting information. Lonely Planet's headquarters staff in Melbourne included a team dedicated to reading both these postings and electronic mail sent to the company. The teams briefed company management on emerging trends in travel and identified updates for guidebooks.

Rob Flynn, the electronic publishing manager of Lonely Planet, believed customers desired personalized travel guides, perhaps including hotel and travel bookings. "In terms of a brand new business, we think it's enormous, and it can't exist outside the electronic world. We have a huge database on places to eat, places to stay, maps, photos, and attractions in every town in the world, and up till now, people haven't been able to make a selective choice," Flynn said.[28] Flynn regarded "reinventing the travel guide" as the next big business opportunity created by the Internet. Lonely Planet had not yet developed a formal process for evaluating proposed e-business initiatives. Steve Hibbard, the company's chief executive officer (CEO), noted that as the CEO he focused on overseeing the creation and implementation of these initiatives, often requiring cooperation from many groups across the organization to succeed.

Lonely Planet, a very successful book publisher in the marketplace, illustrates many of the issues facing traditional businesses today as they consider migrating to the marketspace. For example, Lonely Planet has a large number of products, most of which are distributed via intermediaries through multiple channels to multiple customer segments. Lonely Planet's key assets include a loyal customer base, a well-known brand, motivated and highly qualified writers and editorial staff, a can-do culture with an irreverent style, and a significant amount of intellectual capital. How should Lonely Planet proceed with e-business?

We will discuss the critical issues for Lonely Planet several times in the book. In chapter 12, we will continue the Lonely Planet case study by describing their recent electronic initiatives. We will use our business model schematics to analyze Lonely Planet's challenges in migrating to an e-business model. To assist firms such as Lonely Planet strategizing about e-business, we introduce our notion of atomic e-business models.

E-Business Initiatives and Atomic E-Business Models

Pioneering firms doing business electronically today are incrementally developing business models for e-business. From this evolutionary process, some radical new business models are emerging, including value net integrator, virtual community, and direct to customer. At the same time, some traditional place business models, such as full-service provider, are undergoing radical change to exploit the now ubiquitous electronic infrastructure.

To assist in evaluating the viability of an e-business initiative, we have developed an analytical framework, a modeling methodology, and a set of atomic e-business models. We have identified eight atomic e-business models that firms can combine in multiple ways to create new e-business models. Each atomic e-business model describes the essence of a different way to conduct business electronically. Atomic e-business models are the building blocks for e-business initiatives. Understanding the characteristics of these atomic models allows us to analyze what is necessary to make them work in combination as an e-business initiative. Firms can use the tools described in this book to evaluate potential business models and understand the core competencies necessary for implementation.

Content Provider	Provides content (information, digital products, and services) via intermediaries.
Direct to Customer	Provides goods or services directly to the customer, often bypassing traditional channel members.
Full-Service Provider	Provides a full range of services in one domain (e.g., financial, health, industrial chemicals) directly and via allies, attempting to own the primary consumer relationship.
Intermediary	Brings together buyers and sellers by concentrating information.
Shared Infrastructure	Brings together multiple competitors to cooperate by sharing common IT infrastructure.
Value Net Integrator	Coordinates activities across the value net by gathering, synthesizing, and distributing information.
Virtual Community	Creates and facilitates an online community of people with a common interest, enabling interaction and service provision.
Whole-of-Enterprise/ Government	Provides a firmwide single point of contact, consolidating all services provided by a large multiunit organization.

The diagram in figure 1-1 depicts an e-business initiative. The large box describes the e-business model being implemented in the firm's initiative, which combines some of the eight atomic e-business models. (Firms can illustrate and analyze their e-business model using the schematic described in chapter 2.) The firm implements the model, via a collection of electronic channels, to a specified set of customer segments. The firm's IT infrastructure capabilities (insourced or outsourced) enable the entire e-business initiative.

For example, Amazon.com was launched in 1994 as a direct-to-customer business model for books via the electronic channel of the Internet, aimed at a customer segment of (predominantly male) early technology adopters worldwide. The business model also contains elements of three other atomic e-business models: virtual community, content provider, and intermediary. In Amazon.com's virtual community, customers share information and opinions about books with one another. Amazon offers content (i.e., information) to other organizations that are Amazon's affiliates. In Amazon's innovative affiliates program, other organizations can place an Amazon.com clickthrough on their sites and gain commissions (ranging from 8 percent to 15 percent of dollars spent at Amazon.com) for purchases made by customers who access Amazon.com via their site. More recently, Amazon added elements of two types of intermediary business models: (1) a search agent for locating products that Amazon.com doesn't stock, and (2) online auctions for any type of product.[29]

Amazon illustrates how the atomic e-business models are combined to present a unique value proposition to a target customer segment and how an initial business model is enhanced with the

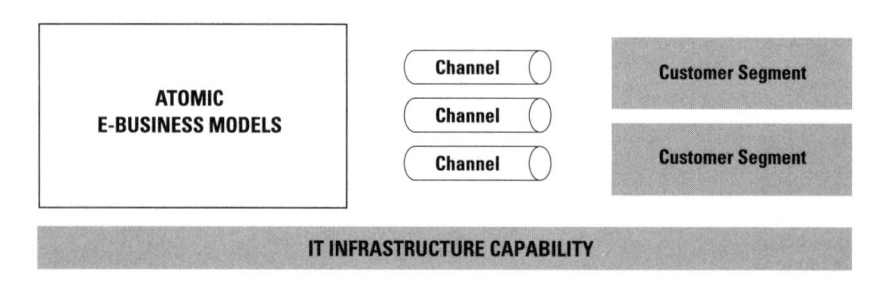

FIGURE 1-1 An E-Business Initiative

addition of further atomic models over time. Amazon also illustrates that some combinations of atomic e-business models may be synergistic or contain conflict. The combination of the four atomic e-business models that make up Amazon may turn out to be nonviable. For example, some major brands, such as Sony and Panasonic, refused to allow Amazon to stock its products, but they have agreed to supply products to its competitors, such as to Circuit City's online store. Amazon.com's online auction site is struggling to establish scale, with 140,000 listings compared to eBay's 3 million listings.[30]

Many traditional firms will launch e-business initiatives in the next few years. Many firms' e-business strategies will include a portfolio of e-business initiatives. Some initiatives will pay off handsomely, while others will fail. The investment strategy will be similar to that of an individual investing in a portfolio of dot-coms. This approach is illustrated by Bruce Leucke, president of interactive delivery services at Bank One Retail Group, who explains that Bank One's Internet strategy is to "[l]everage a broad portfolio of initiatives, employing multiple brands, numerous web alliances, and an unparalleled Internet visibility."[31] Traditional businesses have some major advantages over dot-coms. Harnessing those advantages into e-business initiatives is both the challenge and the opportunity facing traditional firms.

Major Tenets of This Book

Several major tenets underpin this book:

1. E-business will change the ways that all surviving companies do business, and most traditional businesses will evolve from their current business models to a combination of place and space via a portfolio of e-business initiatives.

2. The transition from place to space is difficult for traditional businesses, because they often do not have the appropriate leadership, organizational form, skills, IT infrastructure, customer intimacy and data, reward system, or culture necessary for success with e-business.

3. Many senior managers of traditional firms recognize the importance of e-business, but they are struggling to find effective ways to think about and evaluate potential e-business initiatives.

4. Business model schematics will assist existing firms to define and assess their e-business models. Firms can describe their e-business model using a schematic that identifies relationships between the participants and the flow of dollars, product, and information.

5. A finite set of atomic e-business models forms the building blocks of all e-business initiatives.

6. An e-business initiative can be specified by its combination of atomic e-business models, channels to the customer, targeted customer segments, and IT infrastructure capability necessary to implement the initiative.

7. For each atomic e-business model, the strategic objectives, the sources of revenue, the critical success factors, and the required core competencies necessary for implementation can be specified.

8. Some combinations of atomic e-business models are compatible, while others are incompatible and lead to problems such as channel conflict. These incompatibilities can be identified using our business model schematics and the associated decision rules.

9. Business models come to life when illustrated with examples. Each chapter contains a number of examples and a detailed case study, the associated business model schematics, and an analysis of the model's viability.

10. Business models must be tested in the marketspace via strategic experiments, and they will evolve organically over time, requiring organizations to be far more agile than before.

11. IT infrastructure and the information it contains, particularly customer information, will be a critical success factor for all

e-business initiatives, thus raising the stakes for the management of the firm's IT investments and assets.

12. Firms will need to examine their core competencies, available physical and intangible assets, and likely business models to identify critical building blocks for their future e-business initiatives. Investing in the critical building blocks today can pay off many times over. These building blocks include such things as firmwide customer data, alliance partners, content, skills, and so on.

Terminology Used in This Book

To facilitate our discussion and analysis, we decompose e-business into four levels. This decomposition allows us to focus on different degrees of complexity to suit the topic at hand. The decomposition also allows us to operate in reverse and compose an e-business implementation from its component parts, understanding the capabilities required for each. The four levels of decomposition used in the book are:

1. **Atomic e-business model.** The essence of the way e-business is conducted. There are a finite number of atomic e-business models, which are building blocks of more complex business models. Each atomic e-business model is described by four characteristics: strategic objectives, sources of revenue, critical success factors,[32] and core competencies required.

2. **E-business model.** The combination of atomic e-business models that best describe the firm's e-business activities in a particular initiative. The e-business model includes the roles and relationships among a firm's customers, allies, and suppliers, the major flows of product, information, and money, and the major benefits to the participants. The characteristics of atomic e-business models can be aggregated to describe an e-business model.

3. **E-business initiative.** The unique combination of e-business model, targeted customer segments, channels to those cus-

tomers, and the IT infrastructure necessary to support the initiative. These four aspects are identified as the critical differentiators between one e-business initiative and another. A firm may have one e-business initiative or a portfolio of them.

4. **E-business implementation.** The most complete description of e-business in a firm, including the details of the e-business initiatives plus the many other factors necessary for successful implementation, including financing, pricing, recruitment, marketing, incentives, and so on.

The Structure of the Book

We wrote this book for a broad spectrum of managers of existing firms challenged with thinking about e-business. This book provides a systematic and practical analysis of e-business models, about which there has been much talk but little structured research. In chapter 2 we define a business model and provide a practical framework for understanding both physical and electronic ways of doing business. Chapter 2 also introduces a simple but powerful tool to represent and analyze e-business models: the e-business model schematic. The use of e-business model schematics allows an organization to analyze its current business model and develop and analyze e-business initiatives.

Chapter 3 introduces the concept of the atomic e-business model and gives a brief description of the eight atomic models. The concept of the e-business model initiative is described in detail and illustrated with the proposal for E-StockClub.

Chapters 4 through 11 describe and analyze our eight atomic e-business models in detail. Each atomic e-business model fundamentally differs from the next as a viable way of doing e-business. Each of these chapters contains a short case study of a firm enacting the business model. The rest of each chapter analyzes the business model in order to understand its strengths, weaknesses, and the potential benefits of following it. For each atomic e-business model we probe the following issues:

- E-business model for the firm

- Schematic: a diagram showing the relationships among the major players and the flows of money, information, and products in the business model

- Value proposition of the model to the customer

- Sources of revenue: a description of where value is added and how readily the model can be sustained

- IT infrastructure necessary for each model

- Who in the model owns the three critical assets in e-business: the customer relationship, the data, and the transaction

- Critical success factors for the model to thrive

- Core competencies necessary for the successful implementation of the business model

A firm's ability to rapidly create and implement new business models makes e-business exciting and challenging. Atomic e-business models provide a set of building blocks for new "hybrid" e-business models. There is no complete and accepted classification of e-business models, so we offer ours as a starting place. We are certain there are gaps in our typology and that other atomic models will emerge via strategic experimentation.

In chapter 12 we synthesize the lessons from the preceding chapters on atomic e-business models. We summarize for each model the ownership of the customer relationship, data, and transactions, and what leverage those ownerships create. We summarize in tables the characteristics of the atomic e-business models: the strategic objectives, how money is made and value created, the critical success factors, and the core competencies. We also summarize the IT infrastructure needs for each atomic model based on our study of fifty e-business initiatives. We then focus on composing and decomposing e-business initiatives from the atomic models, using the business model schematics as a tool.

We close the book in chapter 13 by discussing the process of choosing and implementing e-business initiatives in traditional firms. We present a framework to analyze the level of e-business threat and opportunity facing a traditional firm, and we draw links back to the lessons learned about the characteristics of atomic e-business models and their combination in initiatives. We provide a checklist for assessing an e-business initiative and explore the links among business strategy, business models, competencies, and initiatives. We wrap up with our list of the top ten e-business leadership principles for successful place-to-space migration.

CHAPTER 2

E-Business Model Schematics

AS MANAGEMENT educators and consultants, we have lived through, and helped propagate, a number of management panaceas. These panaceas include management by objectives (MBO), strategic use of IT, total quality management (TQM), business process reengineering (BPR), quality circles, activity-based costing, knowledge management, and value-based management. All these solutions have the same noble aim of improving business performance. These fads seem to come out of nowhere, steadily build momentum, and create a huge wave of enthusiasm, as evidenced by converts, conferences, consulting engagements, new projects, and corporate centers of excellence. Careers are often made or broken in the process. In three years or so, the key term begins to slowly fade from public attention. The useful elements of the idea become a permanent part of the manager's tool kit, while the less useful parts evaporate. We may need this endless cycle to distract our attention from the day-to-day issues of management—to reflect and challenge the way we function in firms. The process wastes resources but also creates powerful new ways of thinking. And so it will be with e-business—or is it e-commerce, or e-everything, e.com, or enough! We are putting lowercase *e*'s and dots everywhere as daily reminders of the new way of working. The *e* and dot revolution can declare victory when e-business becomes business and the dot-com becomes the corporation.

The legacies of each management trend are the frameworks, tools, and powerful concepts retained in the management tool kit, such as value chains, process maps, value propositions, critical success factors, and core competencies. A major concept emerging from e-business is the *business model*. In this chapter we introduce business model schematics as a useful tool for analyzing e-business initiatives and for plotting the migration from traditional business to the new electronic world.

Ways to Represent a Business

The way a business is represented, either in words or in diagrams, often facilitates analysis and communication of a change. There are many ways to represent a business, depending on the analytical focus. To clearly understand a business often requires information on:

- **Business strategy:** Who are the targeted customers? What are the products and service offerings? What is the unique and valuable position targeted by the firm? What choices and trade-offs has the firm made?[1]

- **Organizational form or structure:** What is the arrangement of organizational subunits and the accompanying hierarchy of authority?[2] What are the reporting relationships for each manager, the "shape" of the organization, and the division of labor across the organization, the network of organizations, or the team of e-lancers?[3] How do managers balance this collection of rights, privileges, obligations, and responsibilities through incentives, conflict, and conflict resolution?[4]

- **Business process:** What is the key set of activities designed to produce a specified output for a particular customer or market?[5] How do these activities cut across tasks, roles, people, departments, and functions to provide a customer with a product or service? How do managers design, operate, improve, and evaluate the performance of these processes? What intellectual property or competitive advantage is embedded in the firm's processes?

- **Value chain:** How does the firm add value to its inputs? How do the firm's value-adding activities fit with those of the other players in the industry? What information is necessary to manage the boundaries between the firm and other value chain participants?[6] How does the value chain fit with the competitive landscape?

- **Core competencies:** Core competencies are the relatively few sources of intellectual and service strength that are distinctive and create long-term competitive advantage. Core competencies are the collective learnings of firms, especially how to integrate multiple streams of skills, technologies, and processes to adapt to quickly changing opportunities. Although core competencies cannot be consumed, disciplined leadership must envision, invest, protect, and nurture core competencies in-house, and outsource noncore activities to firms for whom they are core.[7]

E-business, with its fast-cycle implementations, heavy reliance on information and alliances, and constantly evolving ways of doing business, requires analytical tools that combine elements of all of the above.

What's Different about E-Business

One of the distinguishing features of e-business is the importance of convergence. E-business requires two forms of convergence: convergence of the technical platform and convergence of business capabilities. At a technical level, e-business uses the convergence of multiple technologies into an integrated electronic infrastructure to conduct business. The Internet, the global telephone system, the communications standard TCP/IP, the addressing system of URLs, personal computers, cable TV systems, databases of product and customer information, multimedia sound and graphics, and the universal use of browsers to access information all converge to enable e-business. Existing IT infrastructure in firms, governments, and homes, which can be connected via the Internet with little further investment, is one of the key drivers for e-business. No one sat down and designed e-business; rather, it emerged once convergence of the technologies made it feasible. Three important developments that contributed to this convergence were the opening of the Internet to commercial activity, the creation of naming conventions for URLs, and the development of an interface that was user-friendly and free (i.e., the browser).[8]

E-business also requires convergence of business capabilities within and among firms—the integration of business processes, workflows, IT infrastructures, knowledge, and data assets. E-business will drive organizations to present a single point of contact to customers via electronic integration and to become nodes in a network of several firms. This integration will occur across previously autonomous business units as well as between firms and their customers, suppliers, and allies.

For example, Hilton hotels, via Hilton.com, has one of the fastest reservation services in the world: The average time to complete a reservation is less than two minutes. Frequent guests have services automatically tailored to their last visit, and meeting planners access the Web site for group reservations and floor plans of venues. Bruce Rosenberg, Hilton's vice president of market distribution, says that, "[T]he web opened up people's eyes about how we can and should do business. We looked at all the business models—every customer segment from the business traveler, the tourist, the meeting planner, the travel agent—and identified an e-business way of doing business with them."[9] Hilton's e-business initiative required information from multiple business units, interactivity among the customer, Hilton.com, and Hilton's existing back-end reservation systems, and a high level of personalization. "We want profiles on the customers, their history with us and what they like and don't like, accessible no matter where they touch us in the world," Rosenberg says. Hilton has very good profiles of members of HHonors (the Hilton frequent-customer loyalty program), but not so good profiles, Rosenberg notes, for the tens of millions of customers that only occasionally stay with Hilton. "The new systems we are building will allow us to have a larger number of profiles and a finer segmentation of our customer base. The web will enable us to reach them cost effectively and develop a deeper personal relationship. We just couldn't do this before by mailing material to them. The budgets weren't there to support it."[10]

Hilton is implementing a direct-to-customer business model via the Web channel, targeting the frequent-traveler segment and providing a single point of contact. All customer segments can use the Web channel, including both individuals and travel agents—with some travel agents bypassed when individuals contact Hilton directly. To implement this e-business initiative, Hilton integrates workflows, reservation systems, call centers, and business processes with the common goal of obtaining more finely segmented customer data. The initiative required a strong vision to evolve to an e-business, many negotiations across business units within Hilton, alliances with other firms, investment in IT infrastructure, and integration of Internet-based application with a large database of segmented customer profiles and various existing reservation systems. This kind of evolution requires a strong culture of working together across areas, a culture not found in all firms.

E-Business Models

Analyzing the impact of a change before its implementation reduces the risk of failure.[11] Problems created by an e-business initiative are often difficult and costly to fix once it is implemented. Managers can use business models to capture the essence of an e-business initiative, combining the elements of the five ways to represent a business mentioned earlier: strategy, form, processes, value chain, and core competencies. A good tool for representing an e-business initiative should also help identify the critical success factors and core competencies necessary for implementation.

We now define business models more formally and propose a way of decomposing business models into their atomic components, which can be recombined in many ways to create and tailor new e-business models. Business language is the living creation of managers, consultants, writers, and others who are searching for a way to describe complex issues. As with many emerging constructs, there is no single, well-accepted definition of business models.

E-Business Models Defined

We define an e-business model as:

> A description of the roles and relationships among a firm's consumers, customers, allies, and suppliers that identifies the major flows of product, information, and money, and the major benefits to participants.[12]

There are many different ways to describe and classify e-business models.[13] We propose that there are a finite number of *atomic e-business models,* each of which captures a different way to conduct e-business. Firms can combine atomic e-business models as building blocks to create tailored e-business models and initiatives, using their competencies as their guide. For example, an outstanding content provider can test new e-business initiatives by combining content provision with other atomic business models.

The characteristics of a *content provider* are typified by AccuWeather (www.accuweather.com). The world's largest commercial weather service, AccuWeather is paid by customers such as America Online, Official Airline Guides, Associated Press, Dow Jones News Retrieval, and CNN Interactive to provide branded digital content used by more than one thousand Web sites, one hundred television stations, and two hundred newspapers. AccuWeather provides accurate and easy to use weather information that is tailored and distributed by customers and allies to consumers via many channels, including Web sites, radio, and television. AccuWeather has accumulated the world's largest concentration of weather-forecasting talent who work with computer, graphics, technical, and support personnel to provide weather content in many forms. Typical of a content provider, AccuWeather employs many professionals (e.g., ninety-three meteorologists and forty-three computer graphics artists) who prepare and disseminate weather information to customers around the world with the strategic objective of becoming the "world's weather authority." Again typical of a content provider, AccuWeather's core competencies include a critical mass of world-class professional skills, the tailored presentation of information, and the use of IT.

The critical success factors for AccuWeather include high brand recognition by consumers as they view AccuWeather content. By delivering accurate, branded content, AccuWeather seeks to change weather information from an undifferentiated commodity to a branded value-added service. Although the typical AccuWeather customer, such as CNN's Web site www.CNN.com, owns the relationship with the end customer, it is critical that AccuWeather's brand is known and valued by the end customer. AccuWeather has achieved this critical success factor today, as 180 million American consumers recognize the AccuWeather name. CNN thus features AccuWeather because its customers know and value AccuWeather. Despite having little direct contact with the end customer, its brand recognition places AccuWeather in a powerful position when negotiating with CNN.[14]

The majority of AccuWeather's revenue comes from payment for content by ally firms who themselves operate *direct-to-customer* businesses and add weather to the value proposition to their customers—the end consumers. AccuWeather's customers also act as allies, by enhancing the demand for AccuWeather's content. Recently AccuWeather made a significant investment in AccuWeather.com to enable online delivery of weather content, thereby combining the content provider and direct-to-customer atomic e-business models. The Web site provides detailed information, examples of weather maps, video streaming, testimonials, and other information to describe AccuWeather's content and facilitate purchase decisions by allies that incorporate weather into a broader set of services (e.g., CNN.com). AccuWeather's new direct-to-customer part of the business model provides free weather information and maps directly to customers and includes a password-protected site for premium users. Premium users pay a monthly fee via credit card and receive access to more detailed and customizable weather information.

E-Business Model Schematics

Through our work with executives, we have developed an *e-business model schematic* to assist analyzing an e-business initiative. The schematic is a pictorial representation, like a map, aiming to highlight the business model's important elements:

- The major entities in the e-business model, including the firm of interest and its customers, suppliers, and allies
- The major flows of product, information, and money
- The revenues and other benefits each participant receives

Firms can analyze an e-business model schematic to deduce:

- whether the model has any major contradictions that may lead to nonviability or conflict,
- the core competencies and key business processes necessary to implement the model,
- the position of each player in the industry value chain,
- the organizational form for implementation,
- the type of IT infrastructure capability required, and
- which entity owns the customer relationship, data, and transaction.

To illustrate the e-business model schematics we will contrast two of the simpler atomic business models: direct to customer and content provider. Figure 2-1 illustrates the direct-to-customer model with the firm of interest, represented by the square, having an electronic connection to the customer, represented by the left-pointing pentagon. The firm whose business model is illustrated is defined as the firm of interest. The customer is the organization or individual to which the firm of interest provides goods, services, or information for consumption. The line joining the two entities in the model represents an electronic relationship. If the line between the customer and firm of interest is solid, the firm owns the relationship with that customer. If the line is dashed, then either

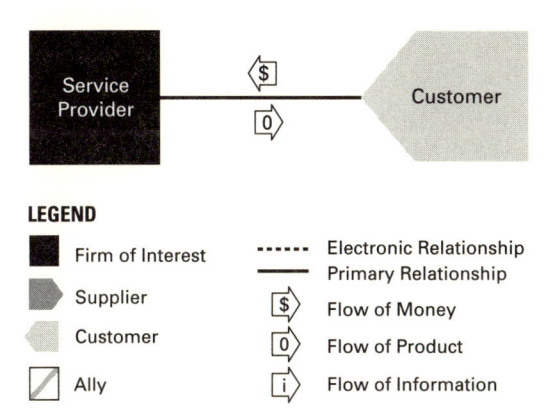

FIGURE 2-1 Direct-to-Customer E-Business Model Schematic

another firm or no firm owns the relationship with the customer. Often but not always this connection is over the Internet, but it may also use other channels, such as call centers.

Figure 2-2 presents a detailed legend for e-business model schematics. The schematics highlight three critical aspects of the business model:

1. **Participants.** Shaded blocks identify the major participants involved in the business model: squares (firms of interest), left- and right-facing pentagons (customers and suppliers), and split squares (allies).

2. **Relationships.** Lines linking the participants represent the major relationships in the model. All of these relationships are electronic and many use the Internet as the infrastructure. A solid line represents the participant owning the customer relationship where the participant knows more about the customer than any other participant (labeled "Primary Relationship" in the legend below the figures). Owning the customer relationship is hard to achieve and implies a "stickiness" or cost to switch providers incurred by the customer. More precisely, the solid line represents the potential to own the customer relationship. Some firms will successfully utilize their position in the model—achieving their potential and owning the customer relationship—and others will fall short.

Firm of Interest
The organization whose business model is illustrated by the schematic.

Supplier
The organization or individual from which the firm of interest obtains goods, services, or information. There is generally a flow of money from the firm of interest to its suppliers.

Customer
The organization or individual who consumes the firm of interest's goods, services, or information. There is often a flow of money from the customer to the firm of interest.

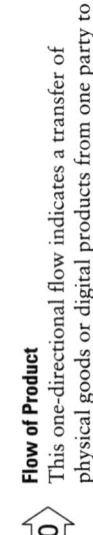

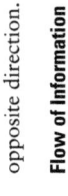

Ally
An organization whose products help to enhance the demand for the firm of interest's products.

Electronic Relationship
A digital connection through which messages flow in both directions. Often, but not always, this connection is the Internet.

Primary Relationship
The firm with the greatest potential to own the customer relationship. Owning the customer relationship provides the firm with the opportunity to know the largest amount of useful knowledge about the customer.

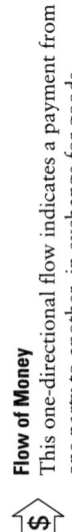

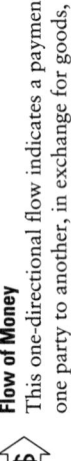

Flow of Money
This one-directional flow indicates a payment from one party to another, in exchange for goods, services, or information. Often there is a flow of product in the opposite direction.

Flow of Product
This one-directional flow indicates a transfer of physical goods or digital products from one party to another. Often there is a flow of money in the opposite direction.

Flow of Information
Messages flow through all the electronic relationships, therefore only those flows of information that are not digital products are represented by this icon. This information is often the result of research about a product or service and is usually free.

FIGURE 2-2 Legend for E-Business Model Schematics

3. **Flows.** The major flows are represented by the arrows: $ (money), 0 (product or service, digital or physical), and i (information that is not a product and thus received free).

The major flows in the direct-to-customer model are the movement of product from the firm to the customer with a reciprocal flow of money. The product provided could include groceries physically delivered to the customer, software downloaded from the Internet, or financial investment advice. The key feature of this model is that the firm of interest provides goods or services directly to the customer. The firm may or may not own the customer relationship. If the firm owns the customer relationship (as illustrated by the solid line in figure 2-1), the firm of interest knows more about the customer's purchase history, demographics, preferences, and so on than any other firm in the industry. A customer has at most one firm who owns their relationship in each area of e-business. Typical areas in e-business where a firm can own the relationship with a B2C customer are PCs, financial services, health, travel, entertainment, and education. A major opportunity of the direct-to-customer model is owning the customer relationship and exploiting the detailed customer information by up-selling (increasing the dollar value of the particular service provided) or cross-selling (selling different but related services to the same customer). In many direct-to-customer models the firm doesn't achieve ownership of the customer relationship and the customer uses many different service providers with similar products at different times without a strong loyalty to any particular one. In this situation, a dashed line in the schematic represents the relationship.

Bypassing (or *disintermediating*) an intermediary, such as a retailer or stockbroker, who was previously part of the chain to the customer is an important feature of the direct-to-customer model. The e-business direct-to-customer connection is often available via a number of electronic channels. For example, an airline implementing the direct-to-customer model can integrate its Web site, call centers, or IVR system with its traditional channels of ticket counters.

Dell Computer Corporation (www.dell.com) pioneered the direct-to-customer e-business model, manufacturing and delivering computer systems directly to the customer. Dell entered the PC market with the direct-to-customer model (see figure 2-3) at a time when existing firms like Compaq and Hewlett-Packard sold exclusively through intermediaries such as distributors or dealers. At the time of Dell's entry into the market, distributor or dealer intermediaries absorbed between 15 percent and 28 percent of the retail price.

Using the direct-to-customer model, Dell can sell at lower prices, build to order, receive payment earlier, and speed up new-product release cycles—without the need to empty and fill the distribution channel. Dell also can build on owning the customer relationship using the customer data collected to provide more tailored and valued services. Nearly fifty thousand Dell customers have Premier

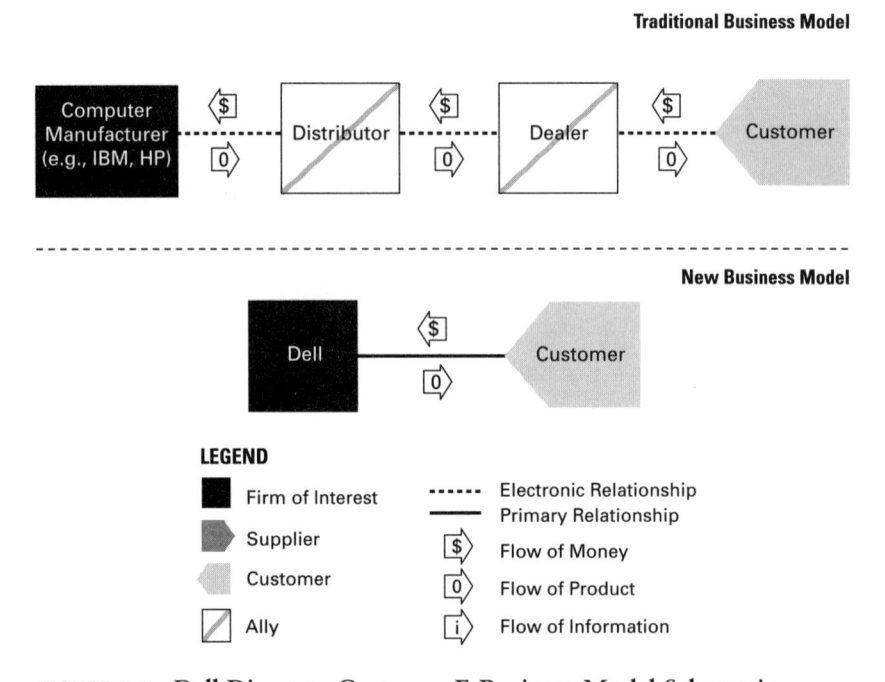

FIGURE 2-3 Dell Direct-to-Customer E-Business Model Schematic

Pages—exclusive customized Web sites for particular business customers. Premier Pages add significant value to Dell products. For example, Dell assists customers to implement standard configurations of PCs. Dell and the business customer agree on a small number of standard computer configurations (e.g., configurations for the customer's administrators, managers, and power users), which are offered on that customer's Premier Page. Employees of the business customer access their firm's Premier Page and order systems directly at a prenegotiated price. Dell delivers and installs the systems with the business customer's standard software already loaded. Dell benefits from being the major supplier and knowing more about the business customer and its installed base of systems. The business customer gains from the lower firmwide purchase costs and the implementation of a standard operating environment for PCs.

By owning the relationship with the customer, the direct-to-customer firm can optimize its value chain position by making information resulting from that relationship available to suppliers. For example, Dell shares its customer orders and forward forecasts with its suppliers to help optimize the suppliers' production runs. Along with other production efficiencies, this level of information transparency allows Dell to build to order and carry very little inventory of finished goods. This high-velocity production process enables Dell, at least for some customer segments, to convert the order to cash very quickly—in less than twenty-four hours for credit card and electronic payments. By comparison, firms such as Gateway and Compaq who sell via intermediaries take sixteen and thirty-five days, respectively, to receive payment.[15]

Competitors of Dell selling systems via intermediaries rely on those intermediaries to pass on customer information, making it more difficult to forecast demand and pass those forecasts to suppliers. Often the intermediary is unable or unwilling to collect and pass on the detailed customer information needed by the manufacturer. In some cases it is in the long-term interests of the intermediary not to pass customer information to manufacturers, because not doing so inhibits disintermediation.

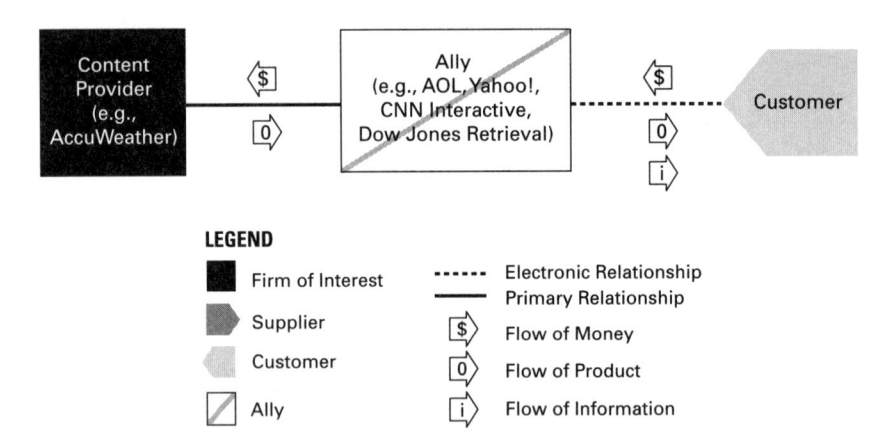

FIGURE 2-4 Content Provider Atomic E-Business Model Schematic

In contrast, a firm using the content provider model (figure 2-4) does not go directly to customers. Instead, the content provider supplies a smaller number of major customers who act as allies. These allies have a direct relationship with the end customer and have the potential to own the customer relationship. The allies may deal with a number of content providers who complement one another and perhaps compete. A portal such as Yahoo! provides attractive content to draw customers to its site. Once at the site, the customer provides revenue to the portal, often indirectly on the basis of advertising or sales commissions. Thus content such as weather, travel information, stock prices, news, and sports results (represented by the arrow labeled *i* on figure 2-4) is often provided by the portal without directly charging the customer. For some segments (e.g., the light user) this pricing structure raises major challenges for content providers contemplating a direct connection to the consumer.

E-Business Stockbroking Business Models

To illustrate the schematics in more detail we look briefly at some of the possible e-business models for stockbroking. Figure 2-5 illus-

E-BUSINESS MODEL SCHEMATICS | 43

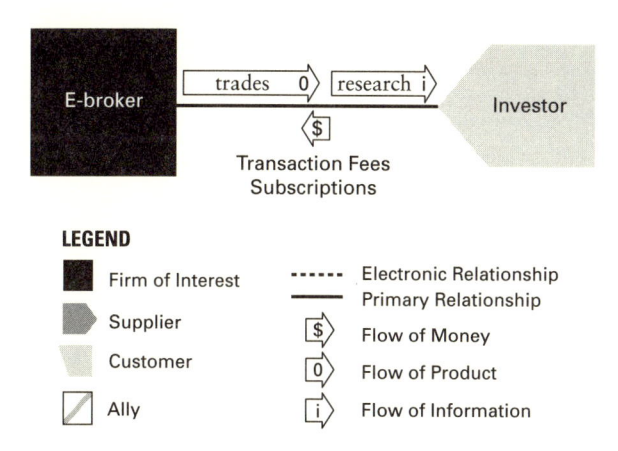

FIGURE 2-5a E-Broking Models / A: Direct-to-Customer

trates the business model schematics of four (A to D) e-business stockbroking (e-broking) models. Models A to D all represent the business from the perspective of the e-broker, and they all exist today.

All e-business model analyses should start with the customer and focus on the value proposition and the sources of revenue. In model A (figure 2-5a), the direct-to-customer model, the investor pays a transaction fee per trade or an annual subscription fee (represented by the $ flow) for trading (represented by the 0 flow). For example, E*TRADE offers trades for around $19.99 on a transaction basis and provides charting, historical information, and some research, but no advice. Merrill Lynch charges an annual fee of fifteen hundred dollars for unlimited trades plus historical information, research, and some advice—all delivered electronically if desired by the customer. In many online stockbroking models, users obtain information free (represented by the i flow), while other information is available only to registered customers in a secure part of the site and is a digital product (represented by the 0 flow).

In model B (figure 2-5b) the full-service financial provider acts as an ally for the e-broker by enhancing demand for the e-broker's services. The full-service financial provider presents an integrated

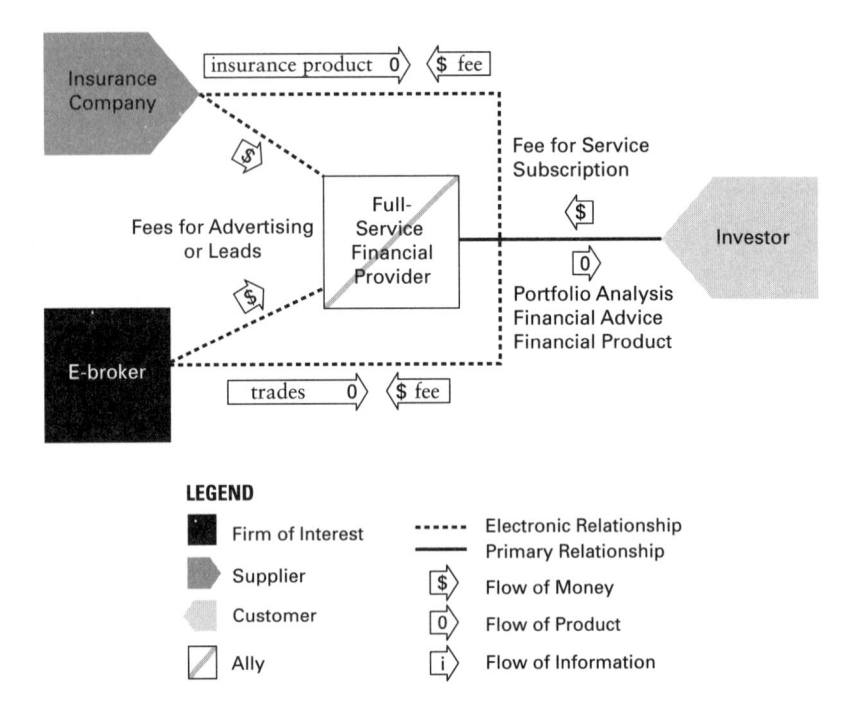

FIGURE 2-5b E-Broking Models / B: Full-Service Financial Provider

offering of its own financial service products and those sourced elsewhere, including e-broking and insurance products. The full-service financial provider may be a financial adviser, a bank, or any other trusted institution.

The full-service financial provider owns the customer relationship with the investor and knows more about that investor than any other participant. The revenue from the investor to the full-service financial provider may be an annual fee, a fee for service, or some combination. A key distinguishing feature is that the full-service provider owns and maintains the customer relationship despite using third-party service providers. We predict many large financial institutions will migrate to this model, exploiting their well-respected brands and large customer bases. They will work hard to own the customer relationship while providing one-stop shopping for financial services. Currently there are few mature

E-BUSINESS MODEL SCHEMATICS | 45

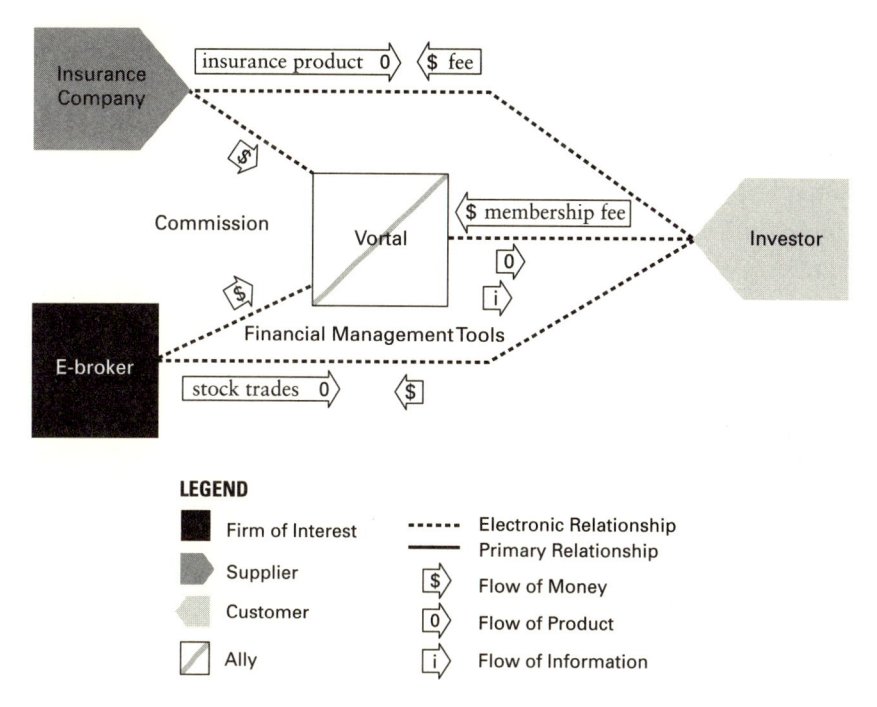

FIGURE 2-5c E-Broking Models / C: Intermediary—Financial Vortal with Fees

examples of full-service providers, although Bank One's Wingspan Bank (www.wingspanbank.com) has many of the features of a full-service provider, as does Prudential Advisor, a service of the Prudential Insurance Company of America (www.prudential securities.com/products_services/pruadvisor.htm).

Model C (figure 2-5c) illustrates e-broking via a specialist intermediary or *vortal*. This rather Star Trekian name means, "portal in a vertical market." The investor uses the vortal as a source of financial information, analytical tools, and perhaps financial advice. For example, the twelve million worldwide users of Quicken's financial management program can access Quicken's electronic one-stop financial services shops. In Australia, Quicken (www.quicken.com.au) offers stock trading under the name of Quick.broker, with execution provided via broker Hartley Poynton at A$19.90 per transaction, including live quotes from the stock exchange, customized portfolios, and charting. Quicken's Insurance Mart provides quotes from three insurers for home and contents policies via a "five-minute quote form." Quicken also provides Morningstar ratings (www.morningstar.com) for mutual funds and a comparison of mortgage, leasing, and other fixed-interest products.[16]

In the United States, Quicken (www.quicken.com) provides clickthroughs to stock-trading services from at least three providers: Ameritrade (www.ameritrade.com), Datek (www.datek.com), and Morgan Stanley Dean Witter (www.online.msdw.com), all of which offer different value propositions and price points starting at eight dollars a trade. Quicken also provides a mortgage-broking service, which arranged $1.2 billion of loans in 1999. Quicken facilitates life and auto insurance policy applications and lists hundreds of mutual funds and other investment products. Quicken provides tools, for example a mortgage finder, to assist decision making as a significant part of its value proposition.

Intuit generated more than $30 million of its revenues in the first quarter of financial year 2000 via the Internet, a doubling over the previous year and already significant compared to total 1999 revenues of $850 million. Intuit derived Internet revenues from advertising (19 percent), transactions (33 percent), and distribution fees (48 percent), increasing by 48 percent, 106 percent, and 188 percent respectively over the first quarter of the previous year. The big increases in revenue from transaction and distribution fees probably include listing fees, referral fees for an introduction, and a larger fee for a completed transaction. Intuit's future will depend more on its ability to attract investors to its site and capture fees for third-party service provision and less on software sales.[17]

Model D (figure 2-5d) is another type of intermediary—a true portal. Yahoo! is the prototypical portal, with over 145 million unique customers worldwide and more than 625 million page views per day.[18] Yahoo! aims to be the place the customer goes to first on the Internet and offers a huge range of content and tools including search engines, news, email, auctions, virtual communities, calendars, and classified advertising. Customers can customize

E-BUSINESS MODEL SCHEMATICS | 47

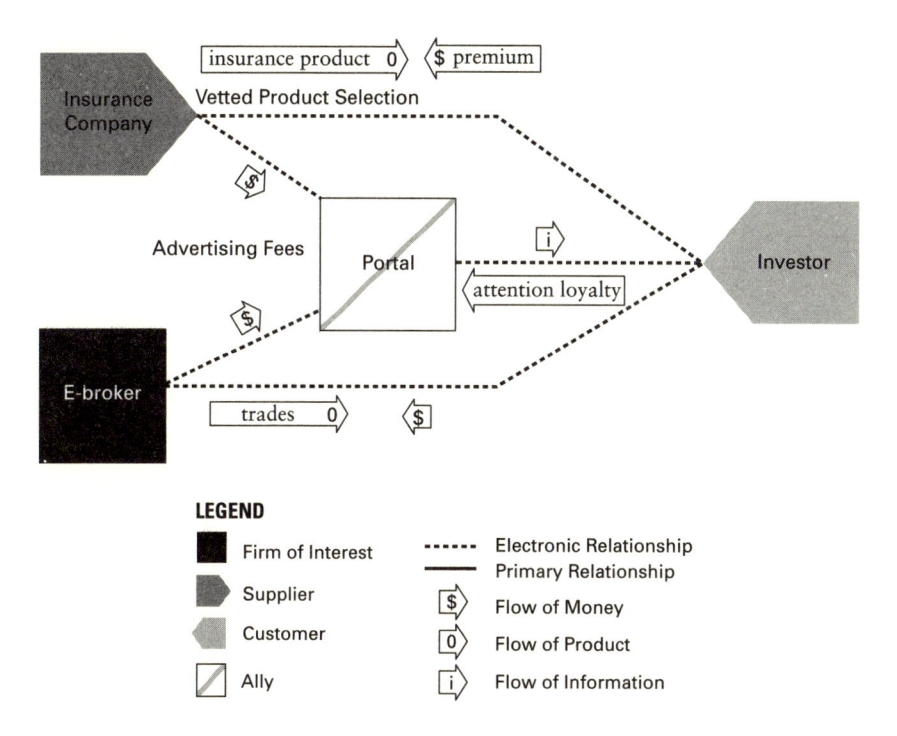

FIGURE 2-5d E-Broking Models / D: Intermediary—Portal with Advertising

their Yahoo! page so that each time their browser is fired up the customized Yahoo! home page appears.

Yahoo! enables customers to click through to e-brokers. For example, in late 1999 Yahoo! offered stock trades at $7.95 via a clickthrough to Suretrade.com. A few months later, Yahoo! provided a clickthrough to E*TRADE with trades starting at $4.95. Quicktrade offers Australian users trades at A$29.95 from St. George Bank. Comparing the schematics of models C and D illustrates the many similarities in the business models, particularly as Quicken continues to evolve from a software provider to a full-service financial intermediary.

These examples of e-business models illustrate several key questions of e-broking viability highlighted by the schematics and summarized in table 2-1.

TABLE 2-1 Summary of E-Broker Business Models

Business Model	A. Direct to Customer	B. Full-Service Provider (FSP)	C. Intermediary—Financial Vortal (FV)	D. Intermediary—Portal with Advertising
Sources of Revenue	Transaction fees and/or Subscriptions Payment for content	E-broker: Transaction fees FSP: Fee for service and owning the customer relationship	E-broker: Transaction fees FV: Fee for owning the customer relationship and being specialized	E-broker: Transaction fees Portal: Fee for delivering potential customer to advertisers and service providers
Owns Relationship	E-broker	FSP	FV	Portal
Level of Intimacy for Primary Customer Relationship	Highly intimate for brokerage and investments	Highly intimate on full financial picture	Medium	Low
Owns Transaction	E-broker	E-broker	E-broker	E-broker
Owns Data	E-broker	E-broker and FSP	E-broker and perhaps the vortal	E-broker
Type of Information Needed to Succeed	Operations cost and prospects and Market intelligence	Customer's total financial picture	Customer profiles and product information	Customer segment profiles and preferences

Sources of Revenue

Determining whether the sources of revenue are realistic is a fundamental question for any e-business model. The sources of revenue in e-broking include the following:

- **Transaction fees.** Transactions fees are the most visible source of revenue for all the e-broker business models in figure 2-5. However, the long-term viability of transaction revenue is questionable, given the commoditization of the product and the associated price competition. Prices as low as $4.95 per trade cannot be sustained without huge volumes, suggesting a major consolidation. Stock trade transaction processing is likely to consolidate into a few major players, resulting in a shared industry infrastructure similar to airline reservation systems or ATM networks. One interesting possibility is the forward integration of stock exchanges such as the NASDAQ into direct stock trading.

- **Information and advice.** Historically stockbrokers provided information and some advice bundled as part of their service, covered by brokerage fees as high as 2 percent of the trade value. As e-business facilitates unbundling of these services, many brokers struggle with how to charge for advice and research. Merrill Lynch's subscription of fifteen hundred dollars per year includes unlimited trades as well as access to research, a personal consultant, and the acquisition of mutual funds and fixed-income products.

- **Fees for services and commissions.** In model B the ally is a full-service provider that makes its money by owning the relationship with the customer. There are many variations, but one common model is that the full-service provider produces a financial plan for the customer on a fee-for-service basis. The full-service broker then receives up-front or trailing commissions for investment products such as a mutual fund provided by the third party. In model C the vortal receives a fee or commission for owning the customer relationship and being specialized. A successful vortal can deliver highly qualified prospects to service providers such as the e-broker.

Creating a strong enough value proposition and customer relationship is a major challenge for the vortal model to ensure an ongoing revenue stream from fees. The strong culture on the Internet that information is free makes this type of information broking challenging.

- **Advertising and listing fees.** In model D the sources of revenue are usually advertising and listing fees, through which the portal is paid by the number of "eyeballs" delivered to advertisers. The portal finds attractive content, both free and paid, to draw people to its site and charges advertisers and service providers such as the e-broker to access its loyal users. The model is similar to that of a traditional free-to-air television or radio station. For example Yahoo! describes its sources of revenues this way:

> The Company derives significant revenues from the sale of advertising elements including placement fees, promotions, banner advertisements, sponsorships, direct marketing, and transaction fees generated from the sale of merchandise on Yahoo! properties. The Company's advertising products currently consist of banner advertisements that appear on pages within Yahoo! properties, higher profile promotional sponsorships that are typically focused on a particular event, such as a sweepstakes, and merchant sponsorship buttons on targeted advertising inventory encouraging users to complete a transaction. Direct marketing revenues result from email campaigns targeted to certain members of the Yahoo! registered community that have indicated a willingness to receive such promotions. Hypertext links are embedded in each banner advertisement, button or directed email to provide the user with instant access to the advertiser's Website, to obtain additional information, or to purchase products and services.[19]

In any e-business model there are three important questions of ownership:

- Who owns the customer relationship?
- Who owns the customer data?
- Who owns the customer transaction?

Understanding and exploiting the ownership of these three assets help us predict the viability of a particular e-business model.

Who Owns the Customer Relationship?

The bold lines in the schematics identify which entity, if any, has the potential to own the customer relationship. In models A to D the entities owning the relationship with the investor know more about the investor's financial needs and history than any other entity. Furthermore, the investor thinks of that entity first when making a decision. For the entity to own the customer relationship (e.g., the e-broker model A in figure 2-5a or the vortal in model C figure 2-5c), it must know more about the investor than any other player and the investor always should consider that service provider first. In model A, the relationship is owned exclusively by the e-broker and is potentially highly intimate, providing a detailed picture of the customer's broking history and investment holdings. The breadth of the relationship in model A is limited to stock trading and similar investments. The bold line represents only the potential to own the customer relationship; in many actual e-business models no entity owns the relationship. Customers cherry pick the best e-broking offering at the time of purchase, exhibiting little or no loyalty.

In model B, the full-service financial provider owns the customer relationship and integrates the services of the e-broker and the insurer. The broader relationship in model B covers the full spectrum of financial services. The electronic relationship from the e-broker is dashed until it joins the solid line, which represents the primary relationship owned by the full-service financial provider. This structure illustrates that the integration of third-party offerings (e.g., that of the e-broker) occurs at the full-service financial provider's Web site. If the investor accessed the e-broker's site directly, the e-broker might someday own the relationship with the customer.

The potential intimacy of the full-service provider in model B is very high, with the possibility of capturing a detailed picture of the investor's complete financial situation over time. If the full-service provider manages this intimacy carefully it creates a valuable digital asset to use for tailoring services to the customer. Some customer segments will happily receive tailored-service offerings that are clearly a good fit for their needs and become loyal customers. Other customers may opt out. A core competency of the full-service provider is to understand customers' preferences and whether they desire additional service offerings.

In model C, the potential for intimacy in the relationship between the vortal and the investor is less than for models A and B. The vortal acts as an intermediary; it has the potential to but may not own the customer relationship. The dashed-line electronic relationship from the e-broker to the investor illustrates that the investor accesses the e-broker's site directly.

In model D the potential intimacy for the portal intermediary is the lowest across the four models. The portal intermediary probably has a stronger focus on transactions than on relationships. Many customers use the portal as an intelligent search engine, and the portal may not capture even the identity of the investor. Thus all relationships are shown by a dashed line indicating no entity owns the customer relationship in this model.

Who Owns the Data and the Transaction?

The key questions about data and transaction ownership are: Who owns the data and thus has access to it for marketing? Who owns the transaction and thus receives a transaction fee? In all four models, the e-broker owns the customer stock trade transaction and receives a fee for completing the transaction. In model A, the e-broker has the potential to exclusively own the relationship, the transaction, and the data. The e-broker will definitely own the transaction and the data about that transaction, and for some segments the e-broker also owns the relationship, which is highly intimate. For other segments neither the e-broker nor any other entity owns the relationship; for example, the investor may use several e-brokers depending on the brokers' current fees.

In model B, the full-service financial provider owns the customer relationship. The stock trade transaction is owned by the e-broker, and the full-service financial provider and the e-broker own the data about that transaction. Over time the financial service provider will build up the most complete picture of the customer's financial picture and will take care to provide the e-broker with only the absolute minimum information set needed to complete the transaction. The e-broker will earn transaction fees and collect data about those transactions, providing some insights about the customer's financial picture, but probably not detailed or complete enough to allow the broker to become the full-service provider.

In model C the vortal intermediary owns the relationship, which is more intimate than for the portal intermediary in model D but less intimate than for the full-service provider in model B. In model C the e-broker owns the transaction, and the e-broker and perhaps the vortal own the data about that transaction. In model D, the portal potentially owns a relatively less intimate relationship with the investor. The e-broker in model D owns the transaction and the data and has a strong likelihood of eventually owning the investor relationship by converting to the structure in model A. The portal will continue to provide prospects for the e-broker in model D, but once it acquires customers, the e-broker will attempt to convert to a direct-to-customer relationship with the investor.

Type of Information

Information is the lifeblood of e-business. The viability of many business models will depend on access to information about customers, products, markets, and costs. The firm's ability to identify, capture, share, and exploit the key information strongly influences business model profitability. As seen in the Hilton example, firms are increasingly seeking detailed and granular information about their customers, particularly customers in their most loyal and profitable customer segments.

Different types of information are critical for the different models (see table 2-1). For example, the direct-to-customer model based on transaction fees (model A) is fast becoming a commodity business. The information critical to succeed includes detail on business process performance and operating costs. A reliable source of prospects to keep up volumes is also critical. In the direct-to-customer model based on annual subscriptions, market intelligence information is critical for success. Merrill Lynch has a huge investment in researchers who produce detailed market intelligence for customers who are prepared to pay a flat fee for access to this information.

A full-service provider (model B) requires information about the customer's total financial picture, enabling accurate matching with needs and service offerings provided both directly and via third parties. For the vortal (model C), the critical information for success includes individual investor profiles and complete and current information about available offerings in the marketplace, allowing the vortal to broker a connection between investors and products. The role of the vortal is strengthened if third-party ratings agencies (e.g., Morningstar ratings for mutual funds) provide independent ratings to aid the customer in selecting and comparing products.

In model D, the portal must focus on segments of its large number of customers, who are interested in a very diverse set of content. A portal needs information on the size of customer segments and their profiles. The portal must deliver detailed information on the segments using their site to advertisers. The more detailed and targeted the segment information collected by the portal, the stronger the value proposition provided to the advertiser, and hence the higher the fees.

The Search for Atomic E-Business Models

Models A to D illustrate three of our eight atomic e-business models: direct to customer, full-service provider, and intermediary. The three business models illustrate very different ways of doing e-business, which fit different business strategies. Implementing the different business models (A to D) requires different core competencies, with different critical success factors, targeting different segments, and requiring different IT infrastructure capabilities. In chapter 3 we explain the concepts of atomic e-business models and e-business initiatives, providing a structured way to analyze future initiatives for an organization.

CHAPTER 3

Atomic E-Business Models and Initiatives

> Things should be made as simple as possible but not any simpler. Problems cannot be solved at the same level of awareness that created them.
>
> —ALBERT EINSTEIN

Atomic E-Business Business Models

Through our research and consulting work, we have identified a small number of atomic e-business models, each of which describes the essence of conducting business electronically. For example, a content provider such as AccuWeather (see chapter 2) is paid to provide branded digital content that other business customers, for example, news services and portals, incorporate into their own services. These models can be used to build understanding of e-business by decomposing more complex e-business models. The atomic business models can also be used as building blocks to create new e-business initiatives.

As e-business matures, firms are becoming less and less likely to implement a single atomic model—although some of our examples get very close. Rather, atomic models are a conceptual framework for understanding the complex reality of e-business. Henry Mintzberg's seminal work, *The Structuring of Organizations,* encouraged our approach. Mintzberg identified five "pure" structural configurations or organizational archetypes. Mintzberg explains his motivations:

> In one sense the structural configurations do not exist at all. After all, they are just words and pictures on a piece of paper, not reality itself. . . . Every theory necessarily simplifies and therefore distorts the reality. . . . The five structural configurations will also exist if they prove to constitute a simple and powerful theory, more useful in some ways than the others currently available.[1]

The motivation for our atomic models is the same: to provide a conceptual framework for understanding e-business initiatives in firms. After boiling down e-business into a finite set of atomic models, we can use the models in at least three ways:

1. **Atomic models as pure types.** Atomic models describe the essence of an e-business model. Understanding the characteristics of the atomic models gives us insights into successfully operating an e-business model of this type.

2. **Atomic models as building blocks.** Managers can combine the building blocks into e-business initiatives. Some combinations of atomic models will be viable, while others will contain inherent conflict and be unstable. Firms can look to these atomic models as potential building blocks when strategizing about e-business initiatives.

3. **Decomposition of e-business initiatives.** Managers can decompose an e-business initiative into its atomic models to better understand implementation requirements.

The advantage of the third use of atomic models is that we can decompose an e-business initiative into better understood atomic business models. By studying firms we can determine the core competencies and the critical success factors necessary to implement an atomic model. For example, a critical success factor for a content provider is branding its content so the consumer is aware of the source and will look for the brand in the future. This critical success factor helps explain the frequent appearance of logos alongside information on the Internet.

By working with firms and studying and classifying a large number of e-business initiatives, we have identified eight atomic e-business models. Our aim was to identify a set of atomic models that were mutually exclusive (and exhaustive) and named to clearly describe their essence as business models. For example, in the direct-to-customer model, a firm takes an order directly via an electronic channel and provides goods or services directly to the consumer. The product may be delivered electronically or physically. Often a direct-to-customer business will bypass an existing player in the channel, as Dell bypassed the retail computer store.

All the atomic models except content provider are equally applicable to B2B and B2C. For example, a full-service provider could be a retail financial services firm, such as Wingspan Bank (www.wingspanbank.com) or Chase (www.chase.com), providing a full range of consumer services including loans, insurance, advice, banking products, credit cards, brokerage, bill paying, and mutual funds via the channel of the Internet.

In chapters 4 to 11 we provide the e-business model schematics and analyze the following:

- How revenues are generated, where value is added, and how readily the model can be sustained.

- The strategic objectives of the business model.

- The value proposition to the customer.

- The critical success factors necessary for the successful implementation of the business model (what must the firm do well to succeed with the implementation).

- The core competencies a firm must nurture and exploit to be successful in implementing the business model. (Core competencies are usually a subset of the critical success factors that we recommend are maintained in the firm and not outsourced. For example, critical success factors for AccuWeather include branding and weather forecasting, but only the latter is a core competency for the firm.)

Combinations of Atomic E-Business Models

Describing an e-business initiative as a combination of atomic business models tells us something about the value proposition to the customer and thus how the firm makes money. Some combinations of atomic business models are compatible and create powerful value propositions. For example, the combination of direct to customer and virtual community has many synergies. Amazon pioneered this combination of business models with chat groups and book reviews provided by Amazon.com customers. Amazon partnered with RemarQ Communities—"the leading provider of online discussion services"—to allow people to share ideas in discussion forums such as the "Author's Corner" and the Oprah Book Club. While clicking to and from the discussion forums, the community member is exposed to Amazon.com advertising and products. If successful, this combination of direct to customer and virtual community will be self-reinforcing, leading to more loyalty and more sales for Amazon.

Other combinations of atomic business models are incompatible, leading to problems such as channel conflict. Many traditional book publishers such as Harvard Business School Press and Lonely Planet face challenges migrating to e-business. The bulk of sales for most book publishers are via bookstores. The bookstore, as an intermediary, compiles a selection of content from multiple publishers to suit the bookstore's target market segments. In an e-business world the publisher can, often for the first time, economically go directly to the customer, an initiative that can create channel conflict. The publisher can also choose to pass on to the customer some of the savings taken from the bookstore's margin, which is as much as 40 to 50 percent of the sale price. We will explore the business models available to publishers such as Lonely Planet in more detail in chapter 12.

A useful analogy for the relationship between the atomic e-business models, e-business models, and e-business initiatives is the relationship between atoms, compounds, and chemical reactions. Atoms are the smallest particle that take part in a chemical reaction. Some combinations of atoms are stable and form compounds, while the laws of chemical reactions prevent other combinations of atoms from occurring. There are a small number of atomic elements and a much larger number of possible compounds. As the field of chemistry developed, new atoms were occasionally discovered, while new compounds are developed frequently.

E-business is developing in a similar way. New atomic e-business models are discovered occasionally—for example, intermediaries such as intelligent search agents that can find the best price for a product. However, new e-business initiatives built from novel combinations of atomic e-business models are developed and tested on a daily basis.

Our objective is to identify a set of atomic business models and describe what we know about their characteristics and their composition into e-business initiatives. Here is where the analogy to chemistry breaks down. In e-business, as with any aspect of management, the best we can hope for are guiding principles, not laws of nature. It would be simpler, but rather naïve, to look for laws of e-business as there are in chemistry. In e-business, value is created through the implementation of an initiative, and that process is much less predictable and scientific than a chemical reaction. A potentially successful business model is only the first step of the e-business journey. Implementing the model, refining the model, and providing and extracting value are where the real work is done. E-business initiatives describe how a firm goes to the marketspace.

E-Business Initiatives

The critical issues in an e-business initiative are the combination of atomic e-business models, the channels to the customer, the targeted customer segments, and the IT infrastructure capability needed (see figure 1-1). The combination of atomic business models explains the business objectives, the relationships, and the flows of the initiative. The customer segments identify the target audience and the value proposition delivered. Channels describe how each customer segment is reached and the richness of the information transfer to the customer. The infrastructure specifies the IT capability required, both internally and externally, to enable the e-business initiative. We will first present an example of an e-business initiative and then discuss each of the four elements in detail.

The E-Stock Club Business Proposal

Imagine E-Stock Club, a proposed wholly owned subsidiary of an existing bank. The business case presents a value proposition in which customers take control of their own investments and control their own destiny, with the bank providing capital. The E-Stock Club business model value proposition emphasizes low-cost straight-through processing in which trade instructions are sent directly to the stock exchange for processing with no delays or price spread manipulation. The E-Stock Club bypasses the traditional broker and offers low transaction costs but no investment advice.

E-Stock Club investor services include:

- up-to-the-minute stock price and trading information with indicators of the depth of demand to sell or buy the stock;

- historical market and stock information with a powerful charting capability;

- independent third-party ratings of a stock's past and future performance, with a table summarizing the buy and sell recommendations of several research firms;

- education, including investment seminars; short primers on topics such as options; books; and classes delivered electronically and physically;

- chat rooms and investment clubs;

- a wide variety of loan products for investors, including margin loans and personal credit lines;
- email service; and
- Internet service provider (ISP) access.

The E-Stock Club has chat rooms on topics such as Internet stocks, futures, emerging markets, gold stocks, mutual funds, and particular stocks. The E-Stock Club encourages members to form and join electronic investment clubs by providing a free email service and a good deal on ISP access. The E-Stock Club uses a range of content providers to supply these services, which are seamlessly integrated into E-Stock Club's Web site (see figure 3-1).

The e-business initiative (figure 3-2) is a combination of the direct-to-customer and virtual community atomic e-business models for like-minded independent investors. The target customer segments are the "active traders" and the "wannabes." Active traders are confident in the market, trade regularly, and account for 8 percent of investors; wannabes are typically young, male, want to be involved in the stock market, and account for 15 percent of investors.[2] New customers will come by "word of mouse" from existing consumers, by limited direct marketing, and via four types of allies: the bank that owns E-Stock Club, portals such as Yahoo!, financial planners, and local accountants.[3] The E-Stock Club particularly wants to target the bank's day-trader and active-trader customers.

Until recently, stockbrokers had exclusive access to the stock market, controlling the path to stock ownership and thus the channel to the investor. In business models such as E*TRADE, the investor can choose to bypass the human stockbroker or financial adviser, doing trades directly via the Internet. The traditional broker channel often targets segments such as the "security conscious" (14 percent), the "active traders" (8 percent), the "confident players" (8 percent), and perhaps the "dabblers" (15 percent).[4]

Delivering the E-Stock Club business model requires a reliable IT infrastructure. In this e-business model the IT infrastructure is the entire business infrastructure and must be reliable, secure, easy

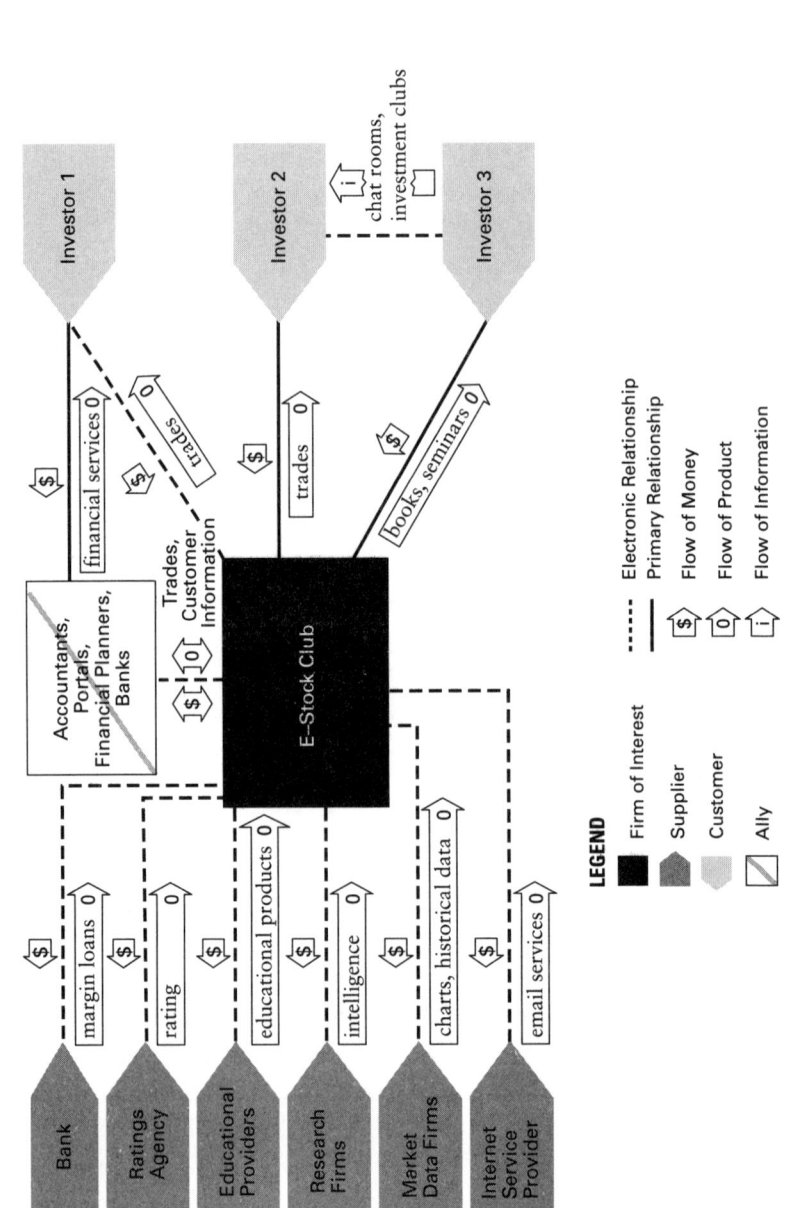

FIGURE 3-1 E-Stock Club Business Model

ATOMIC E-BUSINESS MODELS AND INITIATIVES | 63

	Channels	Segments
ATOMIC E-BUSINESS MODELS ■ Direct to Customer ■ Virtual Community	WWW Phone ~~Broker~~	**Active Traders** (8 percent) **Wannabes** (15 percent)

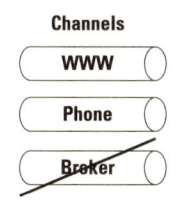

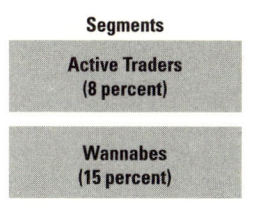

IT INFRASTRUCTURE CAPABILITY

- Straight-through processing to stock exchange
- Transaction payment processing
- Combines multiple sources of online information
- Secure trading with accurate feedback on outcomes
- Reliable 24/7 operations with backup and mirroring
- Rapid development capability
- Firmwide customer relationship database

FIGURE 3-2 E-Stock Club E-Business Initiative

to use, and customizable by the investor. Infrastructure capability requirements include:

- straight-through processing to the stock exchange;
- transaction payment processing;
- combination of multiple sources of online information presented in an easy-to-use Web site;
- secure trading with accurate feedback and reporting;
- reliable twenty-four-hour, seven-day processing operations with backup;
- rapid development capability to incorporate new offerings; and
- firmwide customer relationship database.

The E-Stock Club initiative was presented to the new-products committee of a large bank—and rejected. There were four main reasons:

1. The committee didn't feel that the combination of the virtual community and direct-to-customer atomic e-business models

would work. The committee was concerned that the bank's brand did not engender a feeling of community where customers would come to share financial information. Instead the bank stood for security, integrity, reliability, and perhaps even a bit of detachment.

2. The IT infrastructure requirement of a firmwide customer relationship database was at least one year away. The bank's systems were developed over time on a product basis, with each product system operating on a different and incompatible technical platform.

3. The committee had no data, but they suspected that the two segments targeted by the e-business initiative were not well represented in the bank's current customer base.

4. The committee was concerned that the electronic channels proposed were insufficiently rich and intimate to service the target segments and cross-sell other bank products.

The E-Stock Club illustrates that testing the viability of an e-business initiative requires looking beyond the e-business model. The bank's new-products committee felt that the E-Stock Club e-business model was sound, even attractive. However, the discipline of placing the business model in the context of customer segments, channels, and IT infrastructure requirements revealed problems. Despite a unanimous feeling that the correct decision was made, the committee left the meeting feeling rather dispirited by the bank's inability to address the problem areas important in an e-business world.

Now we will focus on understanding the four elements of an e-business initiative in more detail: target customer segments, channels to the customer, IT infrastructure capability, and, finally, a combination of atomic e-business models.

Customer Segments

Consideration of an e-business initiative should always start with the customer. Specifically, it is important to understand which customer segments are targeted, and what the value proposition is for each segment. Customer segments are groups of similar customers, with enough important differences between the groups that each might merit a separate product or market mix.[5] Segmenting the market requires disaggregating the total market demand into segments with distinct demand profiles and tailoring a different value proposition for each demand profile.[6] Segments represent differences in buying behavior or motivation, and segment members can be described in terms of their background, attitude, income, gender, geography, age, technology savvy, or other criteria and combinations. Customer segmentation is a fundamental skill for traditional-marketplace businesses.[7] Firms such as Disney, Hilton, and Gap are masters at tailoring offerings for targeted customer segments.

In e-business, segmentation becomes even more important than in the physical world because there is often no person to redirect customers if an electronic channel serves them poorly. The typical Internet user profile is changing. In 1995, the Internet user profile was skewed to be primarily Caucasian males with high levels of income and education. Women made up 33 percent of the Internet population in 1995, mainly those women with high income and education levels. In 1999 women composed 46 percent of the online population, and there is early evidence that buying patterns differ by gender. For example, CommerceNet/Nielsen found that of the 4 million online purchasers of software, 3.1 million (78 percent) were male; but of the 2.1 million online purchasers of travel, 1.3 million (62 percent) were female.[8] If sellers are able to further segment their market by other important factors such as income level, number of children, novice versus expert, or time poor versus time rich, powerful value propositions for each segment can be identified.

Perhaps for the first time, e-business offers firms a practical and affordable way to segment current and potential customers. Online tracking programs such as Active Concepts' Funnel Web (www.activeconcepts.com) allow firms to learn much more about customer behavior by digitally storing information about the ways customers navigate their sites. Adding this information to customer purchasing patterns stored in databases leads to careful segmentation. Online advertising companies such as 24/7 Media (www.247media.com) can tailor online advertising campaigns to particular segments and provide immediate data collection and feedback to measure success. Reaching nearly 60 percent of all online users in the United States, 24/7 Media is one of the largest global Internet companies, serving more than 5.5 billion ad impressions per month and hosting more than four thousand sites globally. 24/7 Media has the world's largest permission-based email database, consisting of more than twenty million profiles that can be used to deliver target online banner and email campaigns.[9]

Dell is an exemplar of customer segmentation in e-business and broadly segments its customers as relationship (40 percent), transactional (30 percent), or a blend of both (30 percent). Transactional customers are individuals or businesses seeing each purchase individually, focusing on the economics of the transaction. Whether the transactional customer buys one machine or two hundred, each purchase decision is based on a particular mix of performance specifications, features, and price. Given these customers' lack of focus on brand and continuity, Dell must win them each time they buy. Dell's relationship customers are less price sensitive and focus on a broader definition of value, including issues such as reliability, vendor strength, and standardization of installed technology infrastructure. Popular with the relationship customers are Dell's value-added services such as DellPlus (software installation) and DellWare (one-stop software shopping).[10]

These questions help focus on the customer segments for an e-business initiative:

- What is distinctive about the segments?
- Which customer segments are targeted?
- How big is each segment?
- What is the value proposition for each segment?
- Will our brand be effective for each segment?

Managing the Channels to the Customer

In any e-business initiative, reaching the target customer segments requires careful channel selection and management. A channel is the conduit by which a firm's products or services are offered or distributed to the customer. We propose that for e-business initiatives the channel is considered a feature of the product offer and thus part of the value proposition to the customer.[11] Understanding the characteristics of the target segments for an e-business initiative provides clues for the channel. The suitability of the channel can enhance or diminish the value of the products for each target segment.

Options for offering or distributing products include channels operated by the firm as well as channels provided by a third party such as an agent or intermediary. Matching the value proposition to the target segment is critical for e-business, because there is less likelihood of human assistance. Bruce Leucke, president of interactive delivery services for the Bank One Retail Group, says that Bank One's e-business strategy is to "leverage a broad range of initiatives employing multiple brands, numerous web alliances and unparalleled web visibility."[12] In the words of Bank One CEO John McCoy, "wherever you go on the Internet we will be there." Bank One separates their e-business customers into four segment types using different combinations of channels to deliver a tailored value proposition to each customer segment. Below is a description of these four types:

1. Bank One customers preferring Bank One–branded products and wanting access through many channels including the Internet. For these customers the value proposition is secure, convenient access to Bank One through multiple channels: branches, telephone, relationship managers, ATMs, and bankone.com. Interestingly, 60 percent of bankone.com customers want to use physical banking centers as well as other channels.

2. Internet customers wanting multichannel access to a combination of Bank One and other providers' products. To these customers, Bank One offers the full service of bankone.com

and other Bank One channels as well as partnering with Internet intermediaries such as AOL and Excite to deliver other services.

3. Customers for whom the Internet is more than a channel; it is their primary conduit to the world. These customers are offered a robust set of Internet-delivered services from Bank One via bankone.com.

4. Customers who prefer Internet-only access but want to access Bank One products as well as a full range of other providers. These customers are likely to be attracted to wingspanbank.com, which is an Internet-only financial services provider with banking, money management, stockbroking, and insurance products that sources multiple service providers—all consolidated into a password-protected Web site.

Bank One has thought carefully about its e-business segments, offering a bundle of services and channels attractive to customers in each segment. For example, the first segment is made up of customers wanting full-service provision by a trusted banking partner with whom they have an intimate relationship. These customers want to access Bank One's services via multiple channels depending on their needs at a given time. These customers expect Bank One to know a lot about their financial needs and to treat them knowledgeably, whichever channel they choose. These customers also expect access to personal bankers who can tailor Bank One's services to meet their needs. In contrast, members of the second customer segment want multichannel access to products from both Bank One and other providers. These customers may access Bank One's products directly or via intermediaries, which offer a choice of financial service providers. These customers probably don't want or expect as intimate a relationship with Bank One, and an intermediary may own the customer relationship.

A strength of traditional firms competing with dot-com firms is the multiple channels a traditional firm provides. One bank customer may use the Internet exclusively, while another customer may use multiple channels: the branch for depositing checks and carrying out high-touch activities such as a loan application, and the phone and Internet for paying bills. Each channel has different strengths and weaknesses. The transactions on some channels are more expensive to process than the transactions on others. In chapter 1 we reported a recent Booz•Allen & Hamilton study that put the cost per banking transaction by channel at: branch, U.S.$3.00; telephone, $1.50; ATM, $0.78–$0.42; IVR, $0.30; point of sale, $0.42–$0.24; and Internet, $0.12–$0.06.[13]

Charles Schwab exploited these differences, taking 80 percent of the costs out of 50 percent of its trades—about a $439 million savings in 1999. Online transactions cost only 20 percent of those conducted with Schwab employees in branch offices or by telephone. The cost savings free up Schwab employees for more high-value time with customers and enable global expansion at a lower cost base. Schwab, which began as a place-based business, has exploited these scale economies and maintains only two branches in Europe that serve six hundred thousand customers via the Web, with volumes growing at 25 percent a month, compared to two hundred branches in the United States.[14]

Focusing only on the cost of a channel is tempting, but overly simplistic. Each channel has other important characteristics for e-business, different strengths and potential richness for information transfer between the customer and the firm. This richness works two ways: providing information to customers, and capturing information about customer interactions for later analysis and use.

Table 3-1 summarizes the channels to the customer, identifying their strengths and the richness of the information transfer.[15] Each of the channels has a different strength-to-cost ratio, which must be evaluated for a particular e-business initiative. For example, IVR channels are very effective for repetitive transactions such as balance inquiries and bill paying. IVR offers universal access and is very easy to use. However, IVR is worse than useless for transactions or queries for which it is not programmed. Often there is no simple way customers can determine whether the IVR fits their needs without trying to use it. We all know how frustrating it is to be lost in an endless loop of IVR choices—none of which seems to be right. By contrast, face-to-face contact in a branch, agency, or

TABLE 3-1 Channels to the Customer

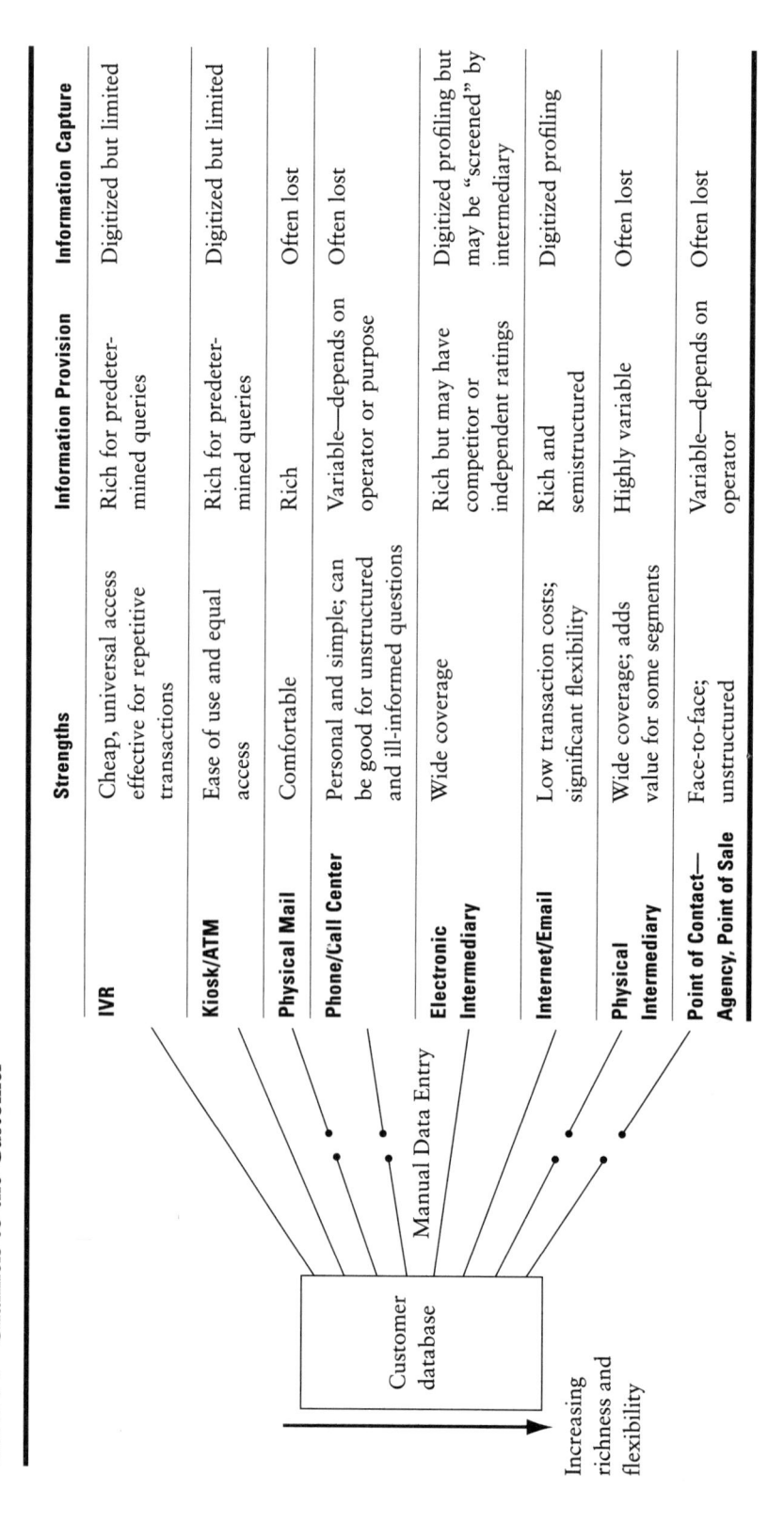

	Strengths	Information Provision	Information Capture
IVR	Cheap, universal access effective for repetitive transactions	Rich for predetermined queries	Digitized but limited
Kiosk/ATM	Ease of use and equal access	Rich for predetermined queries	Digitized but limited
Physical Mail	Comfortable	Rich	Often lost
Phone/Call Center	Personal and simple; can be good for unstructured and ill-informed questions	Variable—depends on operator or purpose	Often lost
Electronic Intermediary	Wide coverage	Rich but may have competitor or independent ratings	Digitized profiling but may be "screened" by intermediary
Internet/Email	Low transaction costs; significant flexibility	Rich and semistructured	Digitized profiling
Physical Intermediary	Wide coverage; adds value for some segments	Highly variable	Often lost
Point of Contact—Agency, Point of Sale	Face-to-face; unstructured	Variable—depends on operator	Often lost

Increasing richness and flexibility →

Customer database

Manual Data Entry

office is much stronger in dealing with unstructured or nonpredetermined queries. However, the cost of the interaction is generally high and the quality of the interaction can be quite variable with long wait times (as anyone who has personally applied for an immigration visa knows).

Call centers combine the strengths of both IVR and face-to-face contact and are excellent for unstructured and ill-formed questions. Call centers are less powerful than face-to-face contact for very complex interactions and also usually require the operator to key in data. The breaks in the lines to the customer database in table 3-1 indicate the channels where a human operator must key data manually. One of the advantages of the IVR, kiosk, and Internet interfaces is that the interactions with the customer are automatically digitized and stored. The cost of keying or scanning data into a firm's systems can be substantial and is therefore often not done. Many important interactions with customers on the phone, face-to-face, or via intermediaries are never recorded. Alas, only the customer remembers the interaction—particularly if it was unsatisfactory!

Integrating all of the channels to the customer to deliver a single picture of the customer's relationship with the firm is a significant challenge for traditional firms in e-business. For example, in the typical bank each transaction system (e.g., checking, mortgage, certificate of deposit) was probably developed at a different time on a different technology infrastructure. Definitions of common data items, such as customer name and address or product name, were probably developed independently for each system, leading to incompatible data architectures. Many banks are now investing heavily in data warehouse systems, middleware (linking Web sites to existing back-end account processing systems), and translation tables to pull together these different platforms and provide an integrated system. Many customers expect not only to access their bank by any channel but also to interact with an informed person who knows the customer's complete relationship with the bank.

E-business raises the stakes for integration across different channels. Bank Internet customers expect that their personalized integrated financial Web page is actually integrated at the back end with online transactions, and therefore contains up-to-date information. Furthermore, the bank customer who uses multiple channels, perhaps on the same day, expects integrated back-end systems with current balances. Providing this level of service and integration is a competitive advantage today, because it enables cross-selling opportunities to all customers and provides rich data for new-product development. Tomorrow this level of integration will just be the price of admission to e-business for any firm.

The channels in table 3-1 are listed in order of increasing richness and flexibility from top to bottom. The potential richness of face-to-face customer interaction is much higher than the richness of IVR or kiosk. Face-to-face contact can include a rich variety of media including voice, text, and diagrams, and it gives the bank employee the opportunity to read the customer's body language and facial expressions. The limited richness of IVR leads to the user's frustration when the options available don't meet their needs. Matching the richness of the channel to the needs of the customer segment is essential in an e-business initiative, particularly if the only channel is the Internet. The increasing popularity of the "click-to-talk" option on the Internet sites of retailers selling products with complex buying decisions is testimony to the need for multiple channels in e-business (e.g., see www.cnet.com).

Another important facet of channel richness is the channel's capacity for information provision and capture. Compare the experiences of interacting with a bank using an IVR, a Web site, and a branch. The information provided by IVR is reasonably rich for predetermined queries; in fact, the structured nature of IVR can help you frame your query or transaction. A Web site is much richer than IVR, with graphics, audio, and video and the ability to click through for more detailed information. A well-designed Web site can provide a rich vehicle for a wide range of semistructured interactions. Web sites are particularly powerful for allowing users to determine how much information they want and in what format (e.g., tables or graphs). The more technically inclined banking customer can explore the fine details of the margin lending product for derivatives, while the customer interested only in a certificate of deposit can get a table of interest rates for deposits of various amounts and durations.

Going to a bank branch for a simple transaction such as a balance inquiry is often frustrating. Long lines and form filling are a high cost to pay for the very small value added from the face-to-face interaction. However, for many people the face-to-face interaction in the branch is important for complex transactions such as choosing bank products. In a good interaction the bank employee can help structure needs and find appropriate products. Unfortunately, face-to-face interactions are not always positive, with poorly trained, overworked, or unhelpful employees resulting in a quite variable customer experience. As the richness of possible information provision increases moving down the table, so does the risk and variability in the interaction. Less rich channels don't vary much in the quality of the interaction from time to time, whereas face-to-face interactions can vary hugely depending on the chemistry of the people involved.

From the perspective of the firm, channels also vary significantly in their ability to capture information for future use. Mail, phone, and face-to-face contact all require a person to key information into a system, and thus potentially rich information is often lost or keyed incorrectly. By contrast, the IVR and kiosk digitize the information of the interaction, but this information is limited to the predetermined services provided by those channels. In those channels in table 3-1 where manual data entry is required, there is a potential for lost information and higher error rates.

The Internet channel provides a potential breakthrough for digitized profiling. For example, Cisco receives over 70 percent of its revenue from its Web site (www.cisco.com) where the online configurator assists the customer to find the right product.[16] Ordering a router from the Cisco Web site via the configurator requires the user to answer a series of questions about the potential use of the router and the systems it connects to. The configurator then leads the user through a series of questions resulting in a design that can then be tested for viability and ordered. The configurator is a very rich provider of information to the user, and it has a much lower error rate for Cisco than human channels. The average error rate in specification via a trained Cisco salesperson or agent is one in four orders, versus one in one hundred orders via the configurator. The cost savings to Cisco from online ordering systems are estimated at $1.5 billion over the last three years. But the cost savings are only the beginning of the value for Cisco. The configurator has the potential to capture very rich information about customer interactions and needs. The attempt by a sufficient number of customers to configure a router not currently available from Cisco could trigger market research for future product development.

IT Infrastructure Capability

IT infrastructure is used in all e-business initiatives to connect different parts of the firm and link to suppliers, customers, and allies. IT infrastructure investments made by firms will be as critical for creating long-term shareholder value as the previous waves of physical infrastructure investments in property, plant, and equipment. In this section we will first define IT infrastructure and then present the findings of our recent study of fifty e-business initiatives and their infrastructure requirements. A complete list of the seventy IT infrastructure services potentially needed for e-business is presented in the appendix.

We define a firm's IT portfolio as its total investment in computing and communications technology (see figure 3-3).[17] This

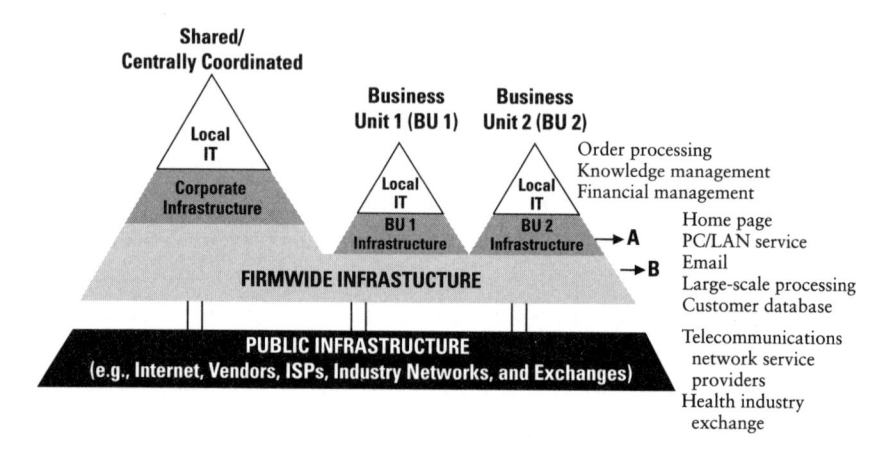

FIGURE 3-3 IT Portfolio for E-Business

Adapted from Peter Weill and Marianne Broadbent, *Leveraging the New Infrastructure: How Market Leaders Capitalize on IT* (Boston: Harvard Business School Press, 1998).

investment includes hardware, software, telecommunications, electronically stored data, myriad devices to collect and represent that data, and the people dedicated to providing these services. The portfolio includes both IT investments implemented by internal groups (insourced) and those outsourced to providers such as IBM Global Services and EDS.

The foundation of the IT portfolio is the firm's longer term IT infrastructure investments, which in turn are linked to external industry infrastructures such as bank payments systems, airline reservations systems, and automotive industry supply chain networks, as well as to public infrastructures such as the Internet and telecommunications networks. The combination of the firm's internal IT infrastructure and the external public infrastructures make up the IT infrastructure illustrated in figure 3-4. These infrastructures are as important for enabling e-business processes as the traditional physical infrastructure—roads, shop fronts, bank branches, share certificates, delivery services, product catalogs—is for enabling traditional commerce.

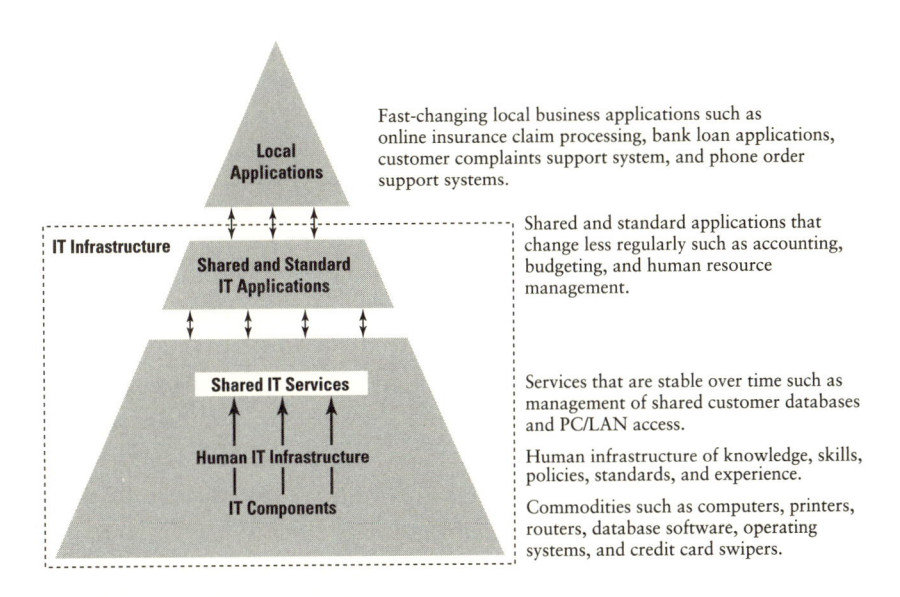

Local Applications: Fast-changing local business applications such as online insurance claim processing, bank loan applications, customer complaints support system, and phone order support systems.

Shared and Standard IT Applications: Shared and standard applications that change less regularly such as accounting, budgeting, and human resource management.

Shared IT Services: Services that are stable over time such as management of shared customer databases and PC/LAN access.

Human IT Infrastructure: Human infrastructure of knowledge, skills, policies, standards, and experience.

IT Components: Commodities such as computers, printers, routers, database software, operating systems, and credit card swipers.

FIGURE 3-4 IT Infrastructure

Peter Weill and Marianne Broadbent, *Leveraging the New Infrastructure: How Market Leaders Capitalize on IT* (Boston: Harvard Business School Press, 1998).

E-business often involves a single electronic point of contact to the firm by a customer. The IT infrastructure must then integrate information from separate business units so that the customer can get to the desired business service from the chosen point of contact (see point B on figure 3-3). Firms taking full advantage of the customer's transaction with one part of the business will also attempt to cross-sell products and services from other parts of the business. Alternatively, the single point of contact could be made for one business unit only at point A in figure 3-3, limiting the cross-selling and information-gathering possibilities to that business unit only.

The various elements of IT infrastructure are presented in figure 3-4. At the base of this framework are the technology components such as computers, printers, database software packages, operating systems, and scanners. These devices are commodities and readily available in the marketplace. The second layer comprises a set of shared IT services. The technology components are converted into useful shared services by a human IT infrastructure composed of knowledge, skills, standards, and experience. This human infrastructure binds the technology components into reliable services that form the firm's IT infrastructure.

The infrastructure services within a firm often include telecommunications network services, management and provision of large-scale computing (such as servers or mainframes), management of shared customer databases, research and development expertise aimed at identifying the usefulness of emerging technologies to the business, and a firmwide intranet. An increasing number of firms have an additional layer of shared and standard infrastructure applications used by all business units. These include firmwide applications that support shared services in functional and support areas such as accounting, human resource management, and budgeting.

The set of infrastructure services required by a firm is relatively stable. Similar services are generally required from year to year with gradual improvements occurring over time to take advantage of new technologies and efficiencies. Occasionally new services are required to support a new initiative. E-business has introduced the need for significantly more and different infrastructure services for most firms. It is likely that after a rush of new services are created for e-business the set of services will again plateau—until the next major trend. In contrast, the IT required for business processes—particularly e-business applications—changes more frequently, often on a quarterly or even monthly basis as business processes are altered to better suit customer needs or in response to competitor activity. In many firms, Web site functionality is increased every month.

The time required to implement a new e-business initiative will depend in part on a combination of the firm's insourced and outsourced infrastructure capability. For example, in building a new Web-based housing loan system, a particular bank needed to use the following IT infrastructure services: mainframe and server processing, customer databases, security procedures and systems, and local area and national communications networks. Having those infrastructure services already in place would have significantly reduced the time and cost to build the loan system. However, the fire wall security services were not in place to support a Web-based application that integrates customer data and credit-scoring systems in the Internet customer interface. Direct customer access was not considered in the initial design of the infrastructure services. The firm had to postpone launching the new initiative until the security services were ready. If the new security infrastructure services are well designed, they will be reused for many other Web applications.

Infrastructure capability is difficult to create, because it is a fusion of technology and human assets.[18] But it can also provide a competitive advantage. We know from our research that firms with greater infrastructure capability have faster times to market, higher growth rates, and more sales from new products, but lower short-term profitability.[19] Building an infrastructure tailored to a firm's strategic context takes considerable time and expertise. While the components are commodities, the management processes to implement the best mix of infrastructure capabilities to suit a specific firm are a much scarcer resource.

The services notion of IT infrastructure is very powerful. The concept emerged from our discussions with business managers grappling with what they were actually getting for their IT investments.

Business managers told us they have great difficulty valuing technology components such as a server or a database package. New IT staff appointments are also difficult to value. However, business managers can more readily value a service, such as the provision of a fully maintained personal computer with access to all firm systems and the Internet. These services can be specified and measured and their costs can be controlled in a service-level agreement. Perhaps most important, managers can price services in the marketplace for comparison. Thinking of infrastructure as services places the customer—the business manager—in charge, rather than the provider, whether it is the information systems group or an outsourcer. The notion of a service also gives the provider much more certainty about what its responsibilities are and allows for more precise planning.

Study of IT Infrastructure Needed for E-Business To understand how IT infrastructure needs may have changed as a result of e-business, we conducted a study of traditional firms that were launching e-business initiatives. The purpose of the study was to identify and define the IT infrastructure services relevant to particular atomic e-business models and their combinations. We sought first to identify and categorize all the IT services relevant for e-business, and then statistically to identify which services were more important for each atomic business model. This section describes the infrastructure services we identified and provides summary results from the study.

We spoke to chief information officers (CIOs), senior IT infrastructure managers, IT managers, information systems planning managers, and e-commerce managers. We studied fifty e-business initiatives in a diverse range of Australian subsidiaries of global firms, Australia-based global firms, and government agencies, including manufacturing, natural resources, financial services, postal, retail, and agricultural resource companies.[20] The appendix describes the study, lists the participating firms, and gives more detailed results.

Using sets of IT infrastructure services from previous work, we expanded the list of services needed to include those we believed were required for e-business.[21] We then piloted and iteratively amended the list by gathering data from companies in questionnaire and interview format until a stable set of services emerged. The result was a list of seventy infrastructure services categorized into the nine areas listed below. The figures in parentheses are the number of services in each area. The table in the appendix presents a complete list of the seventy services with the percentage of firms providing each service and their relative investment.

1. Applications infrastructure (13)

2. Communications management (7)

3. Data management (6)

4. IT management (9)

5. Security (4)

6. Architecture and standards (20)

7. E-channel management (7)

8. IT research and development (2)

9. Training and education in the use of IT (2)

The appendix provides definitions of each infrastructure service area. Table 3-2 summarizes our findings on the provision of these services. Each row represents one area of infrastructure service, with the number of services in parentheses. The numbers in the body of the table are the average firm responses for all the services within each area. The columns in table 3-2 are interpreted as follows:

- The first column is the percentage of firms that provide the service. For example, there are thirteen infrastructure services in the area of applications management. On average these services are provided by 90 percent of firms. The number of firms providing each of the thirteen services within the applications infrastructure area varies, as it does in all areas (see the appendix). For example, 100 percent of firms set policies for Internet use (e.g., employee access and usage login) and 93 percent of firms enforce Internet policies.

TABLE 3-2 IT Infrastructure Services for E-Business

Areas (Number of Services)	Is Service Provided? Percent HAVE	Offered Firmwide (FW) or Business Unit (BU) Percent FW	Percent BU	Relative Investment −10 (lowest) to +10 (highest)	Sourcing Percent IN	Percent OUT	Percent BOTH	Service Used By Percent B2B	Percent B2C	Percent BOTH	Non-E-Business
Applications Infrastructure (13)	90	71	18	3.7	58	22	20	23	1	66	10
Communications Management (7)	81	71	11	3.7	26	44	30	26	2	67	5
Data Management (6)	78	63	15	4.8	54	21	25	17	1	77	5
IT Management (9)	91	80	11	3.8	50	23	27	14	1	84	1
Security (4)	100	93	7	6.1	51	8	41	15	0	85	0
Architecture and Standards (20)	95	91	4	2.7	79	0	21	7	0	93	0
E-Channel Management (7)	51	41	10	4.6	40	31	29	20	4	76	0
IT Research and Development (2)	83	77	7	2.5	56	8	36	16	0	84	0
IT Education and Training (2)	82	71	11	3.9	24	40	36	12	0	76	12

ATOMIC E-BUSINESS MODELS AND INITIATIVES | 81

- The second and third columns are the percentage of firms that offer the services firmwide or only to certain business units. For example, concerning the six data management services, 63 percent of firms provide the services firmwide, whereas 15 percent of firms provide them only to one or more specific business units. The remaining 22 percent of firms do not provide the services.

- The column headed "Relative Investment" is an average of the firm's relative investment in each service area. In the interviews we asked managers whether there would be an increase or decrease in investment in each service in the next year to provide support to e-business initiatives, and we asked them to indicate this on a scale from –10 to +10. A +10 indicates that, relative to other services, the percentage increase in investment in this service was the highest in the coming year. Conversely, a –10 indicates that the service would receive relative disinvestment over the next year. A 0 means no change in relative investment in that service will take place in the coming year. The area with highest relative investment was security, followed by data management and channel management.

- The three columns grouped under the heading "Sourcing" present the percentage of firms providing the services through insourcing, outsourcing, and a combination.

- The four columns grouped under the heading "Service Used By" describe the percentage of firms using the services for B2B e-business, B2C e-business, both B2B and B2C e-business, and not for e-business.

Using statistical analysis of these data we identified the infrastructure services most important for each model. These lists of services are presented in the chapters on each atomic business model (chapters 4 to 11).

Combining Atomic Models into Initiatives

Many e-business initiatives exhibit the characteristics of more than one atomic business model. The average across the fifty e-business initiatives we studied was about two atomic models per initiative. We found that some of these combinations are complementary, or at least viable, while others are in conflict and unstable. The conflict is often caused by one of the following factors and is often easily identified using the business model schematic described in chapter 2.

- **Channel conflict**—in which different customer segments receive different offerings via different channels, causing conflict with intermediaries, allies, and customers. For example, a publisher or an airline that starts an online business to provide products directly to the consumer at discount prices creates channel conflict with the intermediary (i.e., the bookstore or travel agent).

- **Competency conflict**—in which the core competencies and thus culture, reward systems, and structure required for one atomic model are not readily compatible with those of another atomic model. For example, what's required to be a successful content provider—professionalism and the ability to manage relationships with a handful of major customers—is in stark contrast to the transaction-processing capability and customer service management skills needed in a direct-to-customer business with millions of customers.

- **Infrastructure conflict**—in which the IT infrastructure necessary for one atomic model leads to a systems architecture that is not compatible with another model. The content provider and direct-to-customer models again require very different levels of customer data granularity, thus requiring different infrastructure capabilities.

- **Information conflict**—in which the position of the firm gives it access to privileged or private information relative to other allies. For example, when a shared-infrastructure model is combined with a direct-to-customer model, the firm has information about orders made by customers to competitors or allies. This information could be used to the firm's advantage in its direct-to-customer business, leading to a potential conflict of interest.

Questions to Assess the Viability of an E-Business Initiative   The E-Stock Club example illustrates the challenges facing e-business strategists and illustrates how to use business model schematics as an analytical tool. Assessing the viability of any proposed e-business initiative, such as the E-Stock Club, requires answers to at least the following questions:

1. What is the combination of atomic e-business models?
2. What are the sources of revenue, and are they realistic?
3. What customer segments are targeted?
4. What is the value proposition to each customer segment?
5. Who owns the relationship, data, and transaction?
6. What is the likely intimacy of the customer relationship?
7. What are the channels to the customer, and are they capable of supporting the required richness of information provision and capture?
8. What are the critical success factors?
9. What core competencies are needed to succeed?
10. What key information is necessary to succeed?
11. What IT infrastructure capability is required?
12. What conflicts are inherent in the e-business initiative?

We will use this checklist frequently in later chapters.

Lessons from the Atomic E-Business Models

Achieving our goal of being able to analyze and understand an e-business initiative requires us first to understand and analyze each atomic e-business model. Where better to look to understand atomic e-business models than to the dot-coms and to traditional firms as they migrate? Many start-ups began life as very close to pure implementations of an atomic model. Understanding how they operate can give traditional firms insight into how to migrate their business models toward e-business. Jim Harkness of TIAA-CREF, the largest provider of retirement and insurance products for the American education and research communities, summarizes the challenges facing successful firms migrating to e-business:

> We are not going around looking for things that we can do on the Internet. We are looking at the work that is integral to our business and seeing how we can do that better on the web. . . . There is almost nothing you're doing that you can't figure out a way to make it better, faster and cheaper using the Internet. . . . There's almost nothing, there's almost no industry that I can think of today that can't enhance its bottom line in some way using the Internet. . . . To compete effectively in the Digital Age, companies will need to evolve their business models from the tired, command-and-control hierarchies that developed with the Industrial Age to the wired organizations common among companies that have sprung up with the Internet.[22]

The next eight chapters look to existing and successful firms for inspiration and insight. Each of chapters 4 through 11 investigates a different atomic business model to understand its characteristics. These atomic models represent "pure" forms of e-business models that become the building blocks for e-business initiatives. The examples we describe in the upcoming chapters are as close to "pure" implementations of each atomic model as we could find. In some cases we will focus on the aspects of a particular initiative that closely resembles the atomic model, while ignoring other parts. The objective is always to understand what makes each atomic model work.

For each atomic model there is a specific ownership pattern of the customer relationship, the customer data, and the customer transaction. Some models own all three (e.g., the direct to consumer and full-service provider), while the content provider owns none of the three. At the end of each chapter the ownership pattern for each model is identified in a table called, "Who Owns

What?". In general, an atomic model has a higher potential profitability the more of these three assets it owns. The ownership of these three customer assets for each atomic model is summarized in table 12-1. Table 12-2 lists the atomic models in order of potential profitability. Chapters 4 to 11 are presented in order, from the most potentially profitable to the least, starting with direct to customer and ending with content provider.

Potentially most profitable

CHAPTER 4

Direct to Customer

IN THE FIRST three months of the new millennium, American consumers spent more than $7 billion at online retail sites.[1] The number of consumers buying on the Internet rose from 23.3 million during the fourth quarter of 1999, which included holiday buying, to 26.8 million during the first quarter of 2000. Included among the most popular Web sites were both dot-coms such as Amazon.com and the electronic storefronts of traditional retailers such as toysrus.com. Boston Consulting Group (BCG) estimated that online buying by U.S. consumers would continue to rise, reaching $61 billion for the full year 2000.[2] Although this would represent less than 2 percent of total U.S. retail sales, the report also said that by the end of 2000, 10 percent of total U.S. sales of computers, books, music, and videos would occur online. Online sales in Europe are lower than in America but are growing more quickly—up 200 percent in 1999, compared to a mere 145 percent rise in the United States. Although the April 2000 "tech wreck" saw the shares of most Internet merchants crash and brought dire predictions of the failure of many before year's end, the general practice of selling directly to customers online seems certain to grow. In this chapter we will explore the direct-to-customer business model, including the critical success

87

factors and core competencies necessary for success in this deceptively simple e-business model.

In this model, the buyer and seller interact directly. If a purchase is made, the buyer pays the seller, and the seller delivers the goods, either electronically (e.g., software) or physically (e.g., books). It's the electronic version of the ancient marketplace—operating at warp speed.

Direct Success

The potential benefits of the direct-to-customer model are impressive, but success is not assured. Dell, RealNetworks, and Gap illustrate successful direct-to-customer models of different types.

Dell.com

Dell Computer Corporation (described briefly in chapters 1 and 2) challenged the conventional way of selling personal computers (PCs), bypassing dealers and retailers and going directly to business and individual customers.[3] In the original direct model, Dell used the phone and a sales force as the channels to the customer. In 1994, Dell pioneered the use of the Internet as a channel; the Internet now accounts for more than 50 percent of its revenues. Business and individual customers can customize computer systems, order and pay for them, and have the systems—fully configured with software—delivered to their door within a few days. By removing the dealer and distributor, Dell sells equivalent computers at higher margins than the competition. Removing the intermediaries also reduces the time to market for new products by thirty to sixty days relative to competitors, since Dell does not have to empty and fill distribution channels.

A comparison of Dell to its largest competitor, Compaq, shows that over the period 1995–99 the firms' average annual sales growths were 52 percent for Dell and 25 percent for Compaq. Dell's margins were well above Compaq's and 5 percent higher than the industry average overall. The average net income growth over the same period was 80 percent for Dell and 38 percent for Compaq, while average return on equity was 48 percent for Dell and 18 percent for Compaq. Very few firms perform as well as Compaq, but Dell outperformed Compaq on almost every indicator. Dell's "make-to-order" manufacturing strategy reduces inventory levels, with Dell holding six days of stock and Compaq holding twenty-seven days. In 1999, Dell alone accounted for a significant portion of the profits made in the entire personal computer industry, with many competitors actually losing money.

Dell's customers are 90 percent businesses and 10 percent individuals. Dell uses the Internet effectively to deliver different value propositions to different segments within both the B2B and B2C marketspaces. For transactional customers (approximately 30 percent) who need to be acquired each time they buy, Dell offers good value—lower prices for comparative features. For relationship customers (approximately 40 percent), Dell offers many value-added services and customized Premier Pages. Dell has nearly fifty thousand Premier Pages, which business customers use as tailored, secure Web sites designed to add value by increasing management control, standardizing technology, reducing ordering costs, and providing order status and other information. For Dell, migrating to the Internet increased service efficiencies, including the provision of online technical services and information; it also reduced costs. In migrating from place to space, Dell has also achieved sales force efficiencies, freeing up sales staff from taking orders so they can perform more value-adding activities.

RealNetworks.com

RealNetworks (www.realnetworks.com) is a pioneer and recognized leader in media delivery via the Internet.[4] The company develops and markets software products and services enabling users to send and receive audio, video, and other multimedia content over the Internet and corporate intranets. RealNetworks's RealPlayer product, released in 1995, now has a base of over 115 million unique registered users with more than 200,000 new users each day. RealJukebox, which was released in May 1999, already has more than 30 million unique users and supports all leading music formats; thus it can lay claim to being the first universal digital music system. RealSystem software is used by business customers to deliver content on more than 85 percent of all streaming-media-enabled Web pages. The RealNetworks family of Web sites is among the top audio/video destinations on the Web, and it ranks consistently in the top twenty-five most popular sites anywhere on the Internet.

Customers browsing the RealNetworks Web page view a catalog of products available online. Once customers select the "Order and Download Now" link for a chosen product, they are asked to nominate an operating system and prompted to create an account by entering an email address, name, password, credit card details, and billing address. The product is downloaded onto the customer's hard drive, automatically configured during the installation process, and ready to use immediately.

RealNetworks is profitable and had a market capitalization of $4.8 billion as of mid-2000. The company reported record results for the quarter ending March 31, 2000, with net revenues of $53.5 million (an increase of 120 percent from $24.4 million in the first quarter of 1999) and pro forma net earnings (excluding acquisition costs) of $8.8 million. For the year ending December 31, 1999, RealNetworks reported net revenues of $131.2 million, an increase of 98 percent from 1998. Customers downloaded more than sixty-two million unique software packages in the first quarter of 2000, an increase of 175 percent from a year earlier. The Real.com network rose to the eleventh most visited Web and digital media site in February 2000, according to Media Metrix, with close to thirteen million unique visitors.

Gap.com

Gap, Inc. is an apparel manufacturer and retailer established in 1969. Today, Gap is a global company with three distinct brands (Gap, Banana Republic, and Old Navy), more than 110,000 employees worldwide, and over twenty-nine hundred stores in the United States, Canada, France, Germany, Japan, and the United Kingdom. The chain retailer was an early convert to apparel retailing on the Web when it began selling online in late 1997. Its success is attributed to "the same sort of compelling marketing and customer focus" that has brought it success in the bricks-and-mortar world.[5]

Although specific figures are not disclosed, Gap's online sales reportedly tripled in fiscal year 1999. According to the National Retail Federation (NRF), Gap.com was the apparel industry leader in terms of online sales, with estimated sales of $80 to $100 million in the year ending September 1, 1999. In a recent survey by the NRF, households that shopped at Gap.com reported spending an average of $375 at the site over the past year, the highest sales per household of any apparel Web site. While this is only a fraction of Gap's fiscal 1999 sales, which stand at over $9 billion, Gap recognizes the huge growth potential of its Web sales channel. According to Millard S. Drexler, president and CEO, Gap, Inc., has both reached new customers and expanded its market share by extending its brands into the online world.

These examples illustrate the success that is achievable using the direct-to-customer model. Dell can deliver unprecedented customer service and generate industry-leading profits. Dell provides a different and attractive proposition to both relationship (exclusively B2B) and transaction customers (both B2B and B2C). Dell is an exemplar of selling via the Internet, growing online sales from 0 percent to 50 percent of revenue in six years. The move to online sales and the associated efficiencies enabled Dell to achieve industry-leading annual revenue growth while increasing profits.

RealNetworks illustrates the growth and global market penetration possible when introducing a new product that is marketed, sold, and delivered exclusively on the Internet. RealNetworks's digital products have a cost of distribution close to zero. Capturing RealNetworks's level of international sales—more than 25 percent of the firm's revenues come from outside North America—in a traditional firm would require significant investment in overseas offices or dealers. Once an initial sale is made, RealNetworks strives for repeat business: As new products or versions are released, RealNetworks sends emails to registered users offering the new software. As revenues continue to grow, profits on operations should continue to rise beyond their profit in the first quarter of 2000, which was 25 percent of sales.

Gap is using its significant marketplace power to migrate to space. The Gap Web site is promoted at every store's cash register, and online customers can return items purchased from Gap.com to Gap stores. In high-traffic Gap and GapKids stores, "Web lounges" encourage shoppers to migrate to the Web, and Gap holds in-store sales campaigns to get customers' email addresses for online marketing. Online customers have access to all the items in the stores plus a larger range of sizes and added features. The value proposition in space and place are different, although perhaps equally as strong. The resulting customer satisfaction levels are comparable, as evidenced by similar return rates for online and in-store purchases.

Types of Direct-to-Customer E-Businesses

Direct-to-customer businesses fall into four categories. In each category the products or services sold directly to the customer could be physical and delivered by mail or parcel services, or digital and delivered over the Internet. Digital items include products (e.g., software), services (e.g., advice), and information (e.g., stock prices). The four categories are the following:

- Space-based firms (dot-coms) selling their own branded products, such as RealNetworks.

- Place-based firms also operating over the Internet, selling their own branded products. Examples are retailers such as Gap, consultants such as Ernst & Young (recall the description of the online consultant Ernie in chapter 1), catalog companies such as Lands' End (www.landsend.com) and Victoria's Secret (www.victoriassecret.com), and producers such as Gillette (www.theessentials.com) and Nike (www.nike.com).

- Place-based firms selling third-party products both in physical outlets and on the Internet, such as Barnes & Noble (www.bn.com) and Macy's (www.macys.com).
- Dot-coms selling third-party products, such as CDNOW (www.cdnow.com) and Amazon.com.

The potential benefits of the direct-to-customer model are significant for both the customer (lower prices, faster response time, self-service, etc.) and the seller (lower selling costs, online customer data collection, larger geographical reach, etc.). However, turning these potential benefits into profits is not easy.

Direct-to-Customer Profitability

The direct-to-customer model operates in a highly competitive space, particularly for category 3 and 4 firms selling widely available products such as books, CDs, and consumer electronics. The profitability of online retailers varies significantly by category. In a study of 221 "e-tailers," BCG found that only 40 percent were profitable. The study included Internet only, traditional retailers operating online, and catalogers operating online—all of the four categories above. Surveying Internet-only retailers (category 4 above), Forrester Research found only one-quarter made a profit in 1999, leading to predictions that at least half of such retailers would fail before the end of the following year.[6] This early evidence supports the proposition that the Internet increases price competition for commodity items and reduces profitability for retailers selling undifferentiated items.

To put these rates of profitability into context, the Small Business Administration's Office of Advocacy reports that 53 percent of all firms drop out of the economy during the first four years of their operation, and 10 percent of the total population of firms fail each year.[7] We can expect similar failure rates with Internet-based firms. The finding that only 25 percent of direct-to-customer Internet-only businesses return a profit is typical of this type of new venture. The higher rate of direct-to-customer firms overall that make a profit (40 percent, cited above) reflects the result of place-based firms launching Internet businesses.

The Causes of Profitability for Direct to Customer

The BCG study identified some of the causes for lack of profitability.[8] Comparing dot-coms, catalogers that have moved online, and bricks-and-mortar stores operating online, the acquisition costs per new customer were $82 (dot-coms), $11 (catalogers), and $31 (bricks and mortars). The cost of marketing as a percentage of revenue was 119 percent (dot-coms), 6 percent (catalogers), and 36 percent (bricks and mortars). The dot-coms must invest heavily to create a new brand, while the catalogers and bricks-and-mortar operators can simply migrate their brand to space.

Repeat customers and larger unit sales are the keys to success in the direct-to-customer model. The repeat customer requires a much lower marketing cost, and repeat sales build up a relationship and a data profile on that customer. Amazon had a customer base of seventeen million customers as of May 2000 and reduced their cost of customer acquisition to $19, much lower than the average online retailer. The average Amazon.com purchase has increased from $106 in 1998 to $116 in 1999. Focus in these areas led Amazon to announce on February 2, 2000, that its original book business was profitable.[9]

In the BCG study, abandoned shopping carts, the nightmare scenario of both place and space retailers, varied across the three types of firms, with dot-coms reporting that 52 percent of customers abandoned carts, catalogers 66 percent, and bricks-and-mortar operators 76 percent. These data provide good insight into the challenges of the direct-to-customer model. For dot-coms, at least 50 percent of shoppers go to the trouble of placing an item in their shopping basket but for some reason (e.g., the process is too complex, the shipping costs are too high), the shopper doesn't complete the purchase. For catalogers and bricks-and-mortar firms, the rate of shopping basket abandonment is much higher, perhaps indicating that the customer, after shopping on the Internet, then buys via the traditional channel, perhaps from a competitor.

It is still too early to judge the success of the direct-to-customer e-business model. However, we see evidence for significant potential success and profitability with the model. The profitability will vary by category, and we predict that while some entrants in each of the four categories will be profitable, profitability will decline from category 1 to category 4. Selling undifferentiated products online will be the most difficult and the least profitable, because the Internet is a marketplace in which direct comparison on objective criteria, such as price, is easy and cheap. The case study of CDNOW presented later in the chapter illustrates some of these difficulties. Selling differentiated products that can be delivered electronically and have costs of production close to zero will be the most profitable.

The Direct-to-Customer E-Business Model Schematic

The diagram for the direct-to-customer model is deceptively simple, given the many variations already created. The distinguishing characteristic of this model is that buyer and seller communicate directly, rather than through an intermediary. The seller may be a retailer, for example, Wal-Mart (www.walmart.com); a wholesaler, for example, Ingram Book Group (www.ingram.com); or a manufacturer, such as Gillette (www.theessentials.com). The customer may be an individual or a business; the direct-to-customer model covers both B2C firms, such as Amazon (www.amazon.com), and B2B firms, such as W. W. Grainger (www.grainger.com).[10] The model comprises both firms that operate in space alone and those with physical outlets. The model does not attempt to indicate the many options for payment and fulfillment, although both of these activities must be carried out with high quality and low cost in order for an online merchant to succeed.

With any e-business model there are three important questions of ownership: who owns the customer relationship, who owns the data, and who owns the transaction. Each ownership can convey a different type of leverage: influence, information, and revenues. In a typical direct-to-customer e-business model, the firm of interest owns all three critical assets. The direct-to-customer firm can own the customer relationship (represented as the solid line in figure 2-1—i.e., the primary relationship) because the customer is buying directly from the firm. Owning the relationship implies the customer has an element of trust in the firm, giving it significant potential influence over the customer. The customer relationship enables the firm to collect data to profile the customer, who can be encouraged to become a repeat purchaser. By owning the relationship, the firm of interest knows more about the customer (purchase history, demographics, preferences, etc.) than any other firm in the industry. The direct-to-customer firm, as the owner of customer data, has the potential to develop powerful insight into customers' needs and desires. Finally, the direct-to-customer firm owns the transaction. By owning the customer transaction, the firm receives a fee or a profit margin for the item sold.

Existing retailers—including banks, magazines, and travel agents—that go online start out with the initial advantage of already serving customers directly, but they must concern themselves with cannibalization of their existing offerings. For example, the *Boston Globe* already knows how to select, write, and present news in a way that is appealing to readers; these customer-focused skills are translatable from ink on paper to pixels on PCs. But the *Globe* has discovered, like most newspapers, that consumers are unwilling to pay for its online edition (www.thebostonglobe.com). If the online edition is given away free, will paid subscriptions and newsstand sales fall? And if revenue from subscriptions and newsstand sales falls, will the *Globe* still be able to cover its fixed costs?

Manufacturers, wholesalers, and other firms using e-business to skip steps in their existing distribution chain start out with the advantage of additional margin, but they must watch for channel conflict. As described in chapter 1, when Compaq's Australian arm (www.compaq.com.au) began selling to consumers directly over the Internet, one of its major resellers, the Harvey Norman chain, stopped stocking the Compaq brand.[11] Compaq has other resellers, and the extra margin gained from direct sales may ultimately compensate for the profit lost on sales formerly made through Harvey Norman stores, but the episode clearly indicates that the direct-to-customer model contains risk as well as opportunity.

Some of the biggest disasters in the brief history of e-business involve companies using this apparently simple model, particularly companies in the fourth category—dot-coms selling third-party products. Take, for example, boo.com (www.boo.com), an online-only retailer of fashion and sportswear. The company's investors included Benetton, Bain Capital, J. P. Morgan, and Goldman Sachs.[12] After raising $120 million, the company took more than a year to launch its Internet site—and then lasted less than six months before being put up for sale or closure. Boo.com operated in multiple languages and offered the opportunity to spin, zoom, and try on the merchandise. Building a site of such technical complexity meant that the company missed three successive launch deadlines before arriving online. The delays resulted in bad publicity, significant fees for the cancellation of scheduled television advertising, and the loss of value from the print advertising boo.com placed in *Glamour, Details,* and other magazines popular with its twenty-something customer segment. To make matters worse, the bandwidth and computing capacity required to use the site overwhelmed many users' PCs, causing would-be customers to abandon their attempts to purchase merchandise. The site did not work on Apple Macintosh computers at all. Within a few months of its launch, boo.com discounted its products by 40 percent, and its chairman and cofounder left the company. As the money ran low, many of the staff not already made redundant defected, the investors refused to put in any more cash, and the company looked like it was becoming just another fashion victim.[13] Ultimately boo.com's technology was sold to Internet services company Bright Station for $372,500, a small fraction of its development cost.[14]

The troubles of boo.com are an extreme case of the experience of many online retailers: It is difficult to turn a profit on Internet trading alone selling commonly available products. The direct-to-customer model, and indeed all commercial activity on the Internet, is still relatively new, and many industries lose money in their start-up phase. Even award-winning firms appear not yet to have turned a profit. BabyCenter (www.babycenter.com) was given the "retail site of the year" award in May 2000 by the International Academy of Digital Arts and Sciences. BabyCenter was launched in October 1998 and received funding from Intel and a variety of venture capital firms.[15] The company was bought by e-Toys for $150 million in stock in July 1999, just prior to its planned public offering. The site, which sells thousands of maternity and baby products, is attractive, and it may eventually become profitable. However, the parent company's quarterly 10-Q report, filed with the U.S. Securities and Exchange Commission, disclosed that losses were growing even more rapidly than sales, and included the bad news that "WE ANTICIPATE FUTURE LOSSES AND NEGATIVE CASH FLOWS. . . . [B]ecause of our acquisition of BabyCenter, we expect that our losses will increase even more significantly because of additional costs and expenses."[16]

Boo.com was probably undone by its own technical ambitions and the unrealistic expectations created among its prospective customers. Other e-tailers have been undone by a misunderstanding or misapplication of the direct-to-customer business model—or perhaps by a failure to adapt the model as times change. Consider the following case study of one of the Internet's best-known retailers, CDNOW, which is also a category 4 direct-to-customer e-business.

CASE STUDY

DIRECT-TO-CUSTOMER MODEL: **CDNOW**

(www.cdnow.com)

CDNOW was, for a long while, one of the poster children of direct selling on the Internet. An article in the January 1999 issue of *Management Review* said, "Now other electronic retailers like CDNOW are demonstrating that new technologies and changes in consumer preferences are making yesterday's success models obsolete." Another laudatory, although perhaps premature, article said, "CDNOW is one of the pioneers who never crashed and burned. They did it right. They offer the music, the diversity of interests, and best of all they keep it simple. Drawing on their humble beginnings in the early, early days of August 1994, they have built an online market force. They have become the brand name."[17] A special $75 report, "In Search of E-Commerce: Lessons from the Internet's Top Sites," included an entire chapter on CDNOW.[18] From its initial public offering price of $16 in early 1998—despite having lost nearly $11 million on sales of $17 million the year before—CDNOW's shares reached a high of $39.25 before falling back to about $20, where they remained for months. High customer acquisition costs—an estimated $45 to attract each paying customer—were given as one reason.[19]

A visit to the CDNOW Internet site makes both the praise and the problems understandable. The site (www.cdnow.com) offers more than 500,000 CDs and other music-related products and 650,000 sound samples, as well as daily news, features, guides to music genres, and exclusive interviews and reviews by CDNOW's editorial staff. CDNOW offers 30 percent off on best-selling CDs and a selection of new releases. With 3.5 million customers and an average daily audience of over 800,000 people in 1999, CDNOW became one of the most well known and regularly visited music destinations on the Internet.[20] In addition to earning revenues from direct sales, CDNOW leverages its paying customer base by selling advertising and sponsorships—but in 1999 alone the company paid an estimated $108 million to portals such as Yahoo! for placement on their sites.[21] CDNOW merged with competitor N2K, sponsor of the Music Boulevard site, in early 1999, and later in that same year it announced a merger with Columbia House, the music club jointly owned by Sony and Time Warner. The merger fell through in February 2000, but as part of the termination agreement Time Warner and Sony agreed to commit $51 million to prop up CDNOW. CDNOW announced that the amount would go toward debts and operating expenses.[22]

Only one month later, the company's situation appeared dire.[23] CDNOW's annual report, filed with the U.S. Securities and Exchange Commission in late March, revealed that the company's auditors, Arthur Andersen, had written management in January that the company "has suffered recurring losses from operations, and has a working capital deficiency and significant payments due in 2000 related to marketing agreements that raises substantial doubt about its ability to continue as a going concern." An article in *Barron's* claimed that CDNOW had less than a month's cash left, and the company's shares fell to below $4.00.[24] The company announced plans to scale back marketing expenses, but analysts noted that a drop in revenue would be the inevitable result, even though CDNOW was one of the twenty-five most-trafficked sites on the Internet. Soon CDNOW announced that it had retained the services of Allen & Co. to explore strategic options and new sources of funding.

What went wrong? The answer appears to be threefold: competition, technical change, and an unclear, undifferentiated category 4 direct-to-customer e-business model. In June 1997, Amazon announced it was moving into CDs, with an initial stock of 130,000 titles offered at discounts of up to 30 percent. Amazon.com gave music customers the ability to search for CDs in a variety of ways, offering information about products, reviews, customer comments, and RealAudio samples of more than two hundred thousand songs. Within 120 days, Amazon steamed past CDNOW, becoming the largest online seller of CDs.[25] CDNOW also faced competition from scores of other online retailers, local music stores, Wal-Mart, and even supermarkets.

Technologically, CDNOW was challenged by the dramatic rise of MP3, a method for transmitting music over the increasingly abundant Internet bandwidth available free to many university students and company employees. The main MP3 Internet site (www.mp3.com) offers more than a quarter-million high-quality songs from over fifty thousand artists available for free downloading over the Internet, despite the legal cloud over the issue of copyright. As the sharing of CD content rose, the sale of CDs fell, affecting all merchants, but particularly those, like CDNOW, targeting the same technically sophisticated customers who were the early adopters of MP3.

The direct-to-customer business model used by CDNOW may have been right for 1994, but it was outdated by 2000. There was not, and arguably would never be, a "category killer" in the CD marketplace. Broad-line merchants such as Wal-Mart and Amazon viewed CDs as a loss leader, that is, as a branded item that could be sold for a very low price in order to draw customers into physical or virtual stores, where they could perhaps be induced to buy other items. But CDNOW had nothing other than CDs to sell; it could not afford to lower its CD prices to match the prices being offered by others.

As of this writing, the future of CDNOW is very much in doubt. The company was a pioneer adopter of the direct-to-customer model. But its "first mover advantage" did not last for long, if indeed it ever existed. The combined forces of competition, technological change, and an arguably inappropriate business model left CDNOW with plenty of traffic—the company was consistently among the top Internet retailers in terms of the number of unique visitors to its site—but not enough profit from sales, and inadequate revenue from other sources.[26] CDNOW illustrates the dilemma faced by many category 4 direct-to-customer online businesses selling commodity products. Without a large market share or the ability to cross-sell a wide variety of products, the value proposition is relatively weak. Consequently profitability is elusive, with customer acquisition costs high relative to the small average unit sale per customer. If the BCG data are typical, with the cost of marketing for Internet-only retailers running at 119 percent of revenues, it is not surprising that firms such as CDNOW are struggling. Even with a strong value proposition there are other place-based challenges.

Logistics Challenge

One of the major challenges for the direct-to-customer firm selling a physical product is getting the right product to the right address reliably and economically. The American Better Business Bureau identified nondelivery and wrong delivery of goods ordered online as the biggest single source of complaints in e-business.[27] Many Internet entrepreneurs have conceived of attractive Web sites, but they do not have a clear understanding of the complex logistics.

For many traditional retailers, the challenge of home delivery of an assortment of items, each in lot sizes of one, is new and not well suited to distribution centers designed to move goods to their own stores by the pallet load.

As the volume of direct-to-customer sales increases, the number of packages moving is also rising. Forrester Research reports that the number of units to be shipped from online sales will rise from 3 million in 1999 to 2.1 billion in 2003.[28] Two shipping approaches are available to direct-to-customer firms: invest or outsource. A number of firms are building extensive networks of distribution centers and delivery mechanisms, including Amazon and the online grocer Webvan (www.webvan.com). For Amazon this investment is already paying off, with 99 percent of its 1999 Christmas orders arriving on time.[29] Achieving this high level of customer satisfaction requires significant investment and management attention. Besides the major investment in warehouses and delivery systems, Amazon employs two hundred customer service representatives whose job is to "put things right" if they go wrong.[30] Amazon's representatives are authorized to waive shipping charges and make amends with ten-dollar gift certificates.

Direct-to-customer firms can also outsource logistics. Many service providers offer full-service logistics support to direct-to-customer firms. Some logistics companies see delivery of goods ordered via e-business as an opportunity to expand their influence. Federal Express (FedEx) moves more than 3.1 million items a day and has electronic connections with more than 1.9 million customers and a wide range of e-businesses (www.fedex.com). In an attempt to leverage its core competencies, FedEx launched the FedEx Marketplace, "where shoppers gain one-click access to several top online merchants that utilize fast reliable FedEx delivery services." Value America, L. L. Bean, and HP Shopping Village are among the inaugural merchants at FedEx Marketplace.[31]

The importance of fulfillment and logistics for the direct-to-customer business model illustrates the distinction we make throughout the book between a critical success factor and a core competency. Fast and efficient transaction processing, fulfillment, and payment are some of the critical success factors listed at the end of the chapter for the direct-to-customer model—but we do not see logistics as necessary core competencies to be nurtured in-house. Fulfillment could reasonably be outsourced to FedEx, UPS, or many other players.

Channel Management

Having described both success stories and cautionary tales, we turn our attention to the channels used by the direct-to-customer model, drawing on an important distinction identified earlier. Does the firm directly serve customers in both place and space (categories 2 and 3) or in space only (categories 1 and 4)?

Firms that already serve the customer directly generally see the Internet as another channel to reach the customer, possibly at a radically reduced cost or with greater customer intimacy. Firms in this category include many banks, which would much rather have lower net worth customers transact over the Internet than in person, and catalog merchants, which would sooner receive customer orders in digital form than by telephone or mail. An extreme example of this category is Egghead, which in February 1998 decided to close its 250 physical stores and sell software and other goods electronically only.[32] With no costs for bricks and mortar, Egghead was able to reduce its prices by 10 percent to 20 percent. But most firms cannot take the risk of being as radical as Egghead. For these firms, the key to success with this approach is the ability to offer a compelling value proposition via both place and space, capitalizing on the advantages of each channel.

Combining place and space leads to successful models such as Target's Club Wedd (target.com/registries/club_wedd). A future bride and groom first go to the Club Wedd kiosk at a Target store and borrow a bar code scanner. The couple walks the aisles of the store, scanning items that they would like to receive. Their gift list is placed on the Target Web site so that any guest can access it and buy a gift, either online or by visiting a Target store. The bride and groom thus use the touch and feel of the physical store to shop, and the guests use the efficiency of the Internet to buy, armed with knowledge of what the couple wants.

Firms currently dealing with customers only through intermediaries face the challenge of channel conflict, "a situation in which one channel member perceives another channel member(s) to be engaged in behavior that is preventing or impeding it from achieving its goals."[33] One result of channel conflict is that customer segments receive similar offerings via different channels at different prices, causing conflict with intermediaries, allies, and customers. Channel conflict tends to reduce both prices and profit margins, particularly for intermediaries, and it may lead to the refusal of intermediaries to continue selling the products. Channel conflict can be severe enough to make a manufacturer rethink its online strategy. Levi Strauss & Co. (www.levi.com) abandoned its e-commerce site in 1999, primarily because of backlash from retailers. The $5 billion company became an e-commerce pioneer in 1998 when it offered consumers the opportunity to order custom-made jeans online and have the clothing delivered to their doorsteps. Barely a year later, the company ceased selling online and turned all Internet sales back to retailers, such as J. C. Penney and Macy's. While Levi Strauss & Co. insists that retailers were supportive of its online operations, Levi's desire to improve its relationships with retailers was apparently the main reason for its change of strategy.[34]

Channel conflict is not new, but the attraction of e-business to upstream players in the supply chain has raised the stakes for the issue. Channel conflict can be managed, as shown by the example of Estée Lauder, the world's leading skin care and cosmetics company. The company's Clinique Internet site (www.clinique.com) offers direct online sales, but it tries to create a win-win situation with existing channels by also using the site to drive traffic to the stores of retailers selling Clinique products. For example, Clinique Bonus Time, an assortment of many sample-sized and some full-sized Clinique products, is described on the site but available only at retail stores. The site helps shoppers locate nearby stores where the bonus may be obtained. The lingerie manufacturer Maidenform is also pushing online sales, although it believes these will never exceed about 10 percent of overall revenues—less than sales through the company's own outlet stores, which account for 25 percent of revenues.[35] By opening outlet stores, Maidenform has already dealt with channel conflict; retailers who carry its products are well aware that the company also sells directly to consumers, often at prices below retail. Far from being secretive about its Internet site, Maidenform launched an affiliate program to encourage established retailers, and even individuals, to link their own Internet sites to Maidenform's site (www.maidenform.com).[36] Channel conflict is a recurring theme in this book, and in chapter 13 we provide a series of suggestions for reducing its effects.

Whether dealing directly with the customer in the physical world or not, few retailers or manufacturers can afford to ignore the option of direct-to-customer sales. The potential benefits, and the competitive threats, are significant. For some firms, such as Levi Strauss, the channel issues may be difficult to overcome.[37] For others, such as Egghead, the advantages of online sales are large enough to bring about a complete change in the way the firm does business. As an indication of the importance of a combined place-and-space strategy, Egghead announced plans in early 2000 to again build physical stores. Egghead CEO George Orban said that he believed bricks-and-mortar companies were the biggest threat to his now completely online firm.[38] For the majority of firms, the answer will be somewhere in between—an appropriate balance of place and space so that all channels can truly add value for both the firm and its customers. The BCG study cited at the beginning of the chapter revealed that only 38 percent of dollars spent online went to Internet-only retailers. The majority of spending went to organizations that sold from physical stores as well as from a Web site. Such clicks-and-mortar companies will use the Internet to drive traffic to their physical stores, and vice versa. What these firms are trying to develop is not so much an "Internet strategy" as a business strategy with an Internet component. A most important issue is to assure that information flows readily across all the channels used, requiring substantial investment in IT infrastructure.

Infrastructure

The direct-to-customer model requires extensive electronic connection with the customer, including online payment systems. Many direct-to-customer implementations include an extranet to allow customized Web pages for major B2B customers. Operating a direct-to-customer e-business requires significant investment in the equivalent of the store: the Web site. Direct-to-customer businesses spend millions of dollars developing easy-to-navigate and easy-to-use Web sites with the goal of improving the B2B or B2C shopping experience online. Lands' End (www.landsend.com) has devised a feature by which women can build and store a three-dimensional model of themselves to "try on" clothes electronically.

In our field research we found that firms with e-business initiatives containing the direct-to-customer e-business model needed and were investing more heavily in three areas of infrastructure services: application infrastructure, communications, and IT management.

Direct-to-customer firms particularly needed:

- payment transaction processing to process online customer payments;
- enterprise-wide resource planning (ERP) to process customer transactions;
- workflow infrastructure to optimize business process performance;
- communication network services linking all points in the enterprise to each other and the outside world, often using the TCP/IP protocol;
- the installation and maintenance of workstations and local area networks supporting the large number of people required to operate a direct-to-customer model; and
- service-level agreements between the business and the IT group or outsourcer to ensure, monitor, and improve the systems necessary for the model.

Summary of the Direct-to-Customer Model

Strategic Objective and Value Proposition

The traditional business of retail was relatively simple: buy, move, and sell. Buy the right products, move them to the store with customer demand, and sell them at the right price. The e-business direct-to-customer model is potentially fundamentally different: sell, buy, move. E-business enables online retailers to provide huge ranges of carefully specified and described products on their Web sites, take orders, receive payment, and arrange delivery of the item. To the firm of interest, this model offers the prospect of higher margins, expanded markets, and greater information about customers. To the customer, the model offers greater choice, increased convenience, and lower costs. Remarkably, both sets of goals can be achieved simultaneously. At least initially, this model offers the possibility of changing the buyer-seller relationship from a zero-sum game to a situation in which both sides can justifiably feel better off. The direct-to-customer model is potentially one of the most profitable of the models described in this book because the firm owns all three of the customer assets: relationship, data, and transaction. The model is potentially particularly profitable for companies holding large market shares and offering a clearly differentiated value proposition (for example, Dell, RealNetworks, and other category 1 and 2 firms). For firms following the less differentiated models (i.e., firms in categories 3 and 4), profits will be harder to achieve, as the Internet facilitates easy comparison on objective measures such as price. We expect a small number of category 3 and 4 firms to thrive and capture large market share in each retail domain and geographical region. The others will struggle.

Sources of Revenue

The main source of revenue is usually direct sales to customers. Supplemental revenues come from advertising, the sale of customer information, and product placement fees.[39] Higher margins may also be attained either by reducing the cost to serve the customer directly or by cutting steps out of the distribution chain. Illustrating the diversity of the types of revenue, RealNetworks's approximate breakdown of revenue sources in 1999 was consumer media players (40 percent), streaming software for business customers (30 percent), content delivery (20 percent), and advertising (10 percent).[40] In many direct-to-customer models the firm can receive payment at the time of the order and before acquiring or making the product, thereby gaining additional revenues from float on the customer's funds.

Critical Success Factors

Critical success factors are the things a firm must do well to flourish. The following list shows the critical success factors for the direct-to-customer model in any of the four categories.

- Create and maintain customer awareness, in order to build a critical mass of users to cover the fixed cost of building an electronic presence.
- Reduce customer acquisition costs.
- Strive to own the customer relationship and understand individual customer needs.
- Increase repeat purchases and average transaction size.
- Provide fast and efficient transaction processing, fulfillment, and payment.
- Ensure adequate security for the organization and its customers.
- Provide interfaces that combine ease of use with richness of experience, integrating multiple channels.

In addition, firms that serve the customer directly in the physical world as well as electronically must balance the availability of multiple channels with the cost of supporting them, while using the strengths and synergies of both place and space. Firms that continue to work through intermediaries must manage potential channel conflicts.

Core Competencies

Core competencies are competencies necessary for every direct-to-customer firm that should be created, nurtured, and developed in-house. If a direct-to-customer firm outsourced these core competencies, it would reduce its power to maintain its position as owner of the customer relationship. The following list presents the core competencies necessary for direct-to-customer e-businesses.

- Forming and managing strategic partnerships with suppliers, payment processors, fulfillment houses, and others in the supply chain.

- Using the ownership of the customer information assets to understand customer needs, thereby increasing revenues and margins.

- Marketing, prospecting, and selling electronically using banner advertisements, emails, affiliate programs, and click-throughs from allies.

- Managing and integrating online and offline business processes to assure customer value (customers of direct-to-customer firms want fast service and instant gratification; the business processes of the direct-to-customer firm must be capable of processing online quickly and securely).

- Creating unique content to reduce price competition on commodities.

Who Owns What?

	Customer Relationship	Customer Data	Customer Transaction
Direct to Customer	✓	✓	✓

CHAPTER 5

Full-Service
Provider

E-BUSINESS can impact an industry value chain in two opposite ways—sometimes simultaneously. The direct-to-customer model often involves removing intermediaries from the value chain, allowing consumers to serve themselves rather than go through a third party. Some of the best-known e-business firms, for example, Dell and Cisco, illustrate the power of shortening the supply chain when intermediaries do not add value. On the other hand, successful examples of the intermediary model often involve *lengthening* the value chain by inserting an intermediary. For example, Quicken.com acts as an intermediary to allow users of the company's financial management software to buy stocks or mutual funds. The full-service provider model combines the strengths of both the direct-to-customer and the intermediary models, and it is very attractive to many traditional firms in both B2B and B2C e-business.

What Is a Full-Service Provider?

A firm using the full-service provider model provides total coverage of customer needs in a particular domain, consolidated via a single point of contact. The domain could be any major area of customer needs requiring multiple products and services, for example, financial services, health care, or industrial chemicals. The full-service provider adds value by providing a full range of products, sourced both internally and externally, and consolidating them using the channel(s) chosen by the customer.

For example, take the Prudential Advisor, established by Prudential Securities (www.prusec.com), a subsidiary of the Prudential Insurance Company of America. The company's Web site claims, "Prudential Advisor is redefining the full service relationship and bringing together a wealth of resources to support educated investment decisions."[1] Some of these resources are provided by Prudential Securities, and others are provided by Standard & Poor's, Zacks Equity Research, Lipper & Company, and other third parties. The Prudential Advisor aims to provide its customers with their full set of financial needs using both Prudential and third-party products covering cash management, investments, financial advice, research, historical performance information, brokerage, mutual funds, and other services. Transactional services are available for equities and fixed-income securities via Prudential Securities' online PruTrade system, for more than forty families of mutual funds via the PruChoice system, and for cash via the COMMAND cash management account. In addition to delivering information via email and offering online access, Prudential Advisor allows customers to interact in person or by telephone with a live financial adviser—the way all brokerage business was once done. However, unlike the traditional brokerage business, the cost basis of the Prudential Advisor includes transactions—a flat fee per trade—and an annual fee, which is a declining percentage of the assets invested, starting with 1.5 percent for assets of between $50,000 and $250,000, and falling to 0.25 percent for assets in excess of $175 million.

The Prudential Advisor is an example of a full-service provider, in the domain of investment services. According to Prudential Securities, all of a customer's needs for investment information and products are met through the Prudential Advisor. Some of the information and some of the investment products are provided by

Prudential, and other information and other products are provided by third parties. The Prudential Advisor allows Prudential Securities to own the customer relationship, the data about what the customers are doing with regard to investment, and some of the transactions.[2] Prudential Securities thereby gains insight into both the customer's existing portfolio and any investments the customer may consider in the future. This level of insight allows Prudential to cross-sell other products to the customer and also develop or acquire third-party services for customer needs not currently met via Prudential's own offerings.

A third party providing services via Prudential does not own the customer relationship. It is in the best interest of Prudential and other full-service providers to have a strong and comprehensive set of third-party providers, but then to pass to the third party only the minimum data necessary to complete the transaction. The full-service provider wants to own the relationship with the customer and to prevent other firms who act as third parties in this model from attracting the customer away.

Full-Service Provider Atomic E-Business Model Schematic

The full-service provider atomic e-business model schematic (figure 5-1) identifies the firm of interest in the center of the diagram, with suppliers at the left and the customer on the right. The customer's entire needs in the relevant domain—financial services, for example—are met through a close relationship with the firm. Requests for information, orders, and money flow directly to the full-service provider, and then on to third-party providers. For example, if a customer of Prudential Advisor invests in one of the Gabelli family of mutual funds, the purchase information flows through Prudential Securities to Gabelli. The investment confirmation flows back along the same path, and in due course the payment is transferred from the customer to Prudential and then to Gabelli. If Prudential Securities consolidates orders from multiple customers, Gabelli may not even know the identity of its customers or the size of their individual investments in Gabelli funds. Even if Gabelli

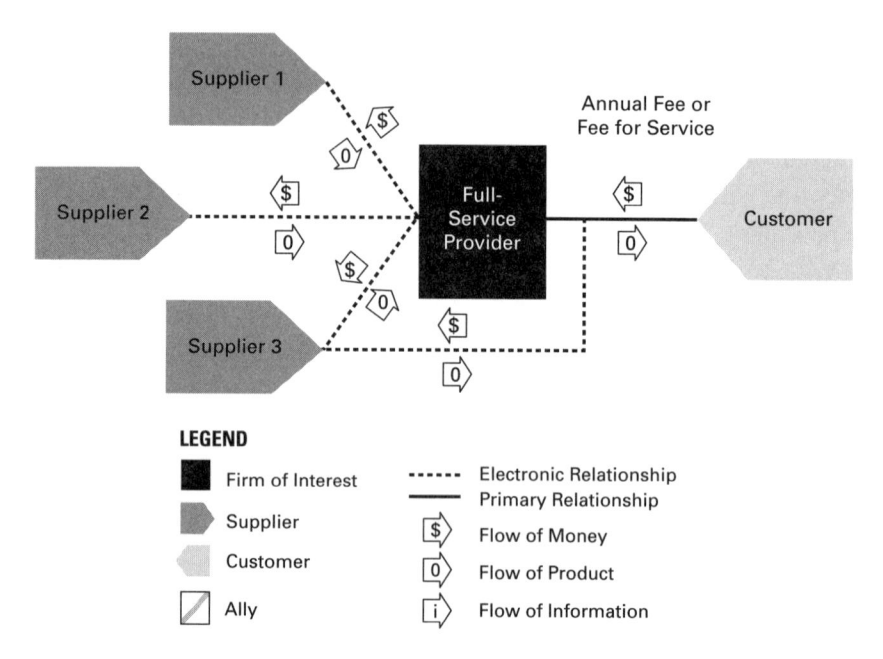

FIGURE 5-1 Full-Service Provider Atomic E-Business Model Schematic

receives individual customer orders, its insight into a customer's investment situation is much less complete than that held by Prudential Securities.

The success of the full-service provider is highly dependent on the strength and intimacy of its relationship with the customer. To thrive, the full-service provider must own the relationship with the customer, thereby knowing more about that customer than does any other player in the model. The profitability of the full-service provider goes up rapidly the more products it provides—either its own or third-party products. To add value for the customer, the full-service provider consolidates a wide range of products and services in the channel of choice. Some customer segments will want to operate exclusively over the Internet, while other segments will want access to multiple channels including face-to-face contact, phone, Internet, and IVR.

Some suppliers' products will be completely integrated into the full-service provider's offerings, and those suppliers will have no direct relationship to the customer (e.g., supplier 1 in figure 5-1).

Other suppliers will have a relationship with the customer but under the umbrella of the full-service provider (e.g., supplier 3 in figure 5-1).

A full-service provider gains revenues from selling its own products, as well as receiving transaction fees or commissions for third-party products that its customers purchase.[3] Some full-service providers, for example, Prudential Advisor, also charge customers a "relationship" or "management" fee, and it is conceivable that some levy a similar fee on suppliers for the privilege of gaining access to the provider's customer base.

B2C Full-Service Providers

The bookseller Barnes & Noble (www.bn.com) is working hard to become a full-service provider. The company is well known for its ongoing struggle with Amazon to dominate the sale of books over the Internet. Like Amazon, Barnes & Noble has expanded to offer much more than books. Rather than flogging wristwatches, home remedies, or power tools, however, Barnes & Noble has adopted a more focused strategy: It is becoming a full-service provider for printed information by extending its direct service offerings and partnering with other suppliers. The domain of this information in printed form extends to posters and greeting cards, e-mail via access to AOL instant messenger, and online book reviews published in leading journals. The customer looking for printed information about a given topic can search for sources on Northern Light (www.northernlight.com), one of Barnes & Noble's partners, which provides Internet citations free and sells electronic copies of articles from more than five thousand sources, including newspapers and wire services. The customer can buy nearly one thousand current magazines and new or used books through Barnes & Noble and its bookstore affiliates and can order a textbook. Along the way, an electronic message or greeting card can be sent, and a poster purchased.

Barnes & Noble delivers on the full-service promise by enabling customers to place their purchases from across the domain of printed information into the same Barnes & Noble shopping basket. The customer pays Barnes & Noble, which delivers a consolidated package. For example, if a search on the Barnes & Noble Web site identifies that a book is out of print, the customer is offered the option to extend the search to a network of hundreds of bookstores that stock used books. The inventory of these bookstores is accessible online, and a search may locate copies of the book in several stores. Each copy is described and priced in detail. A recent search for an out-of-print book written by one of our favorite mystery writers revealed forty-three copies. The copies of the book ranged in price from fifty-five dollars for a first-edition hard cover to seven dollars for a soft cover described as "in good condition with dog eared back cover and creased spine." The customer can choose several used books from several different bookstores, as well as new books from Barnes & Noble, and have the purchase delivered in one package with the entire transaction managed by Barnes & Noble. Barnes & Noble owns the relationship, the data, and the transaction. It is very unlikely that any other bookstore involved in the transaction knows who actually purchased the book or what other books were purchased at the same time.

Like the Prudential Advisor, Barnes & Noble gains revenue by selling its own products—books from its own inventory—as well as by selling third-party products, including magazines and used books. Presumably it keeps a commission for sales of books from other bookstores before passing on the customer's payment. Unlike the Prudential Advisor, Barnes & Noble does not charge an annual fee to customers to participate. On the other hand, the benefit to the customer of this full-service provision in this domain is much less obvious. Day traders aside, customers typically purchase investment products for the medium to long term, and therefore they want each new product purchased to fit with an existing portfolio. There is value to the customer in having information about this financial portfolio in one place, where it may be viewed both by the customer and by a (human) adviser. Much less benefit is obvious for a book portfolio. Barnes & Noble can monitor a customer's buying pattern and attempt to recommend new books written by favorite authors, but it is very unlikely that a customer would enter an entire list of books already owned, or that Barnes & Noble can monitor the customer's responses to books newly read. In this more subjective and personal domain, becoming an enduring full-service provider may be substantially more difficult than in the more quantitative domain of investments.

B2B Full-Service Providers

Full-service providers are equally attractive in B2B e-business, as demonstrated by Chemnet (www.orica-chemnet.com), a unit of the leading Australian chemical company Orica (www.orica.com.au), previously called ICI. Orica-Chemnet sources chemicals from more than two hundred different manufacturers, including its parent Orica, in fifty different countries, and it supplies products and services to more than three thousand corporate customers throughout Australasia. Chemnet's major markets are in building and construction, agriculture, mining, pulp and paper, and manufacturing. The chemicals it supplies include mineral acids, acrylic and methacrylic monomers, superabsorbent polymers, swimming pool chemicals, and specialty cleaning chemicals. Many of Chemnet's suppliers are competitors of other units of Orica, and some of its customers are competitors of still other units of the parent company, for example the Dulux paint business.

In 1999, Chemnet signed a three-year exclusive agreement to supply bulk chemicals and technical service to Kiwi Co-Operative Dairies, the largest dairy products manufacturing site in the world.[4] With an annual turnover in excess of NZ$1.8 billion, Kiwi ranks among New Zealand's top dozen companies. The company produces approximately 28 percent of New Zealand's dairy products, the majority of which go into consumer products. Milk processing requires cleaning processing plants on a daily basis, with very stringent microbiological standards. There is pressure on processing plants to achieve high throughputs, so the time taken to turn plants around on cleaning cycles is critical. Cleaning systems, known as Clean In Place in the dairy industry, require ongoing technical expertise, optimization, and innovation. Chemnet has a team of experts working on-site with Kiwi Dairies to achieve excellence in cleaning and processing. This team is part of Chemnet's full-service provider relationship with Kiwi Dairies in the domain of chemicals and cleaning. Chemnet buys all the chemicals that Kiwi requires, either from Orica or from a third party. Chemnet has the opportunity to add value by finding the best value approach, rather than just the lowest price for a given chemical.

Chemnet can become the full-service chemical provider for a single factory, an entire company, or even a whole industry. As the worldwide chemical manufacturing industry continues to concentrate, and as major users of chemicals increasingly outsource the purchasing of chemical supplies and the maintaining of chemical inventories, Chemnet's opportunities should grow. As these external opportunities increase, so will the internal tensions as Chemnet sells larger volumes of competing products and serves greater numbers of competing companies. Such tensions are inherent in the full-service provider model, for no single organization is likely to have a product range broad enough to serve all of a customer's needs in a meaningful domain, and so third-party products are always part of the picture. And no matter how broad the provider's range, customers are much less likely to trust their entire needs to an organization that supplies only its own products; therefore there will always be competition between the third-party suppliers and the company's internal business units. Effectively managing these tensions is one of the critical success factors of the full-service provider model.

Infrastructure

Virtually all businesses aspire to getting 100 percent of their customers' business, or at least to getting as much of that business as they can profitably handle. Yet the number of full-service providers remains small. Part of the reason for this is infrastructure, and perhaps politics. Take, for example, the Prudential Insurance Company of America (www.prudential.com), the parent company of

Prudential Securities. Prudential offers virtually every financial product an individual could need: investment products; insurance, including life, health, auto, and liability; checking accounts and credit cards; and home mortgages, among other things. However, not only does Prudential Insurance not sell third-party products, but it also does not even sell all of its own insurance products in a strongly coordinated way. The situation of Prudential Insurance is not unusual. In many organizations, layers of systems, each built independently to support a specific product line, make it difficult to consolidate information on a customer basis. Therefore, a unified view of the customer, which is so essential to becoming a successful full-service provider, does not exist, and it cannot readily be created.

The missing piece of infrastructure is often a database containing information about the customer and the products that the customer owns. Without owning these data, a provider does not own the customer relationship, and therefore some of the customer's transactions are likely to take place directly with other providers. All of the important interactions with customers occurring across any channel or business unit must be recorded in the firmwide customer database. A team of analysts then uses the database and other market research data to identify product and service offerings that may be provided directly as self-branded products, along with cobranded products and those sourced from a third party. Implementing a full-service provider model requires an integrated IT infrastructure and architecture linking multiple business units, customers, and third parties with common data definitions and integrated applications.

Our field research identified databases and data warehouses as some of the most important infrastructure services associated with the full-service provider atomic business model. Other important infrastructure services included the following:

- The ability to evaluate proposals for new information systems initiatives to coordinate IT investment across a multi-business-unit firm with the goal of a single point of contact for the customer.

- Centralized management of IT infrastructure capacity to integrate across multiple business units within the firm and third-party providers; the full-service provider model is not readily workable if each business unit optimizes its own IT needs.
- Installation and maintenance of workstations and local area networks to operate the online business linking all the business units and third-party providers.
- Electronic support for groups to coordinate the cross-functional teams required to implement this model.
- The identification and testing of new technologies to find cost-effective ways to deliver this complex business model to the customer across multiple channels.

Developing the appropriate infrastructure for a full-service provider also requires a difficult cultural shift, one that emphasizes and rewards firmwide needs and goals rather than those of the individual business units, and one that requires strong leadership and a different IT governance structure.

Channels and Segments

Many full-service providers must deliver across multiple channels. The transaction cost and potential richness for information provision and capture vary significantly across channels (see table 3-1). Different customer segments will choose different channel combinations that best suit their needs. One of the channels commonly used by the full-service provider is the call center, a powerful channel that offers broad flexibility in the types of strategies that can be implemented, involving both outgoing and ingoing calls.

Domains for Full-Service Provision

For the full-service provider model to thrive, each business or individual customer can have no more than one full-service provider in the relevant domain. This domain will have to be broad enough to allow a full-service provider to include enough products and services to create a strong value proposition. More importantly, the domain will have to be broad enough so that the customer ends up with a manageable number of full-service providers rather than hundreds. That convenience is the primary attraction of a full-service provider—a single place to get all that is needed in a particular domain.

However, the domain cannot be so large that the full-service provider lacks credibility to provide those services. An offer from the local gas station to be the full-service provider of travel services for its customers via the station's Web site is stretching credibility. For the individual customer the potential domains in which we expect to see full-service provider models include financial services, health care, education, entertainment, travel, and government services. The case of GE Supply Company illustrates the potential power of the full-service provider model for the business customer.

CASE STUDY

FULL-SERVICE PROVIDER MODEL: **GE Supply Company**

(www.gesupply.com)

GE Supply Company (GE Supply) is a business unit of GE. GE has consistently been named one of America's most admired companies in annual polls run by *Fortune* magazine, and its CEO Jack Welch has been the subject of numerous laudatory articles and books during his nineteen years as head of the company.[5] Once Welch got turned on to e-commerce, things started to happen fast all across the company, including at GE Supply.

GE Supply offers more than one hundred thousand voice, data, and electrical products from more than two hundred suppliers; the company's motto is, "If it carries power, voice, or data, we carry it."[6] The suppliers include GE, as well as some of GE's competitors, for example, 3M, Lithonia, and Toshiba.[7] GE Supply delivers products from 150 locations in the United States, Mexico, South America, Ireland, the Middle East, and Southeast Asia, from inventories maintained at customer sites, and via GE Supply Net, a Web site enabling customers to request quotations, order goods, and track their orders via the Internet. GE Supply serves electrical contractors, industrial and commercial users, engineer constructors, original equipment manufacturers (OEMs), and utilities.

GE Supply's value proposition combines the immediacy of local delivery and support with the scope and resources of a global firm, including low transaction costs. The company offers a full product line via an online catalog (www.gesupply catalog.com) and inventory system keeping track of stocks at all 150 locations. The online catalog allows searching by item name, GE Supply part number, manufacturer's part number, or Universal Product Code (UPC), as well as by product category. Orders from the online catalog are placed by telephone, rather than over the Internet. GE Supply also offers telephone support from its national sales center, whose staff can assist customers with product selection and application as well as quoting, expediting, and billing.

GE Supply is a full-service provider for electrical supplies, including supplies for voice and data communications as well as more traditional lighting and power applications. The company faces the ongoing challenge of working successfully with outside suppliers who compete with its sister divisions inside GE. For example, the available electronic fluorescent lighting ballasts include those made by Advance Transformer (www.advancetransformer.com), Lutron, and Valmont Electric, as well as by GE's electronic ballast unit.

GE Supply had 1999 sales of $1.8 billion, less than 2 percent of the total revenues of GE. The GE annual report does not disclose the operating results of GE Supply, but in any case it is not clear that those results alone would adequately portray the value of the unit to the parent company. By providing a ready means for customers to compare GE's products to those offered by the competition, GE Supply may well increase the profits of the company's manufacturing units. Such comparisons often include factors other than price. For example, GE Supply's "Parts Supercenter" offers immediate access to over twelve thousand different GE replacement parts, twenty-four hours a day, seven days a week. Competitors offering narrower product lines are not in a position to offer such service for their own products, but in effect they help subsidize GE's service offering, which makes GE products more attractive to the customer. After describing the many benefits of using the firm as a full-service provider for electrical items, GE Supply ends its online profile with the phrase, "That's the power of partnering with a market leader."[8] The business model of GE Supply is shown in figure 5-2.

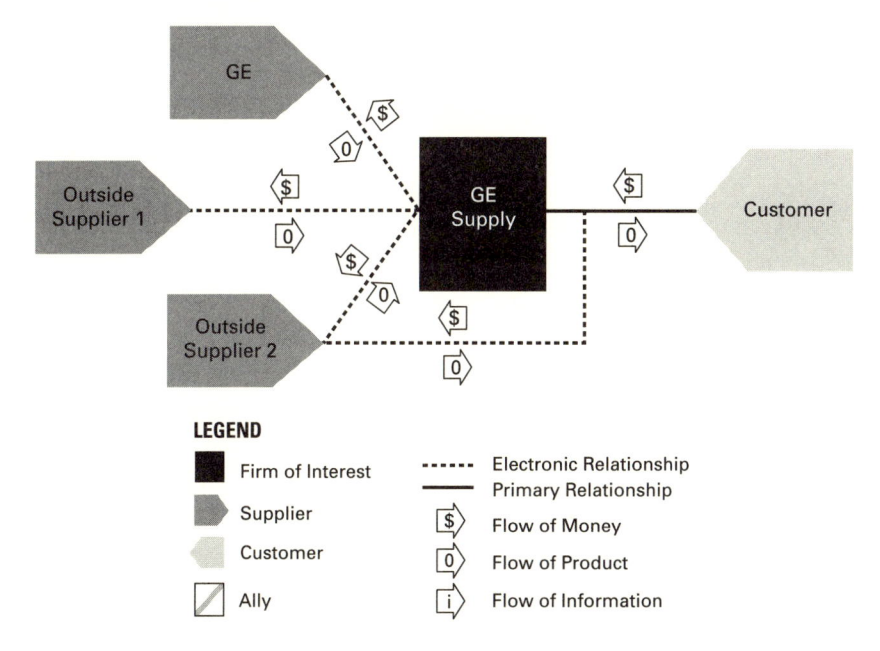

FIGURE 5-2 GE Supply Company Full-Service Provider E-Business Model Schematic

Summary of the Full-Service Provider Model

Strategic Objective and Value Proposition

The full-service provider aims to meet the complete needs of a target customer segment in one domain by integrating the firm's own products and services with those of selected third-party providers. The full-service provider owns the customer relationship, thus knowing more about its customers' needs than any other player in the industry. The firm uses a customer database to identify opportunities for cross-selling products from its existing range and adding new products to the range. Normally each customer will have only one full-service provider in each domain. For individuals, the domains in which full-service providers are most likely to function include financial services, health care, education, entertainment, travel, and government services.

The full-service provider model offers customers lower transaction costs for search, specification, ordering, and fulfillment. In an ideal situation, the customer describes overall objectives—a clean dairy plant in two hours, or a desired combination of financial risk and return—and the full-service provider finds the products and services necessary to meet these objectives at a specified overall cost. Other suppliers are motivated to deal with the full-service provider, even at the risk of losing direct customer contact, in order to make additional sales and be part of a major market presence. These sales may come at a lower price than sales to individual customers, but typically they will come at a lower cost as well, since marketing and billing will be simplified. The full-service provider is also motivated by the prospect of additional sales, but often motivated primarily by the opportunity to capture some of the value it adds by understanding the customer's complete situation. This understanding allows the full-service provider to take a proactive position, rather than simply responding to customer orders. By lowering the customer's overall costs, the full-service provider can further integrate itself into the customer's organization and share in the value created by the partnership.

The customer who chooses a full-service provider must perceive added value in receiving full service from one supplier, as opposed to ordering the same goods directly from their manufacturers. In some cases this value may come from lower prices due to purchasing leverage exerted by the full-service provider. In other cases, such as Orica-Chemnet, the provider adds value by combining different items into a service or by delivering an assortment of goods at one time. Often the provider applies its expertise to help the customer find a better way of meeting its overall needs. The important point is that the successful full-service provider is far more than an online catalog; it is a thoughtful application of business expertise and technology to further leverage a dominant industry position.

Sources of Revenue

A full-service provider gains revenues from selling its own products and those of others, and possibly also from annual membership fees, management fees, transaction fees, commissions on third-party products, advertising or listing fees from third-party providers, and fees for selling aggregated data about customers.

Critical Success Factors

The critical success factors for a full-service provider are detailed below.

- Being a leader in your domain. Prudential Securities, Barnes & Noble, Orica, and GE are all leaders in their field. They are able to supply a large portion of what most customers need in the domain of interest, be it investments, chemicals, or electrical goods. Other suppliers are added to round out the product line, bring in additional revenue, and offer customers some choice, presumably in areas selected by the firm to fit well with its own strengths and strategy. Medium or small suppliers may struggle to succeed with this model, even by gathering together other suppliers of similar size, because they cannot sell enough of their own products to gain sufficient profit to support the overhead of running the model.

- The brand, credibility, and trust necessary for a customer to look to the firm for its complete needs in an area. Successful full-service providers will normally be firms with a long history of trust and customer satisfaction in one of the areas central to the domain. For example, many banks have a sound basis to become full-service providers in the domain of financial services. Similarly, some airlines could become full-service providers in travel.

- Owning the customer relationship in one domain and integrating and consolidating the offering of many third parties into a single channel or multiple channels. A full-service provider needs a strong set of third-party providers covering all the services required for the domain, but it must pass to the third party only the minimum data necessary to complete the transaction. The full-service provider wants to own the customer relationship and must prevent losing customers to third parties that may also have the potential to attain the full-service provider relationship.

- Owning more of the consumer data in the relevant domain than any other player. The full-service provider does not necessarily complete all the customer transactions, but it must own all of the data about customers, their preferences, and their transaction histories. The ability to ethically exploit the ownership of consumer data to provide a full set of services to the consumer is essential for success in this model.

- Enforcement of policies to protect the interests of internal and external suppliers, as well as customers. For example, the incentive and reward systems of the business units or channel managers must be based not only on the success of their areas but on the strength of the total relationship with the customer.

Core Competencies

The core competencies necessary for a full-service provider include the following.

- **Relationship management.** Full-service providers are dependent on their ability to form and manage relationships with customers and with the other major players in the value chain. The strength of the relationship with the customer will largely determine the success of the full-service provider. The relationship will be determined by the strength of the value proposition to the customer and the ability to deliver. The strength of the value proposition will involve the brand, the breadth of offerings, the price-value equation, and the completeness of the consolidation into a single point of contact.

- **Customer and product information management.** This includes collecting, synthesizing, and analyzing information about customer segments and their desires, and matching these with the currently available service offerings while identifying opportunities for new product creation.

- **IT infrastructure.** The full-service provider must develop and integrate firmwide transaction processing, customer databases, electronic links to suppliers, and security. The IT infrastructure capabilities necessary for a full-service provider will be among the largest and most complex for any of the models. The full-service provider infrastructure has to provide seamless integration within a multi-business-unit and perhaps global firm as well as with myriad third-party providers.

- **Brand management and development.** Full service requires a trusted brand to thrive. The brand sets the expectation for high quality and the ability to credibly deliver all the consumers' needs in their domain.

Who Owns What?

The full-service provider is one of three atomic models that own the customer relationship, the data, and the transaction. To succeed, the full-service provider must own the customer relationship and all of the customer data around that relationship, whether or not the firm provides the transaction. The successful full-service provider will own some of the consumer transactions and know about all the rest.

	Customer Relationship	Customer Data	Customer Transaction
Full-Service Provider	✓	✓	✓

CHAPTER 6

Whole of Enterprise

> I want the U.K. to be the world's leading Internet economy.... I am determined that government should play its part, so I am bringing forward our target for getting all government services online [by three years] from 2008 to 2005. This will mean that people and businesses will be able to access government services twenty-four hours a day, seven days a week.
>
> —U.K. PRIME MINISTER TONY BLAIR

> We are very focused on what e-commerce can offer this organization. But you have to migrate your customer base online, and if you move too far ahead you will lose them.
>
> —COLONIAL LIMITED CEO PETER SMEDLEY

> Smedley is now facing a formidable integration risk with these latest acquisitions. When you take subsidiaries into account, he has effectively eight different companies to merge into one computer system.

> Everyone in the industry thinks it is going to be a very big job.
>
> —INSURANCE INDUSTRY CONSULTANT MICHAEL RICE, COMMENTING ON COLONIAL'S STRATEGY

CHAPTERS 4 to 11 describe a wide variety of ways to do e-business. For example, the direct-to-consumer model (chapter 4) caters to customers doing their own electronic shopping, while the intelligent-agent version of the intermediary model (chapter 7) assists customers in having their shopping done for them. Virtual communities (chapter 9) support member-to-member interaction, enabling direct information sharing, while content providers (chapter 11) deliver information indirectly through a third party. The shared-infrastructure model (chapter 8) is adopted by firms in roughly equal positions who can benefit by working together, whereas a dominant firm attempts to further its own strategic goals by becoming a full-service provider (chapter 5). Given the different objectives leading to the adoption of each of the atomic business models, across the multiple business units of any large organization there will likely be a number of e-business models in use.

The use of multiple business models across an organization can create confusion for customers, who may be required to navigate not just different computer systems, but also different ways of doing business. Often customers are treated as different entities by each business unit, and they are asked to carry out repetitive and redundant transactions with different units of the same organization.

An all-too-familiar example of this problem occurs when a customer of a bank or an insurance company experiences a "life event," for example, moving to a new address or taking on a new name after marriage. The customer with multiple products may be required to supply the same information, in a different format, to each business unit for every product—savings account, checking account, credit card, and mortgage for the bank, and life insurance, health insurance, auto insurance, and home insurance for the insurance company. The process is frustrating, error prone, and inefficient for both the customer and the firm.

The problem becomes more complicated if the "business units" are actually government agencies. The citizen with a new home address must report the information to the motor vehicles office, the electoral commission, the water and electricity departments, the welfare and pension offices, the education department, and so on. Each agency may be located in a different building, have different office hours, use different forms, and want the information in a different format. If the agencies are on the Internet, chances are each one got there independently, and their Web pages behave independently as well. Because a significant proportion of government services are information based, an integrated single-point-of-contact approach to electronic service delivery offers dealings with government that are more convenient for individuals and businesses alike. In the marketplace, some banks have achieved a single point of contact for their high-net-worth customers through the use of "personal-banking" models.

Many firms in other industries use the same approach often via a single phone number answered by a call center or an IVR system directing customers to the correct area to meet their current need. More integrated models enable the call center operator to see the customer's full relationship with the firm. For example, software used by a telephone company call center is likely to recognize the caller's number and then to populate the call center operator's screen with a listing of all the phone services the caller has, the caller's payment history, and other important facts. This information is drawn in real time from the separate systems of the independent business units (e.g., cellular phones, residential services, and Internet service provider).

The overall objective of these approaches is to maximize the range of services purchased by each customer. Customers having many of the firm's products, and thus relationships with several business units, are likely to be more profitable and more loyal. Citibank is a leader in implementing this integrated vision, which is embodied in Citibank's long-held objective that a customer be able to interact with Citibank in the same way no matter where that customer is in the world.[1]

Whole-of-Enterprise Atomic Model

The single point of contact for the e-business customer is the essence of the whole-of-enterprise atomic business model. Although many of this model's breakthrough innovations have occurred in public-sector organizations, the model is applicable in both the for-profit and the public sectors. There are two basic implementations of the whole-of-enterprise model: the front-page model and the integrated model.

Front-Page Whole-of-Enterprise Model

Implementing a single point of electronic contact can be as simple as creating an umbrella Web page as a "front page" for the enterprise. Consider Southcorp, the large Australian wine maker that is one of the partners in Artesian Innovations (see chapter 8). Southcorp produces wine under a number of brands, distinguished by region, variety, and price. Although the brands are well known to wine buyers, most may be unaware that their favorite small vineyard is part of the wine giant Southcorp. Each brand has its own Web site (e.g., www.penfolds.com.au, www.seaview.com.au, and www.coldstreamhills.com.au), which isn't necessarily linked to the Southcorp Web site (www.southcorp.com.au). Many consumers are apparently happy dealing with the Web sites individually, but the consumer wanting to see the whole Southcorp wine range would quickly become frustrated moving across sites with different content and formats. For this consumer segment, Southcorp created "Australian Wines of Distinction," a single Web site (www.australianwines.com) providing access to information about all of Southcorp's wines. Southcorp does not sell wine directly to the end consumer, avoiding channel conflict, but the Wines of Distinction Web site enables the user to find a nearby location to purchase wine. Although not particularly sophisticated technically, the Wines of Distinction site provides the customer a whole-of-enterprise view of wines produced by Southcorp, which bills itself as the name behind the brands.[2]

Another example of the front-page whole-of-enterprise model is the Ford Motor Company. Ford's front page (www.ford.com) contains links to the Web sites of Ford, Lincoln, Mercury, Jaguar, Volvo, Mazda, and Aston Martin, all marques owned by Ford. Each of these sites has a distinctive "look and feel" appropriate to the image of the particular brand of automobile; none includes a link back to the Ford corporate home page. Many multiple-business-unit organizations use the whole-of-enterprise model at this very basic level to direct customer traffic. Some firms have migrated from the front-page model to a more integrated but challenging model—but as we will see below, this is not easy.

Integrated Whole-of-Enterprise Model

Beyond the front page, relatively few organizations currently offer an integrated whole-of-enterprise service electronically. For example, a customer could readily receive a good answer to the question, "What options do you offer for a deposit of twenty thousand dollars?" from a teller at any branch of a retail bank. However, customers trying to answer that question by visiting the home page of some major U.S. banks are required to first choose from a list of products, many carrying nondescriptive titles, and then download a file of additional information. For example, Chase Manhattan Bank (www.chase.com) expects the prospective depositor to traverse a maze of pages before arriving at a choice between high-yield savings, certificates of deposit, and money market accounts, each of which is described on still other pages. Although this global bank has a single front page that includes links to the pages of various product groups, the front page is not structured to conform to the customer's framing of the situation. The customer wants to first learn what the best product is, and then to choose one; the bank site expects the customer to choose the products first and then figure out which one is best. Even Wingspan Bank (www.wingspan.com) struggles to deliver, despite describing itself as more than an online bank—in fact, a one-stop resource where one can manage all important parts of one's financial life. On its Web site, Wingspan Bank presents an array of products (checking, loans, credit cards, etc.) rather than a set of solutions. The narrowness of Wingspan's product line keeps the experience from being as frustrating as a visit to the pages of larger banks.

There are two fundamental sources of the deficiency illustrated in this example. First, the information systems in many organizations have been built from a product or business unit perspective, rather than from a customer perspective. Pulling together information from these diverse systems is often difficult, whether it's to answer a query about the best product for a given situation or to present a consolidated report to a customer owning multiple products. Middleware—software that fits between an electronic front end, generally on the Internet, and an organization's existing product-oriented systems—addresses these difficulties in part. However, middleware doesn't address the second source of trouble: a design approach that requires customers to know the products they want, rather than one that helps customers determine their product needs based on their goals.

Whole-of-Enterprise E-Business Model Schematic

In general, the whole-of-enterprise model operates as shown in figure 6-1. In this schematic, the firm of interest is shown in the middle and at the left, and its customers are at the right. The firm of

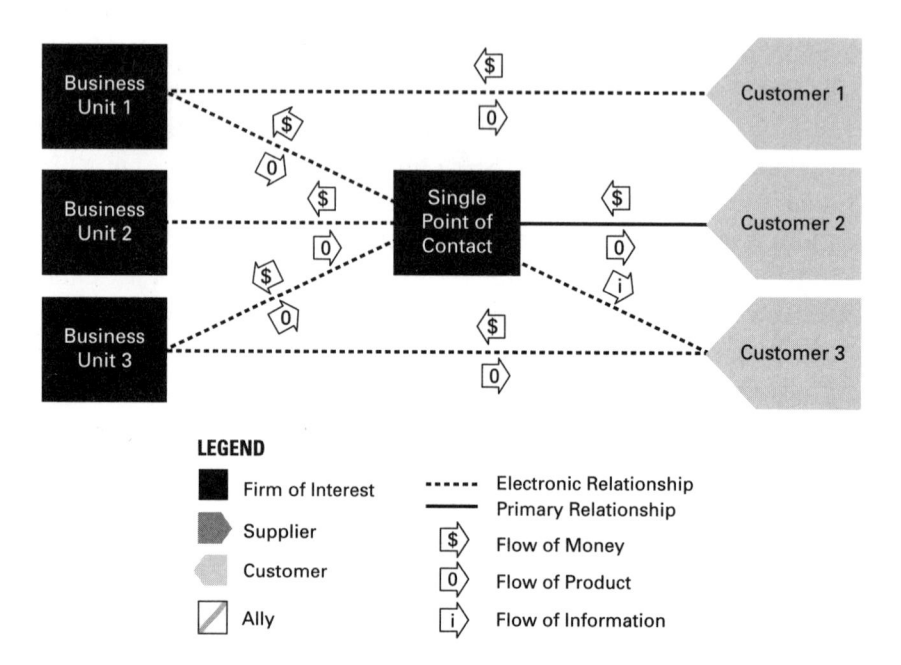

FIGURE 6-1 Whole-of-Enterprise E-Business Model Schematic

interest is represented by four squares—the single point of contact and three business units. Products and dollars flow between the business units and the single point of contact, which may be the corporate center. In the front-page model, communication with customers quickly moves to the business units; in the integrated model, communication with customers continues to pass through a central point. In fact, a customer of a firm that has successfully adopted the integrated model may never know, or need to know, much about the underlying structure of the organization. On the other hand, despite the existence of an integrated model, some customers may prefer to continue to do business directly with some business units, particularly for very simple or very complicated transactions. The diagram indicates such direct customer pathways (i.e., customers 1 and 3), as well as those customer pathways that allow interaction with all business units through a single point of contact (i.e., customer 2).

Whole-of-Enterprise Model in Government[3]

Governments in many countries around the world have pioneered the whole-of-enterprise model. In a recent address to the World Economic Forum, Bill Gates complimented the government of the Australian state of Victoria for being a pioneer in bringing government services to the people.[4] The state's vision is to "ensure that all appropriate Victorian Government services and information be available online, all the time, by the year 2001."[5] The minister for multimedia, Alan Stockdale, commented: "The Victorian Government's aim to have government services available online by 2001 is an ambitious goal, but one which I believe is achievable. Online service delivery—24 hours a day, seven days a week—is going to revolutionise the way government in this state communicates with the Victorian community and the world. The online delivery of government services is an integral part of our Victoria 21 multimedia strategy to position Victoria as a global 'centre for multimedia excellence.'"[6]

The objective is for government services to be accessible from the customer's location at a time suitable to the customer. In this customer-centric approach,

- citizens access all electronically available government services from a single access point;
- access is simple and cheaply available to all in a seamless or transparent manner, from a wide variety of locations, twenty-four hours a day, every day; and
- navigation of government services is set up by subject, as well as by agency—rather than access being aligned solely with the departmental structure of government, which the customer might not readily know.

The last point is a key aspect of the new service delivery concept. In the new Victorian model for state government services, those requesting a government service should need to identify only the service required, and they will not need to know which department or agency is responsible. Two concepts for service delivery were introduced in this new business model for government:

- **Channels:** service groupings aimed at specific customer interest areas—for example, a "business channel" for information and transactions aimed at small businesses.
- **Life Events:** some common occurrence that results in a group of activities. For instance, moving house or turning eighteen results in a group of transactions that are part of the same event for the citizen but are implemented via a number of government departments.

The traditional government business model is illustrated in figure 6-2. In this model, government departments operate as isolated functional silos. It is the responsibility of citizen and business customers to identify the government department(s) responsible for delivering the services they need. In Victoria, as in many places, the identification of the right departments is so complex that professional navigators exist. These navigators include government agencies such as the Community Information Bureau and private navigators such as lawyers and agents.

Figure 6-3 illustrates the result of rethinking government service delivery and identifying of common life events and channels. Channels under way or under development in the Victorian government

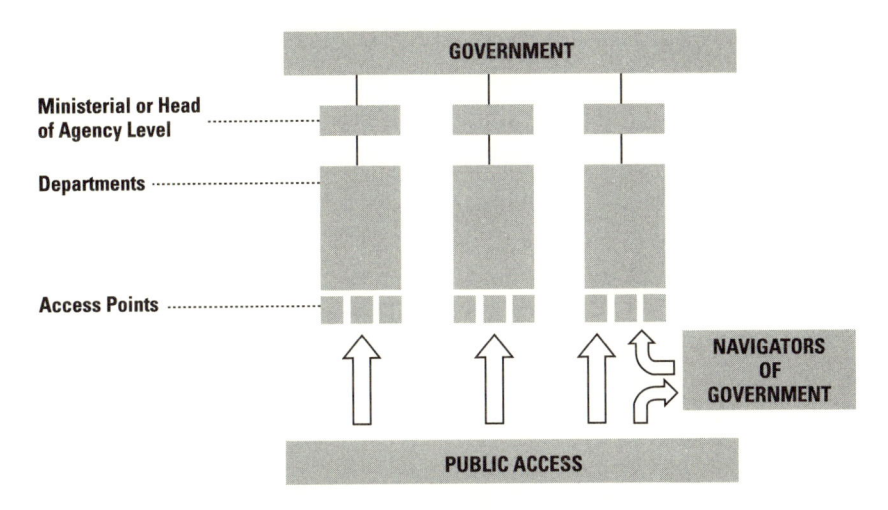

FIGURE 6-2 Traditional Government Model

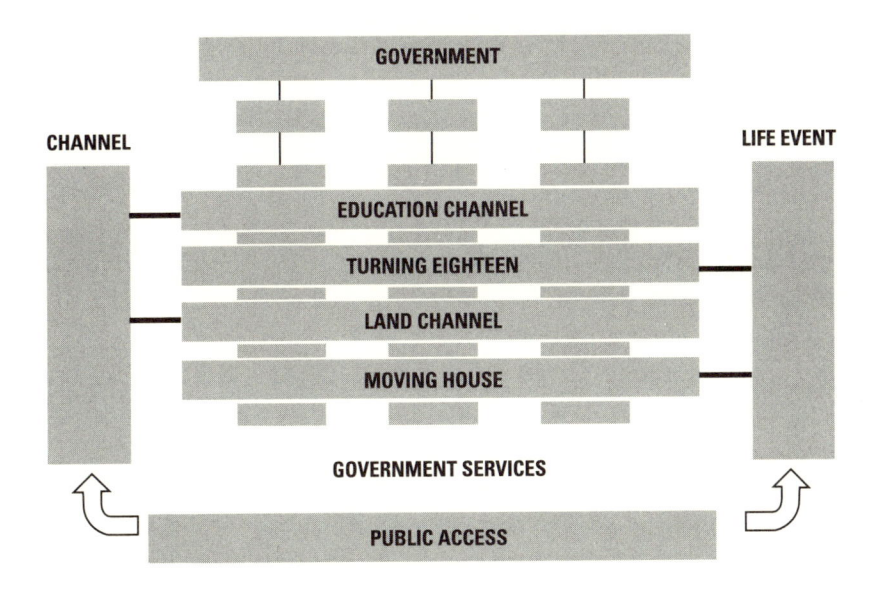

FIGURE 6-3 New Government Model

include the Citizens Channel, the Business Channel (www.business.channel.vic.gov.au), the Land Channel (www.land.vic.gov.au), the Health Channel (www.betterhealth.vic.gov.au), the Tourism Channel, the Education Channel, and the Transport Channel.

Soon after the announcement of the Victorian initiative, all state government departments started to publish information on the Internet, accessible from a single access point at www.vic.gov.au. The first stage of the Citizens Channel was formed by the Victorian Roads Department, the Department of Births, Deaths and Marriages, the Victorian Electoral Commission, two local councils, a water company, and an electricity company. The goal was to enable twenty-four-hour, seven-day service with a wide range of access options, a friendly user interface, and a focus on life events, at no extra service cost to the customer. To provide these access options, the Victorian government undertook the "Maxi" project, the creation of an IT infrastructure that provides government agencies with a variety of electronic delivery methods to service their customers. Maxi delivery methods include public information kiosks, the Internet, and an IVR system. By the time of its first birthday, Maxi was handling more than three times the initial target for transaction volume, far exceeding the transaction estimates in most of the business cases put forward by government agencies at the time they joined the system.

In early 2000, the Victorian Government announced a redesigned site (www.vic.gov.au/onlineservices.cfm) that incorporates the lessons learned since the whole-of-enterprise approach began. Despite considerable initial skepticism, the model appears to be working well for the state of Victoria and its citizens and to be spreading to other governments. As quoted at the start of the chapter, U.K. Prime Minister Tony Blair announced in March 2000 that the United Kingdom would also adopt the whole-of-enterprise model, aiming to get all government services online—through personal computers, telephone, digital television, or a convenient public access point—by 2005. The announcement came just days after Blair set a target of ensuring that every Briton would have access to the Internet within five years. "It is likely the Internet will be as ubiquitous and as normal as electricity is today," Blair said. "We cannot accept a digital divide, for business or for individuals."[7] U.K. Minister Ian McCartney said, "The challenge for the public sector is to innovate and invest in e-business models to help meet growing expectations applied to government services. All citizens will benefit, even those who don't want to use new technology. By making internal processes more effective, front-line staff will be free to provide better services."[8] The first services offered included an online job search, an Internet land registry, and email reminders that tax returns were due.[9]

It may seem puzzling that the whole-of-enterprise model has been adopted most enthusiastically in the government sector, which many believe is characterized by bureaucratic empire building and resistance to change. But by probing we can uncover some likely reasons for this outcome. In the first place, while the agencies of a local, state, or federal government may be diverse, they are rarely competitive, at least at the level of the citizen. There may be significant barriers to cooperation, but only one agency is trying to collect water bills, another to register births, a third to license new drivers, and so on. In a commercial organization, for example, a bank, different business units may in fact compete for each customer's business. Second, the effects of life events are often better defined in a customer's relationship with the government than in a customer's relationship with a business. At a certain birthday a citizen is eligible to apply for a driver's license, at another birthday able to vote, and so on; when a citizen moves house and changes address, a known number of government agencies need to be informed. The effects of birthdays and residential moves in the relationship of a customer to a business may be straightforward, but the commercial implications—the ones in which the business is really interested—are often less clear. The ability of the business to respond to such changes in a way that is valuable to the customer may therefore be constrained.

Infrastructure

For the whole-of-enterprise model, infrastructure needs to link the different systems in the various business units and provide a firmwide perspective for management. Our field research revealed that the following infrastructure services are the most important for implementing the whole-of-enterprise model.

- Centralized management of infrastructure capacity to facilitate integration and capture economies of scale (often a major change in a multi-business-unit firm in which IT management has been decentralized)

- Identification and testing of new technologies to find new ways to integrate the often different systems in many business units into a single point of customer contact

- Management of key data independent of applications and the creation of a centralized repository for firmwide information

- Electronic means of summarizing data from different applications and platforms to manage the complexity arising from a single point of contact for multiple business units

- Development of an ERP service to process the transactions instigated by customers interacting with several different business units, often requiring consolidating or linking several different ERPs in the firm

- Payment transaction processing, either on a firmwide basis or by linking several systems across the business units

- Large-scale data-processing facilities to process transactions from multiple business units, often centralized to achieve economies of scale

- Integrated mobile computing applications, which provide another channel to the customer

In the whole-of-enterprise model there are two significant questions about IT infrastructure: (1) which services? and (2) where to place them? The previous paragraphs describe which services are required. Now we turn to where to place them. For illustration we analyze a whole-of-enterprise e-business model similar to the Victorian government example described above. The IT infrastructure needed for a whole-of-enterprise model is presented in figure 6-4.

The IT infrastructure for a multidepartment government organization, or a multi-business-unit firm, can be represented as a pyramid with multiple layers.[10] Each layer supports all the layers above

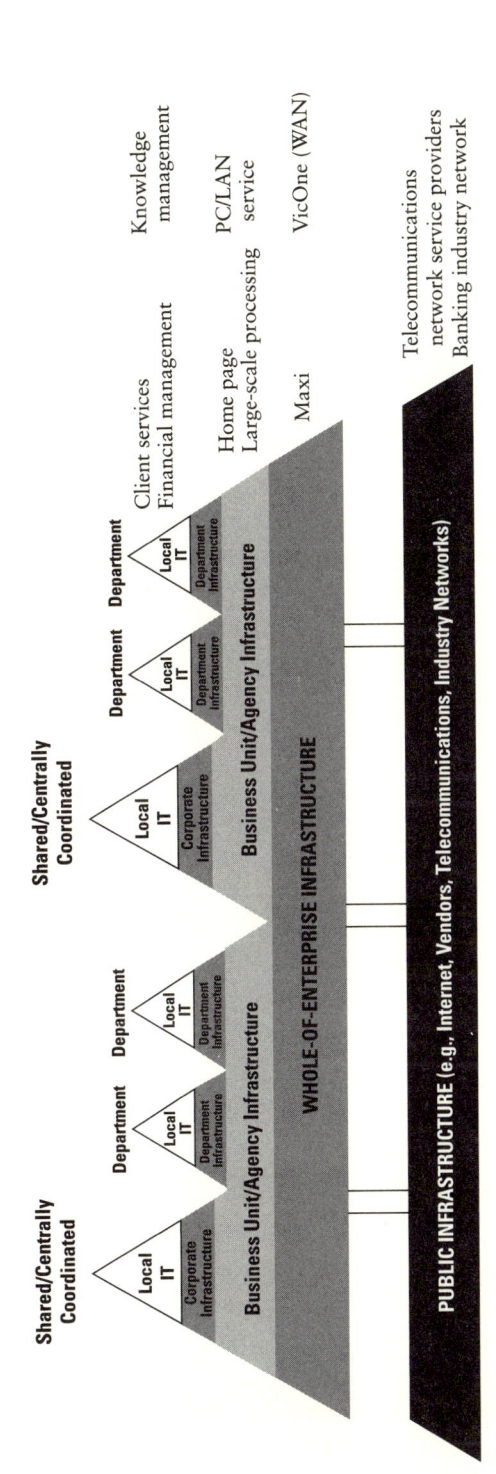

FIGURE 6-4 Whole-of-Enterprise IT Infrastructure

it, and the infrastructure services become more tailored moving up the diagram. For example, the public infrastructure at the base of the model includes the Internet, telecommunications companies, Internet service providers, and vendors, all of whom provide standardized services to multiple customers. The infrastructure for the whole-of-enterprise model for government sits on top of the public infrastructure and uses it to provide government-specific services from all agencies. For example, the Victorian government provides VicOne, a network that allows every government site to communicate with any other government site regardless of location or agency. VicOne encompasses schools, hospitals, libraries, police stations, courts, and departmental offices, and it will eventually include local government, business, and community users. As in all infrastructure investments, the bandwidth and capacity of VicOne had to be decided upon before the precise demand was known. The existence of the VicOne network in fact created new demand, which increased traffic and put pressure on the capacity of the network. This is the typical cycle of any successful infrastructure investment.

On top of the whole-of-enterprise government infrastructure sit the agency-specific infrastructure services, such as an agency intranet and home page. On top of the agency infrastructure sits a department infrastructure, often involving PC/local area network services and standardized financial systems. On top of the multilayered infrastructure sit departmental local applications, which are unique and usually include systems for client services. The government employee sitting at a PC giving employment information to a citizen is thus working though an infrastructure with at least four levels, each providing different services and all integrated via common standards and architectures.

One of the most difficult decisions in a multilayered infrastructure is determining where the infrastructure services should be provided. Should they be standardized across all agencies and provided at the whole-of-enterprise level, achieving economies of scale? Or should they be provided at the individual-agency level, where they can be tailored to specific needs?

The best decision is often a trade-off that must be made uniquely for each organization. However, we can say that to be effective, the whole-of-enterprise model requires at least some of the infrastructure to be provided at the whole-of-enterprise level. The front-page version of the whole-of-enterprise model requires only a relatively thin layer of infrastructure at the whole-of-enterprise level. But the integrated version of the model requires a much thicker layer of services at the whole-of-enterprise level to deliver on the single-point-of-contact experience. This thick layer includes more services than the thin layer.

Investment at the whole-of-enterprise level always requires top-down leadership to support the investment of central funds to build an infrastructure that will be used by all agencies or business units. The placement of infrastructure capability is therefore a strategic decision that should be made by the senior management team. If senior management wish to implement an integrated whole-of-enterprise model, then the services needed must be identified, funded, and provided centrally to enable the agencies or business units to leverage the infrastructure. The business cases for such investment are notoriously hard to quantify convincingly to hard-nosed accountants.[11] Instead, as in the case of the Victorian government, the investments are usually made to enable and implement a vision held by senior management, rather than on the basis of strict financial justification. To make all levels of infrastructure work together often requires significant effort to reach an agreement on IT architectures and standards. We will take up the discussion of where to place IT infrastructure services again in chapter 12.

Challenges in Implementing the Whole-of-Enterprise Model

Although the integrated whole-of-enterprise model is attractive to many enterprises and their customers, the model is not yet common. For many organizations, the potential advantages of the model are apparently outweighed by its costs and risks. The costs arise from the need to reengineer a firm's technical and human infrastructure in order for the whole-of-enterprise model to succeed. Data must at least be mapped, if not standardized, across disparate systems. These systems themselves must at least be interfaced, if not connected or replaced by a unified ERP system. A single customer interface must be designed and built, and then kept current as the underlying legacy systems change. The transactions undertaken by each organizational unit must be cataloged; experiences in the state of Victoria showed that units tended to underestimate the number of different transactions by a factor of at least ten and occasionally one hundred. All of this work on the technology infrastructure takes time and money, both of which are generally in short supply. Only a visionary and disciplined organization will have the resources and the perseverance to create the technical infrastructure necessary for the whole-of-enterprise model.

As difficult as these technical changes may be, the human changes required are even more challenging. Incentive systems must be modified to encourage an enterprise-wide view, and managers of competing business units must learn to cooperate to create the systems necessary for the new business model. The whole-of-enterprise model requires a degree of communication between business units that is much higher than that required, or encouraged, in a traditional "stovepipe" organization. People across the organization must have the time, and the motivation, to share their plans for new products and new processes, or the whole-of-enterprise model will never succeed.

The technical and human obstacles to the whole-of-enterprise model can be overcome, as illustrated by the examples in this chapter. However, the extent of the challenges should not be underestimated; the cost and time required to deal with them must be factored into the decision about whether to adopt the model.

The Future of the Whole-of-Enterprise Model

What is the future of this presently rare atomic business model? As access to the Internet continues to grow, informed citizens and customers will expect, and ultimately demand, that their interactions with all enterprises—government and private—become increasingly electronic. The whole-of-enterprise model allows these interactions to get better, as well as faster, when they move to the Internet.

Despite the implementation difficulties described above, we predict that the whole-of-enterprise model will continue to spread in the government sector. A number of countries have made significant commitments to this model, including Singapore, Malaysia, Japan, and the United Kingdom. The spread may be relatively slow because the cost of creating the model can be significant and the time required to implement it can exceed the expected term in office of a top government official. However, as the notions of channels and life events spread, so should the model itself.

In late 2000, for example, the U.S. government launched a major whole-of-enterprise initiative called FirstGov (www.first gov.gov). FirstGov is "the first-ever government website to provide the public with easy, one-stop access to all U.S. Federal Government resources."[12] FirstGov provides users front-page access to a wide variety of government departments by topic of interest, including agriculture, food, health, and money and taxation. Users can conduct a wide variety of business online, including tracking Social Security benefits, applying for student loans, finding a job, and getting assistance relocating. Links are provided to many state agencies for a wide variety of services such as renewing an auto registration. FirstGov includes some of the channel and life events design pioneered by the Victorian government, while offering access to a much broader set of information. Its creation seems likely to spur efforts by state and local governments across the United States to do business electronically.

Outside of the government sector, the future of the whole-of-enterprise model is less certain. For some organizations, for example, the one described in the case study below, the integrated whole-of-enterprise model will represent an attractive strategic option whose cost will rapidly be recovered through increased revenues. For other organizations, the potential benefits of the integrated model will not be worth the cost of implementing it. Such organizations may implement only a front-page whole-of-enterprise model. For example, organizations such as Ford, whose customers are generally dealing with just one business unit at a time, might find little value in extending the application of the model beyond an Internet front page. The key drivers for an integrated whole-of-enterprise model include a desire to achieve more synergy and cross-selling across previously independent business units, as well as the goal to create a single point of customer contact for firmwide services.

CASE STUDY

WHOLE-OF-ENTERPRISE MODEL: **Colonial Limited** (www.colonial.com.au)

Colonial Limited is a diverse international financial services group, headquartered in Australia but doing most of its business overseas. With businesses in banking, retail insurance, investments, superannuation, funds management, stockbroking, and funds administration, Colonial aims to offer a complete range of products in the financial services domain. Colonial has offices in ten countries and provides its products and services through a range of distribution channels. In Australia, its insurance business is fully integrated with its banking operation, Colonial State Bank.

Colonial's strategy of providing a broad range of integrated financial services is known as *allfinanz,* a German expression for a company that sells all financial services. Colonial itself defines allfinanz as "the seamless integration of Colonial's businesses across individual product streams to assure a single view of each of our customers."[13] Although well accepted in Germany, allfinanz has never been fully tested in the Australian market, and some see it as contradicting the general trend in consumer finance to shop around for financial services. However, early indications are that the strategy is working well; Colonial's cost-to-income ratio for Australian financial services fell from 58 percent in 1998 to 49 percent in 1999, suggesting that the company had become more efficient at operating an allfinanz business. The proportion of Australian customers who purchased products in at least two of the company's three major product streams (banking, insurance, and funds management) increased from 15 percent in 1998 to 21 percent in 1999.

Colonial has added to its product line both by internal development and by acquisition. In 1998, the firm spent more than A$2 billion to buy two large U.K. insurers, Prudential and Legal & General, and in 1999 it purchased Trust Bank of Tasmania and the National Bank of Fiji and formed joint ventures in China and Vietnam. In early March 2000, Colonial merged with the Commonwealth Bank of Australia, Australia's largest bank. Colonial shareholders received a 48 percent premium on the market value of their shares. The merger was expected to increase Colonial's competitiveness in the global financial services marketplace.

Despite Colonial's explicit strategy to provide customers with integrated financial services, and the obvious value placed on this strategy by the Commonwealth Bank, Colonial offers only a front-page approach to the whole-of-enterprise model. The company's Web site (www.colonial.com.au) contains a long list of financial and insurance products available under the Colonial banner, but it offers no way to integrate the holdings of a given customer. The company's 1999 annual report says, "The [Colonial] group expects to introduce a number of e-commerce allfinanz initiatives during the first half of 2000 which will enhance the current e-commerce offering and complement existing physical distribution channels."[14]

Colonial's lack of a true whole-of-enterprise approach, even with the existence of a whole-of-enterprise strategy, is clear testimony to the difficulty of implementing this atomic business model. As the epigraph by Michael Rice at the start of the chapter suggests, pulling together data from the systems of acquired companies is a formidable challenge—and that is the easy part. Much more difficult is assuring that the appropriate processes, incentives, and performance measurement systems are in place to enable people to overcome the natural tendency to focus on their business unit, rather than on the organization as a whole. Whether Colonial will ever implement a deeper version of the whole-of-enterprise model remains to be seen; clearly the intentions of its new parent will influence the outcome. In the meantime, the Colonial example can serve as a reminder of the challenges of implementing the whole-of-enterprise model. Ironically, this difficulty is greatest for precisely those firms that could gain the most from the implementation—namely, firms that have expanded their range by acquiring organizations with offerings outside the firm's existing product set. For such firms, the front-page model, perhaps fitted with an industry-appropriate version of a Cisco-style configurator (see chapter 10), may be the best alternative for the short-to-medium term. Over the longer term, the organization can find ways to pull together information from diverse systems, and it can attempt to determine appropriate life events and their implications for customers.

Summary of the Whole-of-Enterprise Model

Strategic Objective and Value Proposition

In the whole-of-enterprise e-business model, a multi-business-unit organization provides a single point of contact for customers. The customer is then better able to navigate through enterprise-wide offerings to find suitable products and services. The front-page implementation of the model serves as a pointer to the business units. The integrated implementation has a consolidated customer interface that helps customers identify, choose, and acquire services from different business units. The whole-of-enterprise model can increase customer intimacy and service levels, resulting in customers buying a larger number of the enterprise's offerings.

Sources of Revenue

In the for-profit sector, revenues are generated by the provision of goods and services to the customer by the business units. There may also be the opportunity to charge an annual service or membership fee for access to this level of service, as can be done with private banking. Revenue and profit per customer should increase, but these will be at least partially offset by more up-front investment in people, training, and technology.

In the government sector, the motivation is usually twofold: improved service and reduced cost. Service to the community is improved through continuous, round-the-clock operation and faster service times. Government costs can potentially be reduced by sharing more infrastructure and eliminating the need to perform the same transaction (e.g., address change) in multiple agencies. However, the up-front costs of the whole-of-enterprise model in government are substantial, not only in terms of technology infrastructure, but also with respect to reengineering, data standardization, and political capital.

Critical Success Factors

The following list details the critical success factors for the whole-of-enterprise model.

- Changing customer behavior to make use of the new model, as opposed to the customer continuing to interact directly with individual units
- Reducing costs in the individual business units as the direct demands on them fall, and managing the transfer pricing issues that will inevitably arise
- Altering the perspective of the business units to take an enterprise-wide view, which includes broad product awareness, training, and cross-selling
- In the integrated implementation, reengineering the business processes to link into life events at the front end and existing legacy processes and systems at the back end
- Finding compelling and practical life events that customers can use as triggers to access the enterprise

Core Competencies

The core competencies necessary for every whole-of-enterprise model are the following:

- Ability to segment the enterprise's market, identifying which life events are both sufficiently frequent across the customer base and sufficiently meaningful to individual customers

- Leadership skills to move the enterprise from a business-unit orientation to an enterprise-wide orientation, a change that requires the development of a new mind-set and culture that affect almost every aspect of the enterprise, including structure, incentives, investment, performance metrics, the definition of customer service, human resource policies, and technology infrastructure

- Ability to manage complex, heterogeneous information systems environments

- Ability to negotiate (and enforce) agreements among managers of different organizational units

If these core competencies and critical success factors are not present, the whole-of-enterprise model represents just another channel, adding to the expense of running the organization without reducing costs or, especially in the case of government, increasing revenue.

Who Owns What?

	Customer Relationship	Customer Data	Customer Transaction
Whole-of-Enterprise	✓	✓	✓

CHAPTER 7

Portals, Agents, Auctions, Aggregators, and Other Intermediaries

E-BUSINESS is often promoted as an ideal way for sellers and buyers to interact directly, shortening old-economy value chains by "disintermediating" some of their members. Yet some of the most popular sites on the Internet, both for consumers and for business users, are in fact intermediaries—sites that stand between the buyer and the seller. Yahoo!, Jango, eBay, and other intermediaries have become wildly popular on the basis of their seemingly paradoxical ability to add value by becoming an additional link in the value chain. The number and variety of intermediaries are growing at least as quickly as the Web itself. Such growth led *Red Herring,* an electronic newsletter focusing on new e-commerce companies, to proclaim, "Retail is toast!"[1] We do not think retail is finished, but there is no question that the growth of intermediaries will permanently change the value chains of retailers, traditional intermediaries, and consumers themselves. This chapter will examine several kinds of electronic intermediaries, exploring for each the reason that it exists, its current role, and its possible future. To provide structure for this fast developing area, we begin by proposing a framework for describing and distinguishing intermediaries.

Comparing Intermediaries

The Internet is home to a wide variety of intermediaries, each of which provides a different value proposition. Figure 7-1 presents a framework for comparing intermediaries on the basis of the completeness of service offered and the number of buyers and sellers participating.[2] *Completeness of service* is the proportion offered of the full set of services that could potentially be provided by an intermediary. The services include the following:

- **Search:** To locate providers of products and services.

- **Specification:** To identify important product attributes, for example, nine-hundred-megahertz clock speed for a computer or sixty-watt output for a sound system. Specifications reduce communication costs for both buyers and sellers.

- **Price:** To establish the price, including optional extras such as warranties. Options for setting the price include fixed prices, auctions, reverse auctions, and dynamic pricing based on demand or relationships.

- **Sale:** To complete the sales transaction, including payment and settlement.

- **Fulfillment:** To fulfill the purchase by delivering the product or service.

- **Surveillance:** To conduct surveillance of the activities of buyers and sellers in order to report aggregate activity and prices and to inform and regulate the market. This activity can include reporting on the results of completed transactions (e.g., stock market summaries or auction results) and on the depth of the market (e.g., the number of active buyers and sellers and the prices at which they are willing to transact).

- **Enforcement:** To enforce proper conduct by buyers and sellers, including resolving disputes and sanctioning improper behavior. Some intermediaries, such as stock exchanges, have guarantee funds to compensate for any loss.

PORTALS, AGENTS, AUCTIONS, AGGREGATORS, AND OTHER INTERMEDIARIES | 153

Components of Service
Search
Specification
Price
Sale
Fulfillment
Surveillance
Enforcement

Increasing Completeness of Service →

ELECTRONIC MARKETS
e.g., NASDAQ

SPECIALTY AUCTIONS
e.g., Manheim, Sotheby's

ELECTRONIC AUCTIONS
e.g., eBay

SHOPPING AGENTS
e.g., Jango

PORTALS
e.g., Yahoo!

ELECTRONIC MALL
e.g., iMall

Number of Buyers and Sellers →

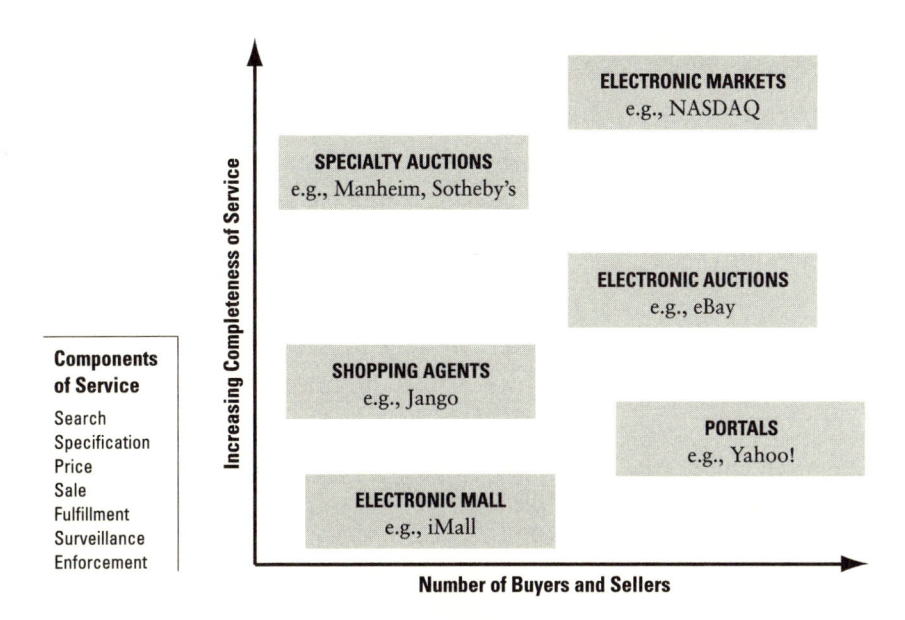

FIGURE 7-1 Intermediary Business Models for E-Business

The other attribute for describing intermediaries is the number of buyers and sellers involved. The more buyers and sellers, the more potential choices the intermediary delivers to its buyer and seller customers. The overall potential value provided by a given intermediary is determined by a combination of its completeness of service and the total number of buyers and sellers it attracts. Electronic markets, such as stock markets, typically provide the full set of services, from search to enforcement. Electronic auctions may leave the specification, and always leave the pricing, sale, and fulfillment, to the customer, so they do not cover as much of the service set, but they do attract large numbers of users.[3] Portals attract even more users, but they tend to offer even fewer services, while shopping agents typically offer more services but are not so popular. The further to the upper right of the framework in figure 7-1 an intermediary is placed, the more potential value it delivers. In the following sections, we will describe the types of intermediaries shown in figure 7-1. We begin with the world's best-known intermediary, the online auction site eBay.

Electronic Auctions

Since launching in 1995, eBay has grown rapidly to become one of the most visited Internet sites, with 1.8 million unique visitors per day.[4] Consumers of all interests and income levels have used eBay's "person-to-person online trading community" to buy and sell items ranging from toys to autos. eBay is free to browsers and buyers, but it charges fees to sellers for listing and selling an item. The listing fee ranges from twenty-five cents to a few dollars, except for vehicles and real estate, which attract higher fees. Additional fees are charged for including boldface type or a photo in a listing, for setting a reserve price, and for placing an item in a "featured auction." If a listed item sells, the seller must pay eBay a percentage of the sale price, ranging from 5 percent of the first twenty-five dollars to 1.25 percent of anything over one thousand dollars. With almost five million items on sale at any given time, and four hundred thousand new items added each day, it is not surprising that eBay had fiscal 1999 revenues of $224.7 million, a 161 percent increase over its fiscal 1998 revenues. eBay's gross merchandise sales (the value of goods traded on the eBay site) for the fourth quarter alone of 1999 climbed to $901 million, almost triple the $307 million reported in the fourth quarter of 1998, and the company's market capitalization was in excess of $17 billion. Net income for 1999 was $10.8 million, a decrease of $2 million from the previous year.

eBay was profitable from the start and deposited its only round of venture capital funding in the bank, where it remained untouched as the company grew. eBay went public in late 1998 at $18 per share and split three for one about six months later. The new shares reached $245 in early 2000 before falling back; the founders of eBay joined the new-economy billionaires' club, and entrepreneurs around the world began investigating variations on the eBay theme.

The eBay business model is typical of an intermediary: At no point during the selling process does eBay take possession of either the item being sold or the buyer's payment for the item. Instead, as the eBay Web site notes, sellers are responsible for bookkeeping, logistics, and collections: "When your auction closes, contact your winning bidder or bidders within three business days. You'll want to confirm the final cost, including any shipping charges, and tell them where to send payment. When the bidder meets your payment terms, you fulfill your end of the agreement by sending them your item. Your auction forms a binding contract between you and the winning bidder or bidders. . . . Breathe easy because the vast majority of buyers and sellers at eBay are honest and reliable."[5]

Following completion of a transaction, each party is encouraged to add compliments or criticisms to the trading profile of his or her trading partner on eBay's "Feedback Forum." eBay's Feedback Forum and other services, such as chat rooms, bulletin boards, and email, are designed to foster direct interaction between buyers and sellers with similar interests, thus promoting a sense of community among customers and encouraging consumer loyalty and repeat usage. These benefits also facilitate surveillance and have contributed to the successful completion of well over 50 percent of all auctions listed on eBay since the site's inception.[6] eBay offers free insurance to buyers of items costing less than two hundred dollars, an escrow service for buyers and sellers of more expensive items, a "safety staff" to resolve issues such as fraud, trading offenses, and illegally listed items, and a dispute resolution service.

As eBay grew, it expanded its services in several directions. The number of auction categories rose from the original dozen to more than four thousand, all suggested by customers. Local auctions were established for many American cities to facilitate the sale of vehicles, real estate, tickets to sporting and cultural events, and other items that are expensive to move or of primarily local interest. Affiliates were formed in Australia, Canada, Germany, the United Kingdom, and Japan. In April 1999 eBay acquired the physical art auction house Butterfield & Butterfield, and in October 1999, it launched eBay Great Collections, which features fine antiques, art, and rare collectibles offered and guaranteed by many well-known auction houses, galleries, and dealers. In early March 2000, eBay announced a strategic alliance with Wells Fargo Bank to develop an online person-to-person payments platform called Billpoint, and an agreement with AutoTrader.com, the world's largest online used-car site, to create the Internet's largest auction-style marketplace for consumers and dealers to buy and sell used cars. The company stepped outside the person-to-person realm in late March 2000 by forming Business Exchange to serve the small-business market—a highly fragmented group of buyers and sellers in a fast-growing business segment. eBay Business Exchange offers goods in thirty-four business-related categories, totalling nearly sixty thousand listings at the time of the launch. The main Business Exchange categories include computer hardware, software, electronics, industrial equipment, office equipment, and professional tools. The company's announcement said, "eBay expects businesses of varying sizes will sell and be successful on eBay Business Exchange, but the company recognizes that its millions of current sellers will serve as the fundamental force behind this business marketplace."[7]

The diagram for the basic business model used by eBay and other online auctions is shown in Figure 7-2. Money flows from prospective sellers to eBay, from buyers to actual sellers, and from successful sellers to eBay. Goods sold move from sellers to buyers directly, not via eBay. Direct interaction among customers is enabled via chat rooms. The chat room and the Feedback Forum give eBay some of the attributes of the virtual community atomic model.

Although not a feature of eBay in particular, in general an auction site could use allies to build traffic. For example, CityAuction (www.utrade.com), an online auction site owned by Ticketmaster Online—CitySearch, encourages Internet users to put a link to the auction site on their home pages. CityAuction pays the "associate" (i.e., ally) $1.50 for each item purchased by buyers who come to the auction site through the associate's link. Associates can recruit other associates, and CityAuction pays the original associate $0.50 for each item purchased by buyers who come through their associates' links. Figure 7-2 therefore indicates the possibility of payments moving from the auction firm to allies.

Like other intermediaries, eBay owns the customer relationship and the data, but not the transaction. The customer relationship is potentially rich, as shown in figure 7-2 for buyer 2 who interacts directly with eBay (but not for buyer 1). The relationship is

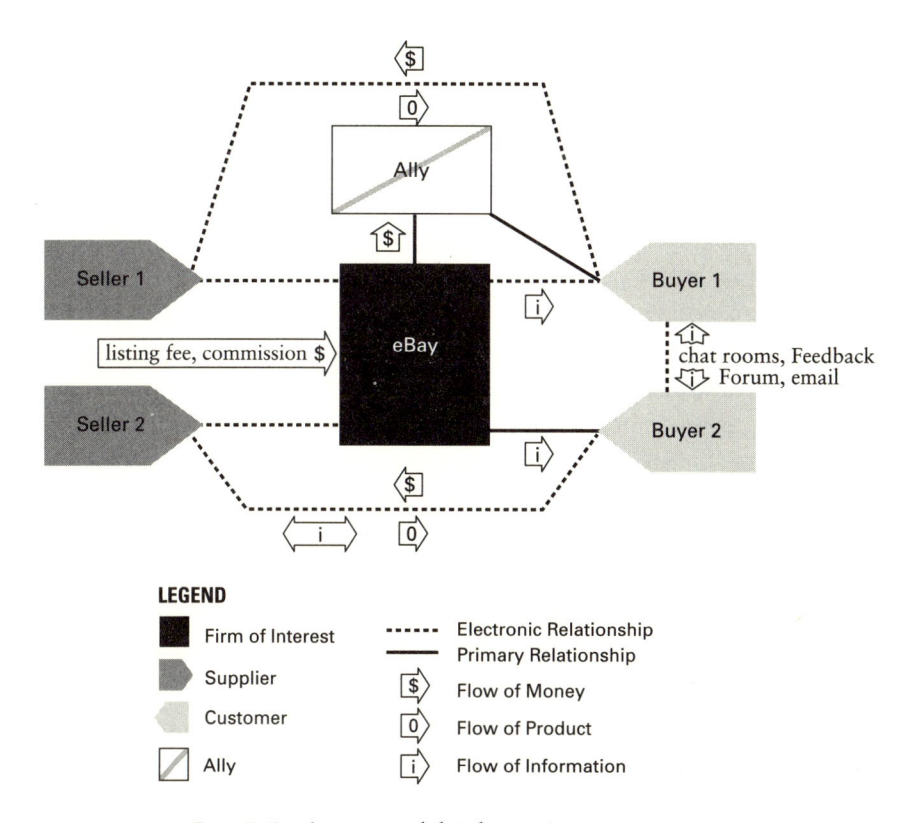

FIGURE 7-2 eBay E-Business Model Schematic

enhanced through the use of chat rooms, newsletters, and even merchandise bearing the eBay logo, available online through the eBay store. The community built up around eBay is undoubtedly one of the firm's most important competitive advantages. Equally, the collection and use of data about customers—what they are buying and selling, and for how much—are a vital part of the eBay model. These data enable eBay to know how much it should be paid when an item sells, and it allows the company to spot trends in items offered or wanted. Not owning the transaction—allowing it to take place directly between the buyer and seller—lowers eBay's operating costs, risks, and working capital requirements, and it allows the company to position itself as a neutral advocate of both buyer and seller, rather than a profit-seeking vendor. As we will see, these same advantages play out for other intermediaries as well.

The success of eBay has led to the formation of numerous other online auction sites, many representing interesting variations on the original eBay formula. Some are specialty auctions (see figure 7-1), which may have more completeness of service than eBay but attract a more limited range of buyers and sellers. For example, the 250-year-old art auction house Sotheby's has followed a clicks-and-mortar strategy, establishing www.sothebys.com. This site offers both online auctions for a wide variety of objets d'art and a guide to the firm's traditional live auctions. Manheim Auctions, another traditional auction house, has extended its physical auctions of used vehicles to the Internet via www.manheim.com, which like the Sotheby's site offers both online transactions and a guide to the company's still-thriving physical auctions held in various locations around the United States.

Auctions.com (www.auctions.com) includes links to merchants for direct, nonauction sales and to a site offering discount home and office furniture. Its Australian affiliate, SOLD.com.au, features RoboBid, a special service that automatically executes a buyer's bids up to a predetermined amount. ReverseAuction (www.reverseauction.com) offers auctions in which the price declines, rather than rises, as the auction proceeds. Sellers set the starting price for their product or service and may also set a reserve price, the lowest price they will accept for the item. Once the auction starts, the price continually declines on screen. Consumers can buy items instantly by clicking on "Buy Now." FreeMarkets (www.freemarkets.com) creates B2B online auctions for buyers of industrial parts, raw materials, commodities, and services. The company has held auctions in product categories including injection-molded plastic parts, metal fabrications, chemicals, printed circuit boards, corrugated packaging, and coal. In a FreeMarkets auction, suppliers compete in real time for the purchase orders of large buying organizations by lowering prices until the auction is closed. In 1999, FreeMarkets auctioned more than $2.7 billion worth of purchase orders and claims to have saved buyers 2 percent to 25 percent on their purchases.[8]

The original eBay model is C2C. With the addition of small-business customers, eBay and other auction sites have expanded into the B2C and B2B spaces. FreeMarkets and similar auction sites are B2B as well. Perhaps the most radical variation on the auction theme is its extension into the C2B realm—auctions in which consumers become the sellers and businesses the buyers. The best-known example of this genre is Priceline (www.priceline.com), which allows consumers to name their own price for items as diverse as airline tickets, hotel rooms, rental cars, home financing, groceries, and gasoline. Priceline describes its service as a "demand collection system" that allows consumers to use the Internet to save money on a wide range of products and services while enabling sellers to generate incremental revenue. Priceline collects consumer demand (in the form of individual customer offers guaranteed by a credit card) for a particular product or service at a price set by the customer, and it communicates that demand directly to participating sellers. Consumers agree to hold their offers open for a specified period, in order to enable Priceline to fulfill their offers from the virtual inventory made available by participating sellers. Once accepted, offers generally cannot be canceled. By requiring consumers to be flexible with respect to brands, sellers, and product features, Priceline enables sellers to generate incremental revenue without disrupting their existing distribution channels or retail pricing structures.[9] The Priceline business model is sufficiently different from other models that the company has been issued a U.S. patent for both the method and the use of "buyer-driven commerce." The approach seems popular; in the first four months of operation of its grocery-buying service, for example, Priceline signed up nearly five hundred thousand customers who made two hundred thousand transactions per week, saving what Priceline estimates to be fifteen dollars per trip to the grocery store. Priceline has announced plans to expand its service to Australia, New Zealand, China and Hong Kong, Singapore, Taiwan, India, Indonesia, Malaysia, the Philippines, India, and Vietnam.

All of these auction models illustrate the general point that intermediaries, although they lengthen the value chain, can be of significant value to buyers and sellers alike. Before exploring other forms of intermediaries, it is worth pausing to ask why this is so. Successful intermediaries offer two potential benefits: lower transaction costs and market making. Transaction costs begin with *search costs*, incurred by buyers and sellers trying to find each other in an increasingly broad and disorganized market. Another type of transaction cost, *decision cost*, is incurred by buyers in evaluating the terms of the seller compared with other potential sellers, and by sellers, in evaluating whether to sell to one buyer instead of another buyer, or not to sell at all. Decision costs are incurred in examining the specifications and the price of objects offered for purchase and sale. Still other sorts of transaction costs, *surveillance costs* and *enforcement costs*, arise because the parties are required to monitor each other to be sure that the terms of the agreement are being met and to take action if the agreement is violated. Reducing these costs is one of the benefits buyers and sellers expect from an intermediary in the physical business world, and these benefits are also sought from an electronic intermediary. As we have seen already, the ability to provide these benefits can be dramatically increased through the use of the Internet and other information technologies. How else could eBay auction nearly five million items simultaneously, thereby creating a site that is attractive to consumers in terms of lowering search costs for nearly anything?

Intermediaries often enable new transactions to take place; that is, the intermediary is able to create a market where none existed before. For example, Half.com (www.half.com) offers an organized online marketplace to buy and sell used goods for at least half off the original list price. Specializing in books, CDs, videos, and computer games, Half.com offered nearly 2.5 million items for sale by early 2000. Half.com is like an open marketplace in which sellers can get rid of used merchandise. But unlike sellers on eBay, sellers on Half.com list their items for a fixed price (which can be no more than half of the manufacturer's original list price), and buyers do not bid against one another. While it is not an auction, Half.com is clearly an electronic intermediary. Half.com processes all payments (which are charged to the buyer's credit card after the seller confirms plans to ship) and sends a check once a month to the seller for all merchandise sold during that period, minus a 15 percent commission. Although markets for used books, CDs, and so on exist on a local basis, a national market depends heavily on the use of IT to lower search costs. The reduction in search costs occurs to the point where potential buyers are willing to use the site, and therefore potential sellers are willing to take the time to list low-value items. Half.com also lowers surveillance costs and enforcement costs by setting policies for the use of the site and collecting feedback on the performance of buyers and sellers. Half.com, and similar sites that facilitate the sale of used goods ranging from heavy equipment to antique porcelain, are enabling new markets for goods that might otherwise be given away, discarded, or scrapped. A sign of Half.com's success in making a new market was its acquisition by eBay in July 2000.

Electronic Markets and Market Makers

The story of Half.com provides a good transition from the topic of auctions to the topic of online markets, in which the selling price may be determined in ways other than bidding. An interesting example of a B2B online market maker is e-STEEL (www.esteel.com). e-STEEL provides the steel industry with a neutral, secure online exchange that can be used by suppliers to expand their marketing reach, grow their customer base, and reduce their transaction costs. e-STEEL is used by buyers to grow their base of suppliers, find better prices, and lower their purchasing costs. e-STEEL does not own any of the products bought or sold on its system, and it is not affiliated with any participant in the steel industry. The company's technology provides customers with the ability to target specific groups for conducting business online, and it provides each customer with the security to block sensitive commercial information from selected members. Customers can also customize pricing, so their trading partners see only the terms they wish to show. The same item can be offered at different terms on a customer-by-customer basis. e-STEEL does not charge a membership fee or any fees to buyers; sellers pay 0.875 percent of the value of each transaction. e-STEEL is not an auction, so pricing information remains private and online negotiations and transactions between buyers and sellers are kept private and secure. However, if a seller chooses, it can post public prices on e-STEEL for all members to view.[10] e-STEEL is fairly typical of market-making intermediaries. It does not own the product, nor does it own the transaction. It does, however, own both the customer data and the customer relationship, which it nurtures by providing industry-related content, discussion groups, and so on.

Market makers create an unbiased environment in which buyers and sellers can find each other and conduct business. Another example of a stand-alone market maker is PolymerSite (www.polymersite.com), which offers buyers and sellers a neutral location for conducting private, sealed-bid negotiations for the purchase of plastic resins and compounds. Alternatively, the site may be a shared-infrastructure model (see chapter 8), owned by a number of suppliers in a specific product category. An example is AutoWeb (www.autoweb.com) for the automotive industry. Yet another form of market maker is a procurement site facilitating the purchasing activities of one or more large buyers. An example of this form is TPN Register (www.tpn.com), originally formed in 1997 by General Electric to facilitate its own purchasing of MRO (maintenance, repair, and operations) items and other indirect products and services. A few years after its founding, TPN Register became a joint venture between GE and Thomas Publishing, a leading provider of product information. TPN Register enables the employees of member companies to search for, find, and order items from approved suppliers. TPN Register claims that, "In doing so, this solution will eliminate paperwork, eliminate maverick buying, improve order accuracy, and relieve professional buyers of the tactical burden of day-to-day paper management. These benefits equate to at least 15 percent savings off a buying organization's current indirect spend."[11] As the joint venture with Thomas Publishing suggests, the success of a market maker is heavily dependent on providing easy access to accurate, timely, and complete information about the items on offer.

Market makers often prosper in large, fragmented industries. BuildOnline (www.buildonline.com) is a pioneering B2B e-commerce site for Europe's £520 billion construction industry. BuildOnline addresses the inefficiencies of the fragmented construction market with a variety of offerings designed to simplify collaboration and transactions. The site offers members a trading platform, project management tools, and a database of supplier information. Since BuildOnline was founded in Ireland in 1998, buyers, specifiers, and suppliers have been quick to adopt it. In its first six months, over 50 percent of Irish buyers signed up for the service, and now an estimated two-thirds of Irish buyers and sellers are registered users. The recent endorsement of four thousand suppliers belonging to the United Kingdom's National Federation of Builders increased the number of registered suppliers to seven thousand. BuildOnline is now managing projects worth more than £125 million. The firm estimates that e-construction can deliver 23 percent savings in European construction and reduce project duration by 15 percent. There are dedicated Web sites for Ireland, the United Kingdom, Spain, Portugal, Italy, Germany, and France. *Time* magazine recently selected BuildOnline as one of only three B2B e-commerce sites to make the list of the "Top 50 Hottest European Tech Firms."[12]

The best-known examples of market makers are stock exchanges, which are becoming increasingly electronic. The Australian Stock Exchange closed its physical trading floor in 1990, and the well-known American NASDAQ exchange has never had one. Futures exchanges for commodities such as wheat, oil, and cocoa also create markets, which exist because the information about a commodity can be separated from the commodity itself. Futures traders do not have to see the bushel of wheat or the barrel of oil; they rely instead on objective information specifying the quantity and quality of these commodities. Electronic market making will be more successful for products such as shares, agricultural commodities, and steel than for products that are not so straightforward to describe.[13]

Electronic share markets such as the NASDAQ or the Australian Stock Exchange are placed on the top right-hand corner of figure 7-1 because they provide very complete service to millions of buyers and sellers. For example, the Australian Stock Exchange provides electronic trading by matching buyers and sellers, market depth information, electronic clearing and settlement, market information and dissemination, surveillance, regulation, and compliance. Most stock exchanges are B2B intermediaries used by brokers; they do not allow retail customers to trade directly. This is likely to change in the future, when stock exchanges could become the equivalent of a shared industry infrastructure. The exchanges could take such action in response to a major threat from ECNs (electronic crossing networks), which are intermediaries for buying and selling equities but "cross" (trade) within their own networks, bypassing the stock exchanges. ECNs have the advantage of lower transaction costs, and transactions on ECNs often do not move market prices as quickly as selling on a stock exchange, which can be a significant advantage to sellers of very large quantities of a given stock. (The case study in chapter 11 includes a description of Instinet, an ECN owned by Reuters.)

Aggregators

Market makers, while important, are essentially passive intermediaries in the electronic marketspace. Aggregators, on the other hand, actively collect and analyze information from multiple data sources, allowing users to compare offerings on a number of dimensions. For example, www.evenbetter.com gathers information about the price and availability of a book from a number of online sources, including Amazon and Barnes & Noble. Frequent fliers can use www.maxmiles.com to collect in one report their frequent flyer entitlements—and then to analyze current mileage offers from various airlines to see what is available. More proactively, www.iship.com collects and compares information from Federal Express, UPS, and others, then allows the user to select a shipper for a given parcel and book a pickup.

Aggregators create new markets, and there is probably room for a number of such intermediaries. Aggregators can earn revenue from both buyers and sellers on the basis of the value they create—both direct value, for example, finding the best way to ship a parcel, and indirect value, for example, identifying opportunities for increased sales or new product offerings. The highest value, however, may arise from the aggregator's ability to analyze the market. What is the best way to price books? Who flies where, and when? Who ships what, from where, and to where? The aggregator is in an ideal position to consider such questions and to earn money from providing the answers. We expect many market makers to evolve into offering aggregation services as well. For example, it is a natural evolution for BuildOnline to provide more services directly, helping buyers find the best value offerings for products they seek.

Electronic Malls

At the lower left of figure 7-1 is another type of intermediary, the electronic mall. The mall does not make a market, but a marketplace—or rather, a marketspace. The electronic shopping mall is patterned on the physical shopping mall, a single site containing a variety of businesses that gather together to benefit from sharing infrastructure expenses and from their proximity to each other. Physical shoppers are attracted to malls by amenities (parking, cafés, entertainment, etc.), the promise of being able to do all of their shopping in one place, and the expectation that the mall owner will exert some selectivity over the shops included. Thus the shopper can to some degree rely on the reputation of the mall to ensure the quality of the shops. Presumably shoppers would be attracted to electronic malls for the same reasons, but it is not clear to what extent these benefits have actually been carried over into the electronic world.

At iMALL (www.imall.com), for example, shoppers can search the mall by products such as laser printers and receive a list of available items with prices. An electronic shopping cart allows customers to shop mallwide and make a single payment. These amenities are presumably of some value to shoppers, although, as we will see below, electronic agents can easily offer them without being restricted to the stores in a single mall. As for a guarantee of quality, at iMALL electronic shoppers can find links to more than fifty computer stores, none of which the typical consumer would be likely to recognize.[14] A special section of iMALL called "Park Avenue" lists a few better-known merchants, including Virtual Vineyards and Barnes & Noble, but the overall impression is of the Internet version of the Home Shopping Network. On one visit the specials on the iMALL home page included an eighteen-inch garnet-and-citrine necklace, inexpensive eau de cologne, and a talking watch. iMALL was founded as one of the Internet's first "shopping destinations" in 1994, a time when the Internet was not nearly as easy to search as now. More than five years later, it is not clear how much value iMALL actually adds beyond that offered by a portal, and indeed in late October 1999 iMALL was acquired by Excite@home, owner of the Excite portal.[15]

The reasons for visiting a physical mall—amenities, one-stop shopping, and the expectation of quality control by mall management—appear to have been largely supplanted on the Internet by competition from other forms of intermediaries and the resulting drive to offer as many shops as possible. i-netmall, for example (www.i-netmall.com), proudly offers more than one thousand merchants, while Mr. Cybermall (www.mrcybermall.com) offers at least as many and allows any merchant to join. Despite Mr. Cybermall's online IQ tests, free personal ads, and other amenities, the online shopper may prefer to use a search engine or a portal instead of wading through a long list of largely unknown shops. On the merchant's side, there may be little incremental value in a listing in a mall that is open to many other merchants, some of which might not be seen as worthy partners.

Nevertheless, at least some physical mall owners feel threatened by the rise of digital malls. John Bucksbaum, the CEO of General Growth Properties (GGP), America's second largest owner of shopping malls, has hedged his company's bets by creating a digital mall, Mallibu.com (www.mallibu.com). Mallibu.com offers amenities (games, movie reviews, news, and free greeting cards), shopping, and home delivery. It also offers a guide to GGP malls across the United States, at which online buyers may collect purchases from central package pickup centers in order to save the delivery charges and other hassles of home delivery. By linking the online mall to physical malls, Bucksbaum believes he has figured out how to "monetize eyeballs" among the thirty-five million people who make 1.2 billion trips to GGP malls each year. "People in the mall are armed with their wallets," Bucksbaum says. "They're consumers, and it's a good place to target."[16]

The value of the electronic mall to shoppers and merchants alike may be undercut by shopping agents, search engines, portals, and other even more virtual organizations. Other threats come from merchants such as Amazon, which are steadily expanding their product offerings under the banner of a brand name that claims to stand for a degree of selectivity over the goods on offer. Commenting on Mallibu.com, Randy Covill, a research analyst, said, "I get the idea, but I'm very skeptical."[17] Seema Williams, an analyst for Forrester Research, notes that many stores already have national Web sites, and that people are most attracted to brand-name stores. "[Electronic] [m]alls don't have the brand strength to attract customers," Williams said.[18] Malls are placed on the lower left of figure 7-1 because they offer relatively incomplete service and appear to attract limited numbers of buyers and sellers. This position perhaps explains the relative decline of online malls as higher-value intermediaries have appeared.

Portals

Yahoo!, one of the best known and financially most successful intermediaries, began as an idea, grew into a hobby, and by the first quarter of 2000 reported revenues of $228 million, an increase of 120 percent from the first quarter of 1999. Net income for the quarter was $63 million. The initial developers of Yahoo!, David Filo and Jerry Yang, both Ph.D. candidates in electrical engineering at Stanford University, started the guide in April 1994 as a way to keep track of their personal interests on the Internet. The company went public in 1996 with an initial public offering (IPO) market capitalization of $30 million; by April 2000 the market capitalization was almost $93 billion.

Yahoo!'s impressive financial results are driven by equally impressive usage statistics. During March 2000, Yahoo!'s global audience grew to more than 145 million users worldwide, including 14 million users in Japan. Yahoo!'s global registration base grew to more than 125 million cumulative registrations for Yahoo! member services. The company's traffic increased to a record 625 million page views per day on average during March 2000, compared to an average of 465 million page views per day in December 1999. Yahoo!'s combined reach among home and work users was 61 percent in the United States during February 2000.[19] Clearly, Yahoo! is a very popular portal, and others, including Excite, AltaVista, and Lycos, are not far behind. Indeed, among the top ten Web sites reported by Nielsen//NetRatings for September 2000, five were portals.[20]

A "portal"—a gateway to the Internet—was initially little more than a collection of useful links presented in an organized way from which users could get directions to other sites.[21] In this initial design, the portal would earn revenues from advertising on its own pages and from clickthrough referrals to the sites listed. To some degree these revenue streams led to conflicting goals for desired user behavior; advertising brings in more revenue the longer users stay on the portal site, while clickthrough revenue is generated the sooner they go somewhere else. Portals such as Yahoo! resolved this dilemma by adding many features—stock quotes, horoscopes, free e-mail, chat rooms, and so on—to their sites, creating a "walled garden" in which users are retained for as long as possible. Clickthrough revenues are still sought, but the portal tries to provide as much as possible itself. For example, Yahoo! Shopping ("thousands of merchants, millions of items") features 10,500 merchants, including such popular offline brands as Macy's, Nordstrom, and Eddie Bauer. Yahoo! Auctions, a free auction service, surpassed 2.5 million active daily listings in March 2000, up from 1.5 million active daily listings in December 1999. The notion of the portal has evolved along with the Internet, coming to mean not only a site from which many other sites can be reached, but also a site on which much can be done.

The phrase *walled garden* was used by George Bell, the chairman and CEO of Excite, to describe that portal's new approach. "We used to think that the faster we pointed people to other sites, the better we were doing," Bell said. "Now our strategy is something like a walled garden. There should be plenty of ways to get out, but there should also be plenty of reasons to stay in."[22] Why would any user choose to view the vastness of the Web through the keyhole of a portal? A consideration of transaction costs provides the likely answer. As one author has recently written, "the Web is still much too confusing for the average person who just wants to e-mail family, get flight information, and perhaps download a dirty picture or two."[23] In the more reserved language of economics, portals reduce search costs, and possibly other transaction costs as well. Users are unlikely to care, after all, about the source of their stock quotes or weather forecasts; they simply want to find the information as quickly and painlessly as possible. The shopping, travel, and other commercial offerings on most portals are easy to find and easy to use. Yahoo! has announced that "Yahoo!'s strategy includes being the world's largest enabler of transactions by providing buyers and sellers the most diverse set of commerce services on the Web. . . . During the first quarter of 2000, Yahoo! enabled more than $1 billion of online transactions through the Yahoo! global network, which includes Yahoo! Japan. . . . During the first quarter [of 2000], Yahoo! also launched Yahoo! B2B Marketplace, a comprehensive directory of variable and fixed-priced listings of equipment, inventory and product listings from business-to-business commerce sites, to enable companies to purchase products and services more cost efficiently and effectively."[24]

As with eBay in the auction space, the success of Yahoo! in the portal space has spawned a wide range of similar businesses, each a variation on the Yahoo! model. Some large companies have adapted the portal model by creating "intranet portals," essentially organization-wide private Web sites, to provide information to employees—so-called B2E commerce. Another type of specialization, of an industry or functional area, has led to the creation of "vertical portals," or *vortals*. A vortal is a cross between a traditional Internet portal, which is offered to a general audience on the Web, and an intranet portal, which is offered to a narrow audience and generally focuses on a specialized topic. Vortals are gathering places for an entire industry, offering news, calendars, the latest research, and discussion groups, in addition to facilitating the meeting of buyers and sellers and enabling the ensuing transactions. VerticalNet (www.verticalnet.com), a producer of software and services to support vertical portals, lists more than sixty vortals on its home page, for industries ranging from solid waste to meat and poultry. Gartner Group estimates that there will be ten thousand vortals by 2001.[25]

Portals, at least under the general definition of "access points for aggregated information," will be a feature of e-business for some time to come. The portal business model will continue to expand, incorporating more and more of the characteristics of the virtual community, direct to customer, and perhaps other atomic business models. The ability to customize a portal (by creating a MyYahoo! or MyExcite home page, for example) allows users to modify the content and format of the information provided by their portal, thus increasing the height of the walls around each portal's garden. There cannot be room for more than a few very large general portals; smaller portals will have difficulty gaining enough advertising or transaction revenue to pay for the content they need in order to hold on to their customers. Vortals, despite their awkward name, will continue to proliferate for a time, but again there is unlikely to be room in any given industry for more than a few vertical portals.

Portals appear on the lower right of figure 7-1 because portals have a potentially large number of buyers and sellers but often provide only a pointer to a place to obtain a product or service, rather than providing the product or service itself. However, with the walled-garden approach, portal companies are recognizing that to increase the strength of their value proposition they must move to the top right of figure 7-1 by providing increased completeness of service.

Intelligent Agents

The final type of intermediary described in this chapter is the newest and least well established, but technically the most interesting. Intelligent agents, also called *bots,* are true creatures of the electronic age. Intelligent agents prowl the Internet, looking for the best deal or price on an item sought by a customer. Information is reported back to the customer in a consistent format, allowing easy comparison and immediate ordering from the supplier of choice. For example, Winerobot (www.winerobot.com.au) searches the sites of Australian online wine retailers, locating information on a bottle or case of wine of a specified variety, region, label, vintage, or price. The customer is transferred to the site of the online retailer once a selection is made.[26] Winerobot charges wine retailers to be included in its searches, and it may also collect a transaction fee when purchases are made.

Winerobot is a specialized example of the intelligent-agent concept, which had its origins in computer science laboratories and has blossomed as the number of online merchants has grown. (See the case study on the shopping agent Jango in the next section.) Intelligent agents reduce customer search costs by carrying out at least the preliminary searching automatically. Reducing search costs is the primary value proposition; for example, the home page of intelligent agent MySimon (www.mysimon.com) claims, "He shops thousands of stores, so you don't have to." Perhaps best of all from the customer's perspective, the intelligent agent works not only quickly and efficiently, but also without charge: There is no known attempt by an intelligent agent to capture some of the value provided to the customer when the agent finds a lower price. Winerobot taps into two potential sources of revenue for an intelligent agent—listing fees from merchants to be included in the search and commissions on sales. The former is somewhat antithetical to an agent's claim to be finding the "lowest prices," and it could over time erode the attractiveness of using the agent. Another potential source of revenue is payments from the merchant, both for display advertising for their listings and for the use of a "one-click" feature that allows customers to more readily purchase from them via the agent's Internet site.

CASE STUDY

INTERMEDIARY MODEL: Jango—Online Shopping Agent (www.jango.excite.com)

The Jango shopping agent allows consumers to search for specific products offered by online stores, auction sites, and classified advertisers (see figure 7-3). The agent is part of the shopping service offered on the Excite portal. Jango will search for products in many categories, including cameras, toys, beauty, health, and collectibles. Books and music are not included; Excite has exclusive relationships with Amazon and CDNOW for those categories. Each available category is further broken down into subcategories (for example, "sports and leisure" includes athletic footwear, camping equipment, fitness equip-

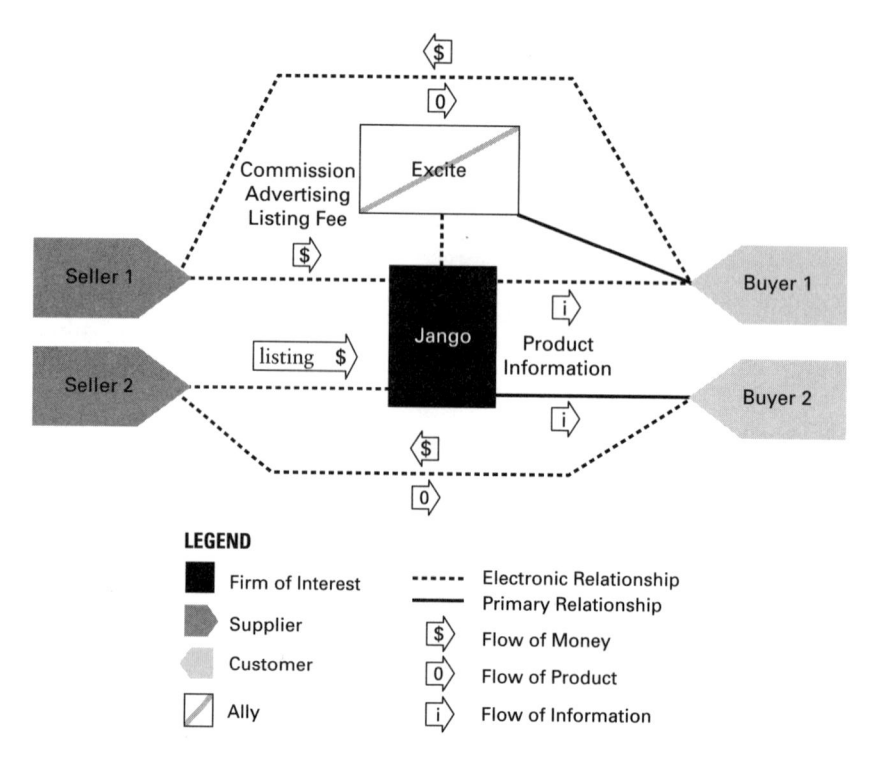

FIGURE 7-3 Jango Intelligent Agent E-Business Model Schematic

ment, golf equipment, skis, and snowboards). The customer goes to a subcategory and selects a product type (e.g., stationary bicycles), then enters the manufacturer's name (e.g., Schwinn) or the product name (e.g., AirDyne), and specifies which of the sources (stores, auction sites, or classified ads) are acceptable. Jango searches for products satisfying the specified criteria and returns its findings in the form of a list that the customer can sort according to price, product, source, or manufacturer. The list often contains as many as fifty merchants selling the product and also includes third-party ratings and reviews of merchants and products to assist in selection. The customer can also click on the name of the product or source to get additional information, or on a button labeled "Buy!" to purchase the item. Any of these actions will bring up a page from the manufacturer or seller within the Jango frame set. Purchases are made from the source, not directly from Excite, but a band at the bottom of the browser window displays the Excite logo, along with buttons that allow the customer to respecify the current search or to begin a new search altogether.

Jango was created by Netbot, Inc., a company founded in May 1996 by University of Washington computer science professors Dan Weld and Oren Etzioni. In October 1997, Excite purchased Netbot for $35 million in stock, and Jango was integrated into the Excite Shopping Channel in time for the 1997 Christmas shopping season. Unlike prior agents, most of which ran on PCs, Jango runs on Excite's servers, pulling information from many sources in real time. This design provides up-to-date information, eliminates the need for the user to download additional software, and reduces waiting time for users who do not have a high-bandwidth connection to the Web.

Jango does not contain explicit advertising. The Product Finder home page does not say anything about how the sites to be searched are chosen, nor about the order in which they are listed, although the different appearance of merchant names (e.g., some are in bold or include logos) suggests differential listing fees. The typical consumer probably assumes that the entire Web is being searched to locate the best deals available, but this is unlikely. There may be some payment to Excite based on clickthroughs to merchants. The other obvious source of benefit to Excite is measured in "eyeballs," that is, in the number of people who are attracted to the Excite portal because of the availability of the Jango-based Product Finder.

The core competencies for Excite/Jango are the ability to select new services that will bring incremental benefits to the site, to integrate those new services into the existing site while maintaining the same look and feel and avoiding customer overload, and to explain such services to nontechnical users. In addition, the organization must have the technical skill to continually refine the agent to incorporate advances in technology.

The critical success factors for Jango include ease of use, timely and accurate fulfillment by merchants from whom products are purchased, and maintenance of adequate infrastructure. Maintaining ease of use requires constant trade-offs with increased product power and flexibility. For example, although the user can enter any manufacturer or product name, in most categories the product type must be chosen from a pull-down menu. Searches are always on the basis of price, although presumably some users would be interested in searching on product quality or other features after specifying a maximum price. Although fulfillment is outside Excite's direct control, shortfalls in this area would undermine consumer confidence in Jango. Excite must therefore be mindful of merchant performance, and it should perhaps consider creating a blacklist of sites that have repeatedly disappointed buyers.

Jango has a powerful value proposition: Multiple sellers are brought together for the buyer to choose from and the products are listed based on objective criteria such as price, features, and independent product reviews. In addition, Excite, the owner of Jango, is following a strategy of technological leadership, demonstrated by the continual development of Excite from a search engine into a full-fledged portal site including weather reports, news, chat rooms, horoscopes, stock market reports, sports scores, and shopping. Jango is not only a technical step forward—the product has won numerous awards for technical quality and innovation—but it is also in keeping with Excite's heritage as a leader in Web searching.

Describing an Intermediary

The general intermediary business model schematic is shown in figure 7-4. The schematic shows the intermediary as the firm of interest, with multiple buyers and sellers and an ally. Usually the sellers pay the intermediary listing fees and selling commissions, as indicated by the dollar flows, and it is possible that the buyer may also pay a purchase or membership fee. Advertisers also provide revenue for intermediaries. In figure 7-4, buyer 1 accesses the intermediary via a customer relationship held with an ally, which receives a finder's fee or commission from the intermediary. The intermediary owns the relationship with buyer 2, and it knows more about buyer 2's preferences than any other player. The intermediary may sell aggregated information to advertisers, but it

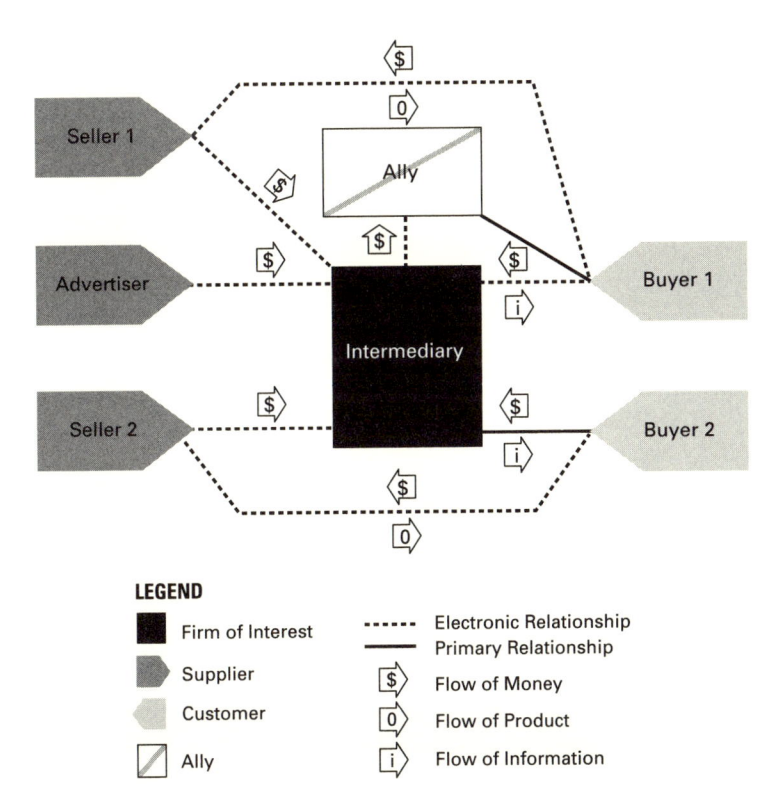

FIGURE 7-4 Intermediary Atomic E-Business Model Schematic

makes money primarily by concentrating information. Transactions occur directly between the seller and the buyer. Intermediaries come in many types, and we have identified six of the major classes of intermediaries in figure 7-1. As a general principle, the further toward the top right of the framework an intermediary operates, the stronger the customer value proposition and the more potentially profitable the business model.

Customer Segments

The examples suggest that intermediaries exist right across the spectrum of e-business—B2B, B2C, C2C, and even C2B. This should not be surprising, since intermediaries exist in great variety in all aspects of traditional commerce. Some intermediaries—for example, the auction site eBay and the portal Yahoo!—serve the general consumer and business markets on both the buy side and the sell side. Other intermediaries aim for a narrower segment, such as the bakers, dentists, or purchasing agents targeted by the vortals in their respective industries. To some degree the giant auction and portal sites use their "associates" programs to target more specialized markets; a link on the page of a military history museum, for example, can lead directly to the relevant auction or information. As information becomes more symmetric and intermediaries have to rely on lowering transaction costs, rather than on possessing more information, the advantages of scale are likely to dominate.

Channels

The intermediaries we have examined serve customers primarily via the Internet, although eBay and other auction sites will take bids over the telephone, presumably to serve those customers who use their PCs for job-related tasks but can use the telephone while executing those tasks. As wireless applications protocol (WAP) spreads, it is likely that intermediaries will operate almost entirely electronically.

Infrastructure

Intermediaries generate value by concentrating information and bringing together buyers and sellers, operating entirely in space and thus relying on IT as the primary infrastructure. Our field interview data revealed that the most important infrastructure services for firms pursuing the intermediary atomic business model are the following:

- Knowledge management, including knowledge databases and contact databases that enable the codification and sharing of knowledge in this highly information-intensive business

- Enforcing Internet and email policies to ensure proper and consistent use of electronic channels to buyers, sellers, and intermediaries

- Workstation networks to support the products and services of this all-electronic business model

- Centralized management of e-business applications, ensuring consistency and integration across product offerings

- Information systems planning to identify the most effective uses of IT in the business

- Information systems project management to ensure that business value is achieved from IT investments

Additional infrastructure services required by intermediaries also relate to their need to search for information on behalf of their customers, to store information, and to keep information secure. Searching is especially important for agents, but it is needed by every portal and market maker as well. Databases of customer, supplier, and transaction information are crucial to an intermediary's success, which is often based on matching buyers and sellers, or at least allowing them to locate each other. As in any market, in electronic markets information security must be enforced in order to prevent one party from gaining an unfair advantage over another.

What Do Intermediaries Mean for Existing Businesses?

The continuing rise of intermediaries will impact all existing businesses with regard to pricing and customer relationships, and it will impact some businesses even more fundamentally. Intermediaries such as auctions and shopping agents will certainly increase price transparency, leading to changes in customer behavior and pricing strategy. For example, Geoff Dahlsen, the managing director of the Winerobot shopping agent described earlier, expects comparison shopping to increase dramatically. "Think of the consequences," Dahlsen says. "People won't be able to say they are the cheapest any more when they blatantly are not, and only the cheapest [online] retailers will make the sales."[27] Although Dahlsen may overstate the pace and depth of change, there can be little doubt that shopping agents, market makers, and auctions will make prices much more visible, allowing buyers to bargain more effectively. The impact will be particularly severe for companies that have been exploiting information asymmetries to support differential pricing. It seems only a matter of time—and probably not much time—before an electronic intermediary makes such price differences unsustainable, severely disrupting some firms' economics.

There is more to most purchasing decisions than price alone. However, these nonprice attributes will increasingly be gathered and made available, both directly and via shopping agents, allowing buyers to comparison shop for quality, reliability, reputation, and other characteristics in addition to price. Sellers will have to adapt to a world of symmetric information, objectivity, and transparency.

One standard response to such threats of "commoditization" is for the seller to draw closer to customers, creating relationships such as "strategic partnerships." Unfortunately for many producers, this too will be made more difficult by the rise of intermediaries. The most valuable strategic partner for a customer may well be an intermediary, who will strive to own the customer and the data, although not the transaction itself. The companies who use

TPN Register to source MRO items, for example, would probably name TPN as their strategic partner, not the actual suppliers of the goods. The providers who choose to sell through TPN and other intermediaries—and most producers will ultimately be forced to do so in order to maintain business—will face a growing challenge in attempting to establish close links to their ultimate customers.

Another potential impact results from the activities of eBay, Half.com, and others who make a market in used goods. Such intermediaries can reduce search and other transaction costs to the point that efficient, nationwide markets form for goods that might otherwise be discarded. The immediate impact will undoubtedly be felt by physical dealers in used goods—used bookshops, used auto dealerships, and so on. But the more important impact may well be on the primary producers of the goods. If a used copy of a book can be found online with no more effort than a new copy, then publishers' sales seem certain to fall. Similarly, if used cars, tractors, and porcelain vases can readily be located online, together with objective descriptions of their condition, the amount of new goods purchased should decline. Or will it? One model of the behavior of industrial customers is that some will buy new equipment if they can get a good price for the equipment they already own. Indeed, some manufacturers (such as Caterpillar, a manufacturer of heavy equipment—www.caterpillar.com) have embraced the opportunity to sell used goods as a way of increasing sales of new models. This phenomenon will undoubtedly play out differently for consumer goods than for industrial goods, and differently again by industry.

The Future of Intermediaries

As noted in chapter 4, some advocates of the direct-to-customer atomic business model have argued that e-business will allow unlimited direct connections between buyers and sellers, creating a world without intermediaries. Although this may be technically possible, we think it is not going to happen. Intermediaries of the types described in this chapter play an important value-added role in facilitating e-business, and we believe their number and variety will continue to grow.

In each of the major categories of intermediary, there will ultimately be a few major players and a large number of niche players. The categories will continue to evolve and blur; already Yahoo! is a portal, an auction site, and a mall. The value-added framework (figure 7-1) suggests that the winners will be intermediaries providing completeness of service to a large number of buyers and sellers.

Summary of the Intermediary Model

Strategic Objective and Value Proposition

An intermediary makes its living by bringing together buyers and sellers, and then getting paid on the basis of whatever business they transact. Buyers and sellers are motivated to use intermediaries, in both the physical world and the virtual world, to achieve lower search and transaction costs. The intermediary is motivated to attract more users and to increase its range of services to expand the total value it adds to the transaction process.

Sources of Revenue

An intermediary may earn revenues from buyers, sellers, or both. Sellers may pay a listing fee, a transaction fee, a sales commission, or some combination. Similarly, buyers may pay a subscription fee, a success fee, or a sales commission. A promising basis for revenue, value added by the intermediary (e.g., cost savings from list price), is not popular yet perhaps because the baseline is difficult to establish. As buyers gain experience, and, more important, as data are generated and analyzed, value added will probably become a more common basis for intermediaries' fees.

Critical Success Factors

The chief requirement for survival as an intermediary is sufficient volume of usage to cover the fixed costs of establishing the business and the required infrastructure. Attracting and retaining a critical mass of customers is therefore the primary critical success factor. Another important critical success factor is building up infrastructure just quickly enough to meet demand as it increases. The notoriety given to eBay's periodic service shortcomings is evidence of the importance that both buyers and sellers attach to having enough resources in place to meet their needs. A third critical success factor is owning the customer relationship and producing an intermediary site with a high degree of "stickiness" (need or desire to return to the site). Part of achieving a sticky site is utilizing the ownership of customer data. Intermediaries, like many other place-based businesses, are just learning how to use the vast amounts of customer data they own. Using the data to analyze their customers into clear segments will be a matter of survival for intermediaries as their inevitable consolidation occurs.

Core Competencies

All intermediaries require the ability to collect, synthesize, and utilize information about products, prices, and other market factors. Even auctions and market makers, although they do not control what is offered for sale and do not set prices, must observe what is being offered, categorize it for easy search, and promote it to customers likely to be interested in it. For intermediaries, the ability to objectively specify in precise, well-understood, and repeatable terms the characteristics of an object offered for purchase or sale is essential. The early electronic markets have been made in steel, polymers, shares, and other items that are easy to describe. If online markets are to continue to expand into new product categories, their makers will have to assist customers in developing descriptions for the categories. A further core competency is the ability to balance service completeness with customer volume, so as to optimize the value delivered. Increasing either dimension entails costs and the potential loss of customers who are not willing to pay for the additional services provided; the balancing act is therefore a difficult one. Finally, intermediaries must be excellent analyzers of customer data, spotting trends and identifying changes in preferences and sizes of customer segments.

Who Owns What?

	Customer Relationship	Customer Data	Customer Transaction
Intermediary	✓	✓	✗

CHAPTER 8

Shared Infrastructure

> Not only is it unprecedented for GM, Ford and DaimlerChrysler to come together to form this type of joint venture, but it's also the largest Internet business ever created. Nobody will be better. Nobody will be faster. Nobody will offer more to everyone involved.
>
> —GM WORLDWIDE PURCHASING GROUP VICE PRESIDENT HAROLD R. KUTNER[1]

IN THE WORLD of e-business, hypercompetition is the norm. Bright-eyed "e-entrepreneurs" compete first for venture capital, then for staff, and then for the attention of an expanding but fickle market. Although the Internet is sometimes said to create a "level playing field," most of the players are constantly trying to tilt the rules in their favor. In this Darwinian environment, it might seem unlikely that cooperation of any sort would ever occur, much less be sustained. But when the conditions are right, the benefits of an electronic alliance—cooperation among competitors by sharing infrastructure—can be significant enough to overcome competitive barriers.

Artesian Innovation

Artesian Innovation (www.artesian.com.au) is a joint venture formed in January 2000 by Lion Nathan, Southcorp, and United Distillers & Vintners (DIAGEO) as a B2B e-business venture serving the A$70 billion Australian hospitality and retail liquor industries. The three partners, who together hold 30 percent to 40 percent of the Australian market for alcoholic beverages, spent A$10 million setting up the operation. Lion Nathan (www.lion-nathan.com.au) holds about 40 percent of the Australian beer market, Southcorp (www.southcorp.com.au) is Australia's biggest wine producer, and United Distillers & Vintners (www.diageo.com) has about 40 percent of the Australian spirits market as the distributor of nineteen of the world's top one hundred liquor brands, including Smirnoff vodka, Johnnie Walker scotch, and Tanqueray gin. Peter Maher, the general manager of the Artesian Innovation joint venture, noted that its restaurant, pub, and retail customers "would be able to select products from a range of suppliers but make one order, one payment, and receive one delivery; access information about previous orders, promotions, tasting notes, and products; and receive sales data. Suppliers would receive market data and analysis helping them understand how to better service their customers."[2] Over time the three partners hope to include other brands of alcoholic drinks—that is, their competitors' products—and to add complementary products such as food, glassware, and cleaning services. Artesian expects to earn revenue by charging suppliers a fee to develop, maintain, and operate the customer interface. The partners also hope to benefit through improved efficiency of dealing with existing customers and attracting new customers for their products.[3]

Although not stated explicitly, an additional goal of the Artesian partners was probably to counteract the efforts of another e-business venture, List (Liquor Industry Services Technology) (www.list.com.au). Founded in 1998 and backed by a major Australian telecommunications carrier as well as by wealthy individual investors, List aimed to simplify the supply of wine to Australian restaurants. List was essentially an intermediary (see chapter 7), allowing restaurants to order from many suppliers via the Internet. List earned subscription fees from the restaurants and transaction fees from the suppliers.

Which business model will prevail? After hearing the surprise announcement of the creation of Artesian Innovation, Frank Wilden, the head of List, said, "They are the three giants of the liquor industry. Although we are dwarfed by them it doesn't diminish our resolve to create a truly independent portal. The problem with Artesian, even if you take a benign view of their action, is that it is self-serving. Instead of having a community of common interest, we will end up with a situation where restaurants have to go to thirty different Internet sites." The head of a large independent supplier agreed: "As a distributor I would be loath to give my details to a competitor." But Artesian Innovation general manager Maher was confident: "It's a clear mandate from the [three] investors that this is not just a vehicle for the partners."[4]

Is Artesian Innovation a viable stand-alone business, or is it primarily an attempt by three large players to forestall competition and secure their own positions? By the time Artesian Innovation was announced, Foster's Brewing Group, Ltd., which holds more than half of the Australian beer market, already had an e-business pilot running in three Australian states, and two other large Australian wine groups, BRL Hardy Limited and Orlando Wyndham Group Pty. Ltd., were said to be close to announcing their own e-business plans.[5] Numerous wine retailers had established Web sites, and several new entrants, such as the publicly listed Wine Planet (wineplanet.com.au), were offering alcoholic beverages to consumers over the web. For the three joint-venture partners, perhaps any revenue earned from sharing Artesian Innovation's facilities with other suppliers will simply be a bonus atop the more basic goal of establishing a direct connection to their customers. Regardless of motivation, however, the Artesian Innovation example points clearly to another atomic e-business model: shared infrastructure.

Shared-Infrastructure Atomic Business Model

In the shared-infrastructure atomic business model, the firm of interest—shown at the center of the diagram in figure 8-1—provides infrastructure shared by its owners, shown at the left. Other suppliers, who are users of the shared infrastructure, but not owners, are also shown at the left of the diagram. Generally the owners (and the other suppliers) are competitors, at least in a general sense, as are Lion Nathan, Southcorp, and United Distillers & Vintners, the owners of Artesian Innovation. The shared infrastructure generally offers a service that is not already available in the marketplace, and it may also be a defensive move to thwart potential domination by another major player.

Customers who access the shared infrastructure directly (e.g., customer 2 in figure 8-1) or via allies (e.g., customers 1 and 3) are given a choice of suppliers and value propositions. The owners and the nonowner suppliers are generally represented objectively.

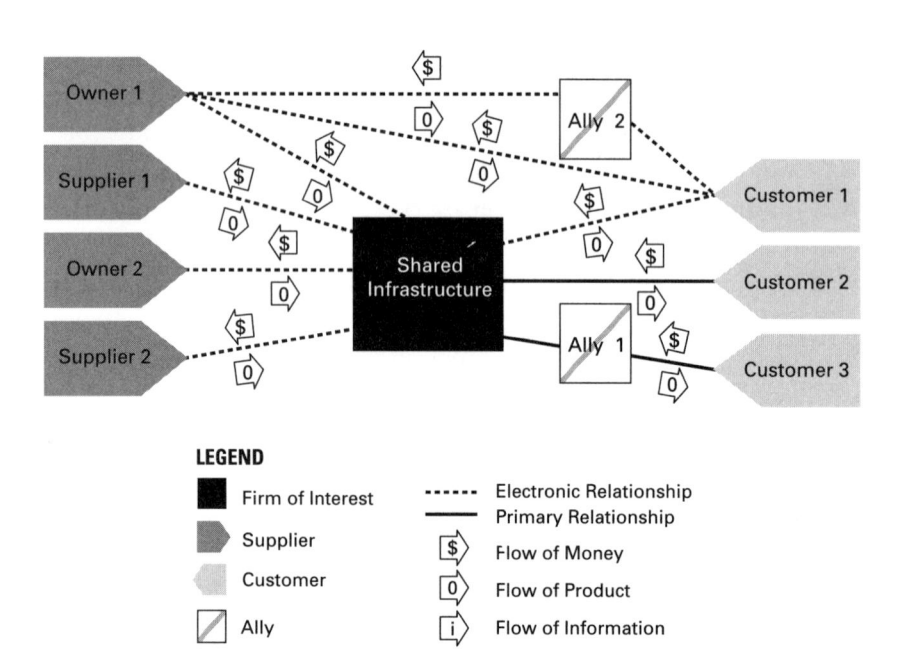

FIGURE 8-1 Shared-Infrastructure Atomic E-Business Model

In some situations, goods or services flow directly from the shared infrastructure to the customer. In other situations, a message is sent by the shared infrastructure to the supplier, who then completes the transaction by providing the goods or services to the customer. The suppliers, both owners and nonowners, are paid either by the shared-infrastructure firm or directly by the customer.

In many shared-infrastructure models, other players own the relationship with the customer. For example, in the ABACUS airline reservation system (started by a group of Asian airlines) example described later in this chapter, the travel agent, not ABACUS, owns the relationship with the traveler. In this situation, the shared infrastructure owns the relationship with the intermediary, as indicated for customer 3 in figure 8-1.

The shared-infrastructure e-business model is interesting because the sharing is done among firms that compete fiercely in other dimensions but agree to cooperate in a particular electronic realm. In principle, nothing prevents firms from banding together to provide any infrastructure service, for example, a large data center—but in practice, the difficulties of cooperating with competitors often outweigh any advantage gained through joint provision of a generic service already available on the open market. The advantage to be gained from jointly providing a generic service would be primarily, or perhaps solely, lower cost. In most cases, the market for generic infrastructure services is already so well developed that any such cost advantage is likely to be both small and short-lived, and thus not worth the effort required to achieve it by bringing together a group of competitors. Companies wishing to achieve economy in the provision of a generic infrastructure service are usually better advised to go to an outsourcer than to try to set up an alliance with competitors.

A more powerful criterion for selecting an infrastructure service better provided jointly is that customers would find some advantage. This implies that the service is visible to customers, in the way that Artesian Innovation is visible to restaurants, pubs, and retail liquor stores. An order-entry and information-reporting system is an example of this sort of shared-infrastructure service.

Automotive Industry

An example illustrating the features of the shared-infrastructure business model is the system announced in early 2000 by America's largest automakers, some of their dealers, and IBM, Motorola, and Intel.[6] The as-yet unnamed system will keep dealers in touch with car owners by providing the owners a variety of services, including access to home or work computers from their vehicles and instant notification of impending vehicle failure. The apparent aim is to build customer loyalty by keeping dealers in constant contact with car owners, including making available pricing and product information. In announcing the system, which will be ready for the 2003 model year, GM Chairman John F. Smith Jr. said that the automakers were abandoning their earlier efforts to bypass dealers by setting up factory-owned stores that would sell cars over the Internet. By establishing a shared infrastructure instead, the manufacturers and dealers hoped to defeat the dot-com auto businesses, including autobytel.com, CarsDirect.com, Inc., and InvoiceDealers.com, that are based on cutting the dealers out of the sales process. Apparently the automakers and dealers, often fiercely competitive both horizontally and vertically, found it advantageous to make common cause against the new entrants, whose success was based partly on finding a lower price and partly on near-universal consumer distrust of car makers and their dealers.

Automotive manufacturers are cooperating to compete on the back end as well, with the announcement of joint ventures in managing supply chains. As stated in note 1, Ford, GM, and Daimler-Chrysler have combined forces to form a B2B integrated supplier exchange that will be the world's largest Internet-based virtual marketplace. The new enterprise will offer open participation to auto manufacturers around the world and to their suppliers and dealers as well. The three partners will have equal ownership in the business, which will operate independently from its parents. Jac Nasser, president and CEO of Ford, said, "Today's announcement is an exciting example of how the Internet is transforming every piece of our company and our industry. . . . We'll push this transformation even further to bring sustainable benefits to our customers, suppliers and dealers."[7]

The president and COO of General Motors, G. Richard Wagoner Jr., also commented on the industry's efforts to build independent exchanges and the decision to cooperate to compete: "As we continued to build our separate exchange sites, we quickly realized traditional, individual, stand-alone models weren't the winning strategy for us, our industry, our suppliers and, ultimately our customers. By joining together we can further increase the pace of implementation.... We are excited about the opportunity to build on what each of us started separately and create the best trading exchange in the world."[8]

Each of the three partners had made significant progress in building their own exchange, with Ford's Auto-xchange and GM's TradeXchange already operational. General Motors, Ford, and DaimlerChrysler apparently see stronger potential benefits from cooperating on supply-chain logistics than from competing. If the "Big Three" are successful, other car manufacturers will have a strong incentive to participate in this huge electronic market. With shared-infrastructure models, we often observe that after the parties have announced the high-level principles of the agreement publicly and with great fanfare, the hard work of negotiating the details can take months or even years to complete. By way of illustration of the complexities involved, several months elapsed after the three auto firms agreed to cooperate before the name of their initiative (COVISINT—COllaboration VISion INTegrity) was finally announced.

Another interesting example of shared infrastructure owned by competitors is the Amsterdam Internet Exchange, AMS-IX (www.ams-ix.net). AMS-IX provides a way for Dutch Internet service providers (ISPs) to interconnect and exchange traffic with one another at a national level. The exchange is owned by, and connects, seventy-eight major Dutch ISPs, including @HomeBenelux, GTS Ebone, and Global One. AMS-IX is governed by a general meeting at which each participating ISP has one seat, by an executive board elected by the members, and by an administrative committee and a technical committee. AMS-IX creates efficiencies by replacing a large number of one-to-one connections between individual ISPs. The exchange's home page spells out a number of other advantages: "[AMS-IX] . . . is structured as a transparent and democratic Association, [and] operated by a neutral operator under a not-for-profit aim. It also functions as a test-bed for innovation (e.g. multicasting and IPv6, new versions of protocols). As a result the AMS-IX has become one of Europe's larger Internet Exchanges, thus keeping a major part of Dutch Internet traffic within the Netherlands."[9] The final phrase makes clear that a competitive motivation is present, in this case operating on a national level: the desire by Dutch ISPs to keep their traffic within their own country.

Motivations for the Shared-Infrastructure Business Model

Although shared-infrastructure models are generally operated on a for-profit basis, the alliances tend to have motivations beyond profit alone. These motivations include the following:

- Demands by customers for a single channel to access multiple service providers. We have observed this trend in many industries, including travel, hospital supplies, automobiles, and insurance. Often a major player leads with an innovative system and then competitors follow, perhaps incrementally improving functionality. Soon customers are faced with multiple and incompatible systems, and eventually they demand single-channel access to all providers.

- Response from competitors when a major player innovates and creates competitive advantage. One response to a major innovation is for other competitors to cooperate to create a shared industry infrastructure to nullify the innovator's competitive advantage.

- The opportunity to reduce costs by sharing infrastructure investments. Many stock exchanges, such as the Australian Stock Exchange, were started by a group of stockbrokers who cooperated to create a bigger market and to share the transaction and record-keeping costs. Over time these exchanges have taken on more of the functionality originally performed in the backroom operations of the individual brokers, thus reducing their costs. This process of increasing shared infrastructure in stockbroking is likely to continue, with some stock exchanges ultimately offering direct-to-customer trading.

Like many of the business models described in this book, shared infrastructure is not completely new. The first attempts at establishing shared electronic infrastructure may have been in the air travel industry.[10] In the United States, American Airlines introduced its SABRE reservations system in early 1962, and Delta Air Lines finished its own system six months later. Pan American, Eastern, TWA, and United Airlines soon followed with their own individual systems. Travel agents who wished to use multiple systems were required to install different equipment for connecting to each. A common airline reservation system was first proposed in 1967 by the Donnelly Company, publishers of the "Official Airline Guide"; this proposal was abandoned because the potential participants could not agree on financing. In 1972 the American Society of Travel Agents (ASTA) proposed to develop a common system for travel agents. Worried that such a system would require the carriers to pay the travel agents for use of the system, American Airlines and other airlines formed a task force with ASTA and hardware suppliers to consider the development of a joint system. The task force met for more than a year, during which time United Airlines continued to push aggressively its own reservation system, APOLLO. Three weeks after the January 1976 task force recommendation for a joint system, United withdrew from the task force and announced that its proprietary APOLLO system would be made widely available. American soon followed suit, and the notion of an industry-wide shared system was forgotten. As American, United, and other airlines developed their systems, they eventually included the schedules of other airlines, including their competitors. In this sense, the use of the infrastructure was shared, but the ownership never was: The systems, until recently, remained the exclusive, and often very profitable, property of single carriers, creating competitive advantage for them.

Running a computer reservation system (CRS) is a complex and profitable business. A CRS is a channel to the travel agent, an airline productivity tool, a potential source of competitive advantage, and a business in its own right, with annual returns on investment as high as 83 percent. There is also a strong first-mover advantage in CRS, derived from factors including scale economies, access to booking information, and screen display bias. The first-mover advantage can be significant, with the American first movers, United and American, having up to 70 percent market share resulting in both companies having three times the net cash contributions of the next largest CRS.[11] The barriers to cooperation are therefore high, but as the following case study illustrates, they can be overcome.

CASE STUDY

SHARED-INFRASTRUCTURE MODEL: **ABACUS Asian Airline Computer Reservation System**

Before 1986 the Asia-Pacific region had no dominant CRS.[12] United and American had attempted to enter the region with their APOLLO and SABRE systems, but they had not achieved significant penetration. In 1986 United Airlines bought some Pacific routes from PanAm and began marketing the APOLLO system strongly in Asia. In response, local Asian airlines such as Singapore Airlines and Cathay Pacific Airways, Ltd. aggressively promoted their single-owner systems by increasing functionality and reducing prices. However, these actions did not reduce the threat from APOLLO, which offered the ability to book on multiple airlines via a single user interface. Travel agents in the Asia-Pacific region, like those in the United States years earlier, preferred APOLLO's approach to the alternative of separately accessing different systems via expensive multi-hardware investments. In addition, the significant competitive experience of APOLLO in the United States gave United an edge over the local Asian carriers.

According to Neo Boon Siong of the Nanyang Technological University in Singapore, "The combination of increasing competition and rapidly evolving technologies led to an enrichment of functionality in U.S.-based CRSs to the point where they were recognizably superior to other CRSs. . . . Asian carriers faced challenges including the move towards deregulation in many countries and increasing direct competition with U.S. carriers. Without a strong CRS of their own Asian carriers faced the threat of conceding worldwide dominance to the U.S. carriers."[13]

In 1987 five Asian airlines—Singapore Airlines, Cathay Pacific, Japan Airlines Company, Ltd. (JAL), Qantas, and Thai Airlines—formed a steering committee to spearhead the development of a new CRS to serve the interests of the carriers in the Asia-Pacific region. Many Asian airlines are national carriers, owned in part or wholly by their home country's government and linked with national centers that promote travel and investment in their country. These relationships created a complex set of stakeholders in the negotiations to set up an Asian CRS. For example, by December 1987 there was already disagreement over where the CRS would be located. Soon afterward, JAL and Qantas pulled out and the Thai government suspended involvement.

Established in 1988 by the two remaining partners, Singapore Airlines and Cathay Pacific, the joint reservation system ABACUS is now used by over ninety-three hundred travel agencies in eighteen countries across Asia and has enjoyed annual growth of 30 percent in each of the last three years. In addition to airline schedules and fares, cruise schedules and prices, and other travel information, ABACUS provides access to more than fifty car rental companies and over forty thousand hotel properties worldwide. ABACUS has a 90 percent market share in these eighteen countries, placing it in the dominant position in Asia. Figure 8-2 presents the business model schematic for ABACUS.

Although the addition of new partners was often challenging, requiring detailed negotiations, by October 1990 ABACUS had signed up ten participating carriers, and by 1992 it broke

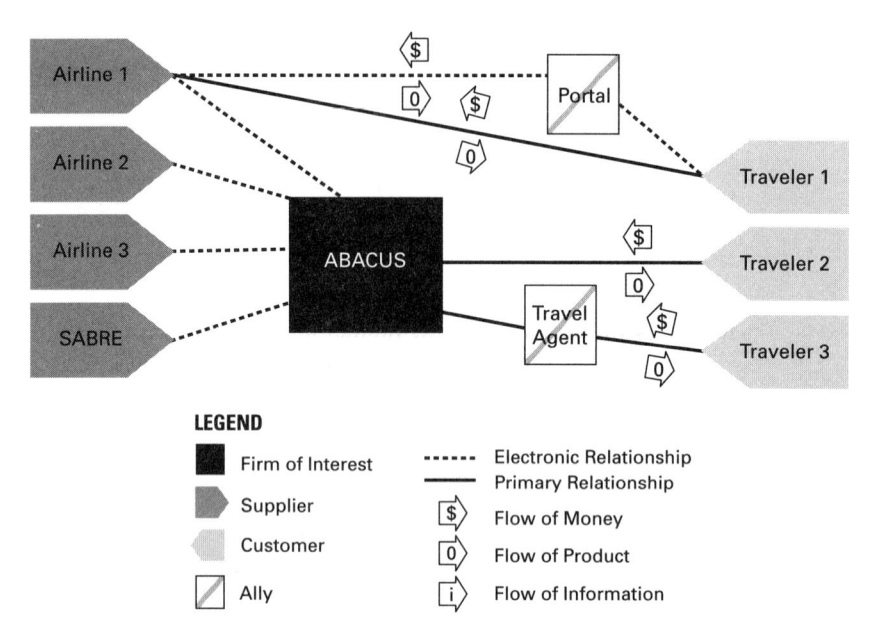

FIGURE 8-2 ABACUS E-Business Model Schematic

even financially. By 1994, there were twelve partners: All Nippon Airways (ANA), Cathay Pacific Airways, China Airlines, EVA, Garuda Indonesia, Dragonair, Malaysia Air, Philippine Airlines, Royal Brunei Airlines, SilkAir, Singapore Airlines, and Thai Airlines. JAL and Qantas were not partners, having developed their own reservation systems.

Once established and dominant, ABACUS moved aggressively to optimize its technical infrastructure. In 1998 ABACUS formed a joint venture with Sabre (www.sabre.com), a U.S.-based global CRS, known for technology leadership, that grew out of the American Airlines SABRE system. ABACUS announced at the time, "The new ABACUS system combines the regional strength of ABACUS with the technology of the SABRE Group."[14] The alliance represents another major accomplishment for ABACUS and its founders, who have been successful with ABACUS in many ways:

- Domination by an American CRS in Asia was prevented

- ABACUS became a successful business in its own right

- ABACUS is sufficiently dominant to partner with one of the CRSs that it was established to protect against

ABACUS is now owned by ABACUS International Pty. Ltd., a Singapore-based provider of travel information and airline reservation services. ABACUS International Holdings, which has a 65 percent stake in ABACUS International P/L, is jointly owned by the twelve Asian airlines. The other 35 percent of ABACUS International P/L is owned by Sabre Group. ABACUS thus achieved a sufficiently powerful market position that it could form an equity-based alliance with Sabre to gain advantage from the technology base of an organization that it once feared.

Why did ABACUS succeed in Asia when attempts at a shared system failed in the United States? One explanation may be that the lack of success of a shared-infrastructure service in the United States, and the resulting massive expenditure on the development of individual systems, was a motivational learning experience for the Asian airlines, encouraging them to set aside their competitive instincts in favor of cooperation. In addition, airline reservation technology had become considerably more mature during the decade or more that passed between the U.S. task force report and the founding of ABACUS. An investment in ABACUS in 1988 looked much less technically risky than the investment in the proposed U.S. joint system in 1976.

The decision by the airlines to cooperate rather than compete was probably motivated by a combination of greed and fear. An American CRS that controlled the electronic channel to the travel agent could relegate the Asian airlines to secondary positions. The American CRS operator would know more about travel bookings and trends than any of the Asian airlines, placing the airline that owned the CRS in a powerful position in competitive battles in Asia. In the short term, there were also significant economies of scale available by consolidating travel reservations into a single, unbiased, and efficient system.

The ABACUS Web site (www.abacus.com.sg) describes the organization's grand vision for the future. ABACUS wants to serve a wider community and be less dependent on airlines for revenue. ABACUS also wants to become a repository of travel and tourism data, and to mine those data, turning them into useful information for travel agents and others. ABACUS will enable travel consultants, travelers, information service providers, and end consumers to use technology to facilitate the best travel arrangements. ABACUS certainly faces challenges in the future, with some airlines going direct to customer via their own Web sites, as illustrated by traveler 3 in figure 8-2. Airline 3 owns the customer relationship with traveler 3, bypassing ABACUS. ABACUS may choose to more aggressively pursue their direct customer relationship by bypassing the travel agent, as illustrated by traveler 2. Nevertheless, the organization has achieved a great deal through the use of the shared-infrastructure business model.

A Torturous Process to Decide What to Share

Even though there was strong motivation for the Asian airlines to cooperate, there were many details and issues of vested interests to negotiate. The location of the headquarters, data centers, and associated investments was one of the first issues to resolve, with each of the national governments wishing to attract the initial investment to its own country. There were large start-up costs to bear, and some airlines took a wait-and-see attitude before committing to the new system. Many issues arose regarding compatibility with existing systems used by travel agents in the various partner countries. Still more decisions were required about the fee structure, the ownership of data (particularly booking and passenger load details), and finally the distribution of profits. The overarching principle was that there would be no bias to any partner, and control would be distributed among the partners. After lengthy negotiations, a stable structure was reached, which involved sharing both equity and management control.

In ABACUS, as with any shared infrastructure, some of the most difficult decisions were about what to share and what to compete on. The ABACUS partners created a level playing field in a number of critical areas that were traditionally bases for competition, including:

• *Information:* Information on aggregate demand, bookings, load factors, paid travel, industry trends, transfers, and other data contained in the CRS is shared with all partners.

• *Objectivity:* The airlines agreed to represent their products objectively, attempting to eliminate any bias.

• *Access:* ABACUS provides a single point of access through which the airlines' common customers—the travel agents—access the airlines' offerings, effectively creating an electronic market where multiple buyers and multiple sellers meet.

• *Investment and return:* Investments and dividends are shared among the partners. The investment in infrastructure, particularly IT infrastructure, is significant. Sharing the infrastructure cost spreads the cost and reduces the development risk for any one airline.

• *Control:* Management control and development of future strategy are shared among the partners via management boards and other mechanisms.

Partners in the shared-infrastructure business model also have to agree on where they will compete. For example, the ABACUS partners continue to compete on these factors:

• *Schedules and pricing:* Each airline determines its own schedule and pricing, and the CRS has rules about how schedule and price changes are entered in the system.

• *Brand:* The relationship to the customer and brand are fundamental to competition among the airlines. The existence of an unbiased CRS may explain the pioneering efforts of the airlines with loyalty programs and more recently with direct-to-customer Web sites. Given that the CRS channel to the customer is cooperative and thus carries no bias (or differentiation), other ways of differentiating are required.

• *Service:* Airlines compete strongly on customer service, particularly after booking, including all direct-to-airline contacts such as check-in, baggage, connections, and changing travel plans after commencement.

> The details of what is shared and what is the basis for competition often predict the success or failure of a shared-infrastructure business model. Sharing too little removes the need for the model. Sharing too much reduces the partners' abilities to differentiate and compete.

Infrastructure

The shared-infrastructure business model requires competitors to cooperate by sharing IT infrastructure and information. This level of cooperation requires agreement on high-level IT architectures as well as operational standards for applications, data communications, and technology. Effective implementation of the shared-infrastructure model also requires enforcement of these standards, and most shared-infrastructure models have a joint committee to set and enforce the standards. Another role of these committees is to implement the policies of the shared infrastructure about what information, if any, is shared and what information is confidential to partner firms. Our field research revealed that the most important infrastructure services required by firms implementing the shared-infrastructure atomic business model all concerned architectures and standards:

- Specification and enforcement of high-level architectures for data, technology, applications, communications, and work that are agreed to by alliance partners
- Specification and enforcement of detailed standards for the high-level architectures

Channels and Segments

A shared infrastructure offers a new channel for its customers to reach its owners; Artesian Innovation is an archetypal example. The channels that the alliance itself uses, however, may well include face-to-face contact as well as telephone, email, and so on. It is no surprise that the general managers of the three Artesian

Innovation partners were pictured, in the press stories cited earlier, sitting in a bar holding glasses of their respective products. No matter how high-tech its product, a shared infrastructure will still need to be managed and governed in a traditional way.

The richness of the channel (see chapter 3, particularly table 3-1) to the customer is a major issue for partners in a shared-infrastructure business model. The partner airlines in ABACUS agreed on an objective representation of their flights on the system. In effect, the richness of the channel was reduced to the lowest common denominator, so that no one airline has the ability to provide more information than any other airline. If an airline is able to get the customer to visit its own Web site directly rather than via the shared-infrastructure site, much more richness in the two-way communication is possible. The direct channel to the customer will appeal to some consumers who are loyal to the particular airline or have no alternative. The huge investment in airline loyalty programs is partly driven by the motivation to counter the objective listing of competing products on an electronic market enabled by a shared infrastructure. Once the channel is standardized, with products compared objectively, providers have to look for other ways to create an appealing value proposition.

Part of the motivation for forming an alliance is to reach new segments of the market. For example, the founders of Artesian probably hope to sign up retail customers who are not currently buying directly from any of the three partners. The ease of submitting a single order to all three major providers may cause some customers to move from dealing with intermediaries to dealing directly with the three partners. More important for the future, a shared infrastructure allows the partners to provide a single point of contact direct to the customer, disintermediating channel partners such as dealers, agents, and perhaps retail stores.

Shared-infrastructure models were being proposed long before the advent of the Internet, and the reasons for forming them in the past are the same as today: to lower costs, to block potential competitors, and to serve customer segments who find value in a combined approach. The Internet has made forming such alliances easier technically, but the political and personal barriers appear to remain as substantial as ever.

Summary of the Shared-Infrastructure Model

Strategic Objective and Value Proposition

Multiple providers choose to cooperate in some areas in order 1to compete more effectively overall. The providers agree to share infrastructure investments and the aggregate information in the shared systems. The motivation is often to reduce cost via economies of scale or to make a defensive move against a potentially dominant player. The shared-infrastructure model is often started by a small group of competitors, with others waiting to see if the model works and joining later. If successful, the shared-infrastructure business model can capture almost complete market share and provide a powerful barrier to entry for alternative providers.

Sources of Revenue

Revenues can be generated both from membership fees (e.g., from other suppliers who use Artesian Innovation, and from auto dealers who use the joint industry system) and from transaction fees (e.g., from the retailers who use Artesian Innovation). The alliance may be run on a nonprofit basis, as with AMS-IX, or on a profit-making basis, as with Artesian Innovation. Not-for-profit shared infrastructures are typically open to all eligible organizations and distribute any excess revenues back to their members. The for-profit models are typically owned by a subset of the firms in a given segment, which split up any profits among themselves. Other sources of revenue include information dissemination, equipment provision, and fees for providing logistics to fulfill the service. Pricing is often a source of contention, particularly between equity holders and nonequity users of the system. Nonequity users may complain that transaction fees are too high, discriminating particularly against smaller participants and unfairly benefiting the owners, who receive profit distributions.

Critical Success Factors

Critical success factors for the shared-infrastructure model include the following:

- No dominant partner that gains more than any other partner.

- An unbiased channel and objective presentation of product and service information.

- Critical mass of both alliance partners and customers. In the nature of infrastructure investments, these shared infrastructures will have high fixed costs, which must be spread across a sufficiently wide base to enable the alliance to be viable.

- Management of conflict among the ongoing e-business initiatives of the alliance partners. In the case of Artesian Innovation, this might mean that the three joint venturers would no longer run independent order entry systems.

- Compilation and delivery of accurate and timely statements of the services and benefits provided to each member of the alliance. Without this information, the members—who are, after all, competitors—are much less likely to continue to support the alliance. In particular, information must be provided to support the agreed arrangement for the splitting of costs, whether on the basis of traffic, revenue from new business, or some other measure. Ideally such information would be reported along with statements of the cost of obtaining an equivalent service from a nonalliance vendor.

- Interoperability of systems. Many shared-infrastructure systems connect directly to the customer at the front end and to the supplier or partner at the back end. To succeed, common standards are needed for data, telecommunications, and other components. For example, in the airline reservations industry there have been significant problems with incompatibility of travel agent systems.

Core Competencies

The core competencies for a shared-infrastructure model are:

- The ability to deliver the infrastructure service(s) around which the alliance was formed. For example, Artesian Innovation must in fact be able to deliver order-entry services, the car makers' and dealers' system must really be able to connect automobile owners to their dealers, and so on. Electronic alliances formed from scratch have the opportunity to build these capabilities; those formed around the existing abilities of one or a few firms must be sure that they have or can acquire the ability to serve a broader set of stakeholders.

- The skill to manage a focused coalition of competitors, generally having diverse backgrounds, resources, and goals. Bringing together competitors and agreeing on what to share and where to compete takes patience and strong negotiation skills. It has become commonplace to describe certain tasks—managing programmers, for example—as being like "herding cats"; running a shared infrastructure can be something like herding mountain lions.

- Efficiently running complex infrastructures to attract participants. Once ABACUS established its dominant position, it was able to partner with Sabre to provide a low-cost IT infrastructure and to help maintain technological superiority. It is telling that ABACUS did not merely outsource to Sabre but rather chose an equity partnership, effectively keeping the skills of running complex infrastructures close to home.

Who Owns What?

	Customer Relationship	Customer Data	Customer Transaction
Shared Infrastructure	✗	✓	✓

CHAPTER 9

Virtual Community

> The notion of community has been at the heart of the Internet since its inception.
>
> —ARTHUR ARMSTRONG AND JOHN HAGEL

VIRTUAL COMMUNITIES deserve our attention, and not merely because they are the clearest, and perhaps the last, surviving embodiment of the original intent of the Internet. By using IT to leverage the fundamental human desire for communication with peers, virtual communities can create significant value for their owners as well as for their members. Once established, a virtual community is less susceptible to competition by imitation than any of the other atomic business models.

Businesses have been quick to recognize the potential value of a sense of community as a way of enhancing their e-business efforts. Many commercial Web sites, although established principally to sell goods and services or to provide information, also allow users to communicate with one another, either directly or via a bulletin board. For example, the Edmunds.com, Inc. site (www.edmunds.com), "where smart car buyers start," incorporates a "Town Hall," "where smart shoppers talk about cars, trucks, and related consumer issues." Amazon.com offers "Amazon.com Community," "a gathering place where you can share your passion for everything from the Beatles to bath toys . . . and it's a way to keep connected with your favorite friends and family." The Web site of American fast-food purveyor Taco Bell includes a bulletin board, on which fans exchange views on cuisine, prices, "stupid Taco Bell managers," and other topics.[1]

Although the virtual community is often combined with other atomic models, our focus in this chapter will be on the virtual community as a stand-alone model. The schematic for this atomic business model is shown in figure 9-1.

In this business model, the firm of interest—the sponsor of the virtual community—sits in the center, positioned between members of the community (at the right of the diagram) and suppliers

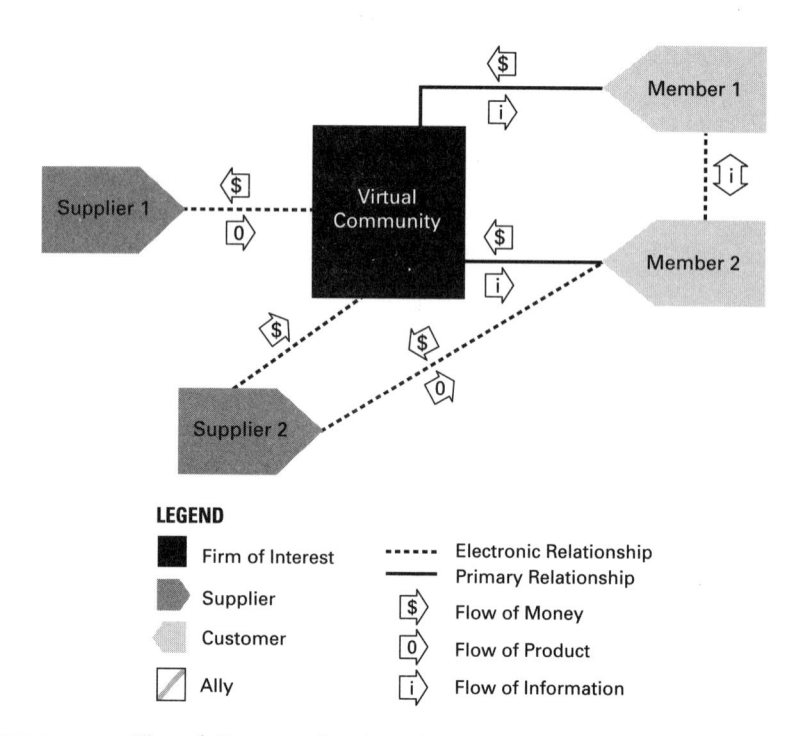

FIGURE 9-1 Virtual Community Atomic E-Business Model Schematic

(at the left). Fundamental to the success of this model is that members are able, and in fact are encouraged, to communicate with one another directly. Communication between members may be via email, bulletin boards, online chat, Web-based conferencing, or other computer-based media, and it is the distinguishing feature of this model.

The sponsoring firm may gain revenues in a number of ways, indicated in figure 9-1 by the flow of dollars from members and suppliers to the firm of interest. Members may pay to be part of the community, although this is not common. Almost always, the community site contains advertising and links, targeted at community members, for which the sponsor may be paid. For example, Parent Soup (www.parentsoup.com), a virtual community for parents, features advertising for beauty products, auto loans, long-distance telephone service, and baby portraits. Fishing.com—"your online community for all things sportfishing!"—includes classified ads for boats, fishing rods and reels, and links to bait-and-tackle shops, guides, and fishing charters. The home page of The Motley Fool (www.motleyfool.com), a Web site that says it "exists to educate, amuse, and enrich the individual investor," includes links to Amazon.com and AOL, as well as advertisements for Compaq and the Internet infrastructure provider GlobalCenter, Inc. Figure 9-2 represents the virtual community of The Motley Fool.

The community sponsor may also be paid for clickthroughs to advertisers' sites, and it may receive a flat fee or percentage commission for sales made to community members. Such sales are indicated in figure 9-1 by the flow of product from suppliers directly to members. The sponsoring organization has the potential to own the relationship with the customer. In order to sustain and improve its relationship with suppliers, the sponsoring organization may furnish them with information about the size and general demographics of the membership base, although maintaining the privacy of individual members is an important objective for all virtual communities. The sponsor may also gain revenue by selling goods or services directly to community members. The Motley Fool offers a variety of investment books and newsletters, for example, as well as investment software.

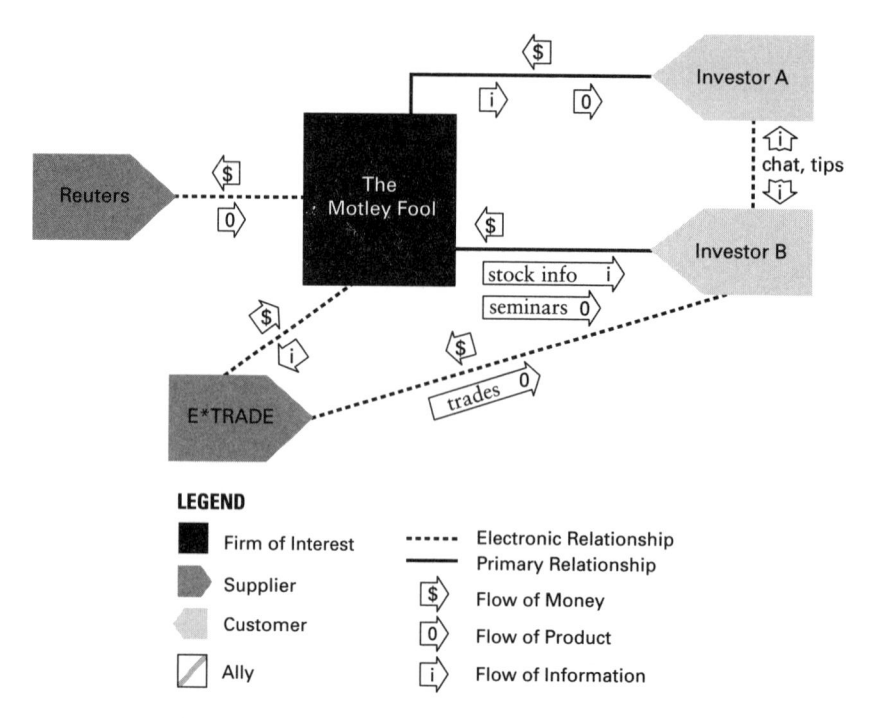

FIGURE 9-2 The Motley Fool E-Business Model Schematic

Revenue generation and links to useful information are characteristics that distinguish a virtual community from an electronic mailing list set up by a community of interest—for example, chess players (tom.cuy.net/chess), or Japanese neurosurgeons (www.sm.rim.or.jp/~amagasa/fnml/html). For example, Parent Soup offers links to published articles on children's health and education, as well as its own hints on creating a healthy parent-teacher relationship and a bulletin board for breast-feeding mothers. Fishing.com offers up-to-the-minute fishing reports and a database of seven thousand patterns for flies. Likewise, The Motley Fool's site offers links to stories from CNET Networks, Inc., Reuters, and other outside sources, in addition to content created by the "100+ people who work and play at Fool Global HQ." The profit-motivated sponsoring organization continually searches for products and services that can be offered to members on favorable terms because of the collective buying power of the community. Members of Parent Soup, for example, are offered discounts by online merchants Petopia (www.petopia.com), Babygear.com, and iMaternity.com, and they receive special offers from department stores Macy's and Nordstrom. Members of Fishing.com can get free email and have access to a discount bookstore featuring fishing-related titles.

Virtual communities are positioned to benefit very strongly from the network effect, by which the community becomes progressively more valuable as it grows.[2] All networks—human as well as electronic—benefit from this effect, as long as they do not become constrained by capacity. The larger a virtual community becomes, the more interested new members become in joining, so long as the growing membership continues to share the common interest around which the community was formed.

Many virtual communities encourage visitors to become members—and to provide the additional information inevitably required for membership—by granting members privileges not given to casual visitors. For example, anyone can read the message boards on The Motley Fool's site, but only members are allowed to respond to messages. Members are also allowed to select favorite message boards, and to customize the presentation of information from those boards. The Motley Fool also has sections, for example "My Portfolio," accessible only to registered members. Parent Soup says, "Membership is free, safe, and comes with cool stuff," the latter including free email, a free personal home page, and access to a menu maker, a pregnancy calendar, and a daily online crossword puzzle. Fishing.com emails free fishing reports to members who disclose their favorite species and fishing method.

A virtual community generally does not own the transactions done by its members, and it owns at most only some of the data about its members and their transactions. However, by encouraging a sense of community and formal membership, a virtual community can completely own the relationship with its members. The more a virtual community knows about its members, the more leverage is possible from owning the relationship.

Infrastructure

Virtual communities depend on IT to exist. In particular, the creation and continual enhancement of an Internet site is essential if a virtual community is to survive. Many virtual-community sites include not just static content and links, but also tools of interest to potential members. For example, Parent Soup includes a period calculator and a baby name search engine, while Fishing.com includes tide and weather reports. The Motley Fool's site provides stock quotes and an "online PEGulator" to help determine the value of growth stocks. These technological tools make the community site more useful, and therefore more attractive to potential members.

Our field research revealed that the infrastructure services most important for the virtual-community business model are the following:

- Training in the use of IT for members of the community. Such training enhances the value of the community to the members but is challenging to deliver at a distance.

- Application service provision (ASP) to provide the specialized systems virtual communities need such as bulletin boards, email, and ISP access. Typically virtual communities use ASPs rather than develop the technical skills in-house.

- IT research and development, including infrastructure services for identifying and testing new technologies and for evaluating proposals for new information systems initiatives, to keep the community attractive and leading edge.

- Information systems planning to identify and prioritize potential investments in IT in this completely online business.

- Installation and maintenance of workstations and local area networks to support the electronic world of the virtual community.

In addition to these infrastructure services, a few others are likely to be important to virtual communities. Many community members are concerned about maintaining the privacy of their identities and of any communication they might have with other members, so a virtual-community Web site must provide a measure of information privacy. Most community sites include a privacy statement outlining the degree of privacy that is provided. For example, Parent Soup follows the privacy policy of its parent, iVillage:

> Except as provided herein, iVillage will not sell to any third party your name, address, email address and member name, unless you provide your informed consent, except to the extent necessary to comply with applicable laws, police investigations, or in legal proceedings where such information is relevant. iVillage allows access to database information by third parties providing technical services, such as email, but only to the extent necessary to provide you with those services. In those instances, the third party is bound by these terms. Your informed consent shall be in the form of an "opt in" or similar policy. You understand and agree that iVillage may disclose to third parties your zip code, gender and/or age, but only in the form of aggregated information. . . . iVillage reserves the right to offer you third party services and products based on the preferences that you identify during the registration process and based on your subsequent preferences; such offers may be provided to you by iVillage. iVillage reserves the right to terminate your iVillage email account if iVillage learns that you have provided iVillage with false or misleading registration information.[3]

Planet Out Corporation, which bills itself as "the leading Internet media company offering a vibrant, welcoming and safe community for all gay, lesbian, bisexual and transgender people as well as their family and friends," sponsors a virtual community, Planet Out.com. The privacy statement on this community's site starts out simply: "PlanetOut feels very strongly that private information should remain private. We will never willfully disclose personally identifiable information about our users to any third party without first receiving that user's permission." It appears, however, that on the PlanetOut site permission to use the information is given by members if permission is not explicitly withdrawn:

Membership on PlanetOut is completely optional. PlanetOut's registration form requires users to give contact information (for example, an email address) and demographic information (e.g., ZIP code, age). On our join form, required fields are marked with an asterisk. We use this information to send members information about PlanetOut (e.g., a weekly newsletter); members may opt-out of receiving this information. This information may be used to tailor a member's PlanetOut experience by delivering content specific to your interests. At times, PlanetOut may rent names, mailing and email addresses to carefully selected organizations. This information is rented on a single-use-only basis. Members may opt-out of these programs by selecting "don't share my mailing address" and/or "don't share my email address" on our registration form. Aggregate demographic information collected through the registration process is shared with advertisers and other partners. This aggregate information is not traceable to an individual user.[4]

PlanetOut.com members who fail to read the fine print may be surprised at the degree of information sharing to which they have implicitly agreed. PlanetOut.com is already a relatively long-lived virtual community; perhaps the sponsoring organization has a very clear understanding of the kind of advertising and other information that the members want to see, or at least of the kind of "selected organizations" that members do not mind hearing from.

Channels

By their nature, most virtual communities have just one channel to the customer: the Internet. However, many virtual communities have clickthroughs from other organizations, often portals or other intermediaries. Community members may, of course, communicate with each other via telephone or mail or face to face, but these channels apply to individual members rather than to the overall community.

Customer Segments

Virtual communities always begin with a segment in mind: women, parents, investors, engineers, or fishermen, for example. The common interests of this segment are intended to bring together in space members from diverse physical locations. The challenge for virtual communities is to balance the benefits (e.g., advertising revenue) of serving a broad segment with the attractiveness to members of having a narrow one. A well-designed virtual community can achieve the best of both worlds by offering some general information to a broad segment and creating subcommunities for narrower segments. Parent Soup contains specific sections for women hoping to become parents, for expectant parents, and for parents of toddlers, school-age children, and teenagers. Parent Soup itself is a subcommunity of iVillage.com, a virtual community that bills itself as "the women's network." U.S.-based Fishing.com includes subcommunities, complete with their own message boards and other features, for anglers in the United Kingdom and Australia, as well as for devotees of fly-fishing. The Motley Fool has subcommunities for retirees, U.K. investors, and those trying to get out of debt. Each of these subcommunities is accessible from The Motley Fool's main page, and each includes content, tools, and message boards of particular interest to the target audience.

Governance

Like any community, a virtual community requires governance. That is, it must have rules about the rights, responsibilities, and behavior of its citizen members. The relatively simple Web site of Fishing.com includes the following rules for posting to its message boards:

> The Rules of The House:
> Please keep posts relevant to the topic at hand.
> No Advertising. This will result in your being banned from the entire site.

> Message Size is capped at 4k. (4096 characters, which should be plenty).
>
> This is your resource and we'll do our end to keep them [sic] fast, clean, and available, if you do your end and respect the resource. :-)[5]

The low involvement of Fishing.com in community governance is in keeping with its apparently low investment in a relatively straightforward site. The much more elaborate iVillage.com site, on the other hand, is governed by an extensive set of "Terms of Service" for all of the Women's Network (TWN), including in very small part the following:

> You alone are responsible for the content of your messages, and the consequences of any such messages. iVillage reserves the right to terminate your registration if it becomes aware and determines, in its sole discretion, that you are violating any of the following guidelines.
>
> Any use by you of any other subscriber's information, personal or otherwise, for any commercial purpose or to obtain direct financial gain (e.g. mass marketing) is prohibited. Any such use shall be deemed to be a violation of these Terms of Service. TWN is to be used by you for your personal use only. Commercial uses of TWN are strictly prohibited unless prior written consent from iVillage has been granted. You agree that you will not use TWN for chain letters, junk mail, 'spamming,' solicitations (commercial or non-commercial) or bulk communications of any kind including but not limited to distribution lists to any person who has not given specific permission to be included in such a list.
>
> You further agree not to use TWN to send or post on message boards or any place on TWN, any message or material that is unlawful, harassing, libelous, defamatory, abusive, threatening, harmful, vulgar, obscene, profane, sexually oriented, threatening, racially offensive, inaccurate, or otherwise objectionable material of any kind or nature or that encourages conduct that could constitute a criminal offense, give rise to civil liability or otherwise violate any applicable local, state, national or international law or

regulation, or encourage the use of controlled substances. iVillage reserves the right to delete any such material from TWN. iVillage will cooperate fully with any law enforcement officials and/or agencies in the investigation of any person or persons who violate the Terms of Service contained in this Section. . . .

You agree not to impersonate any other person or entity, whether actual or fictitious, including impersonating an employee or consultant of iVillage. You further agree not to use an inappropriate member name of any kind.[6]

On the very elaborate site of The Motley Fool, the "Fool's Rules" include:

The Motley Fool champions active and open debate among our members. All we ask is that it's done in a lawful and civil manner. Accordingly, you agree to use The Motley Fool for lawful purposes only. You may not use or allow others to use your Fool membership to:

Post or transmit any content that is abusive, vulgar, obscene, hateful, fraudulent, threatening, harassing, defamatory or which discloses private or personal matters concerning any person;

Post or transmit any material that you don't have the right to transmit under law (such as copyright, trade secret or securities) or under contractual or fiduciary relationships (such as nondisclosure agreements);

Post, transmit or link to sexually explicit material;

Impersonate any person, or falsely state or otherwise misrepresent your affiliation with a person or entity;

Post or transmit any advertising, promotional materials or other forms of solicitation including chain letters and pyramid schemes;

Intentionally violate the laws, rules, and regulations of the U.S. Securities and Exchange Commission and the national or other securities exchanges, especially and including the rule against making false or misleading statements to manipulate the price of any security;

Intentionally violate any other applicable law or regulation while accessing and using our site;

Offer, sell or buy any security; and

Post or transmit any file that contains viruses, corrupted files, "Trojan Horses" or any other contaminating or destructive features that may damage someone else's computer.[7]

The much higher degree of governance imposed by Parent Soup and The Motley Fool is a clear indication of their much higher levels of investment in the sites, and their corresponding aversion to the risks of inappropriate use. All of the examples, however, illustrate that governance of a commercially successful virtual community is significantly more developed than the peer enforcement of "netiquette" that characterizes voluntary mailing lists and list servers.

Gaining New Members

How does a virtual community grow? How can visitors to a virtual community's Web site be screened, and how can those visitors who would add value to the sponsoring firm, and to the community as a whole, be convinced to join? The answers to these questions are of great concern to all virtual communities, for without new members—if only to replace members who move or lose interest—a virtual community, like a physical community, will die.

Virtual-community philosopher Howard Rheingold has noted, "Unless you create a place of value to people that they trust and they come to, then you're not going to be able to sell them anything."[8] The general question of creating trust in an Internet organization has been studied, and some of the lessons from that research are particularly relevant to virtual communities.[9] The following recommendations have been adapted from the general research findings to apply to a virtual community.

1. Make clear what the community is about. Many virtual communities indicate their purpose in their name. There can be little doubt about the common interest of members of Fishing.com, Agriculture.com, or Parentsoup.com, for example.

2. Specify the obligations of membership. Fishing.com, Parent Soup, The Motley Fool, and PlanetOut all emphasize, at the top of their home pages, that membership is "FREE!"

3. Create a sense of personal connection. Both PlanetOut and Parent Soup have photos on their home pages, the latter of children and the former of an attractive young person who may be presumed to be a member. Fishing.com has a picture of a fish.

4. List the benefits of membership, including access to content as well as to other members.

Sustainability

As with many questions about e-business, the full answer to the sustainability of virtual communities won't be known for some time. However, both experience and theory support the notion that virtual communities are sustainable over the long run. In early 1997—eons ago, in Internet years—*Business Week* published a special report on Internet communities. The article featured virtual communities for gays, mothers, "twentysomethings," farmers, and home gardeners.[10] All five sites were alive and apparently well four years later, an admirable record in the constantly shifting virtual world.

The sustainability of a virtual community results from offering an attractive mix of information, communication, and interaction, and from updating the features of the community site as technology evolves. A virtual community has an advantage often missing in a purely commercial site: the allegiance of its members to each other as well as to the site itself. For example, Electric Minds ("E-Minds"), the virtual community started by researcher and philosopher Howard Rheingold, faced bankruptcy when the advertising-supported site failed to bring in enough revenue.[11] A potential investor, Durand Communications, Inc., came forward, and E-Minds members were encouraged to pose questions about the potential buyer's plans and technological capabilities. A news story pointed out that although Rheingold could agree to sell the assets of E-Minds, he could not promise that the people who made up the community would go to a new E-Minds. Durand carefully weighed the feedback from E-Minds members before deciding to proceed with the purchase.[12] Durand itself was purchased by Webb Interactive in early 1998. The E-Minds virtual community lives on, apparently on the basis of advertising, links, and business for its new parent company.[13]

The stickiness created by interpersonal affiliation is the reason that so many commercial sites have tried to create a sense of community among their customers. The bond of common interests—whether in fishing, parenting, gardening, or farming—will most often be far stronger than the bond built around happening to shop at the same site. While Amazon.com customers who meet in cyberspace may form lasting personal relationships, their relationships to Amazon.com may weaken. Members of a true virtual community, on the other hand, may well remain loyal to the site as long as their common interests endure. The implication for current and prospective virtual communities, therefore, is to seek new members aggressively and to quickly link new members with old in order to create a human connection that transcends the explicit benefits of membership.

The examples given in this chapter illustrate three variations on the virtual-community atomic business model:

Examples	Features	Comments
The WELL (see case study in this chapter)	Fee-based, communication only (no advertising or links)	Probably viable only as a feature of a larger site, which will attract members and share infrastructure
Fishing.com Parent Soup	No fee, revenue earned from advertising and links	Viable if balance between sense of community and revenue-earning features can be maintained
The Motley Fool	No fee, revenue from advertising and links, plus direct sales to members	Viable but over time the sense of community may be lost

The Future

The notion of the virtual community has clearly caught on. A search engine found more than 360,000 references to that phrase on the Web, and a quick check of the results revealed virtual communities for philatelists, small-office and home-office owners, and Superman collectors,[14] among many, many others. Virtual-community professionals even have their own (physical) conference, VirComm.[15] The virtual community appears to be here to stay in the e-business world. Although some Web pioneers might decry the impact of commercial considerations on the early notion of the Internet as a collection of naturally formed and self-governing communities, the combination of a profit-motivated sponsoring firm and time-pressured members with a desire to communicate seems powerful indeed.

CASE STUDY

VIRTUAL-COMMUNITY MODEL: The WELL

(www.well.com)

Although The WELL, LLC. perhaps the earliest and certainly one of the best-known virtual communities, has undergone significant change since its founding in the pre-Internet era, it continues to thrive. Describing itself as "a cluster of electronic villages on the Internet, inhabited by people from all over the world," The WELL is unusual in being supported completely by member fees (ten to fifteen dollars per month) and carrying no advertising or links. In 1999 The WELL was purchased by Salon.com, an Internet content provider covering news, technology, entertainment, books, parenting, sex, travel, and health. The WELL describes its operations as follows:

> The WELL has more than 260 featured subject areas called Conferences which range from the technical and specific to the abstract and surreal. Each Conference has a distinct flavor and

crowd, and regulars check-in frequently—in some cases every day—to offer expertise, play word games, indulge in gossip and banter, or to debate and pursue ideas. Hosts of each Conference stimulate new discussions and help orient newcomers. Unlike real-time chat, The WELL makes it easy for users to converse wherever and whenever they choose, easily returning to the conversation hours, days, or even weeks after they last checked-in.[16]

Members of The WELL also create their own private conferences, to which others are admitted by invitation only. Despite having only seven thousand paying members at the time of the purchase by Salon.com,[17] The WELL's status as a pioneering virtual community has led to it being extensively researched, analyzed, and occasionally lamented.[18] The organization once ventured into the provision of computer services, including Internet access, and the development of Internet conferencing software, but it spun off those businesses in 1996 and returned to its roots as "a members-only online discussion community which continues the tradition of intelligent conversation." As a relatively small part of a well-known content provider, The WELL will probably survive. But in a world of free Internet access, free chat rooms, and free membership in interest-focused virtual communities, the number of people who will pay to join an unscreened and unmoderated conference is probably quite small.

Summary of the Virtual-Community Model

Strategic Objective and Value Proposition

The virtual-community model offers members the opportunity to interact electronically with like-minded individuals and to both create and consume content relevant to a topic of personal or professional interest. In effect, the sponsoring firm has created an "attention aggregator" amidst the fast-paced and constantly changing marketspace. The fact that membership is usually free adds to the value perceived by members. Advertisers and merchants can gain access to a group of active Internet users known to be interested in a given area, and therefore predisposed to certain goods and services. Lower customer-acquisition costs are likely to justify spending on advertising fees and sales commissions.

The sponsoring firm may view its virtual community as a stand-alone profit-seeking activity (e.g., Parent Soup), as one part of a business that's composed of several other atomic models (e.g., Amazon.com), or as an adjunct to place-based business. Amazon.com sees the virtual community as a way of bringing additional traffic to its Web site and, over the long term, increasing revenue. Place-based firms, such as Taco Bell, sponsor virtual communities to increase customer involvement and loyalty.

Sources of Revenue

A sponsoring firm can gain revenue from:
- membership fees (The WELL),
- direct sales of goods and services (The Motley Fool),
- advertising (PlanetOut and many other sites),
- clickthroughs (Parent Soup and many other sites), and
- sales commissions (Fishing.com and many other sites).

A firm sponsoring a virtual community as an adjunct to its other activities may receive no direct revenue at all from the virtual community. Rather, the firm receives less tangible benefits, such as customer loyalty and increased knowledge about its customer base.

Critical Success Factors

The critical success factors for a virtual community include:
- Finding and retaining a critical mass of members
- Building and maintaining loyalty with an appropriate mix of content and features

- Maintaining privacy and security for member information
- Balancing commercial potential and members' interests
- Leveraging member profile information with advertisers and merchants
- Engendering a feeling of trust in the community by its members

Core Compentencies

The core competencies for this model include:

- Building a lasting sense of community
- Sourcing or creating attractive content at an economically attractive price
- Discovering member needs and understanding the value members attach to meeting those needs

Who Owns What?

Virtual communities vary in their level of ownership of customer data, with some knowing many demographic and behavioral details about individual members and others knowing little about individual members but having a broad profile of member segments. In general, virtual communities own the customer relationship but not the customer data or transaction.

	Customer Relationship	Customer Data	Customer Transaction
Virtual Community	✓	✗	✗

CHAPTER 10

Value Net
Integrator

TRADITIONALLY, most firms operate simultaneously in two worlds: the physical and the virtual. In the physical world, goods and services are created in a series of value-adding activities connecting the supply side (suppliers, procurement, and logistics) with the demand side (customers, marketing, and shipping). Goods move along the *physical value chain* from supplier to producer to consumer, passing through intermediaries along the way. In the parallel virtual world, information about the members of the physical value chain is gathered, synthesized, and distributed along the *virtual value chain*.[1]

E-business provides the opportunity to separate the physical and virtual value chains. Value net integrators take advantage of that split and attempt to control the virtual value chain in their industries by gathering, synthesizing, and distributing information. Value net integrators add value by improving the effectiveness of the value chain by coordinating information. A pure value net integrator operates exclusively in the virtual value chain, owning few physical assets.

To achieve the gathering, synthesizing, and distributing of information, the value net integrator in figure 10-1 receives and sends information to all other players in the model. The value net

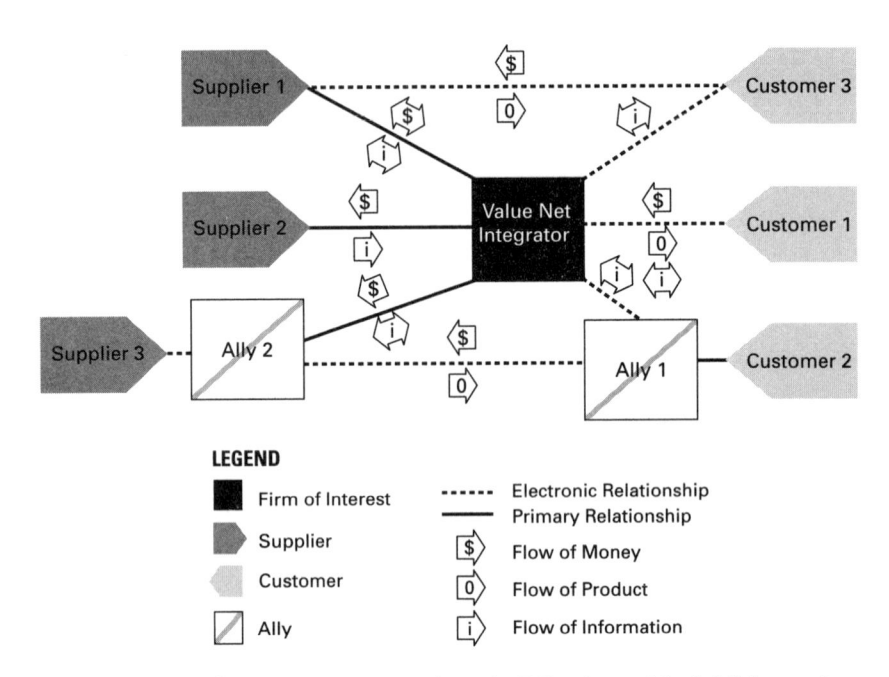

FIGURE 10-1 Value Net Integrator Atomic E-Business Model Schematic

integrator coordinates product flows from suppliers to allies and customers. The product flows from the suppliers to customers may be direct (supplier 1 to customer 3) or via allies (supplier 3 to customer 2). In some cases the value net integrator may sell information or other products to the customer (e.g., customer 1). The value net integrator always strives to own the customer relationship with the other participants in the model, thus knowing more about their operations than any other player. The value net integrator model is evolving quickly and new variations are emerging every week. The business model schematic in figure 10-1 is only one of many possible variations.

Coordinating the Value Chain

Denis Eck, the CEO of Australian retailer Coles Myer, talks about turning the U.S.$15 billion retailer into a new style of media company, whose primary asset will be information. Coles Myer owns a series of retail brands including Kmart, Target, Coles Supermarkets, and Myer Grace Department Stores, which together hold a 20 percent share of the retail market in Australia. If Eck is successful, Coles Myer will control the virtual value chain in retail, operating as a value net integrator able to coordinate the activities of the other players in the chain.[2] Eck's ambition is not without precedent; other companies have already evolved into very sophisticated value net integrators. For example, Seven-Eleven Japan has revolutionized the Japanese retail industry with their value net integrator model, and Cisco is well placed to do the same for telecommunications products.

CASE STUDY

VALUE NET INTEGRATOR MODEL: **Seven-Eleven Japan**

A powerful example of a value net integrator that coordinates a value chain is Seven-Eleven Japan,[3] operating in the highly regulated Japanese retail market. Japanese retailing was traditionally dominated by large manufacturers, who set prices, forecast demand, took returns of unsold goods, and provided a series of rebates to retailers in return for loyalty, holding inventory, and achieving sales targets. Goods were distributed through three or more levels of national and regional wholesalers, delivering to many thousands of small retailers. Living in a small apartment with little storage capacity, the typical Japanese retail customer makes purchases on a daily basis and has strong loyalty to local stores.

These industry conditions were ideal for Toshifumi Suzuki to introduce Seven-Eleven convenience stores, which he describes as "stores where you can a find a solution for any of your daily life problems."[4] The convenience store business is competitive in Japan, with one convenience store for every two thousand people. Seven-Eleven Japan has more than eight thousand stores and is the most profitable retail business in the country. Seven-Eleven's value proposition to the consumer is simple: easy access, warm and friendly environment, consistently high quality, and a highly targeted product range, with 70 percent of the three thousand lines carried in the typical store new each year, and product prices about 10 percent higher than supermarkets.

Stores send orders electronically at 10 A.M. daily, with deliveries the same day at 3 P.M. Seven-Eleven Japan has developed a combined-delivery system, in which similar products from different suppliers are centralized in a combined-delivery center. Through the use of this facility over a period of eighteen years, Seven-Eleven has reduced the number of deliveries to each store from seventy per day to nine. The value proposition to the franchisees, often a couple running their own business, is that Seven-Eleven will provide a huge range of products to select from, strong buying power, coordinated deliveries, and the advice of field counselors who visit two or three times a week to help owners get the most out of their stores. For this assistance and the Seven-Eleven brand, franchisees pay 45 percent of their gross profit to Seven-Eleven. The other major Japanese convenience stores charge franchisees around 33 percent of gross profit.

Seven-Eleven also coordinates the distribution system by identifying an exclusive wholesaler for each region who is guaranteed large volumes and a long-term relationship. To participate, regional wholesalers must continually improve their operational performance. "It was tough for us because we had to make a huge investment to upgrade our information systems for [them],"[5] one manager at a Tokyo-based wholesaler commented. The information is collected by Seven-Eleven, synthesized, and distributed back to the wholesalers and manufacturers. A salesman at Tokyo Style, a large garment maker that produces an exclusive line for Seven-Eleven, explains, "Their information system is so good that we can instantly find out which goods of ours are selling and for how much."[6]

Seven-Eleven is a highly evolved value net integrator. Seven-Eleven founder Suzuki explains, "We are not in the retail business but rather the information business."[7] Seven-Eleven headquarters has access to the daily sales of every item in each of its six thousand stores by the afternoon of the day following the sale. Seven-Eleven doesn't own any part of the physical value chain—no inventory, no stores, no warehouses, no manufacturing plants. Instead, Seven-Eleven controls the virtual value chain and the data within it. Seven-Eleven doesn't even own most of the IT necessary to run its business: IT is outsourced to Nomura Research Institute. Seven-Eleven collects and synthesizes information, and then distributes it to stores, wholesalers, and manufacturers to increase profitability for all the players by better meeting the needs of the consumer.

The Seven-Eleven Japan business model schematic is presented in figure 10-2. Seven-Eleven is the only player in the value chain to have access to information about all the major entities, from the manufacturers through to the customers. Seven-Eleven collects and distributes information from all the entities in the model, represented by the double-headed arrows labeled with an *i*. Seven-Eleven uses that information to determine consumer tastes and demand and then to order products to be manufactured, distributed, and delivered to the retail franchisees. Seven-Eleven coordinates the value chain by

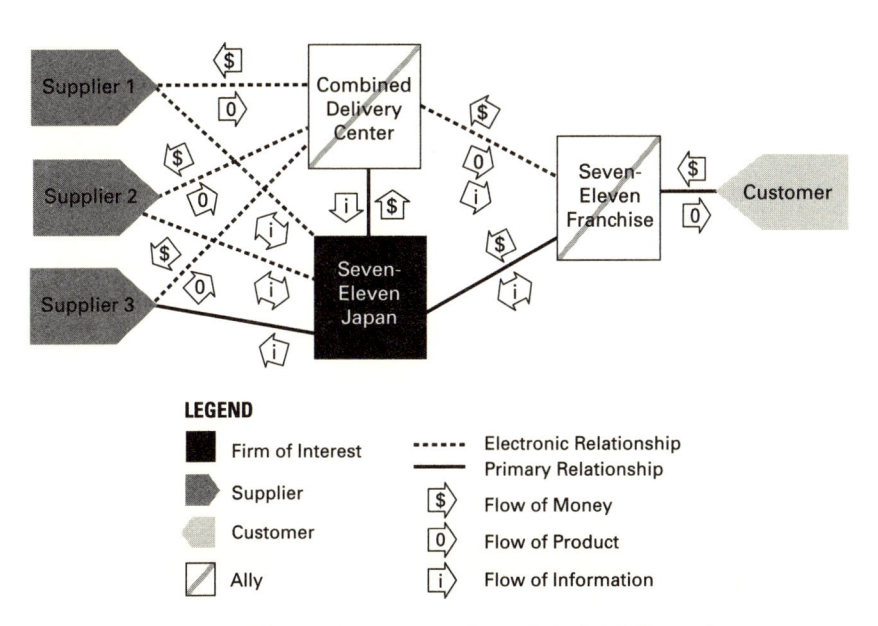

FIGURE 10-2 Seven-Eleven Japan E-Business Model Schematic

brokering the information to the other players in return for revenue, exclusivity, or fast fulfillment. For example, Seven-Eleven coordinates the different manufacturers to deliver to the combined-delivery centers that deliver to the stores in four types of vans classified by the temperature of the goods: frozen, chilled, room temperature, and hot.

Seven-Eleven receives the great bulk of its revenue as royalties from affiliate shops. Seven-Eleven owns the relationship with the franchise stores, with the exclusive combined-delivery wholesalers, and perhaps with some of the suppliers as well. Owning the relationship means that Seven-Eleven knows more about the other organizations' capabilities, capacities, inventories, and cost structures than any other entity. The franchise store owns the relationship with the consumer but effectively passes over data ownership to Seven-Eleven, delivering the data via an electronic connection directly from the store. Effectively, Seven-Eleven is the only player who can see into the entire value chain from end to end.

Seven-Eleven owns the customer data but not the customer relationship or transactions, which are owned by the store. This is the typical ownership pattern for value net integrators. This ownership pattern represents a highly evolved e-business model, since money is made without owning any physical assets.

Seven-Eleven's strategy has continued to deliver increasing profits, and it has been rewarded on the Japanese stock market with share prices increasing from five thousand yen in March 1999 to fifteen thousand yen in January 2000. To further utilize the store infrastructure and widen its control of the virtual value chain, in 2000 Seven-Eleven introduced dream-7.com. In partnership with Sony, NEC, Mitsui, and others, Seven-Eleven will install in-store terminals to be used to purchase a broad range of goods online. The stores will serve as distribution and collection points for the goods.[8] The in-store terminals will include a digital printer, a scanner, a smart card reader, and a mini disk drive that will allow customers to buy favorite songs and get them delivered immediately. Seven-Eleven Japan expects this to generate revenues of 10 billion yen in 2000, rising to 300 billion yen (U.S.$2.9 billion) in 2003.[9]

CASE STUDY

VALUE NET INTEGRATOR MODEL: Cisco Systems (www.cisco.com)

Cisco's television advertisements repeatedly ask the question "Are you ready?" as they promote the use of the Internet.[10] The ads reinforce the human benefit from the Internet as it changes the way we work, play, and learn. Cisco promotes the Internet for a very good reason: The company controls about 80 percent of the market in the "plumbing of the Internet." Cisco sells routers and other devices that effectively act as electronic traffic cops, directing the flow of packets of information on the Internet. Cisco sells these devices over the Internet, through a direct sales force, and via a wide range of resellers and channel partners.

The purchasers of Cisco products are almost exclusively other businesses, which use the devices to operate and control their networks. Every firm with a significant IT investment needs routers to connect internal networks to one another, as well as to the Internet and to other external networks. Configuring a router correctly for a given customer's needs is a technical task requiring significant expertise. Cisco's resellers and channel partners are certified to provide value-added services to customers, and they generate 70 percent of Cisco revenues. For example, a Gold Certified Cisco partner offers a complete solution to any networking requirement, including configuration, training, installation, and service.

When a direct customer or reseller orders routers, switches, or other equipment from Cisco via fax or telephone, one in four orders has an error in pricing or configuration. For orders placed via the Cisco Web site, the error rate drops to one in one hundred. The Web site leads the customer through the purchase and configuration process via the Cisco configurator. The configurator software asks questions about the way the device will be used, and thereby helps the customer specify the product correctly. Once a design is complete, the customer can test it for feasibility and place an order. The Cisco Web site with its configurator has the following advantages:

- Reduces selling cost, saving $1.5 billion in the last three years

- Removes the need to answer order status queries by providing this information online

- Saves as much as $25 million a month in shipping and administrative costs by downloading software

- Allows self-service twenty-four hours a day

- Frees up sales staff for higher-value-added activities

- Enables global expansion without bricks-and-mortar offices. In the United States, 50 percent of Cisco's orders are received electronically, while in South America and Australia, 90 percent and 70 percent are electronic, respectively

- Provides digitized market research information about what customers want, as opposed to what they finally buy

- Reduces order cycle time by three to five days compared to ordering by fax or telephone

Cisco has been equally innovative at the supply end of the business model. Cisco has established a virtual manufacturing system, partnering with key suppliers and contract manufacturers like Selectron and Flextronics. These partners are so electronically linked to Cisco that the demarcation between the firm and its suppliers is blurred. About one hundred of Cisco's first-tier partners are connected to the firm's ERP system so they can share orders, forecasts, and specifications.

Cisco didn't achieve this level of electronic integration overnight. Here is a summary of the major steps:

- 1996: Pricing, configuration, and order status data viewable online.

- 1997: Configuring, pricing, and ordering online.

- 1998: Cisco's selling system integrated with their largest customers' purchasing systems.

- 1999: Customer-specific tools available for service providers, small and medium enterprises, large firms, and resellers.

Largest customers can access Cisco's manufacturing systems and schedule their own orders.

- 2000: Multivendor solutions to integrate the ordering of related third-party products.

Cisco has maintained its market position, in part, by product leadership. Cisco does not rely solely on in-house research and development. Rather, with forty-two acquisitions in the last three years, Cisco partially outsources research and development.[11] Cisco's business model schematic, presented in figure 10-3, is a combination of the content provider, direct-to-customer, and value net integrator atomic models. Currently Cisco operates in both the physical and virtual value chains. Cisco designs, markets, manufactures, sells, and distributes products. Cisco sheds risk at the customer end by using resellers to install and support and the configurator to reduce errors and collect market information. Cisco sheds risk at the back end by outsourcing

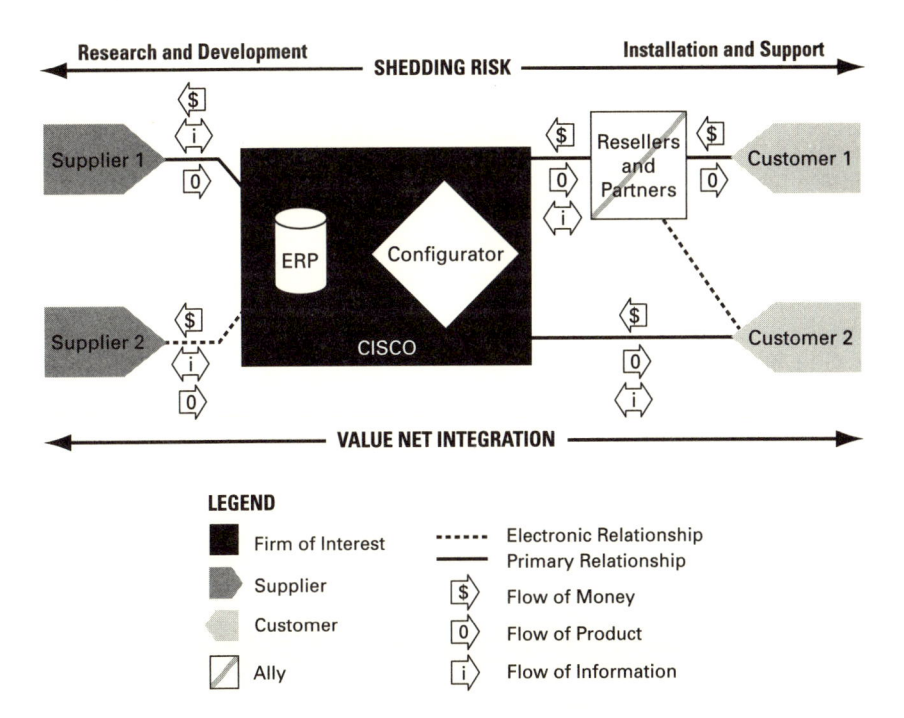

FIGURE 10-3 Cisco Systems Atomic E-Business Model Schematic

some research and development via acquisitions and creating a tightly integrated manufacturing and supply network.

Cisco avoids channel conflict, despite maintaining both direct and reseller channels (see figure 10-4) in several ways. Cisco has 80 percent market share, so the options for purchasers are limited. More important, Cisco's products require technical skills to implement. Some customers have these skills available, but many do not, and they therefore happily choose to use—and pay for—the services of a reseller. Using channel partners reduces Cisco's need for staff to handle field support. Clear segmentation has also helped reduce channel conflict. Cisco focuses on three segments: service providers, small- to medium-sized companies, and large enterprises and resellers. Each segment has tools on the Web site and a configurator tailored to its needs. It will be interesting to see if channel conflict continues to be a nonissue, since Cisco could capture margin by going direct in some segments.

In early 2000, Cisco became the second-largest corporation in the world in terms of market capitalization, behind General Electric. In valuing Cisco, we believe the market places significant weight on the intellectual property captured in the configurator, the brand, and the network of tightly linked suppliers and resellers who make up Cisco's value chain. Cisco has made

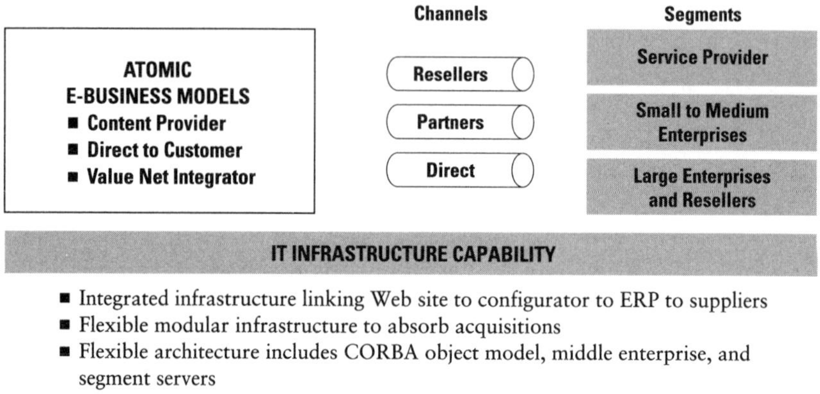

ATOMIC E-BUSINESS MODELS
- Content Provider
- Direct to Customer
- Value Net Integrator

Channels
- Resellers
- Partners
- Direct

Segments
- Service Provider
- Small to Medium Enterprises
- Large Enterprises and Resellers

IT INFRASTRUCTURE CAPABILITY

- Integrated infrastructure linking Web site to configurator to ERP to suppliers
- Flexible modular infrastructure to absorb acquisitions
- Flexible architecture includes CORBA object model, middle enterprise, and segment servers

FIGURE 10-4 Cisco's E-Business Initiative

significant progress toward owning the virtual value chain in its industry. Unlike Seven-Eleven Japan, Cisco still owns physical assets, including some manufacturing plants and inventory. However, it is in an excellent position to slowly outsource them all. Shedding more physical assets is one way that Cisco could maintain its relatively high margins. Cisco's plans for 2000 to integrate products from third parties so customers can order everything from one place is an aggressive further move toward the value net integrator model.

The Value Net Integrator As a Highly Evolved E-Business Model

Seven-Eleven Japan is an example of an almost pure value net integrator, which operates exclusively by controlling and brokering information. A value net integrator is perhaps the most highly evolved of our atomic e-business models. A firm using this model has withdrawn from (or never operated in) the physical world of moving products, and thus it has pulled costs out of its business. Value net integrators that once operated in the physical value chain incrementally withdrew by increasing the use of outsourcing. Cisco still operates in the physical world, selling routers directly to consumers and resellers as well as manufacturing products and holding inventory. However, the company has the potential to adopt—and we observe them moving toward adopting—more of the value net integrator model as they outsource more and more of the physical value chain. Cisco's configurator, containing much intellectual property about configuring their products as well as consumer preferences, places them in a strong position to become a pure value net integrator. By opening up their ERP to their suppliers and understanding their suppliers' capabilities, Cisco can move to a value net integrator business model of collecting, synthesizing, and distributing information similar to Seven-Eleven. Cisco has made major strides in this direction by its aggressive acquisition strategy, effectively outsourcing research and development. In the future

Cisco could own only its strategy, brand, configurator, and product list, outsourcing the rest. Cisco would then make money as a value net integrator by collecting, synthesizing, and distributing information.

Infrastructure

The value net integrator succeeds in its role by gathering, synthesizing, and distributing information. Thus, for a value net integrator, data and electronic connectivity with allies and other players are very important assets. Our field research suggests that the most important infrastructure services required for a value net integrator include:

- middleware, linking systems on different platforms across the many players in the value net;
- a centralized data warehouse that collects and summarizes key information for analysis from decentralized databases held by several players across the value net;
- specification and enforcement of high-level architectures and detailed standards for data, technology, applications, and communications to link together different technology platforms owned by different firms;
- call centers to provide advice and guidance for partners and allies in getting the most value from the information provided by the value net integrator; and
- high-capacity communications network service to support the high volumes of information flowing across the value net.

Since most transactions are done by others, security is generally not of great concern for the value net integrator, but privacy is important, and it must be among the infrastructure services available.

Summary of the Value Net Integrator Model

Strategic Objective and Value Proposition

Traditionally most industries have operated in relatively linear value chains, with products and services moving from player to player. With the increasing use of e-business, value networks are emerging with multiple connections among players, breaking down the traditional chain. This chapter has described the value net integrator, which gathers, synthesizes, and distributes information to improve the operation of a value net in an industry segment. The value net integrator owns few physical assets but has rich information on the needs and capabilities of the other players and customers. Often the value net integrator will also own a strong brand and may have once been a player in the physical world of the industry. The value net integrator may be using information as part of a broader strategy to increase revenues and profits from the sale of physical goods, whether those goods be Bento boxes in Tokyo or Internet routers in Manhattan. We see many firms with direct-to-customer atomic models adding and perhaps migrating to be value net integrators, taking advantage of their strong brand and powerful position in the value net.

Sources of Revenue

In this model, exemplified by Seven-Eleven Japan, revenues are generally earned by fees or margins on the physical goods that pass through the industry value net. By using information about consumers, the value net integrator is able to increase prices by meeting consumer demand. By using information about suppliers, the value net integrator reduces costs by cutting inventories and lead times. The value net integrator atomic model may be combined with other models, creating opportunities for other sources of revenue, such as commissions on direct sales.

Critical Success Factors

The critical success factors for the value net integrator atomic business model are listed below:

- Reducing ownership of physical assets while retaining ownership of data

- Owning or having access to the complete industry virtual value chain

- Establishing a trusted brand recognized at all places in the value chain

- Operating in markets where information can add significant value, such as those that are complex, fragmented, regulated, multilayered, inefficient, and large with many sources of information, and that require specialized knowledge

- Presenting the information to customers, allies, partners, and suppliers in clear and innovative ways that provide value

- Helping other value chain participants capitalize on the information provided by the value net integrator

Core Competencies

The core competencies of a value net integrator are the following:

- Managing relationships with customers and all other major players in the value chain

- Managing information: collecting, synthesizing, distributing, and presenting information

- Linking the IT architecture to strategic objectives

- Developing and managing the brand

- Analyzing and interpreting information from multiple sources

- Identifying and using levers of influence, rather than direct control
- Evaluating cost and customer benefit of various types of information

Who Owns What?

	Customer Relationship	Customer Data	Customer Transaction
Value Net Integrator	✗	✓	✗

[handwritten: Potentially least profitable ro...]

CHAPTER 11

Content Provider

> AOL Time Warner will be a premier global company delivering branded information, entertainment and communications across rapidly converging media platforms and changing technology.
>
> —PART OF THE ANNOUNCEMENT OF THE MERGER OF AOL AND TIME WARNER, JANUARY 10, 2000

THE MERGER between America Online (AOL) and Time Warner was another chapter in the ongoing debate about which is more important and more valuable: content or customer relationships. AOL has tens of millions of customer relationships, and Time Warner is one of the best-known branded content providers on the planet. Together they create a formidable combination that is more powerful than either company alone. AOL Time Warner's brands include AOL, *Time*, CNN, CompuServe, Warner Brothers, Netscape, *Sports Illustrated*, *People*, HBO, ICQ, TBS, Digital City, Warner Music Group, Spinner, *Fortune*, *Entertainment Weekly*, and Looney Tunes. Mr. Gerald

(Jerry) Levin, the CEO of Time Warner, said, "This strategic combination with AOL accelerates the digital transformation of Time Warner by giving our creative and content businesses the widest possible canvas. The digital revolution has already begun to create unprecedented and instantaneous access to every form of media and to unleash immense possibilities for economic growth, human understanding and creative expression."[1]

What Is a Content Provider?

Like many terms associated with e-business, *content provider* has different meanings to different people. We define *content provider* as a firm that creates and provides content (information, products, or services) in digital form to customers via third parties. The physical-world analogy of a content provider is a journalist, recording artist, or stock analyst. Digital products such as software, electronic travel guides, and digital music and video are examples of content.

Weather

A virtual-world example of a content provider is Weathernews Incorporated (WNI), the world's largest private meteorological-services organization (www.weathernews.com). WNI provides weather information directly to shipping companies, offshore oil producers, media outlets, and, via the Internet, portals such as Yahoo!. WNI thus combines the direct-to-customer and the content provider business models. The weather content—data and graphics—at www.weather.yahoo.com is provided by WNI, whose logo and hyperlinked name appears at the top and bottom of each Yahoo! weather page. A user who clicks on one of these links is taken to the WNI sales page, which lists account managers for various products and regions. This symbiotic arrangement has benefits for both Yahoo! and WNI, and it is not clear who is, or should be, paying whom. In the physical world, WNI is paid for providing weather information to *USA Today,* the *Los Angeles Times,* and other newspapers.²

Providing valuable and time-sensitive content such as weather reports and forecasts is a competitive industry. Weather Services International (www.wsicorp.com), AccuWeather (www.accuweather.com), and the Weather Services division of Data Transmission Network Corporation (www.wx.com) all supply content similar to that provided by WNI. WX.com allows the owners of other Internet sites to link to its site without charge, and it will even create for them, free, a custom link page showing the five-day forecast for a given location and carrying a WX.com advertising banner.³ Custom link pages with more information, and information delivered directly to a customer's Web site, attract a fee.

These weather services typify the content provider business model. The essence of their businesses is providing accurate and easy-to-use content—weather information—that is distributed to end consumers via many channels, including the Internet and television. By delivering accurate, branded content, the weather services seek to change weather information from an undifferentiated commodity to a branded value-added service. Although the services' customers, for example, Yahoo! or CNN.com, own the customer relationship with the consumer, it is critical that the weather services' brands are known and valued by the consumer. AccuWeather, for example, has achieved this critical success factor: 180 million Americans recognize the AccuWeather name.

As with many e-businesses, content providers can occupy intermediate positions in the supply chain. In particular, the customers of a content provider can themselves be content providers. For example, the portal and search engine Lycos obtains the weather information displayed at weather.lycos.com from Weather Services International; the provider's name and logo, but not a link to its site, appear at the bottom of the Lycos weather pages. In turn, Lycos itself is a content provider to Juno Online Services, a large American ISP. The company's home page (www.juno.com) notes that the Juno site is "powered by Lycos," and users who click on "Check the Weather" are taken directly to weather.lycos.com. In announcing the arrangement, Lycos President and CEO Bob Davis described the general motivation for using a content provider: "By allying with Lycos, service providers like Juno are able to augment existing services and enhance Web content for their users. Together, Lycos and Juno are giving Internet consumers a richer, more personalized Web experience."[4]

Providing information via a third party is an atomic business model that is different in essence from the other models, as is clear from the content provider schematic as shown in figure 2-4.

The content provider—the firm of interest—is shown at the left end of the value chain. A content provider typically works with multiple third parties; Weather Services, for example, provides content to America Online as well as to Lycos. These third parties generally pay the content provider for its product and information and pass this information along to their own customers. The third parties may, like Juno, be paid by customers, as shown in the diagram, or may, like Lycos, be supported by advertising and other indirect sources of revenue. In any case, the third party owns both the relationship with their customers and any transactions that these customers engage in. The issue of data ownership can be more complicated. Passive content delivered to a third party (e.g., Yahoo!) and accessed on the third party's Web site generates no consumer information for the content provider, and generally the content provider does not own any consumer data. Indeed the content provider is usually dependent on the third party, who often owns the relationship with the consumer, for feedback and demographic data.

In general the content provider owns *none* of the end-customer relationship, transaction, or data. The content provider is the only atomic model with this pattern of ownership. To succeed, the content provider has to be a world leader in its area of content, and it often employs large numbers of specialist professionals. Not owning any of the customer assets—relationship, data, or transaction—makes the content provider very reliant on third parties. On the other hand, content providers typically have a relatively small number of direct customers, and therefore they do not incur the costs of managing relationships with millions of consumers.

Sometimes a provider of active content—for example, the weather stickers offered free by Weather Services—can generate and capture information about the ultimate destination and use of its product.[5] If the handover is more complete—for example, when a Juno user is sent directly to the Lycos weather page—then the opportunities for owning customer data increase further. The privacy statement on the Weather Services site tells users, "From time to time, WX.com will perform statistical analysis using data provided by you for the purposes of: determining interest in various services provided by WX.com, [to] inform advertisers of the effectiveness of their marketing campaigns, and to better serve your information needs."[6] So although third parties certainly have the greater opportunity to gather and own customer data, it is sometimes possible for a content provider to collect part of this crucial information.

Financial Content

It is not surprising that some of the most eagerly sought content is financial. For example, Morningstar (www.morningstar.com) provides mutual fund, stock, and variable-annuity investment information. An independent company, Morningstar does not own, operate, or hold any interest in mutual funds or stocks, but it provides data on more than ten thousand mutual funds and eight thousand stocks. Its products are available in print, on the Internet, and on CD-ROM. Morningstar sells content to allies such as stockbroking and other financial services firms, and to media organizations including CNN, CNBC, the *New York Times,* and the *Wall Street Journal.* Morningstar also operates a direct-to-customer model for institutional and corporate investors and individual consumers.

Morningstar's comments tend to be concise and pointed; for example, regarding the Strong Discovery Fund, the company said, "Despite a recent uptick in performance, this fund is still a dud," while the Fidelity Magellan Fund was described as, "No longer your grandparents' large-blend fund."[7] Morningstar also rates mutual funds, awarding five stars to the funds it rates most highly and zero stars to the funds at the bottom of its list. Morningstar is unusual among content providers in that it also actively seeks to attract consumers directly to its Internet site. A free membership allows consumers to track, manage, and analyze up to fifty portfolios with up to fifty securities in each, and to receive an analysis of how well those holdings work together to meet the consumer's investment goals. A premium membership (the direct-to-customer model), at $9.99 per month, allows access to additional analyses of stocks and mutual funds, delivers email alerts of news relevant to an investor's portfolio, and offers advice about investing for retirement.

The majority of Morningstar's business, however, comes from content distribution via third parties. The relationship between Morningstar and The MutualFundWire.com (www.mutualfundwire.com), which delivers information to mutual fund professionals, is typical. Under this arrangement, announced in late April 2000, Morningstar provides editorial and data content, and exclusive banner advertising links, to The MutualFundWire.com. "Morningstar's information will be a valuable new resource for the InvestmentWires community," said Sean Hanna, president and publisher of InvestmentWires, publisher of The MutualFundWire.com. "This information will enable our visitors to quickly research fund performance and their portfolios."[8] As part of the sponsorship, Morningstar will have the exclusive rights to advertise its online investment advice service, Morningstar ClearFuture, via banner ads on MutualFundWire.com. There will also be a link to the Morningstar premium service.[9] This arrangement is a good example of the relationship between a content provider such as Morningstar and a third-party ally such as InvestmentWires. Although the full financial arrangements between the two parties were not disclosed, Morningstar is receiving at least advertising and potential premium memberships in return for its branded content. InvestmentWires increases the attractiveness of its MutualFundWire.com site by having Morningstar's content on the site.

Morningstar is also an interesting example of a provider of another type of valued content: performance ratings. Morningstar's star ratings for hundreds of mutual funds are used by individual and institutional investors to objectively assess the performance of a fund. In the nonfinancial performance-rating arena, BizRate (www.bizrate.com) gathers direct customer feedback and transactional information after every purchase from more than thirty-six hundred online merchants, including Amazon, Dell, QVC, and Wal-Mart Online. BizRate's ratings appear on Consumer Reports Online, AltaVista, GO Network, Go2Net, Snap, Citibank, iChoose, Brodia, Dealtime, and CNET. Such ratings are a way of differentiating retailers on quality-of-service metrics, allowing consumers to focus on quality comparisons as well as price comparisons. BizRate does not allow stores to pay for listing or placement on its site, and it does not accept sponsorships. Instead, it generates revenues by helping consumers buy online and by helping stores study and better understand how to serve the needs of consumers buying online. BizRate sells aggregated market research information about consumer preferences, and it also receives commissions from stores for referrals from its Web site. BizRate promises to pass these commissions back to consumers in the form of rebates on further purchases; BizRate keeps three dollars of each commission.

Both Morningstar and BizRate have combined the content provider model and the direct-to-customer model. These organizations avoid conflict with their third-party distributors—some of which are also among the firms whose performance is being rated—by not accepting advertising or sponsorships or in any other way appearing to favor one distributor over another.

Why Do Content Providers Exist?

If content providers don't own the customer relationship, transaction, or data, why do they choose to distribute their product through third parties? Content providers generally want to focus on what they are good at, which is developing content—films, weather forecasts, travel information, educational material, and so on. Content providers also want to avoid the expense of developing a customer-friendly, retail front end for what is essentially a wholesale backroom operation. The skills required for content provision via third parties are quite different from the skills required for content provision directly to consumers. The content provider requires a high measure of professional and technical skill, for example, being able to convert a stream of raw data from a weather satellite into information that is meaningful and tailored to the needs of their allies. These allies in turn add value to or combine with other information for customers. Direct-to-customer distribution requires considerably more insight into changing patterns of consumer behavior, including the value placed by the customer on an overall basket of information and services. Another distinction between the two modes is the number of third parties involved. Direct providers must deal with a much larger group, which obligates them to monitor and influence many more relationships than providers who deliver information through third parties. The difference in required skill sets may explain why many content providers decide to take the lower revenue, but perhaps the higher leverage and lower risk, that come with dealing through third parties rather than directly with consumers.

Like Morningstar, many content providers also incorporate direct-to-customer models in their business model. The Web sites of WNI (www.wni.com), Weather Services division of Data Transmission Network Corporation (www.wx.com), and Weather Services International (www.wsicorp.com) are colorful, consumer-oriented sites offering a wide variety of content in an assortment of styles. These content providers have taken on the cost of providing information directly to end users as well as to intermediaries. Similarly, MapQuest.com—the "#1 Web site for consumers to get online, interactive maps and driving directions," according to its Web site—provides those maps and driving directions directly from its site as well as being a content provider for Sears, Borders books, Walgreens, Blockbuster, AOL, Bank of America, American Express, Yahoo!, and Travelocity. Quote.com offers a free, easy-to-use Web site accessed regularly by about a half million direct users,[10] in addition to distributing branded content through the Internet sites of Charles Schwab, Fidelity, and other brokers. In a few cases, for example, the advertisements of DoubleClick (see below), the content being provided may not actually be wanted, forcing the content provider to work through third parties.

A content provider can, of course, avoid at least some portion of the expense that would otherwise be required for marketing its information product. With marketing reportedly composing as much as 70 percent of the spending of many dot-coms, the savings could easily make up for the drop in margin that may accompany a choice to distribute through an intermediary rather than directly.

Content providers often work through allies because of the specialized nature of the content being provided. Although end consumers could go to separate sites for weather reports, driving instructions, and other information, it is not likely that many would do so, even if the information were free. Most consumers do not want to learn the details of connecting to many individual sites, then gathering small amounts of data from each site, and finally combining the results. There is a continuing role for intermediaries (see chapter 7), and an equally durable role for content providers.[11] By working through an intermediary, a content provider can greatly expand the number of users with ready access to the information it offers. A content provider can collect reasonable usage fees from a small number of third parties, but collecting micropayments from a large number of individual users is so expensive as to be impractical. Most content providers generate the bulk of their revenues from a relatively small number of allies. The direct-to-customer sites may not be significant revenue generators, but they are designed to reinforce brand presence and recognition.

DoubleClick (www.doubleclick.com), "the global Internet Advertising Solutions company," is in the unusual position of providing content—advertisements—that the end consumer probably does not want to see. It is doubtful if anyone would voluntarily go to DoubleClick's Web site to view this content, so the company must work through third parties. DoubleClick claims to have pioneered the "network model" of advertising on the Web, through which the company delivers more than seventeen billion ads per month to Internet users, all via banner ads on the Web pages of third parties. DoubleClick allows customers (advertisers) to target ads by geography, user interest (e.g., sports or finance), and type of site (e.g., portal or news). For example, a user investigating luxury cars on the AutoByTel site (www.autobytel.com) might see a banner advertisement from Jaguar on the first visit to the site, and an ad from Mercedes-Benz on the next; a user investigating passenger cars would see Ford and Chevrolet advertisements instead. DoubleClick provides ads from its central server to fit the chosen criteria and avoid duplication. DoubleClick's revenue grew by about 250 percent from 1998 to 1999, to exceed U.S.$316 million; like many dot-com companies, its losses grew even faster, reaching U.S.$55 million in 1999.

Infrastructure

Content providers must excel at tailoring and manipulating their core content to meet the specific needs of customers. Content providers must categorize and store their content in well-indexed modules so it can be combined and customized to meet customer needs via a wide variety of channels. Customers and transactions tend to be relatively few, at least compared with the number of end consumers and their transactions. Often complex and unique IT infrastructures are needed to support the particular needs of the specialized professionals employed by the content provider (e.g., weather forecasters at WNI, map makers at Lonely Planet, financial analysts at Morningstar). Our field research identified the most important infrastructure services:

- Multimedia storage farms or storage area network infrastructures to deal with large amounts of information, including images, maps, and video, which are the assets of a typical content provider.

- A strong focus on architecture, including setting and enforcing standards particularly for work (e.g., business processes), applications, and telecommunications to link with the allies using their content.

- Detailed data architectures to structure, specify, link, manipulate, and manage the core intellectual property (i.e., the content) in content providers' own systems and when transmitted to their customers.

- Workstation network infrastructures to enable the fundamentally online business of a content provider.

- A common systems development environment to provide compatible and integrated systems, ensuring the systems can provide content across multiple channels to their customers.

Channels

Because their information product is delivered to consumers by third parties, content providers have little say in the channel to the customer. Content providers must produce their products so they can be distributed via whatever channel the ally requires. Often the same content must be reconfigured for different channels. As additional channels to end consumers are created, content providers will undoubtedly extend their wholesale offerings into these channels as well.

Segments

Although many organizations engage in e-business to expand the number of customer segments they serve, those who take up the content provider model may be seeking to specialize and restrict this number. By working through allies, content providers can operate simpler and more focused organizations. Many content providers do serve end consumers directly, but they may not spend much on advertising this capability. Instead, content providers can directly target a relatively small group of third parties—Yahoo!, AOL, Lycos, and so on—all of whom arguably fall into the same customer segment. A key lesson from content providers is that the opportunity for disintermediation offered by the Internet need not be taken. Some organizations are better off working with and through third parties, rather than trying to serve directly the extremely large and diverse set of end consumers theoretically available over the Internet.

Who Distributes the Content to the Customer?

Having explored some of the reasons for the existence of content providers, we now turn to the reasons for the existence of their allies—the third parties who distribute their content. Some of these third parties, particularly portals such as Yahoo!, are described in chapter 7, which analyzes the intermediary atomic business model. Others—for example, Charles Schwab, using quotes from Quote.com, or Borders, using maps from MapQuest.com—are essentially direct-to-customer (chapter 4) or full-service provider (chapter 5) organizations, both in the marketplace and in the marketspace. Such organizations typically provide information from the content provider—a map to the nearest store or a stock quotation—free, to stimulate additional business. These third-party sites do not exist primarily in order to distribute content, but such content can be an important part of their success. Presumably, some of the third parties would find the content—stock quotations, for example—so important that they would generate that content themselves if they could not obtain it from someone else. Obtaining the content from a specialized provider allows these organizations to focus on their core competencies—managing funds, creating the right ambience to stimulate the sale of books—while satisfying their customers' needs for timely, accurate, and useful information.

Information and Physical Goods as Content

So far in the chapter we have defined content provider as a firm that provides information or digital products to customers via a third party. This definition leads to the critical success factors, core competencies, and infrastructure required for success with the content provider business model. These same requirements are also important for many organizations that provide physical content to customers via third parties. Consider Springs Industries, Inc. (www.springs.com), a manufacturer of bedding, bath, window, and other home fashion products. Springs's products are sold under brand names such as Wamsutta, Springmaid, and Regal through retail stores including Bloomingdale's, Macy's, Kmart, Sears, and Target.[12] In the physical world Springs provides content (sheets, towels, curtains, and so on) via third parties (the retail stores).[13] A visit to the Springs Web site makes clear that the company is focused on the characteristics of content providers: modularization and branding. Perhaps equally important is what Springs does *not* do: sell products directly on the Internet. To do so would be to invite channel conflict. Instead, the Springs site offers many pointers to retail outlets that carry its products, including a store and dealer locator system.

Many, perhaps most, manufacturing organizations selling through independent dealers or retailers can be considered content providers. The Web sites of companies making such diverse products as office furniture (www.steelcase.com), clothing (www.levi.com) and consumer products (www.gillette.com) exhibit the characteristics of content providers: branding and modularization. We believe that many organizations involved in physical content provision can profitably take onboard the findings and recommendations in this chapter as they consider e-business.

The Future

The growth of the Web has created a large number of content providers, so it is no surprise that content aggregators have begun to appear. For example, iSyndicate (www.isyndicate.com) describes itself as "the preeminent content syndication service on the Internet, distributing a broad selection of written, graphical, audio and video content from more than 700 sources, to a vast and diverse network of 169,329 Web sites."[14] iSyndicate's sources include

Reuters, Rolling Stone, CBS Sportsline, and TheStreet.com,[15] while its customers include GeoCities, Xoom.com, theglobe.com, Netscape, Clairol, PeopleSoft, Nintendo, Nortel, and NationsBank. These customers receive content from iSyndicate and seamlessly integrate it into their Web sites, maintaining the sites' branding and page layout. Will the future then include only a very few "super-aggregator" content providers, which gather content from aggregators, which in turn bring together content from subaggregators, and so on? The continuing consolidation of global media companies suggests that this is indeed the future.

As we learn how to digitize more and more products and services, it will become possible to select, buy, and deliver them via the Internet. The music industry is undergoing a major revolution as the ability to deliver music digitally using MP3 becomes possible (www.mp3.com). Money, for example, a mortgage, can also be delivered digitally, and the entire process of applying for and receiving the funds can also be digital. It will soon be common for other products and services to be delivered digitally, including consulting, tax advice, and counseling. One of the challenges for the future is whether the providers of these services (e.g., consulting firms, accounting firms, and psychologists) will choose to become content providers rather than pursuing the direct-to-customer models of today.

One of the premier content providers that has changed its business model to embrace e-business is Reuters.

CASE STUDY

CONTENT PROVIDER: **Reuters**

(www.reuters.com)

According to its Web site header, Reuters is in "the business of information." The company provides financial information and news, offering an extensive range of information products to online information services, the print media, television and radio stations, and various government and private organizations. The information includes real-time trading data on securities, commodities, futures, and options from various markets and exchanges; general and specialized news; securities transaction products; and information databases, applications, and management systems. Reuters provides data on more than 940,000 stocks, bonds, and other financial instruments, as well as on forty thousand companies, to its subscription base of over 521,000 users in 52,800 locations worldwide. Reuters estimates that more than forty million individuals on nine hundred Web sites see its information daily.

After some hesitation, Reuters—founded more than 140 years ago to gather and report information to newspapers—has fully embraced the Internet, offering "a range of major initiatives designed to accelerate its use of Internet technologies, open up new markets and migrate its core business to an Internet-based model."[16] On February 8, 2000, Reuters CEO Peter Job announced that the company would spend $800 million to migrate its services to the Internet over the next four years. Following this announcement, the price of Reuters stock increased 33 percent in two days.

This new business model provides Reuters with access to a much wider market and the realization of greater cost efficiencies. As CEO Job pointed out, "Reuters's strategy is for anyone, anywhere, anytime, to have access to personalized information services."[17] To maximize the advantages from these opportunities, Reuters expanded its capabilities through spin-offs and alliances and embarked on an extensive branding campaign.

Reuters's vision is to "deliver its real-time information products more cost effectively to certain market segments using Internet technology and an e-commerce business model."[18] To achieve this, Reuters is focusing on three business areas: Reuters Financial, Reuterspace, and Instinet. Reuters Financial includes Reuters Inform and Reuters Trading Solutions, and it is the division responsible for the development and sale of information products for professionals in financial institutions and their clients. In late 1999, Reuters Inform launched its first real-time news and information product delivered and supported entirely on the public Internet. The first modules are targeted at the global agrimarkets and the North American power market. Both modules include comprehensive market prices, breaking news, charts, weather maps, and customer bulletin boards. Reuters Inform is a first step in Reuters's drive to deliver its real-time information products directly and more cost-effectively to certain market segments using Internet technology and the direct-to-customer e-business model. The company saw the Internet as ideally suited to the needs of smaller and geographically dispersed markets throughout the world. Reuters Inform offers significantly lower delivery and administrative costs, online customer support, easy product upgrades, and direct billing by credit card.[19] The overall strategy is to "link Reuters Inform to Reuters Trading Solutions to predict and satisfy the e-business needs of the financial markets."

Reuterspace groups businesses and assets together to realize Internet-enabled opportunities for Reuters to reach wider audiences at work and at home through fixed or mobile devices. Reuterspace includes the firm's initial business, information gathering for print media. Instinet is the world's largest electronic agency brokerage firm and a member of eighteen equities exchanges in North America, Europe, and Asia. Instinet clients can communicate, negotiate, and trade electronically, either directly with one another using Instinet's block brokerage service or by linking to exchanges.

Reuters is still the world's largest international news and television agency, with twenty-one hundred journalists, photographers, and camera operators in 184 bureaus serving 154 countries. News is gathered and edited for both business and media clients in twenty-three languages. Approximately thirty thousand headlines, including third-party contributions, and over three million words are published daily under the Reuters brand.[20]

Reuters is expanding beyond the pure content provider model by adding elements of the direct-to-customer and intermediary business models. The comments from its managers reported above point to the reasons: lower administrative, support, and delivery costs; access to an expanded market; and firsthand knowledge of the workings of the new economy. In adding the new business models, Reuters focused on the critical success factors the models require. For example, in the first few months of 2000 Reuters embarked on significant marketing campaigns, including global television and print advertising campaigns for Instinet, all of which focused on Reuters brands. The firm also created numerous joint ventures, including those with FTSE International, Microsoft, and VentureSource.[21] Reuters's continued evolution into e-business illustrates the pattern of strategic experiments that we believe is the appropriate way forward for traditional firms entering the e-business world.

Summary of the Content Provider Model

Strategic Objective and Value Proposition

A content provider delivers, via third parties, information and digital products to be integrated into the parties' own offerings to their customers. The importance to these businesses and consumers of such content varies from very high (stock quotations on the Internet site of an online broker) to marginal (maps to the nearest Wal-Mart), emphasizing the need for content providers to understand both customer behavior and their own costs. Content providers must be among the world's best at what they do and generally employ teams of professionals generating world-class content. Equally important, the content provider's brand must be recognized as world-class. Content providers must be able to provide their product at a price-to-quality ratio below what it would cost their customers to generate the content themselves. End consumers of the content are attracted to the third parties' Internet sites, and stimulated to do more business with the third party, by the presence of the content.

Sources of Revenue

The primary source of revenue for a content provider is fees from its third parties or allies. These fees may be based on a fixed price per month or year, or on the number of times the third party's own customers access the content. In some situations, the fees paid are lower for content branded by the provider, and higher for unbranded content, which then appears to the customer to have been generated by the third party itself. Some content providers, for example, Morningstar, also have a direct-to-customer business, the customers of which pay a fixed or usage-based fee for direct access to the content. Such content providers must offer some value-added service to these direct customers, who would otherwise access the content free via a third party.

Critical Success Factors

To succeed, a content provider must provide reliable, timely content in the right format and at the right price. The critical success factors for this model include the following:

- **Branding.** Users of www.schwab.com or www.nationsbank.com see the phrase "quotes provided by Quote.com"[22] next to each stock quote, while Web surfers seeking the nearest Wal-Mart or Borders bookstore find "MapQuest" in the top left corner of their online maps.[23] Weather report and forecast providers WNI, Weather Services International, Weather Services division of Data Transmission Network Corporation, and AccuWeather carefully attach their names to the content delivery. The service agreements of content providers often forbid the removal of this identifying information. These organizations are so intent on branding because they recognize that the value, and hence the price, of their content is due in part to their reputation.

- **Recognized as best in class.** Content providers must strive to be the best in the world or in their region to thrive. The significant costs for the content provider are in the generation of the content by teams of professionals. As the cost of access to, and distribution of, content continues to fall, the business of content provision will be global and very competitive, with relatively low switching costs for customers. There will be significant concentration in content provision, particularly for factual information such as stock prices. Being known as best in class will be critical for content providers to thrive. There will be room for local content providers that specialize in local knowledge, but the number of global content providers will become quite small.

- **Network.** A critical success factor for content providers is establishing and maintaining a network of third parties through which content is distributed, as well as a network of content suppliers and creators. No content provider can own, or even control directly, either of these networks. Rather, these vital networks must be built and maintained on the basis of influence, exerted both through marketplace forces such as pricing and through social levers growing out of personal contacts.

Core Competencies

The successful content provider must have at least three core competencies maintained and nurtured in-house rather than outsourced.

- The fundamental core competency of a content provider is expertise and leadership in its field, whether stock analysis, weather forecasting, news, travel information, or financial data. Being a leader requires significant investment in human expertise. Nurturing, educating, and codifying this expertise will create an environment that will attract professionals to join the firm.

- The content provider must also be able to modularize, store, retrieve, combine, and deliver content so that it can be distributed in a large number of ways. Each third-party distributor may want different amounts of content in a different format, and the content provider must meet these varying requirements in an economical way. The ability to modularize content is a good sign that its characteristics have been thoroughly understood; without building and maintaining this metaknowledge, a content provider will have a difficult challenge in the evolving marketspace.

- A related competency is the ability to understand the value that third-party providers and their end consumers place on content, and to price it accordingly. Information generally has a time value; yesterday's stock quotes have very little value, quotes with a fifteen-minute delay have more value, and real-time quotes are more valuable still. But just *how* valuable? The successful content provider must keep abreast of the competition and the customers and demonstrate valuable uses for its content.

Who Owns What?

	Customer Relationship	Customer Data	Customer Transaction
Content Provider	×	×	×

CHAPTER 12

Combining Atomic Business Models into Initiatives

CHAPTERS 4 through 11 describe the eight atomic e-business models in depth. The chapters deliberately focus on firms that are reasonably close to pure implementations of each atomic model. For example, AccuWeather is an almost pure implementation of the content provider model becoming a world leader and authority in creating and disseminating weather content via portals and news services. In the remaining two chapters, we apply the lessons learned from the atomic business models to creating e-business initiatives in existing firms.

In this chapter we summarize for each model the ownership of the relationship, the data, and the transaction, and what leverage those ownerships create. We summarize the characteristics of the atomic business models: the strategic objectives, how money is made and value created, the critical success factors, and the core competencies. We also discuss the IT infrastructure needs for each atomic model, based on our study of e-business initiatives (see chapter 3 and the appendix). We then focus on composing and decomposing e-business initiatives using the atomic models. Finally, the case study of Lonely Planet continues, illustrating the company's careful migration from place to space via several major e-business initiatives.

Chapter 13 closes the book by discussing the process of designing and implementing e-business initiatives in traditional existing firms. We present a framework and scorecard to analyze the level of e-business threat and opportunity facing an existing firm. We draw links to the lessons learned about the characteristics of atomic business models and their combination into initiatives. We provide a checklist for assessing an e-business initiative and explore the links among business strategy, business models, core competencies, and success. We wrap up the book with our list of the top ten e-business leadership principles for successful place-to-space migration.

Atomic Models as Building Blocks

The atomic e-business models can be used in at least three ways:

1. **Pure types.** Atomic models describe the essence of an e-business model. Understanding the characteristics and requirements of the atomic models provides insights into the requirements for successful operation alone or in combination with other atomic models.

2. **Building blocks.** This set of atomic building blocks can be combined into e-business initiatives. Some combinations of atomic models will be viable, while others will contain inherent conflict and be unstable. The e-business activities of a particular firm may be described as a portfolio of e-business initiatives.

3. **Decomposition of e-business initiatives.** A proposed e-business initiative can be decomposed into atomic models to better understand the requirements for implementation. Comparing what is required for the implementation of each atomic model in the initiative with the firm's current capabilities is a good start in a gap analysis.

Lessons from Atomic E-Business Models

We summarize the characteristics of each atomic model before discussing how to combine them. For each model this summary includes: the schematic, the ownership pattern (relationship, data, and transaction), characteristics, and the infrastructure capabilities required for implementation.

E-Business Model Schematics

Each of the preceding eight chapters presented and analyzed the schematic for an atomic business model. A useful starting point for combining atomic models into an initiative is merging these generic atomic schematics. Part two of the Lonely Planet case study presented later in this chapter illustrates the process of combining schematics into an e-business initiative. All of the eight models are appropriate for both B2B and B2C e-business, except for content provider, which is exclusively B2B.

Ownership of the Customer Relationship, the Data, and the Transaction

In any e-business model, whether atomic or hybrid, there are three important questions of ownership: who owns the end customer relationship, the data, and the transaction. The pattern of ownership of these three assets for the eight atomic models is summarized in table 12-1 and described in detail below.

The Relationship Firms that own the customer relationship usually have the most powerful position in a business model, and the most to lose. Owning the relationship implies the following:

- The customer is a repeat purchaser from the firm.
- The firm has a set of historical data to profile the customer.
- The customer has an element of trust and brand recognition regarding the firm.

- The firm has more potential influence over the customer than other players in the model.
- The firm has the potential to earn a fee from third parties whose services are used by its customers as a result of influence by the firm.

The business model schematics identify which entity, if any, owns the relationship with the consumer. For example, in figure 2-5a, the e-broker holds the relationship with the customer, providing a detailed picture of the consumer's broking history and investment holdings. In figure 2-5b, the financial service provider holds the relationship, integrating the services of the e-broker and the insurer for the customer. The potential intimacy of the full-service provider in model B is very high, with the possibility of capturing a detailed picture of the investor's complete financial picture over time. If managed carefully, this intimacy could become a valuable asset in offering tailored services to the consumer. Owning the relationship implies that the firm also has the potential to own or co-own the customer data (see table 12-1).

TABLE 12-1 Ownership of Customer Relationship, Data, and Transaction

	Relationship	Data	Transaction
Content Provider	✗	✗	✗
Direct to Customer	✓	✓	✓
Full-Service Provider	✓	✓	✓
Intermediary	✓	✓	✗
Shared Infrastructure	✗	✓	✓
Value Net Integrator	✗	✓	✗
Virtual Community	✓	✗	✗
Whole of Enterprise/ Government	✓	✓	✓

(OWNERSHIP OF CUSTOMER)

Establishing an intimate customer relationship is a critical success factor of many of the atomic models. The models vary in potential intimacy; however, the full-service provider model is potentially much more intimate than the shared-infrastructure model. Moreover, two implementations of the same atomic model (e.g., direct-to-customer) can vary in intimacy. The level of customer intimacy achieved will largely predict the stickiness of the customer relationship and the success of the initiative. In strategizing with partners firms should strive for, and definitely not cheaply relinquish, the opportunity to own the customer relationship.

The Data   The owner of customer data has the potential to develop powerful insights into customers' needs and desires. Online businesses such as Dell, Amazon, and Barnes & Noble have the potential to track business and household customers' previous purchases and movements through their Web sites and other firms' linked sites. For some segments, utilizing customer data to deliver personalized offerings will be the path to significant profits. In a number of the atomic models, some of the customer data are co-owned. For example, when a customer buys a product via an intermediary, important data are generated and are often co-owned by the intermediary and product vendor. A firm may own only the data (as in the value net integrator), the data and the relationship (as in the intermediary), the data and the transaction (as in the shared-infrastructure), or all three (as in the direct-to-customer).

Owning the customer data implies that:

- the firm captures the data electronically and has the potential to analyze them at either the customer or the segment level, and
- the firm has more potential insight about the customer than other players in the business model.

The Transaction   Firms owning the customer transaction receive a fee or a profit margin for any service provided, including the sale of a product, the provision of information or advice, or a professional service.

Owning the transaction implies that:

- the firm receives revenue from the transaction;
- the firm also owns the customer data related to that transaction, but perhaps no other customer data, unless the firm also owns the customer relationship; and
- if the firm also owns the relationship (as in the direct-to-customer model), then in the mind of the consumer the firm has the exclusive responsibility for completion of the transaction. If the relationship is owned by another party, the customer will probably hold the other party, or perhaps the firm jointly with the other party, responsible for completing the transaction (as in the shared-infrastructure model).

Owning each of these three assets brings different types of leverage. Owning the customer relationship brings the leverage of influence. The customer looks to the relationship holder for trust, recommendations, and tailored advice. Owning the customer data brings the leverage of insight as the firm has detailed information about the history and needs or likes of the customer. Owning the customer transaction generates the leverage of revenue for service. In the example of buying a Palm Pilot from Dell via the intermediary Jango, the relationship is owned by Jango, the data are co-owned by Dell and Jango, and the transaction is owned by Dell. This is a typical pattern of ownership for an intermediary. It is also possible and potentially still profitable not to own any of the three customer assets, as is the case for the content provider model. However, as a general rule, the more of these three assets the firm exclusively owns, the more powerful and potentially profitable the model.

The assertions that owning more of these three assets is potentially more profitable and that owning the relationship creates more leverage than owning either of the other two are expressed in table 12-2. This table presents the atomic models in descending order of potential profitability. The double check marks represent

TABLE 12-2   Atomic Models Listed by Potential Profitability

	OWNERSHIP OF CUSTOMER		
	Relationship	Data	Transaction
Direct to Customer	✓✓	✓	✓
Full-Service Provider	✓✓	✓	✓
Whole of Enterprise/ Government	✓	✓	✓
Intermediary	✓	✓	✗
Shared Infrastructure	✗	✓	✓
Virtual Community	✓	✗	✗
Value Net Integrator	✗	✓	✗
Content Provider	✗	✗	✗

the potential for a particularly powerful ownership of the asset. The most potentially profitable atomic models are the direct-to-customer and the full-service provider, both of which own all three assets and may have particularly strong and intimate customer relationships. The direct-to-customer firm owns all three assets and thus has all three types of leverage, with a potentially intimate customer relationship and the strength of potentially owning all the customer's transactions in the model.

The full-service provider owns the relationship with the customer in a chosen domain (e.g., financial services) and meets the customer's complete set of needs directly and via third parties, thus collecting a more complete data picture of the customer. We see the direct-to-customer model as potentially more profitable than the full-service provider. Both models have strong customer relationships, but the extra revenue generation from owning the transaction (more immediately tangible than owning data) elevates the direct-to-customer model in terms of profitability. In the long term the full-service provider will probably overtake the profitability of the direct-to-customer model because of the strength of the broader data asset. Consequently, we expect many successful direct-to-customer firms to evolve to full-service providers.

The next most potentially profitable model is the whole-of-enterprise model, in which all three assets are owned but the customer relationship is less strong than in the first two models. The intermediary and virtual-community models have similar ownership structures, owning the relationship and some of the data, but not the transaction. Intermediaries generally own more customer data than virtual communities and thus are more potentially profitable. Virtual communities have to balance the dual objectives of creating a sense of community and leveraging the ownership of the customer data. Thus virtual communities tend to devise systems that are less aggressive toward data ownership than intermediaries.

As with any strategy, real value is determined by the success of the implementation, so table 12-2 represents only the *potential* profitability of each atomic model. Particular implementations of the models may be relatively more or less profitable, but on average we suggest the order of potential profitability is predictable—or at least as predictable as anything to do with business strategy and business models! Combining the models will create different dynamics, as we will discuss below.

Strategic Objectives and How Money Is Made

The strategic objectives and patterns of how money is made were discussed in some detail for each atomic model in the earlier chapters. Table 12-3 presents a summary of this information. As an example, consider the shared-infrastructure model, in which multiple providers choose to cooperate in some ways in order to compete more effectively. The providers agree to remove competition in some areas, sharing infrastructure investments and the aggregate information resident in the shared systems. The motivation is generally either to reduce cost via economies of scale or to make a defensive move against a potentially dominant player. The shared-infrastructure model is often started by a small group of competitors, with others waiting to see if the model works and then joining

TABLE 12-3 Strategic Objectives and How the Model Is Made for Each Atomic Model

Chapter	Business Model	Strategic Objectives	Sources of Revenue or Value
4	Direct to Customer	• Offer a lower price or be more customer-intimate than the marketplace • Bypass other value chain participants • Increase geographical reach without a physical infrastructure or sales force • Facilitate competition based on objective measures, such as price or independently rated quality	• Income for services provided to customers • Lower cost channel of distribution • Increased margin via bypassing intermediaries
5	Full-Service Provider	• Own the primary customer relationship • Meet the complete needs of a target customer segment in one domain (e.g., financial services, travel, etc.) • Integrate the firm's own products and services with a selected set of third-party providers	• Annual membership fees • Fees as a percentage of assets under management • Transaction fees • Margins on in-house products • Commissions on third-party products • Advertising or listing fees from third-party providers • Fees for selling leads or aggregated data about customers

(continued)

Chapter	Business Model	Strategic Objectives	Sources of Revenue or Value
6	Whole of Enterprise	• Implement a single point of contact for certain customer segments of a multiple-business-unit enterprise • Organize by life events or areas of interest so that the customer is able to navigate through the enterprise-wide offerings • Act as a pointer to various business unit offerings • Help the customer identify the need for, choose, and acquire services provided by a number of different business units	• In the for-profit sector: provision of services to the customer by the business unit; annual service or membership fees are possible • In the government sector: improved service (e.g., 24/7), reduced cost from sharing more infrastructure and removing the need to perform the same transaction (e.g., address change) in multiple agencies
7	Intermediaries	• Provide a single point of access, bringing together buyers and sellers • Make a market by concentrating information	• Transaction fees • Listing fees • Referral fees on the basis of clickthroughs • Sales commissions
8	Shared Infrastructure	• Multiple providers cooperate in some areas in order to compete more effectively • Remove competition in some areas sharing infrastructure and aggregate industry information resident in those shared systems • Reduce cost via economies of scale • Make a defensive move against a potentially dominant player • Provide a powerful barrier to entry for alternative providers	• Membership fees from shared-infrastructure customers • Transaction fees from alliance partners and customers • Sale of data summarizing customer and partner activity • Proprietary equipment rental • Logistics services

9	Virtual Community	• Build a community of members around a common interest • Capture increasing returns as community grows	• Membership fees • Advertising revenue from third parties (e.g., vendors) wishing to gain access to the community • Clickthrough fees or commissions on purchases made by members • Sale of aggregate or profile data on members • Direct sale of goods and services
10	Value Net Integrator	• Coordinate the value net (or chain) by gathering, synthesizing, and distributing information • Occupy a central position in an industry value net (or chain) with the best access to information • Improve the effectiveness of the value net (or chain) by working with other participants	• Franchise fees or a share of profit/revenue of other value net participants from controlling the virtual value chain • Share in increased revenues or decreased costs of the members of the value net
11	Content Provider	• Develop and provide information or digital product content via allies • World-class in an area of expertise	• Monthly fees for content • Fees for content or pages accessed by end consumer

later. If successful, the shared-infrastructure business model can capture almost complete market share, creating a powerful barrier to entry for alternative providers.

Revenues can be generated both from membership fees and from transaction fees. The alliance may be run on a for-profit or nonprofit basis. Nonprofit alliances are typically open to all eligible organizations and distribute any excess of revenues over costs back to their members. The for-profit models are typically owned by a subset of the firms in a given segment—Australian distributors of alcoholic beverages, for example—who divide up any profits among themselves. Other potential sources of revenue include information dissemination, equipment provision, and the logistics around fulfillment of the service (e.g., shipping and handling fees).

Critical Success Factors and Core Competencies

Table 12-4 presents a summary of the critical success factors and core competencies for each atomic model. Continuing the illustration, the shared-infrastructure model must achieve a critical mass of both alliance partners and customers and present product data objectively rather than favoring any one participant. In the nature of infrastructure investments, these electronic alliances will have high fixed costs, which must be spread across a sufficiently wide base to enable the alliance to be viable. Any one partner dominating or gaining major advantage will discourage the other participants and reduce the success of the model.

The core competencies listed in table 12-4 are necessary for every shared industry infrastructure business and should be developed, nurtured, and maintained in-house. For a shared-infrastructure business to outsource these competencies would reduce the effectiveness of the business. For example, to achieve the critical success factor of critical mass, the skill to manage a focused coalition of competitors, generally having diverse backgrounds, resources, and goals, is required. Bringing together competitors and agreeing on what to share and where to compete takes patience and strong negotiation skills.

TABLE 12-4 Critical Success Factors and Core Competencies for Each Atomic Model

Chapter	Business Model	Critical Success Factors	Core Competencies
4	Direct to Customer	• Create and maintain customer awareness directly or via intermediaries • Increase repeat customer purchase rate and size of the average transaction • Reduce customer acquisition costs • Manage potential brand and channel conflicts • Offer fast and efficient service, including transaction processing, logistics, and payment • Insure adequate security for organization and customers • Provide interfaces that combine ease of use with richness of experience • Balance availability of multiple channels with cost of supporting them • Enable easy and secure payments	• Form and manage strategic partnerships with suppliers, fulfillment houses, and others in the supply chain • Use customer information to increase sales and service • Use marketing and effective customer prospecting • Manage business processes and systems integration • Create own content
5	Full-Service Provider	• Be a leader in the domain (e.g., financial services) • Create the brand, leadership, credibility, and trust necessary for a customer to look to the firm for its complete needs in an area • Own the customer relationship in one domain; integrate and consolidate the offerings of many third parties into a single channel or channels	• Form and manage strong, enduring relationships with customers • Create a strong value proposition involving brand, breadth of offerings, price/value equation, and completeness of the consolidation into a single offering • Collect, synthesize, and analyze information about customer segments and match these with existing and new service offerings

(continued)

Chapter	Business Model	Critical Success Factors	Core Competencies
5	Full-Service Provider *(continued)*	• Own more of the customer data in the domain than any other player • Manage tension between internal and external products • Create and enforce policies to protect interests of internal and external providers as well as customers	• Develop and integrate firmwide transaction processing, customer databases, and electronic linkages to suppliers and security • Develop and nurture a trusted brand to set the expectation to credibly deliver all the customer's needs in one domain; scan the environment to identify third-party products and establish partnerships • Maintain and use a customer relationship database; anticipate changes in customer needs
6	Whole of Enterprise	• Change customer behavior to make use of the new enterprise-wide model • Reduce costs in the business units as the direct demands on them fall; manage transfer pricing • Take an enterprise-wide view that includes broad product awareness, training, cross-selling, and incentives • Identify compelling and practical life events that customers use as triggers to access the enterprise • Reengineer business processes to link to life events at the front end and to existing legacy processes and systems at the back end	• Identify channels and life events that are meaningful to customers • Move the enterprise from a business-unit orientation to an enterprise-wide orientation • Manage complex, heterogeneous system environments • Negotiate (and police) agreements among managers of different organizational units

7	Intermediaries	• Attain a critical mass of users
• Capture data on customer needs; complete any uncompleted transactions
• Scale up infrastructure quickly
• Increase level of service completeness over time
• Own customer relationship, resulting in high level of "stickiness"
		• Evolve a business model that meets changing customer expectations
• Achieve the desired level of service completeness
• Perform customer information analysis and segmentation
• Collect, synthesize, and use information about products, prices, and customer needs
8	Shared Infrastructure	• Share benefits equitably with no dominant partner
• Present product and service information objectively
• Achieve a critical mass of both alliance partners and customers
• Manage channel conflict with the ongoing e-business initiatives of the alliance partners
• Compile and deliver accurate and timely statements of the services and benefits provided to each member of the alliance
• Create and maintain systems' interoperability
		• Deliver the infrastructure service(s) around which the alliance was formed
• Manage a focused coalition of competitors, generally having diverse backgrounds, resources, and goals
• Run complex infrastructures efficiently
9	Virtual Community	• Find and retain members who share a common interest
• Build loyalty to the community by providing attractive content
• Maintain privacy and security of member information
• Balance commercial potential with members' interests
• Leverage member profile information with service providers
		• Discover customer needs and understand the value customers attach to meeting those needs
• Build an enduring sense of community
• Source attractive content

(continued)

Chapter	Business Model	Critical Success Factors	Core Competencies
10	Value Net Integrator	• Reduce ownership of physical assets while retaining ownership of data assets • Own or have access to the complete industry virtual value chain • Establish a trusted brand recognized at all places in the value chain • Operate in markets where information can add significant value, such as those that are complex, fragmented, regulated, multilayered, inefficient, large with many sources of information, and require specialized knowledge • Present the information to customers, allies, partners, and suppliers in clear and innovative ways that provide value • Help other value chain participants capitalize on the information provided by the value net integrator	• Manage relationships with customers and all major players in the value chain • Manage information assets by collecting, synthesizing, distributing, and presenting information • Link the IT architecture to strategic objectives • Develop and manage the brand • Analyze and interpret information from multiple sources • Identify and use levers of influence, rather than direct control • Evaluate cost and customer benefit from various types of information
11	Content Provider	• Provide reliable, timely content in the right format and at the right price • Brand content to create customer recognition • Be recognized as best in class • Establish a network of allies through which content is disseminated	• Provide leadership and expertise in the field • Maintain a critical mass of professional content creators • Modularize, store, retrieve, combine, and distribute content at a reasonable cost • Understand marketplace value and pricing of content

IT Infrastructures

In chapter 3 we described our study of the IT infrastructure services necessary for implementing e-business initiatives. We visited and interviewed either the CIO or the infrastructure manager in large firms that are collectively implementing fifty major e-business initiatives. The overall results are summarized in the appendix. The chapters on each atomic business model listed the most important infrastructure services needed for the success of the model.[1] Table 12-5 summarizes the critical infrastructure categories for each atomic business model. The table indicates the most important areas of infrastructure service; each area has between two and twenty services. Other infrastructure services will be needed to implement each of the atomic models, but these services are the most important by relative investment levels. For example, all atomic models use security services, but in no model is it the most important area. For a detailed list of the infrastructure services needed for each atomic model see the end of the chapter on that model (chapters 4 to 11).

Direct to Customer The direct-to-customer model requires significant investment and reliance on three areas of infrastructure service: application infrastructure, communications, and IT management (see table 12-5). In the area of application infrastructure, implementing a direct-to-customer model requires investment in payment transaction processing (see Appendix: Service 1.13), ERP (Service 1.8) and workflow (Service 1.12) infrastructure services. These three services all relate to the task of automating and integrating the firm's systems; the payment-processing systems collect the funds, and the ERP systems process the transactions. The workflow infrastructure is necessary to optimize business process performance. The direct-to-customer model typically services many customers, who generate millions of transactions a month. ERPs are typically the transaction-processing engine for these firms, and any e-business initiative thus requires extensive investment in ERP integration, fine tuning, and data management.

Three other infrastructure services are very important for the direct-to-customer model: communication network services, which link all points in the enterprise to one another and to the outside

TABLE 12-5 Summary of IT Infrastructure Investments for Atomic Models

Atomic E-Business Models	Application Infrastructure	Communication	Data Management	IT Management	Security	Architecture and Standards	Channel Management	IT Research and Development	IT Education
Number of Services	13	7	6	9	4	20	7	2	2
Content Provider	✓✓	✓	✓	✓	*	✓	✓		
Direct to Customer	✓✓	✓	✓	✓✓	*				
Full-Service Provider	✓	✓	✓	✓	*		✓	✓✓	
Intermediary	✓✓	✓	✓	✓✓	*				
Shared Infrastructure					*	✓✓			
Value Net Integrator	✓	✓	✓		*	✓	✓✓		
Virtual Community	✓			✓✓	*			✓	✓
Whole of Enterprise	✓✓	✓	✓✓	✓	*			✓	

✓✓ = very important   ✓ = important   * = required

world, often using the IP protocol; the installation and maintenance of workstations and local area networks (LANs), supporting the large number of people required to operate a direct-to-customer model; and service-level agreements between the business and the IT group or outsourcer to ensure, monitor, and improve the systems necessary for a direct-to-customer model.

Full-Service Provider The full-service provider model requires significant integration between multiple business units within the firm and a series of third-party providers, all packaged into a single offering to the customer. For many firms, achieving this level of integration requires a significant increase in the centralized management of IT infrastructure capacity, including capacity management and tracking. This change has a technical component, moving from managing multiple systems, often on different platforms across multiple business units, to a centralized model integrating or linking multiple systems. The change also needs a more difficult cultural shift to emphasizing and rewarding firmwide needs and goals rather than those of the individual business units, requiring strong leadership and a different IT governance structure.

The move to centralized governance and management of IT also requires evaluating proposals for IT initiatives and identifying and testing new technologies for business purposes. A centralized service for evaluating proposals is required to coordinate IT investment across a multi-business-unit firm with the goal of a single point of customer contact. The full-service provider model is not workable if each business unit optimizes its own IT needs. Providing electronic support to groups is another important service to facilitate the cross-business-unit teams needed for the model, which are supported by increased investment in the installation and maintenance of workstations and LANs. The move to a more centralized infrastructure is expensive in dollar terms and time-consuming in organizational terms, requiring leadership, cooperation, and often a change in incentive schemes to reward firmwide performance.

Whole of Enterprise The whole-of-enterprise model also enables a single point of customer access to a multi-business-unit organization, often organized by life events or topics of interest. Implementing this model effectively also requires centrally managed infrastructure capacity and identifying and testing new technologies for business purposes. Implementing the whole-of-enterprise model doesn't usually require the high level of integration of applications and platforms that the direct-to-customer model does. Instead, the whole-of-enterprise model needs services that summarize data from the different applications and platforms to provide a firmwide perspective. This firmwide perspective is often achieved via the electronic provision of management information and the management of key data independent of applications, perhaps in a data warehouse or similar system. The whole-of-enterprise model also requires significant investment for transaction processing including: ERP, transaction payment processing such as EFT to receive payment, and large-scale data processing to reduce the cost of transactions.

Intermediary Intermediaries generate value by concentrating information and bringing together buyers and sellers. To manage this highly information-intensive business requires infrastructure services supporting knowledge management such as knowledge databases and contact databases that enable the codification and sharing of knowledge. The intermediary e-business model, more than many of the other models, is fundamentally an electronic business trading in information about buyers and sellers. The products and services are all electronic and the business relies completely on IT, investing heavily in workstation networks. Intermediaries also invest heavily in infrastructure services to manage and get value from IT, including information systems planning and information systems project management. As most of the communication with customers, suppliers, and allies is electronic, intermediaries invest heavily in workstation networks and policies for the use of email and the Internet.

Shared Infrastructure The shared-infrastructure business model requires competitors to cooperate by sharing IT infrastructure and information. This level of cooperation requires agreement on high-level IT architectures as well as operational standards for applications, data communications, and technology. Effective implementation of the shared-infrastructure model also requires enforcement of these standards, and most shared-infrastructure models have a joint committee to set and enforce the standards. Another role of these committees is to implement the policies of the shared infrastructure about what information, if any, is shared and what information is confidential to partner firms.

Virtual Community The virtual-community model brings together a group of members around a common interest. To maximize the effectiveness of the community, members should be well informed and educated on the use of the technology. Similar to the intermediary, the virtual community is an online business, and it therefore invests heavily in IT management infrastructure services including information systems planning and workstations and LANs. Many virtual communities outsource the IT required to support the community to application service providers. Technology for supporting virtual communities is specialized, and the managers of these communities often prefer to focus on nurturing the community and designing the services rather than providing the technology platform. To keep their communities attractive and leading edge, managers of virtual communities invest heavily in the infrastructure service area of IT research and development. This area includes both infrastructure services for identifying and testing new technologies and the service for evaluating proposals for new information systems initiatives.

Value Net Integrator The value net integrator succeeds in its role by gathering, synthesizing, and distributing information. To collect and analyze information from many sources, value net integrators need centralized data warehousing in order to summarize data from decentralized databases. Heavy investment is also made in middleware to link systems on different platforms and in telecommunications network services. To function, a value net integrator requires IT infrastructure services that link together different technology platforms owned by different firms. Achieving this integration requires high-level architectures to increase compatibility.

Content Provider Content providers deal in large amounts of information including images, maps, and video, requiring significant investments in storage farms or storage area networks. Content providers require a strong focus on architecture, including setting and enforcing standards particularly for data, work, applications, and telecommunications. Content providers, like intermediaries, are fundamentally an online business and invest heavily in workstation network infrastructures. Content providers must excel at tailoring and manipulating their core content to meet the specific needs of customers. Content providers of digital products must categorize and store their content in well-indexed modules so it can be customized to meet customer needs via a wide variety of channels. To provide compatible and integrated systems, content providers invest heavily in common systems development environments. Customers and transactions tend to be relatively few, at least compared with the number of end consumers and their transactions.

Combining the Atomic Models

To illustrate the combination of atomic models into an e-business initiative and analyze the opportunities and challenges faced by a traditional firm migrating to e-business, we return to the case study of Lonely Planet.

CASE STUDY

LONELY PLANET PUBLICATIONS: **Traveling from Place to Space, Part 2**

(www.lonelyplanet.com)

Lonely Planet, a successful book publisher in the physical marketplace, illustrates many of the issues facing traditional businesses as they consider migrating to the marketspace. Lonely Planet has more than five hundred titles, most of which are distributed via intermediaries through multiple physical and electronic channels to multiple customer segments, including backpackers and time-poor ex-backpackers with money. Lonely Planet's key assets include a loyal customer base, an internationally known brand, motivated and highly qualified writers and editorial staff, and a significant amount of intellectual capital embedded in Lonely Planet's people and documents. How has Lonely Planet proceeded with e-business?

In early 1999, Lonely Planet announced its first public venture into e-business. Lonely Planet formed a joint venture with eKorp.com (now eKit.com), a Silicon Valley telecommunications start-up, to produce eKno, an interactive communications service for international travelers.[2] eKno included a free email account, a global voice mail account accessible via free-call numbers in forty countries, and inexpensive international long-distance calls. The service was promoted on the Lonely Planet Web site and by tear-out cards in Lonely Planet guidebooks. Bryan Rowe, the CEO and founder of eKorp.com, predicted that the service would generate revenues of A$7 million in 1999, A$37 million in 2000, and A$1 billion in 2004. Rowe estimated that telecommunications usage in the travel segment was about U.S.$10 billion per year. "We think that for international travellers the ability to access a voice mailbox and leave messages for their parents and/or friends back home will prove very attractive," Rowe said. "Similarly, the ability to leave messages for travellers which they can pick up at their own convenience will also be very attractive."[3] Lonely Planet receives a percentage of revenue generated from the promotion of eKno in Lonely Planet books and on the Lonely Planet Web site.[4]

In mid-2000, Lonely Planet CEO Steve Hibbard described the company's experience with eKno as a "mixed bag." "The service is growing at 20 percent per month," Hibbard said, "but it has not met the original 'hockey stick' revenue projections. Eighty percent of the people who try the service once continue to use it, but getting people to try the service has been more difficult than expected."[5] Lonely Planet had always intended to use the eKno mail service as a platform for other products, since the service provided a means for regular contact with the company's customer base. However, even as Lonely Planet worked to integrate eKno fully into its Web site, eKorp began providing travel content on its own site. The potential for a service such as eKno to become the global all-in-one budget communication service for independent travelers was clear. The question was whether Lonely Planet's version of the service would prevail over those offered by eKorp's competitors, or indeed by eKorp itself and the other resellers of eKorp's services.

A second Lonely Planet e-business initiative was driven by the explosion in handheld computers, the manufacture of which were expected to exceed twenty-five million by 2001. A product of Lonely Planet called CitySync, "the personal digital guide to urban adventure," was created; it allowed owners of a Palm Computing, Handspring, or other Palm OS Connected Organizer to load up their handheld devices with Lonely Planet city guides. The city guides contained all the types of information typically found in a book version, including attractions, hotels and restaurants, transportation options, safety tips, and quick tours in a growing number of CitySync cities. All information in the CitySync guides was searchable and hyperlinked. CitySync customers could easily sort, view, and annotate this information on their handheld computers. By mid-2000, CitySync cities included Chicago, Hong Kong, Las Vegas, Paris, San Francisco, Sydney, Los Angeles, New York City, Bangkok, London, Miami, and New Orleans. For U.S.$19.99, digital information about a city could be downloaded in seconds to a customer's PC and then to a handheld device. Free trials were available, in the form of software that was fully functional for twenty-four hours before it self-destructed. The information could also be purchased on a CD-ROM from retail outlets. Lonely Planet provided content, branding, and distribution for CitySync, and it retained rights to the content. An outside organization called Concept Kitchen was hired to do the necessary programming for CitySync and to provide technical support.

Steve Hibbard feels it's still too early to tell whether the offering will be a success. The Web site (www.citysync.com) attracts lots of visitors, and online sales of CitySync increase each week. Nevertheless, Hibbard believes that older forms of distribution might ultimately prove more important than the Internet. "Delivering a CD-ROM in a box may remain a big part of the business," Hibbard said, pointing out that some potential customers for CitySync either were not connected to the Internet or were not comfortable downloading information or paying online.[6]

The travel content in both eKno and CitySync is drawn from Lonely Planet's extensive store of travel-related information. Traditionally, the company developed its books using decentralized, text-based systems that were not linked to any central database. Content was thus stored in a variety of locations and formats, resulting in inefficiencies, including the occasional production of duplicate material. Moreover, very little of Lonely Planet's traditional content was accessible via the Internet. In mid-1999, Lonely Planet began the Knowledge Bank project, with the ultimate goal of transferring all of its intellectual property to a standardized and centralized database. All information—text, images, and maps—would eventually be stored digitally, in a format that included highly accurate data about physical locations. The Knowledge Bank is intended to enable Lonely Planet to more easily maintain and update current information, to tailor information for specific products, and to eliminate duplicate research and storage. The Knowledge Bank also offers various longer term business opportunities, including the ability to license and syndicate content to outside organizations.

Ron Gallagher, the first staff member assigned full-time to the Knowledge Bank project, was given a three-part brief: organize Lonely Planet's existing content, try some experiments with new technology, and write up the lessons learned. Gallagher observed that even Lonely Planet's most extensive guidebooks held only a small fraction of the information gathered by writers in the field; in order to list five restaurants in a given city, for example, an author had probably visited twenty. Thus, instead of focusing on the text of Lonely Planet's existing publications, Gallagher set out to make better use of field research data. Aiming initially at an "out-to-eat" guide for Melbourne, Gallagher developed a paper-based template for collecting information about restaurants. This marked the first time that Lonely Planet had required its writers to collect information in any particular format. When he reviewed the answers to the template question "Smoking?" Gallagher found twenty-seven different responses across a sample of 430 restaurants. To establish greater consistency, and to get the field data into a more convenient form, Gallagher equipped authors with handheld devices programmed to accept only a limited range of responses to each question. When the data about a site—restaurant, hotel, attraction, and so on—were transferred from the author's handheld device into the Knowledge Bank database, they were labeled with the precise latitude and longitude of the site.

"Our main problems," Gallagher said, "are determining which places to choose, and how deep to go. We collected forty-two data items about the restaurants in Melbourne, for example, and that may be too many fields. Our next guide, for Sydney, will use only twelve data items. Eventually, it could be possible to produce all of our publication products out of a single database—but before that can happen there must be high confidence internally in the Knowledge Bank. The information we're collecting can be accessed over the Internet, but my main focus is still on facilitating the internal sharing of information."[7]

Considering eKno, CitySync, and the Knowledge Bank, Steve Hibbard commented, "We don't have an integrated, company-wide plan for using new technology. Instead, we are using 'skunk works' and strategic experiments. As CEO, my role in supporting new initiatives can be crucial. Although others do 99 percent of the work, my 1 percent can make the difference. A major challenge will be introducing these new technologies while maintaining the unique Lonely Planet style, voice and brand positioning—these are essential to the success of any new Lonely Planet business initiative." Hibbard continued, "One of the challenges of e-business initiatives is whether we should relax the business case requirement for new titles of meeting a 50 percent gross margin threshold. With an e-business initiative the revenue stream is so hard to predict that we can't be confident about the revenue or the gross margin."[8] Another issue facing Hibbard is how, or indeed whether, to convert the two million unique monthly visitors to the Lonely Planet Web site into a revenue stream. Recent tracking of the Web site visitors in comparison with the sales of books revealed the following breakdown.

Region	Web Visitors (percent)	Book Sales (percent)
North America	70	38
Asia Pacific	15	22 (Asia 10, Australia 12)
Europe	15	40

Lonely Planet Business Model Schematic

Lonely Planet has approached e-business via a series of initiatives, as well as an investment in the major building block needed for future initiatives: the Knowledge Bank. There are four major initiatives.

1. The Lonely Planet Web site, which includes upgrades to currently published guides, the Thorn Tree community chat room, and links to useful information sites, but contains no advertising or links to vendors other than eKno. The Web site is targeted to all Lonely Planet customer segments but is particularly useful to the traveler on the road. The breakdown of Web site visitors listed previously shows the disproportionately high use of the site by Americans relative to book sales.

2. The eKno product, an interactive communications service for international travelers, which is targeted at all customer segments but particularly at backpackers who will be on the road for long periods and thus hard to contact.

3. The CitySync product, enabling owners of handheld devices to pay for and download city guides containing

information about attractions, hotels and restaurants, transportation options, safety tips, maps, and quick tours in a growing number of cities. The CitySync product is targeted to the time-poor, cash-rich Lonely Planet customers who already own handheld devices and travel mainly to cities.

4. The Knowledge Bank project, which aims to digitize, index, standardize, and make available all Lonely Planet content (text, images, and maps) to be used electronically or physically.

To analyze Lonely Planet's migration to e-business we will use the business models introduced in chapter 2. Combining the first three e-business initiatives above with the existing book and content business generates the e-business model schematic in figure 12-1. The business model for Lonely Planet is a combination of three atomic e-business models:

• *Content provider:* Lonely Planet creates branded and unbranded travel content that is distributed through a number of allies, including the sale of books via electronic and physical bookstores such as Amazon.com and Borders. Lonely Planet content is sold to allies like Travelocity and Yahoo!, which use it to attract visitors or to sell travel services. If any player owns the customer relationship with travelers C and D (in figure 12-1), it's the ally, not Lonely Planet, even though much of the content is branded. Other users of travel content, such as publishers of in-flight magazines, also purchase Lonely Planet content. The content Lonely Planet supplies to allies ranges in quantity from one photograph or map to an integrated package of material—text, photos, maps, and diagrams.

• *Virtual community:* Lonely Planet has created a thriving virtual community that revolves around their Web site, which receives three million hits a day from two million unique visitors a month. The center of the virtual community is the Thorn Tree bulletin board, on which travelers and potential travelers post more than fifteen hundred messages a day. The uses of the

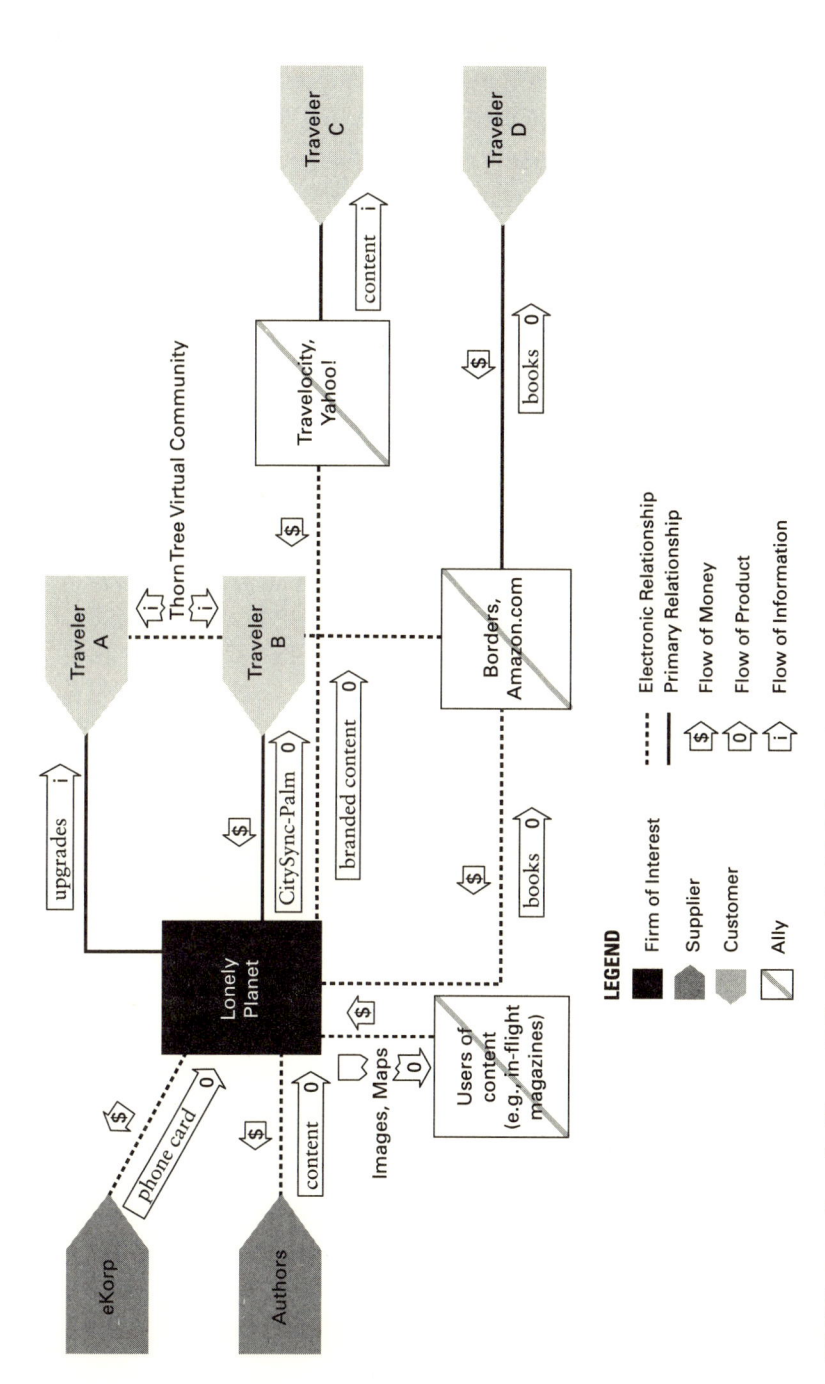

FIGURE 12-1 Lonely Planet E-Business Model Schematic

bulletin board are limited only by the imagination, and many Lonely Planet virtual community members are very imaginative. Members are not required to register but often identify themselves or at least provide an email address. The Thorn Tree is used extensively for travelers on the road to share up-to-the-minute travel information. For example, we found very helpful postings on Thorn Tree about the trail ahead during a recent trek in the Himalayas. Thorn Tree users are not shy about providing feedback to Lonely Planet about their recent offerings or initiatives. For example, typical comments on Thorn Tree about the new CitySync product range from "wonderful new product" to "Lonely planet has finally sold out." Lonely Planet has succeeded in creating a thriving, dedicated, and frank travel community.

- *Direct to customer:* Lonely Planet has made a careful entry into the direct-to-customer business model. Both the CitySync and eKno products provide services direct to consumers. eKno is a new product offering for Lonely Planet, while CitySync is a product extension using a new channel. Lonely Planet also sells books via their Web site, but only at the full recommended retail price plus shipping. Sales of books direct to end customers are very small. The direct-to-customer model is also used to provide upgrades of guides to travelers during the typically two- or three-year cycle between new editions. Direct interaction with consumers requires a different set of competencies for Lonely Planet, including potentially dealing with millions of consumers rather than with a smaller number of allies. Direct-to-customer requires payment to be collected and physical or electronic distribution. For the eKno and CitySync products, Lonely Planet has formed alliances with eKorp and Concept Kitchen, which handle much of the consumer interaction. Lonely Planet provides the content and carefully retains stewardship of the brand. Introduction of these direct-to-customer products mark the first time Lonely Planet has had the means to communicate directly with travelers on the road, and they offer many exciting opportunities.

The schematic in figure 12-1 is a combination of three of the business model schematics (content provider, virtual community, and direct-to-customer). Decomposing figure 12-1 into the three atomic schematics reveals a number of interesting issues for Lonely Planet.

• *Channel conflict:* The potential for significant channel conflict exists for Lonely Planet with the same products (books or content) being sold via multiple channels. Lonely Planet has worked hard to minimize channel conflict by selling books on their Web site only at the recommended retail price, thus not undercutting their retail resellers. Most retailers hold only a small selection of the five hundred Lonely Planet titles, and for the many titles they do not hold, channel conflict is minimal. The CitySync product is also carefully positioned to reduce channel conflict, since it targets a specific segment (time-poor, cash-rich travelers) with a new offering that is somewhat different from the existing Lonely Planet city guidebooks. However, over time there may be some conflict between CitySync and products such as customized guidebooks.

• *No vendors in the virtual community:* Comparing the atomic model schematic for the virtual community in chapter 9 with the part of figure 12-1 that represents the virtual community (the part touching travelers A and B) flags a major difference. In the atomic model for the virtual community (figure 9-1) there is a link from a vendor (supplier 2) directly to a member (member 2). The virtual community forms a relationship with supplier 2, which then offers its products and services to members. The virtual community usually receives a fee or commission on sales, represented by the flow of money from supplier 2 to the virtual community. As indicated in figure 12-1, Lonely Planet has not created these alliances with vendors to sell to virtual community members. This decision raises the question of whether Lonely Planet should generate profit from the virtual community directly or consider it a cost of brand building.

- *Owning customer relationships:* Figure 12-1 illustrates the potential to own a number of customer relationships with travelers. Yahoo! owns traveler C's customer relationship and Amazon.com owns traveler D, but Lonely Planet potentially owns travelers A and B. This is a new opportunity for Lonely Planet, and a key strategic decision will be whether they should endeavor to build that customer relationship. Building the relationship requires collecting detailed information about travelers A and B over time and slowly moving all those customers' purchases and interactions to be direct, rather than through intermediaries (e.g., Borders).

- *The need for content to be delivered across multiple channels:* One particularly clear insight from figure 12-1 is that Lonely Planet will need to be able to deliver all its content over a number of different channels. This insight strongly supports Lonely Planet's initiative through the Knowledge Bank to get its content digitized, indexed, and ready for whatever unpredictable future e-business will bring.

- *Core competencies and critical success factors:* A scan of the critical success factors and core competencies for each of the three atomic models pursued by Lonely Planet quickly reveals some potential conflicts and gaps. For example, the critical success factor for a direct-to-customer model of fast and efficient service including transaction processing, logistics, and payment is an area where Lonely Planet will need to invest. Building competencies in the new areas must be done while still modularizing, storing, retrieving, combining, and distributing content at a reasonable cost and establishing a network of allies through which to disseminate content, both of which are needed by a content provider. Balancing and allocating resources between these somewhat competing competencies will be major task for Lonely Planet's management team.

Challenges Facing Lonely Planet

A number of other opportunities and challenges face Lonely Planet and any other business migrating to e-business—particularly those businesses with a product that could potentially be delivered electronically. Specifically:

1. Managing channel conflict and ally anxiety if Lonely Planet continues to build the direct-to-customer business. We will discuss some general approaches to channel conflict in chapter 13.

2. How Lonely Planet makes investment decisions for completely new e-business initiatives. It will be very difficult to build a convincing case that a new e-business product will meet the 50 percent gross profit threshold. Instead, the firm will need to consider these initiatives as strategic experiments with seed funding and minimal investment, perhaps through alliances. If these initiatives are successful, Lonely Planet will need to quickly support and integrate them by investing capital and management attention.

3. Lonely Planet has a huge opportunity to reinvent the travel guide by creating customized guides that cover only a traveler's desired destinations, having content tailored to the traveler's interests, and delivering the guides and their updates electronically and on the road.

4. A further question is how, if at all, Lonely Planet should attempt to derive revenue from the two million individuals who visit their Web site each month. Selling third-party products or accepting advertising would be a big change for the company's brand image, and it would move them toward either an intermediary or a full-service provider model.

Portfolio of E-Business Initiatives Plus Building Blocks

We believe Lonely Planet's approach to e-business is sensible and potentially useful to many other firms. Lonely Planet has invested in a portfolio of e-business initiatives for different target customer segments. The failure rate will probably be higher than for its traditional products, but the upside potential is also much greater. Having a portfolio of these initiatives will reduce the overall risk of e-business investment, and one initiative may well be the harbinger for the future of the Lonely Planet business.

The exact form of successful e-business for Lonely Planet is uncertain and perhaps unpredictable. However, there is no doubt that the Lonely Planet content will need to be delivered in customized packages down many different channels. Thus, creating the Knowledge Bank is a sound investment that will pay off many times over. Like any infrastructure investment, the Knowledge Bank's costs will be hard to justify and will take some time to pay off, but the sheer existence of the Knowledge Bank will stimulate new ways of doing business. A hard decision will be how to index the content and which technology platforms to use.

CHAPTER 13

Choosing and Implementing an E-Business Initiative

TRITE ADVICE abounds for senior executives to "act fast or die" or "just get started" with e-business. Fueling this frenzy of advice was the high market valuation of dot-coms, many of which had yet to make a profit and most of which were experiencing the challenges familiar to all start-up businesses: achieving positive cash flow, arranging logistics, finding and retaining personnel, negotiating supplier arrangements, and creating a brand. Many dot-coms will fail or be acquired—but a few will dominate their markets and become the commercial powerhouses of the future. All the attention paid to the dot-coms in particular, and to e-business in general, was a wake-up call to traditional firms that put tremendous pressure on senior executives to act decisively, demonstrating to the market that they are e-business savvy.

This final chapter lays out a way forward for existing firms, balancing the opportunities and threats of e-business with the traditional firm's assets and liabilities. The way forward begins with a test of the threat and opportunity from e-business for a particular firm, indicating the level of urgency for action. We then provide a framework for e-business strategizing, linking the firm's strategic intent and competencies with e-business building blocks and a portfolio of e-business initiatives. One of the results of this strategizing is a series of proposed e-business initiatives requiring evaluation. We present a framework for evaluating a particular e-business initiative, identifying the risks and the potential pressure points. The book closes with our top ten leadership principles for senior management, who must guide their firms into a world combining the best of the old—place-based business—with the best of the new—space-based e-business. This is a watershed time for traditional firms—an opportunity to rethink their business models; because the market will expect and tolerate change inspired by e-business, it will be unforgiving of firms not migrating, at least in part, to space.

Test for the Level of Threat or Opportunity from E-Business

We have found the following structured approach very helpful to test for the size of threat or opportunity e-business creates for a firm. In our minds there is little difference between e-business threats and opportunities. Other firms threatening a firm's livelihood are a strong signal that there are also real opportunities. Indeed all firms already have many valuable assets for doing business electronically. In our experience a successful traditional firm is generally in as good a position to capitalize on e-business opportunities as a new entrant. Capitalizing on the opportunity may require changing the business model. In fact, we believe that new business models will be needed by many agents, including travel agents, real estate agents, stockbrokers, and insurance agents. Capitalizing will also require new skills and a clear understanding of the firm's core competencies and its value proposition to particular market segments. Most important of all, capitalizing on e-business will require strong, clear leadership by senior management.

To provide an indication of the level of opportunity and threat for your firm, we suggest you work though the following ten issues. Each issue was chosen because of the impact of e-business on cost or value delivery.[1] The larger the potential impact on your firm or your customers, the greater the potential threat or opportunity from e-business. Taken together, your answers provide a good indicator of the level of threat and opportunity. For each issue read the description in the text and then indicate on a scale of 1 to 5 whether the answer to the question is very small (1) or very large (5) for either your customers or your firm in creating value for your customers. Place your answer in table 13-1.

Digitally Describe or Deliver

How large is the potential to digitally describe or deliver your products? Firms selling products more easily described (books, CDs) or delivered (software, music) digitally face significantly higher opportunity and threat from e-business. The major recording companies (e.g., Sony) may well survive and even thrive, but only if

TABLE 13-1 E-Business Opportunity or Threat Indicator

How large is the:	Very Small				Very Large
potential to digitally describe or deliver your product?	1	2	3	4	5
potential to generate price or cost reductions via Internet technologies?	1	2	3	4	5
potential to undermine customer loyalty (to counter brand identification or switching costs)?	1	2	3	4	5
gap between actual and potential customer self-service?	1	2	3	4	5
potential and practical geographical reach for your product?	1	2	3	4	5
potential for dynamic pricing?	1	2	3	4	5
potential of knowledge management?	1	2	3	4	5
online customer base?	1	2	3	4	5
opportunity for online product customization?	1	2	3	4	5
power or importance of channel intermediaries?	1	2	3	4	5
	Total:				

they move quickly to use the opportunity of MP3- and Napster-style technology to deliver customer value. If the major companies don't respond, new e-businesses, or perhaps the recording artists themselves, will gain a strong foothold. Major record labels need to migrate to a combined place-and-space strategy, drawing on the advantages of both the physical world (e.g., record stores) and the virtual world (e.g., online distribution and customization).

Price/Cost Structure

Relative to the current way of doing business, how important are Internet technologies for reducing costs in creating and delivering products to your customers? For example, the cost of a standard banking transaction, such as obtaining an account balance or moving money between accounts, is between twenty-five and fifty times less via the Internet than via a branch (see chapter 1).

Customer Loyalty

How large is the potential for competitors to undermine the loyalty of your customers? Loyalty has two important components: brand identification and switching costs. If customers have high brand identification, based on lifestyle, personality, product features, or emotional benefits, they will be more loyal. If the switching costs for a customer to move from a firm to its competitor are high, then the customer will also be more loyal. Switching costs are high where there are significant requirements for registration, documentation, or changing third-party arrangements, as there are in moving banks. Loyalty programs raise switching costs, as does significant involvement by the customer to personalize the firm's offerings (e.g., accounting services). The higher the potential to undermine customer loyalty, the greater the threat and opportunity created by e-business.

Customer Self-Service Gap

How large is the gap between your current and the potential customer self-service? Customer self-service is defined as providing an attractive value proposition to customers who can help themselves when they want the service. For example, if there are segments with an unfulfilled desire to self-serve without queuing in branches or waiting on the phone, the gap is large and the potential for e-business is greater. If the Internet offers a new opportunity for customers to help themselves (e.g., retail brokerage or travel bookings), the threat or opportunity is larger. Your answer to the following question is a good, if often painful, indicator: How much do your customers dislike dealing with your firm in person?

Geographical Reach

What is the difference between your firm's current geographical reach and its potential reach via the Internet? The larger the gap, the greater the threat or opportunity from e-business. If the potential and practical reach is much larger than the current reach, there is significant opportunity for revenue growth without a proportional increase in selling expenses. For example, Cisco's Internet sales are significantly higher as a percentage of total sales in South America (90 percent) and Australia (70 percent), where the company does not have as large a physical presence as in North America (50 percent).[2] Any potential increase in geographical reach must be practical. Many firms' geographical reach is limited by other countries' regulations, tariffs, or the cost of transporting the product—not just by a lack of technology or imagination in senior management.

Dynamic Pricing

How large is your potential loss to the firm if its product is not sold by a certain time? An airline seat or a hotel room is highly perishable, leaving the provider with no revenue if not consumed by a given date. If a firm's products are highly perishable and their value reduces to zero on a certain date, there is significant opportunity to sell via auction or dynamic pricing. The Internet offers unprecedented ability to dynamically adjust the price for products depending on supply and demand. This ability not only allows firms to fill unused capacity by reducing prices, but also provides the opportunity to raise prices when demand is high and supply scarce.

Knowledge Management

How large is the potential for your firm to benefit from better knowledge management? Knowledge management can generate customer value in at least two ways. First, it can do this by codifying the knowledge resident in individuals, documents, and procedures, and making it available firmwide and perhaps to customers, as in Ernst & Young's Ernie product (see chapter 1). Second, it can generate customer value by identifying the firm's knowledge resources—people, documents, and so on—and making them more easily identifiable and accessible from within the firm as well as by customers. The higher the potential for knowledge management to add value, the larger the threat and opportunity created by bringing knowledge assets online for access within the firm or by customers.

Online Customer Base

What percentage of your current customers are already online at work, at home, or both? Over time this percentage will undoubtedly increase, but the size today will indicate the immediate level of threat or opportunity from e-business. If a customer base already has significant online segments, it is certain that a current competitor or new entrant will offer them a similar product directly or as an intermediary. Keep in mind that not knowing the answer to the question of the percentage of customers online is also a major threat.

Customization

How large is the opportunity for online customization of your product? Consider the following two components when answering. (1) How important is customization in generating value from your product? (2) Can any or all of the customization be done online? We define customization as products allowing design or tailoring to meet customer needs that are not satisfied by standard product offerings. Some products for which customization is important but hard to do online (such as a tailor-made suits) are relatively unthreatened by e-business. The providers of other services requiring customization that can easily be done online—for example, mortgages and holiday travel—may be greatly threatened by new e-businesses.

Channel and Intermediary Power

How large is the power or importance of channel intermediaries in your traditional business? Powerful or important channel intermediaries demand lower prices, influence customer choice, and retain the customer relationship, often without sharing important customer data. Such intermediaries include large retailers (e.g., Wal-Mart or Macy's), manufacturers' agents, and financial advisers. Powerful channel intermediaries can influence the customer to use a competitor's product or may not do your product features justice at the point of sale, thus posing a potential threat. Direct connection to the customer either for influence or purchasing is an opportunity for responding to powerful intermediaries.

After entering your ratings for each question into table 13-1, total the numbers. The highest score is 50 and the lowest 10. Based on our experience, the following general interpretations indicate the urgency of action required:

> **40–50:** Your business requires a major rethinking of its strategy, business model, customer value propositions, position in the value chain, and potential source of profits. This process should result in significant and immediate investment in e-business building blocks, several important e-business initiatives, as well as major organizational change.
>
> **30–39:** Your business faces threats and opportunities in some segments, requiring a rethinking of the business model, customer value proposition, and potential source of profits. This process is likely to result in significant investment in long-term e-business building blocks and a portfolio of initiatives focused on the customer segments under threat or providing opportunities. Many of these initiatives will probably involve

either bypassing traditional intermediaries or providing your services via full-service providers or intermediaries.

20–29: Your core business is not under immediate threat from e-business, but there are definitely opportunities to be explored. The urgency is not great and e-business issues should be integrated into the normal business strategy process. However, a few key building blocks, probably based on your core competencies (e.g., the Knowledge Bank project for Lonely Planet described in chapter 12), should be created, requiring significant long-term investment and leadership. A small portfolio of e-business initiatives should be launched to learn more about the potential of e-business and to help identify the building blocks.

10–19: Recheck your answers and arithmetic! Then ask someone else in your firm to complete the analysis. If you both agree on the result then think about product and service extensions for your businesses that are e-business enabled. Or pass this book to someone who may need it more!

E-Business Strategizing

Once the level of threat and opportunity from e-business and thus the urgency to act are established, the process of strategizing can begin. Every consulting firm has developed an e-business offering to help firms migrate from place to space. Some of these offerings are better than others, but all of them will stimulate thinking about the impacts of e-business. We offer a simple framework (see figure 13-1) for e-business strategizing that should be useful for many firms, particularly for those with scores on the opportunity-and-threat indicator of between 20 and 39.

Because e-business has the potential to make fundamental change, we suggest starting with the firm's strategic intent rather than the current strategy (how business is done today). The strategic intent of a firm specifies its long-term, stable goals—a worth-

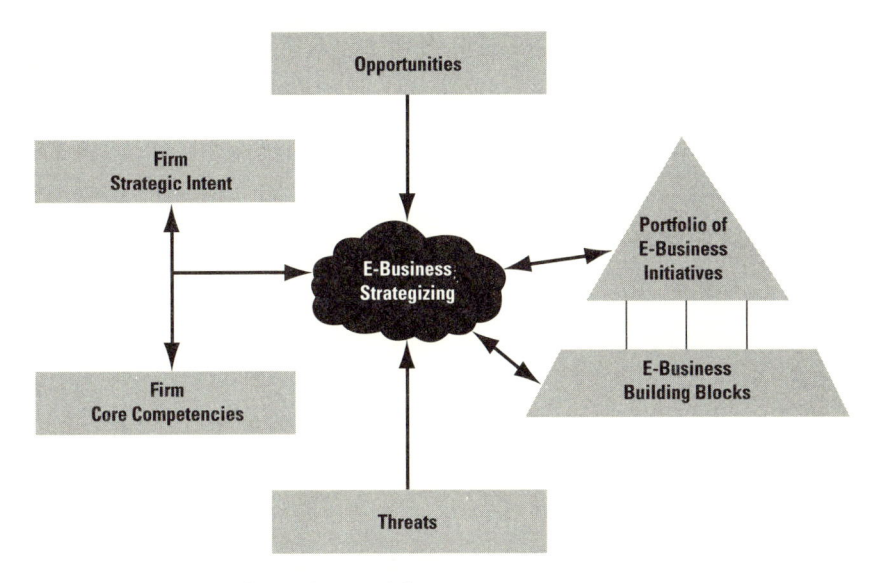

CHOOSING AND IMPLEMENTING AN E-BUSINESS INITIATIVE | 299

FIGURE 13-1 E-Business Strategizing

while destination and one where a firm desires to be.[3] The destination should require a stretch for the firm. The situation of RACV, an Australian, membership-based insurance and roadside services firm similar to AAA, illustrates this approach.[4]

RACV's strategic intent is for membership to be essential for all Victorians and for RACV to be the preeminent member organization. More than 66 percent of Victorian households—1.35 million people in all—have RACV basic roadside services. RACV aims to provide a total range of motoring, insurance, finance, and assistance products and services, which make it easy for the firm's 1.6 million users of their roadside service to meet all their motoring and insurance needs from the one organization. But only 40 percent of drivers use those other products and services at present.

To be successful, RACV must first refine its core competencies in customer relationship management, customer needs and data analysis, cross-selling, cost control, and innovative product design and sourcing; then it must invest in the necessary e-building blocks. E-business presents RACV with many threats and opportunities, including the potential launching of GM's innovative concierge OnStar service in Australia. OnStar (www.onstar.com) provides a wide range of services to its in-car customers via a cell phone and global positioning system. OnStar organizes roadside assistance; books theaters, restaurants, and hotels; provides route support; and provides information and access to hundreds of other services.

In general, e-business building blocks are derived from a firm's core competencies.[5] In e-business, as in any other business, investing in unique capabilities provides competitive advantage. Thus, building blocks derived from a firm's core competencies provide a unique platform for future e-business initiatives. Also, the more of the necessary building blocks in place, the faster time to market for the e-business initiative.

We believe firms can identify many of the critical building blocks necessary for their future e-business initiatives based on their competencies. To illustrate, we present the likely building blocks for the core competencies often found in a direct-to-customer model:

Core Competencies	Typical E-Business Building Blocks
• form and manage strategic partnerships with suppliers, fulfillment houses, and others in the supply chain	• develop a network of personal contacts with other players in the supply chain • detailed information and insight on the capabilities, profitability, and value added of other players in the supply chain
• use customer information to increase sales and service	• customer databases tracking a detailed level of purchases over time
• marketing and effective customer prospecting	• sales force capable of exploiting detailed customer information to up-sell and cross-sell
• manage business processes and systems integration	• process management expertise and discipline including metrics for process performance • activity-based costing • an integrated information systems portfolio (e.g., ERP)
• create own content	• invest in the research and development of unique content by a world-class team of professionals

E-business strategizing also results in a portfolio of e-business initiatives. The strategic importance and the size of the investment in the portfolio will depend on the extent of the firm's e-business threat and opportunity. Higher scores on the opportunity-and-threat indicator suggest significant investment, with a larger number of major initiatives. For best results we have found that e-business strategizing needs a team of people with the following attributes:

- Customer-facing people with an understanding of the strategic intent of the firm
- Technologists who have worked for the firm for some time
- Practical marketing-oriented people
- Senior managers who have the most to gain
- Supportive customers keen to take advantage of the potential of e-business
- Results- and finance-oriented people such as the chief financial officer

The number of people is less important than good coverage of these skill sets. An external consultant with a strong tool kit for managing diverse groups dealing with challenging issues can facilitate the process. We suggest that strategizing begin from two different places in figure 13-1: strategic intent and core competencies. Half the group can review table 12-3 (strategic objectives and sources of revenue for each atomic model) and identify which models are suited to the firm's strategic intent. The other half of the group can review table 12-4 (core competencies for each atomic model) and identify the models that fit the firm's current core competencies. Bringing together the list of atomic models resulting from these independent analyses is an excellent starting point for planning an e-business initiative.

There will be no shortage of ideas for e-business initiatives. The next challenge is evaluating each initiative. Before preparing a formal business case complete with discounted cash flows, budgets, accountabilities, and measures of success, we suggest passing the initiative through an evaluative process.

Evaluating an E-Business Initiative

To explain how to evaluate a proposed initiative, we return to the description in chapter 1 of an e-business initiative having four components (see figure 1-1): a combination of atomic e-business models delivered via one or more channels to targeted customer segments supported by a tailored IT infrastructure capability.

E-Business Model

Most e-business initiatives combine two or three atomic business models. Some combinations of atomic models are synergistic, while others are in conflict or unstable and require very careful handling during implementation. To help understand the opportunities and challenges in creating an e-business initiative, we suggest the following steps:

1. Identify the atomic models that make up the initiative. Using the schematics for the atomic models, create a business model schematic (similar to figure 12-1) for the initiative. Start by combining the atomic model schematics, and then tailor the initial model for the particular firm.

2. From tables 12-3 and 12-4, compile lists of strategic objectives, sources of revenues or value, critical success factors, and core competencies. Answers are needed to the following questions:

    - Are the strategic objectives clear, achievable, and credible?
    - Are the sources of revenue realistic, sustainable, and sufficient?
    - Who owns the customer relationship, data, and transactions?
    - How strong is the potential customer relationship?
    - Is the firm capable of achieving the critical success factors?
    - Does the firm have the core competencies required?

3. **Assess the hybrid business model for synergies and conflict.** Look up the potential synergies or conflict in table 13-2. Our study of fifty initiatives statistically identified the typical effect of the combinations of pairs of atomic models.[6] We assessed the four areas of potential conflict or synergy in an e-business model (described in chapter 3): channel, competency, infrastructure, and information. The effects of combining pairs of atomic models can be described as one of four results:

- **Synergistic:** For example, combining direct-to-customer and virtual community is naturally synergistic. Firms using the direct-to-customer model want to create loyalty and passion for their products. Supporting a virtual community is an excellent way for a direct-to-customer firm to cement the link with end consumers by providing a place where people can congregate and discuss the products. The direct-to-customer firm can use the virtual community for market

TABLE 13-2 Synergy and Conflict between Atomic Models for an E-Business Initiative

	CP	D2C	FSP	I	SI	VNI	VC	WOE
Content Provider (CP)		STOP	⚠	⚠	□	STOP	□	□
Direct to Customer (D2C)			□	□	STOP	□	✓	✓
Full-Service Provider (FSP)				✓	⚠	⚠	✓	□
Intermediary (I)					⚠	⚠	□	✓
Shared Infrastructure (SI)						□	□	⚠
Value Net Integrator (VNI)							✓	⚠
Virtual Community (VC)								□
Whole of Enterprise (WOE)								

STOP = clear conflict   ⚠ = caution possible conflict   ✓ = clear synergy   □ = neutral research and product feedback and in many other ways. The combination works equally well for B2B or B2C customers, although the communities will have very different characteristics. Potential synergies exist in all four areas: channel, competency, infrastructure, and information.

- **Neutral:** The two atomic models are neither clearly synergistic nor in conflict. For example, the combination of content provider and shared-infrastructure models is neutral in terms of the four types of potential conflict or synergy.

- **Caution:** The two atomic models are potentially in conflict, and the initiative must be handled carefully. For example, combining the full-service provider and shared-infrastructure models causes potential conflict particularly in the areas of information and competency. The full-service provider may have access to very valuable sales or customer identity information. If the other participants in the shared-infrastructure model see their partner using information gathered from the shared infrastructure in pursuit of a full-service provider model, they will withdraw from the shared infrastructure. Exactly this type of conflict occurred often in the early days of travel computer reservation systems, which were dominated by United and American Airlines. The conflict led to legal action and eventually government regulation. It is often possible to manage this type of conflict via negotiation with partners and transparency with customers.

- **Stop and consider:** When the two atomic models are in clear conflict, the cause is usually a combination of the four areas of conflict. For example, the combination of content provider and direct-to-customer can result in channel, competency, infrastructure, and information conflicts. (Later in the chapter we return to the question of how to manage channel conflict.) The two models also have very different needs for information, infrastructure, and competencies—for example, managing potentially millions of small customers in the direct-to-customer model versus a few large customers for the content provider.

Customer Segments

The customer is the most important single issue in an e-business initiative. In particular, it is essential to decide which customer segments will be targeted and to determine the value proposition for each segment. Segmentation is even more important in e-business than in the physical world, because there is often no person to redirect or help customers if they are poorly served by one channel. Clear answers are needed to the following questions:

- Which customer segments are targeted?
- How big are the segments?
- What is the value proposition for each segment?
- How effective will our brand be for each segment?

Channel to the Customer

In any e-business initiative, reaching target customer segments requires careful channel selection and management. A channel is the conduit by which a firm's products or services are offered or distributed to the customer. The value of particular products is enhanced or diminished depending on the suitability of the channel for each target segment. Traditional firms competing with dotcoms have the advantage of multiple channels to offer customers a choice of place or space.

Each channel has different characteristics, strengths, and weaknesses. Table 3-1 summarizes the potential channels to the customer and the potential richness of the information transfer. One of the significant challenges in e-business, particularly for traditional firms, is integrating all of the channels to the customer to deliver a single picture of the customer's relationship with the firm. E-business raises the stakes for integration across different channels. Clear answers are needed for the following channel questions:

- Are the channels capable of supporting the type of customer relationship identified in the value proposition for each segment?

- Are the channels capable of supporting the richness and flexibility of information provision required for each value proposition?

- Are the channels capable of supporting the breadth of information capture required to deliver each value proposition and to support the desired intimacy of the customer relationship?

- Is there potential channel conflict with intermediaries, allies, or customers?

Managing Channel Conflict   The potential for channel conflict with e-business is very real. The Internet offers a new channel to the end consumer, and firms can choose to bypass existing channel partners, causing channel conflict. For example, the same end consumer could be offered two different value propositions via the direct or intermediary channel as described in the Cisco example in chapter 5. More difficult to handle is channel conflict in which an end consumer is offered very similar value propositions directly and via an intermediary, but at different prices. This type of conflict can lead to alliance breakdowns, such as Harvey Norman retail stores' public announcement that it was dropping Compaq computers from its offerings when Compaq opened direct-to-customer stores (see chapter 1).

Some producers have launched and then withdrawn direct-to-customer e-business initiatives. A *Computerworld* article recalled that Levi Strauss had announced it would be the sole retailer of its brand on the Internet.[7] As described in chapter 4, Levi Strauss soon revisited the decision, citing channel relations concerns and sagging sales. Instead, Internet sales were moved to the Web sites of Macy's and J. C. Penney. This type of channel conflict is difficult to handle, and many firms will try different strategies, possibly changing positions as the situation evolves.

What are the options, and how can channel conflict be avoided?[8]

- **Segment by customer:** Identify a segment of customers to target online directly and continue using intermediaries for the other segments. For example, a computer vendor chooses to serve corporate and medium-sized business customers directly, while using intermediaries for individuals, solo operators, and home offices.

- **Segment by product:** Segment customers by product and distribute some products directly and other products via traditional channels.

- **Redefine dealer's role:** Define the role of the retailer (or dealer) to display, test-drive, and configure the product, and the producer takes all orders directly. Tentative moves toward this business model are being made in the auto industry. Vauxhall (www.vauxhall.co.uk) in the United Kingdom has moved in this direction, offering car purchases from home in cooperation with dealers.

- **New brand:** Develop a new brand or rebadge existing products to sell directly, giving them different value propositions than the products sold via retailers.

- **Direct all leads to distributors:** Establish an informational Web site with product descriptions and perhaps a virtual community, and pass on all sales leads to the retail channel—perhaps taking a commission along the way.

- **Retreat:** Retreat from selling similar products, because the resulting price war is unwinnable. Move to value-added services or higher-value, higher-margin offerings.

Channel conflict is not new, and over time businesses have found win-win ways of working together to service the customer. The importance of dealing with channel conflict and the radicalness of the response increase with the level of threat and opportunity, identified in table 13-1.

IT Infrastructure Capability

IT infrastructure is the platform in all e-business for connecting different parts of the firm and linking to suppliers, consumers, and allies. The IT infrastructure investments made by firms are as critical for creating long-term shareholder value as the previous waves of physical infrastructure decisions of location, buildings, and plant. Having in place the necessary IT infrastructure building blocks significantly reduces the implementation time for e-business initiatives.

In studying e-business initiatives, we identified seventy different IT services in nine categories (see the appendix). The goal of our study was to identify and define the IT infrastructure services most important for each atomic e-business model. The check marks and stars in table 12-5 represent the most important infrastructure service categories for each atomic business model.[9] Note that the infrastructure services related to security were required for all atomic models.

After identifying the atomic business models in a proposed initiative, use table 12-5 and the section "IT Infrastructures" in chapter 12 as the starting points to compile a list of your firm's critical infrastructure services. E-business initiatives often require fifteen or twenty new firmwide infrastructure services. Many of the same infrastructure services will be required for different e-business initiatives. IT infrastructure is too important for the success of e-business to be left to the IT group alone. Rather, it must be a senior management responsibility, involving business and IT professionals working together to specify the required infrastructure capability.[10] The IT professional's role is to turn those requirements into technical specifications for services that will be provided internally or by outsourcers.

When specifying the IT services required, business and IT management should carefully develop measures for each service. These measures become the basis for service-level agreements to assess the performance of the IT provider, whether internal or outsourced. If the service is vital and not a commodity, we recommend using an internal IT group. Outsourcing places more barriers in the way of the difficult process of integrating the IT provider and the business. Firms that outsource more IT have longer times to bring new products to market.[11] The longer time is probably because outsourcing adds another layer of complexity to the communications between the business and the provider. If the service is mission critical, then the firm should nurture and develop the skills required to manage this asset within the organization as a core competency.

If the service is a commodity, or if the firm's business strategy is to be the low-cost producer, then the firm should test the marketplace to identify the best source, because outsourcing often results in lower IT costs. A firm should outsource as many of the services as possible, using performance-based contracts for relatively short periods once it has specified service levels. Where IT is a core competency, the number of services outsourced will be fewer and focused on commodities such as PC/desktop maintenance or standard telecommunications networks. Other firms, particularly those with a cost focus, should outsource more of the services. Where time to market and synergies between business units are important, the services critical to achieving these goals should be retained in-house (for example, managing shared customer databases).

Firms should never outsource the decision rights or the setting of the IT architecture to any other group, be it a service provider or a consultant. Drive the architecture from the strategic intent of the firm. IT architecture is a key decision for the firm's e-business position, and outsourcing it would be like outsourcing the decision of what core competencies the firm should have. Setting architectures requires a partnership between the business and IT management. Only outsource the provision of the service once the architecture is set.

Top Ten Leadership Principles for E-Business

These leadership principles provide advice for senior managers wanting to derive business value from their e-business initiatives. These principles synthesize the findings of our research and our observations of successful e-business leaders. We suggest senior managers use the top ten as a checklist to inform and audit the way they manage and govern e-business.

1. **Migrate toward e-business, combining the strengths of both place and space.** E-business offers new and exciting ways of doing business for firms and their customers. E-business can increase customer satisfaction levels, potentially offering

customized twenty-four-hour service delivered worldwide on a single-point-of-contact basis. For many firms, the economics of e-business are irresistible, with transaction costs reduced by 75 percent or more. All firms need to begin migrating to e-business with the urgency and pace determined by the size of the threat and opportunity. Senior management must lead this strategizing and migration; the opportunities and threats are too large to delegate the responsibility down to a level where the person cannot say no!

Most traditional firms will migrate their businesses to a combination of place and space. Different and tailored value propositions are needed for each customer segment. Some segments will want only clicks, others will want bricks, and many will want a combination. For many large successful B2B and B2C businesses, the full-service provider atomic model (see chapter 5) is attractive because it leverages the firm's brand and customer relationships. The full-service provider model is a combination of clicks and bricks, requiring integration across physical and electronic channels and delivering a seamless single point of contact for customers.

Successfully migrating to a clicks-and-mortar business model is a major change, affecting almost every aspect of a firm including channel and intermediary management, customer segmentation, organizational form, incentives, skills, IT infrastructure, culture change, and a convergence of business processes, workflows, infrastructure, and data assets. The migration is both exciting and challenging, and it will bring into question the very essence of your business. What *really* are our firm's core competencies? Are these competencies world-class? How do we nurture these competencies? What is our position on the industry value chain? Is our current profitability sustainable?

2. **Identify e-business assets and liabilities and the size of the threat and opportunity.** Carefully identify the firm's specific e-business assets and liabilities. Typical assets and liabilities for a traditional firm are presented below. Then identify the

Assets	Liabilities
brand recognition	pricing and cost structure
cash	mindset: skills, culture, and incentives
transaction processing and logistics experience	lower (potential) growth
market power with customers and suppliers	non-integrated IT
existing customer relationships and databases	channel conflicts
proven implementation skills	lack of agility

nature and size of the e-business threats and opportunities (see table 13-1). The combination of these two factors provides a strong indicator of the urgency of the migration from place to space. For most traditional firms, the lists of e-business assets and liabilities will be substantial. The list of e-business assets is reassuring, as many of the traditional business assets such as brand, transaction processing, and logistics experience will be as useful in an e-business world as in a physical world. These capabilities put many traditional firms in a powerful position to launch e-business initiatives—if only they can actually leverage the assets. Often the problem is that the years of effort devoted to creating these assets have also brought a set of liabilities. For a traditional firm to thrive in an e-business world requires dealing with the liabilities on the right-hand side of the list of assets and liabilities presented previously, while simultaneously leveraging the assets on the left-hand side.

3. **Invest in a portfolio of e-business initiatives.** Given the uncertainty of the future of e-business, take the lead from the portfolio approach used so successfully in financial markets. An investor looking at the dot-com sector will typically buy a portfolio of stocks and keep a close watch on their performance. The investor expects high variability in the performance

of any one stock in the portfolio. Many stocks will fall in value, perhaps to zero. Others will break even in investment terms, often after a bumpy ride. A small percentage of the stocks will enjoy meteoric rises and deliver huge returns on investment, giving a positive return for the portfolio as a whole. The same approach should be applied to a portfolio of e-business initiatives.

For firms migrating to e-business, the size and importance of the portfolio of initiatives will depend on the magnitude of the e-business threat and opportunity. The number of e-business initiatives in a firm varies markedly. Firms with lower e-business threat and opportunity will have two or three major e-business initiatives, while firms at the high end of the threat/opportunity spectrum may have ten or more major initiatives.

E-business initiatives have a relatively higher volatility than many other projects, and they require the governance structures and project management techniques more often found in research and development projects. Unlike research and development projects, however, the success of an e-business initiative will often be clear relatively quickly. If successful, the online market will respond quickly, often straining the resources and capabilities of the initiative and requiring top management attention.

4. **Identify and invest in e-business building blocks based on core competencies.** The savvy investor will invest in learning more about the dot-com sector; he or she will read, collect performance data, chart, join chat groups, and attend seminars. The investor is gaining competencies on which he or she hopes to capitalize when unpredictable opportunities present themselves. We advocate the same approach for firms: Build a series of competencies that are certain to be needed in an e-business future, regardless of the exact business models that eventuate. We saw this building block approach in the Lonely Planet case study (see chapter 12). Lonely Planet is not sure which e-business business models it will ultimately pursue,

but the firm is sure that it needs its travel content (text, images, video, maps, etc.) stored in an integrated Knowledge Bank. Whatever the product or the distribution channel (bookstores, handheld devices, Web sites, etc.), Lonely Planet can access, integrate, and distribute content electronically. The Knowledge Bank is one of Lonely Planet's building blocks for the e-business future.

The decision to invest in each building block is similar to the decision of an investor to buy a financial option that can be exercised in the future. Investing in a capability now provides the ability to build e-business initiatives more quickly later. Determining the right building blocks for a firm is one of the most important e-business leadership activities for senior management. Deciding which building blocks to create requires senior management to ask hard questions about the firm's competencies in an e-business world. Creating the wrong building block produces an option that will never be called, and thus it adds cost without adding value.

5. **Create a culture of strategic experimentation.** E-business initiatives managed within traditional firms often take two forms: strategic experiments and big bang. Many firms are well practiced at big bang implementations. However, creating a culture of strategic experimentation is often new and challenging for many management teams. Despite their substantial assets of cash, technology, brand, management experience, and market power, good managers often struggle when doing something different from what has made them successful in their current business model.[12]

A culture of strategic experimentation requires recognition that the information to make a decisive and relatively certain e-business investment doesn't exist. Instead of careful deliberate analysis, fast, inexpensive, and flexible strategic experiments are needed. A strategic experiment is typically an e-business initiative based on a good idea with an internal champion to drive it. Typically, initiatives are run as skunk works within the traditional firm by managers who are passionate about e-business. Resources and people are pulled from all over the firm, and the initiative often affects many different functional areas or units in some way.

The key attributes of a strategic experiment are the following:

- There is limited detailed analytical work.
- The business case is brief, with clear checkpoints and limits to the investment.
- There is an expectation that the initiative will evolve and change in scope during implementation and beyond.
- If successful, management attention and investment requirements escalate rapidly.

The strategic experiment is a powerful way to add to a firm's portfolio of e-business initiatives. E-business allows fast market testing of a new initiative. If successful resources and attention can be focused on the initiative, it can be as if the firm had designed it as a major strategic thrust at the outset. If the initiative doesn't receive customer support, it may be canceled, with little lost other than some seed funding. The successful use of strategic experiments, however, does require a different mind-set, one that tolerates failure and rewards innovation. Strategic experiments require a very different approach to in-project and postimplementation reviews. A review examining what went well and what can be learned for the future is required. The review must avoid becoming a witch-hunt in which guilty parties, or perhaps scapegoats, are pilloried, potential organizational learning is lost, and the disincentives for any form of innovation are clearly broadcast in the firm.

6. **Analyze the business model, channel, segments, and IT infrastructure capability when evaluating each e-business initiative.** When evaluating the potential of a proposed e-business initiative, four important areas (see figure 1-1) must be in harmony to succeed. An e-business initiative must clearly articu-

late the combination of atomic business models delivered via specific channels to targeted customer segments supported by a tailored IT infrastructure capability. The combination of atomic business models explains the business objectives, the relationships, and the flows of the initiative. The customer segments identify the target audience of the initiative and guide the way the business model is shaped and the value proposition delivered. Channels describe how each customer segment will be reached and the richness of the information transfer to the customer. The infrastructure specifies the IT capability required, both internally and externally, to enable the e-business initiative.

Most e-business initiatives will be a combination of two or more atomic business models. Some of these combinations are synergistic while others are in conflict or unstable. To help evaluate an e-business initiative, we suggest developing and analyzing a business model schematic (see chapter 2). The schematic can be analyzed to deduce:

- whether the model has any major contradictions leading to nonviability,
- the core competencies and key business processes necessary to implement the model,
- the position in the industry value chain or net,
- some indications of the organizational form necessary for implementation,
- the type of IT infrastructure capability required, and
- which entity owns the consumer relationship, data, and transaction.

7. **Protect and utilize what you own: relationships, data, and transactions.** In any e-business model there are three important questions of ownership: who owns the relationship, who owns the data, and who owns the transaction. The generic ownership of these three assets for the eight atomic e-business

models is summarized in table 12-1. Firms owning the customer relationship, and thus knowing more about that customer than any other player in the business model, usually have the most powerful position in the business model—and the most to lose.

The owner of customer data has the potential to develop powerful insight into its customers' needs and desires. Many firms own customer data, but they don't use them effectively. Owning the customer data implies the firm captures the data electronically and has the potential to analyze them at both the customer and the segment level. In a number of the atomic models, some of the customer data are co-owned. The firm may own only the data (as in the value net integrator business model), own the data and the relationship (as in the intermediary), own the data and the transaction (as in the shared infrastructure), or own all three (as in the direct to customer).

Firms owning the customer transaction receive a fee or a profit margin for the service provided. The service could be the sale of a product, the provision of information or advice, or the provision of a professional service. Owning the transaction implies that the firm also owns the customer data related to that transaction, but perhaps no other customer data, unless the firm also owns the customer relationship.

Owning each of these three assets creates different types of leverage. Owning the customer relationship provides influence where the customer looks to the relationship holder for trust, recommendations, and tailored advice. Owning the customer data provides insight, as the firm has detailed information about the customer. Owning the customer transaction generates customer revenue for service. Owning all of these assets—the relationship, data, and transaction—is more powerful and profitable than owing less than three. However, profitable businesses exist owning just one (e.g., the value net integrator) or even none of these three assets (e.g., the content provider).

When considering a new e-business initiative, a firm should analyze whether it will gain or lose leverage from these three sources—relationship, data, and transaction—relative to its current place-based business. Jealously protect and leverage what you currently own and be reluctant to give up ownership of these assets to another player.

8. **Lead the determination of the required IT infrastructure capability.**[13] Together business and IT management must link the IT infrastructure to the strategic intent of the firm. The link is two-way: strategic intent driving IT infrastructure decisions, and the technology capability providing opportunities for new business models. Business managers should write the IT infrastructure capabilities sections of their business plans with the help of IT managers or consultants. Forcing business management to take responsibility will ensure solid linking between the strategic intent and the IT infrastructure. In addition, the corporate IT group must be responsible for providing firmwide infrastructure to facilitate economies of scale, sharing of information, cross-selling, firmwide e-business, and integration. Use mechanisms such as IT councils to govern the firmwide infrastructure and check for synergies among the business unit portfolios. These governance structures are even more important when IT is outsourced.

    Manage the IT infrastructure and the e-business applications that use the infrastructure separately, because they have different characteristics. Infrastructures have longer lives, are shared by multiple e-business initiatives and applications, and must be in place before the precise business needs are known. In contrast, e-business applications will often change and are specific to an initiative, function, or business process. Different approaches to specification, justification, management, and evaluation are necessary for infrastructure and applications. Therefore, separate processes for management are necessary, but the two processes must be interlinked.

9. **Understand the characteristics of the e-business business models.** All organizations will be affected by e-business. Understanding e-business and the characteristics of the possible business models is the responsibility of all senior management. Senior managers are best positioned to integrate

knowledge of the business with the opportunities and threats of e-business. However, the catalyst will often be younger people more familiar with technology and e-business and with less invested in the traditional and currently profitable way of doing business.

The atomic e-business models described in this book are a conceptual framework for understanding e-business initiatives. After boiling down e-business into a finite set of atomic models, we can use the models in at least three ways:

a. *Atomic models as pure types.* Atomic models describe the essence of an e-business model. Understanding the characteristics of an atomic model gives insight into what is required to successfully operate a business model of that type.

b. *Atomic models as building blocks.* The building blocks can be combined into e-business initiatives or hybrid models. Some combinations of atomic models are viable, while others contain inherent conflict and are unstable. Firms can look to these atomic models as potential building blocks when strategizing about e-business.

c. *Decomposition of e-business initiatives.* A proposed e-business initiative can be decomposed into its atomic models to better understand what will be required for implementation. The core competencies and critical success factors necessary to implement each atomic model are summarized in chapter 12 (see table 12-4).

We do not claim the eight atomic models are fully descriptive of the e-business possibilities. We are not even sure they are a stable set. However, they are mutually exclusive and are observable in e-business initiatives by traditional firms, and thus they are good place to start. We fully expect new atomic models to emerge.

10. **Prepare to acquire dot-coms that are a good fit when they have cash flow problems.** There are many interesting business models being implemented by dot-coms with funding from

venture capital or IPOs. As the stock market continues to adjust the stock prices of these dot-coms, a number of these businesses will become distressed, making them excellent takeover targets.

Identifying a list of potential takeover targets will educate senior management about the interesting e-business business models in their industry. As the stock market sentiment turns against dot-coms—and the signs are already here—then good buying opportunities present themselves for traditional firms that have studied the marketplace and have cash in the takeover chest.

A Final Word

Observing online business models over time, we have noticed a pattern of e-business model evolution. Many e-business initiatives began with one or two atomic e-business models and have grown in functionality by adding several other atomic models. We believe that over time there will be a merging of e-business business models, with each initiative having aspects of several atomic models. The transparency of e-business strategies, which can be viewed on many firms' Web sites, reduces the time a firm can expect to enjoy an IT-enabled competitive advance. Until the arrival of the Internet, the average period of IT-enabled competitive advantage, before competitors responded and nullified the advantage, was about three years.[14] We expect that time to reduce significantly, affecting the approach to evaluating business cases for e-business initiatives. Projects taking longer than a year to create a positive net present value must include the effect of competition in the analysis.

Returning to the chemistry analogy, we anticipate only a small number of new atomic e-business models to emerge in the future. We expect a relatively stable set of compounds (i.e., combinations of two to four atomic models) to form. We also look forward to an evolution to compounds that contain the most profitable atomic e-business model combinations. Some likely candidates for profitable combinations would include: full-service provider plus virtual community; value net integrator plus direct to customer plus virtual community; and whole of enterprise plus intermediary.

Finally, we foresee the migration from the Old World to the New World to continue with the time-honored family pattern of funding. The immigrants to the New World will need financial support from those remaining in the Old World. Eventually the new immigrants will fund the retirement of the Old World members of the family—but combining the best of both worlds will create the richest result. Studying the evolution of firms implementing e-business models will provide clues about future firm profitability, good investment vehicles, and the next generation of business.

APPENDIX

IT Infrastructure Services for E-Business

THIS APPENDIX contains definitions, detailed data, and the names of the firms that participated in our study of IT infrastructure services and e-business. We gratefully acknowledge the time and cooperation of the participating firms and the work of Peter Raisbeck of the Melbourne Business School. We studied fifty e-business initiatives in fifteen firms, all of them Australian subsidiaries of global firms, Australia-based global firms, or government agencies. A list of the companies is presented first, followed by a breakdown of the atomic business models found in the e-business initiatives studied. The fifty e-business initiatives had a total of eighty-nine occurrences of the atomic models, with direct to customer the most common. We conducted an analysis to identify the infrastructure services associated with each atomic business model. Brief descriptions of the nine areas of infrastructure services are provided, followed by a detailed table describing the seventy infrastructure services.

Participating Firms

The following firms participated in the study:

- Ajax Fasteners, www.ajaxfast.com.au (the largest fastener and tool company in Australia)
- ANZ (Australia and New Zealand Banking Group Limited), www.anz.com.au (a global bank)
- Ausdoc, www.ausdoc.com.au (information management, facilities management, freight, storage, and distribution)
- Australia Post, www.post.com.au (Australia's government-owned national postal service)
- Barwon Water, www.barwonwater.vic.gov.au (large regional water utility)
- BHP, www.bhp.com (global resource company with business units including petroleum, minerals, and steel)
- Email metals, www.email.com.au/products/products.htm (manufacturer and distributor of sheet metal, bar, plate, pipe, valves, and chain)
- Ford Australia, www.ford.com
- Fosters/Carlton and United Breweries (CUB), www.fosters.com.au
- General Motors Acceptance Corporation (GMAC), www.gmacfs.com
- Macquarie Bank, www.macquarie.com.au (investment bank, also providing a range of retail financial services)
- Mattel, www.mattel.com
- Melbourne Water, www.melbournewater.com.au (large city water utility)

- Southcorp Holdings, www.southcorp.com.au (maker of wine, water heaters, and packaging)
- Woolworths Ltd., www.woolworths.com.au (retailer with business units including Safeway Supermarkets, Big W, and Dick Smith Electronics)

Atomic Models Represented

The atomic models were implemented in the fifty e-business initiatives studied with the following frequencies:

ATOMIC MODEL	TOTAL
Content Provider	12
Direct to Customer	33
Full-Service Provider	5
Intermediary	13
Shared Infrastructure	5
Value Net Integrator	14
Virtual Community	1
Whole of Enterprise	6

Categories of IT Infrastructure Services

Applications Management

An application is a software program that resides on a computer for the purpose of translating electronic input into a meaningful form. Applications management includes purchasing software, developing proprietary applications, modifying applications, providing installation and technical support, and other tasks related to ensuring that applications are meeting the needs of the organization.

Communications Management

Communications management focuses on all technology that facilitates communication both within the organization and with the outside world. It includes the management of hardware and software to facilitate communication via computer, telephone, facsimile, pagers, mobile phones, and other communication and messaging services. It includes the cabling and any other communication linkages required to create an effective communications network, in addition to the necessary hardware and applications to meet the needs of the organization. This category includes the management of wide-area-network facilities.

Data Management

Data management refers to the way the organization structures and handles its information resources. Data may be sourced from internal or external databases. Data management includes data collection, database design, sorting and reporting information, creating links to external databases, assuring data compatibility, and other activities surrounding the effective management of electronic information.

IT Management

IT management includes many of the professional and strategic activities of the IT group including negotiations, information systems planning, project management, and other tasks. Information systems project management is the coordination and control of all the activities required to complete an information systems project.

Security

Security refers to the need to protect data, equipment, and processing time. Organizations restrict access to certain data and protect data and applications from manipulation or contamination.

Recovery refers to the need for a plan to maintain computer operations and information should a disaster occur.

Architecture and Standards

IT architecture is a set of policies and rules that govern the use of IT and plot a path to the way business will be done in the future.[1] In most firms it provides the technical guidelines rather than rules for decision making. An architecture has to cope with both business uncertainty and technological change, making it one of the most difficult tasks for a firm. A good architecture evolves over time and is documented and accessible to all managers in the firm. Each architecture decision needs a sound business base to encourage voluntary agreement and compliance across the business. A standard is a detailed definition of the technical choices to implement an architecture. Five elements of architectures and standards were studied: data, technology, communications, applications, and work. We also distinguished between specifying architecture or standards and enforcement.

Channel Management

Channel management was included to recognize that new and emerging technologies allow direct connections or distribution channels to customers. We were interested in finding out which electronic channels were important and how IT departments managed the technologies inherent in these channels.

IT Research and Development

The information systems market develops rapidly, particularly with the rise of new e-business technologies. It is thus necessary to continually test applications and hardware to assist with planning decisions. IT research and development includes identifying and testing new technologies for business purposes and evaluating proposals for new information systems initiatives.

Training and Education in the Use of IT

We define training as formal classes, individual training, and technology-based self-training programs for users ensuring hands-on computer proficiency levels meeting corporate requirements. We define information systems management education as education aimed at senior levels in the firm designed to generate value from IT use.

Table of Detailed Study Results

The following table presents the detailed data from the study of IT infrastructure services for e-business. The first column of figures is the percentage of firms that provide the service in each area. There are thirteen infrastructure services in the area of applications infrastructure. The percentage of firms that provided each service is shown. For example, 86.7 percent of firms provided middleware linking applications on different platforms (service 1.9).

The second column of figures indicates the firm's relative investment in each service area. In the interviews we asked the senior managers to indicate, on a scale from –10 to +10, whether their firm will increase or decrease spending on each service in the next year to provide support to e-business initiatives. A +10 indicates that, relative to other services, the increase in spending on this service would be the highest in the coming year. Conversely, a –10 would indicate that the service would receive relative disinvestment over the next year. A 0 means no change in relative spending on that service. The service that was highest on the relative-investment rating was "centralized management of infrastructure capacity" (service 1.6). Only one service—electronic data interchange (2.6)—had a relative disinvestment compared with the previous year.

APPENDIX | 327

TABLE A-1 IT Infrastructure Services and E-Business Survey Data

	Applications Infrastructure	Percent Having 89.8%	Relative Investment (−10 [lowest] to +10 [highest]) 3.7
1.1	Internet policies *(e.g., employee access, URL logging)*	100.0	1.7
1.2	Enforce Internet policies	93.3	1.9
1.3	Email policies *(e.g., inappropriate and personal email, harassment policies, filtering policies)*	100.0	1.8
1.4	Enforce email policies	93.3	1.9
1.5	Centralized management of e-business applications *(e.g., centralized e-business development, common standards and applications, single point of access, and multimedia applications)*	100.0	4.5
1.6	Centralized management of infrastructure capacity *(e.g., server traffic)*	100.0	7.3
1.7	Integrated mobile computing applications *(e.g., laptop dial-up and ISP access for internal users)*	100.0	4.2
1.8	ERP services *(shared and standard enterprise resource planning system)*	92.3	5.9
1.9	Middleware linking systems on different platforms *(e.g., integrating Web "shopfronts" to ERP systems)*	86.7	7.1
1.10	Wireless applications *(e.g., Web applications for wireless devices)*	69.2	3.0
1.11	Application services provision *(e.g., applications used by business units and centrally provided)*	75.0	2.6
1.12	Workflow applications	64.3	2.7
1.13	Payment transaction processing *(e.g., electronic funds transfer)*	92.9	3.7

		Percent Having	Relative Investment (−10 [lowest] to +10 [highest])
Communications		**81.3%**	**3.7**
2.1	Communications network services (e.g., full-service Internet protocol [IP] networks linking all points within a business)	100.0	4.7
2.2	Broadband communication services (e.g., higher bandwidth activities such as video)	71.4	2.4
2.3	Intranet capabilities (e.g., an intranet to support a variety of applications including publishing, company policies, directories, message boards, etc.)	100.0	6.0
2.4	Extranet capabilities (e.g., providing information and applications via Internet protocol [IP] to a select group of customers and suppliers)	93.3	6.4
2.5	Workstation networks (e.g., workstation networks, local area networks and point of sale [POS] networks)	100.0	2.8
2.6	Electronic data interchange (EDI) linkages to customers and suppliers	84.6	−0.1
2.7	Electronic support to groups (e.g., groupware)	20.0	2.0
Data Management		**78.0%**	**4.8**
3.1	Manage key data independent of applications (e.g., centralized product data)	100.0	5.2
3.2	A centralized data warehouse that summarizes key information from decentralized databases	86.7	4.5
3.3	Data management advice and consultancy	69.2	3.7
3.4	Electronic provision of management information (e.g., executive information systems [EIS])	71.4	4.3
3.5	Storage farms or storage area networks (e.g., major storage separate from local area networks and workstations)	86.7	4.6

APPENDIX | 329

		Percent Having	Relative Investment (−10 [lowest] to +10 [highest])
Data Management *(continued)*		**78.0%**	**4.8**
3.6	Knowledge management (KM) *(e.g., contact database, KM architecture, knowledge databases, and communities of practice)*	53.8	6.3
IT Management		**90.9%**	**3.8**
4.1	Large-scale data processing facilities *(e.g., mainframe)*	92.9	2.5
4.2	Server farms *(e.g., email server, Web servers, and printer servers)*	100.0	4.8
4.3	Installation and maintenance of workstations and local area networks	100.0	3.2
4.4	Information systems (IS) planning *(e.g., forward business plans and capacity strategy)*	86.7	3.3
4.5	IS project management	93.3	3.4
4.6	Negotiate with suppliers and outsourcers *(e.g., centralized and negotiated pricing for software)*	100.0	4.1
4.7	Service-level agreements *(e.g., agreements between corporate IT or outsourcers and business units)*	80.0	4.5
4.8	Common systems development environment	78.6	2.5
4.9	Pilot e-business initiatives *(e.g., pilot Web "shopfronts" managed in conjunction with business units)*	86.7	5.9
Security		**100.0%**	**6.1**
5.1	Security policies for use of IS *(e.g., data protection, access privileges, and hacker protection)*	100.0	5.9
5.2	Enforce security policies for IS	100.0	6.1
5.3	Disaster planning for business applications	100.0	6.5
5.4	Firewall on secure gateway services	100.0	5.7

	Architecture and Standards	**Percent Having 95.5%**	**Relative Investment (−10 [lowest] to +10 [highest]) 2.7**
6.1	Specify architectures (data) *(create a blueprint and set high-level guidelines for the way data will be used and integrated)*	92.9	3.0
6.2	Specify architectures (technology) *(create a blueprint and set high-level guidelines for the way technology will be used and integrated)*	100.0	2.9
6.3	Specify architectures (communications) *(create a blueprint and set high-level guidelines for the way communications technology will be used and integrated)*	100.0	3.2
6.4	Specify architectures (applications) *(create a blueprint and set high-level guidelines for the way information technology applications will be used and integrated)*	100.0	3.5
6.5	Specify architectures (work) *(create a blueprint and set high-level guidelines for the way work will be conducted)*	84.6	2.5
6.6	Enforce architectures (data) *(enforce compliance with high-level data architectures)*	92.9	2.9
6.7	Enforce architectures (technology) *(enforce compliance with high-level technology architectures)*	100.0	2.5
6.8	Enforce architectures (communications) *(enforce compliance with high-level communications architectures)*	100.0	2.8
6.9	Enforce architectures (applications) *(enforce compliance with high-level applications architectures)*	100.0	3.1
6.10	Enforce architectures (work) *(enforce compliance with high-level work architectures)*	84.6	2.5

	Architecture and Standards *(continued)*	Percent Having 95.5%	Relative Investment (−10 [lowest] to +10 [highest]) 2.7
6.11	Set standards for IT architectures (data) *(set standard operating environment [SOE] to implement data architectures)*	92.9	2.5
6.12	Set standards for IT architectures (technology) *(set SOE to implement technology architectures)*	100.0	2.7
6.13	Set standards for IT architectures (communications) *(set SOE to implement communications architectures)*	100.0	2.7
6.14	Set standards for IT architectures (applications) *(set SOE to implement applications architectures)*	100.0	2.8
6.15	Set standards for IT architectures (work) *(set SOE to implement work architectures)*	84.6	2.5
6.16	Enforce standards for data architecture	92.9	2.2
6.17	Enforce standards for technology architecture	100.0	2.2
6.18	Enforce standards for communications architecture	100.0	2.3
6.19	Enforce standards for applications architecture	100.0	2.5
6.20	Enforce standards for work architecture	84.6	2.5
	E-Channel Management: provide electronic channel to customer or partners to support multiple applications.	51.3%	4.6
7.1	EFT/POS	50.0	5.7
7.2	Kiosks	30.0	1.7
7.3	Web sites	100.0	6.9
7.4	Call centers	85.7	4.0
7.5	IVRs	33.3	2.0
7.6	Mobile phones	30.0	1.3
7.7	Mobile computing *(e.g., via dial-up)*	30.0	2.0

		Relative Investment Percent Having	(−10 [lowest] to +10 [highest])
IT Research and Development		**83.3%**	**2.5**
8.1	Identify and test new technologies for business purposes	80.0	2.3
8.2	Evaluate proposals for new IS initiatives	86.7	2.6
IT Education		**82.1%**	**3.9**
9.1	Training and use of IT	85.7	3.9
9.2	Management education for generating value from IT use	78.6	3.8

Notes

PREFACE AND ACKNOWLEDGMENTS

1. The notion of moving from a marketplace to marketspace was popularized by the pioneering work of John Sviokla and Jeff Rayport in two articles. See J. Rayport and J. Sviokla, "Managing the Marketspace," *Harvard Business Review* 72, no. 6 (1994): 141–151; and J. Rayport and J. Sviokla, "Exploiting the Virtual Value Chain," *Harvard Business Review* 73, no. 6 (1995): 75–85.

CHAPTER 1

1. Cost-to-income ratios are commonly used by banks to measure profitability. The ratio is the cost of operations divided by the total bank income (i.e., net interest income plus fee income).

2. Prior to the introduction of the Internet, business was conducted face-to-face, by telephone, mail, or facsimile, or via proprietary computer networks.

3. B2B e-business is where a business is buying, selling, or acting as an agent for another business electronically. Estimates by eight authorities on the percentage of e-business that is B2B vary from 61 percent to 90 percent, with an average of 78 percent. Because the building blocks for B2B e-business are more firmly in place, B2B e-business is likely to continue to dominate B2C in dollar terms, and the Gartner Group predicts it will be 71 percent of total global sales transactions by 2004. See Gartner Group (www.gartner.com),

"Triggering the B2B E-business Explosion," 31 January 2000, <http://www.gartner.com>.

4. This definition was influenced by the work of many others including: Professor Detmar Straub at Georgia State University who pointed out the importance of substitution of information for the physical business process; J. O'Brien, "Glossary" in *Management Information Systems: Managing Information Technology in the Internetworked Enterprise* (Chicago: Irwin/McGraw-Hill, 1999), G6; U.S. Department of Commerce, *The Emerging Digital Economy II* (Washington, DC: U.S. Department of Commerce, 1999); Organization for Economic Co-operation and Development (OECD), *The Economic and Social Impacts of E-business: Preliminary Findings and Research Agenda*, 1999, <http://www.oecd.org/subject/e_commerce/summary.htm>; A. Brandenburger and B. Nalebuff, *Co-Opetition* (New York: Doubleday, 1996); and during much debate among the Melbourne Business School students in the subject "E-business: Strategy and Implementation."

5. Complementors were described by A. Brandenburger and B. Nalebuff, in their excellent book *Co-Opetition*. A complementor is an organizational entity whose activities enhance demand for the products and services of another enterprise.

6. U.S. Department of Commerce, *The Emerging Digital Economy II*, 3.

7. Internet: A global network of networks through which computers communicate by sending information in packets. Each network consists of computers connected by cables or wireless links. IP (Internet Protocol): The protocol that governs how computers send packets across the Internet. TCP (Transmission Control Protocol): A computer protocol that allows one computer to send the other a continuous stream of information by breaking it into packets and reassembling it at the other end and that resends any packets that get lost in transit. TCP uses IP to send the packets, and the two together are referred to as TCP/IP.

8. T. Berners-Lee and M. Fischetti, *Weaving the Web* (New York: HarperSanFransisco, 1999), 213.

9. OECD, *The Economic and Social Impacts of E-business*.

10. Ibid.

11. A. Giraldo, F. Gens, and J. Gantz, *The State of the Internet Economy—Trends Forecast, 1998–2003: Investments Will Fuel Commerce*, IDC W20368 (Framingham, MA: IDC, 1999).

12. See <http://www.internetindicators.com/executive_summary_oct_99.html>, "The Internet Economy Indicators," June 2000 & October 1999 reports.

13. The attention paid to B2C e-business is well deserved. CommerceNet and Nielsen Media Research have conducted an Internet demographic survey since 1995. In 1999, around ninety-two million North Americans over the age of sixteen were online, fifty-three million of whom had used the Internet to shop—to find product and price information—and then had purchased offline. Twenty-eight million people had purchased online, with one million purchasing at least once a week. The widespread use of the Internet for window-shopping means that product and service producers who continue to sell through intermediaries will still need to provide detailed product information directly to the consumer online.

14. In a study of fifty-four businesses over a five-year period we found that 57 percent of IT investment was infrastructure. Firms that invested more in IT infrastructure than their competitors have faster time to market for new products and higher revenue growths but low profitability in the first two years. For details see P. Weill and M. Broadbent, *Leveraging the New Infrastructure: How Market Leaders Capitalize on Information Technology* (Boston: Harvard Business School Press, 1998), 58. The evidence for the significant payoff of public-sector infrastructure is summarized in P. Weill, "The Role and Value of Information Technology Infrastructure: Some Empirical Observations," in *Perspectives on the Strategic and Economic Value of Information Technology,* eds. R. D. Banker, R. J. Kauffman, and M. A. Mahmood (Middleton, PA: Idea Group Publishing, 1993), 547–72.

15. The research from the Center for Research on E-business at the University of Texas shows that in Quarter 1, 1999 (compared to Quarter 1, 1998), revenues in the infrastructure layers grew between 50 percent and 61 percent, whereas the Internet commerce layer grew by 127 percent. Thus leveraging the infrastructure investment has commenced. For details see <http://www.internetindicators.com/executive_summary_oct_99.html>.

16. As reported in C.V. Callahan and B. Parsternack, "Corporate Strategy in the Digital Age," *Journal of Strategy and Business,* second quarter 1999, <http://www.strategy-business.com/research/>. Callahan and Parsternack's article summarizes a study by Booz•Allen & Hamilton entitled "Competing in the Digital Age: Will the Internet Change Corporate Strategy?" <http://www.strategy-business.com>. The study involved 525 survey responses, interviews at fifty companies, and two thought leadership panels.

17. Premier Pages are secure, tailored areas for major customers on the Dell Web site that provide a predetermined set of Dell and third-party products at prenegotiated prices. Dell customers can use the Premier Pages to implement a standard operating environment for desktop products. See several Dell news releases including: "Dell Announces Premier Dell.com," press

release, 8 September 2000, <http://www.dell.com/us/en/gen/corporate/press/pressoffice_us_2000.htm>, in which Premier Pages was renamed Premier Dell.com; V. K. Rangan and M. Bell, "Dell Online," Case 9-598-116 (Boston: Harvard Business School, 1998); M. Dell and C. Fredman, *Direct from Dell: Strategies That Revolutionized an Industry* (New York: HarperCollins, 1999).

18. A. M. Chard, "Knowledge Management at Ernst & Young," Case M291 (Palo Alto: Stanford University Graduate School of Business, 1997), <http://www.ernie.ey.com>.

19. See "E-commerce Poster Child Grows Up," *Datamation*, B. Roberts, August 1998, <http://www.datamation.com/ecomm/08ecom.html>; A. Reinhardt, "Meet Cisco's Mr Internet," *Business Week*, 13 September 1999, <http://www.businessweek.com/1999/99_37/b3646001.htm>.

20. See <http://www.quicken.com>; M. Dobbie, "Quicken's One Stop Shop," *Personal Investor*, May 1999, 96; D. C. Johnson, "Jostling of Share for E-Mortgages," *New York Times*, 31 May 1999; S. Hamm, "This Intuit Hunch May Pay Off," *Business Week*, 15 June 1998, 78.

21. As reported by B. Howarth in "Strategy: Compaq the Shopkeeper Treads on a Few Toes," *Business Review Weekly*, 1 October 1999.

22. *IBIS Industry Outlook Reports: K7321 Banks*, October 1999, <http://www.ibis.com.au>.

23. As reported in P. Hudson, "Bank Tellers Fall Victim to ATMs," *The Age*, 15 September 1998, 3.

24. I. Rubin, "Automation Technologies Offer Branches a New Strategic Life," *Banking Systems and Technology* 36, no. 8 (1999): 48.

25. As reported in Callahan and Parsternack, "Corporate Strategy in the Digital Age," which summarizes the Booz•Allen & Hamilton study, "Competing in the Digital Age: Will the Internet Change Corporate Strategy?".

26. Bank of Montreal Group of Companies, *1999 Annual Report* (Montreal: Bank of Montreal Group of Companies, 1999), 45.

27. OECD, *The Economic and Social Impacts of E-business;* "Can Pay Won't Pay," *The Economist*, 14 February 1998.

28. Rob Flynn, interview by authors, late 1999.

29. As of April 24, 2000, Amazon's market capitalization dropped to $16.9 billion, which was 13.5 times that of Barnes & Noble. For details on Amazon see K. Brooker, "Amazon vs Everybody," *Fortune*, November 1999, <http://www.fortune.com>; A. Stone, "An Investor's Guide to Online Booksellers," *Business Week*, 10 June 1998; P. Ghemawat and B. Baird, "Leader-

ship Online: Barnes and Noble vs Amazon.com (A)," Case 9-798-063 (Boston: Harvard Business School, 1998). Amazon.com's and Barnes & Noble's Web sites are at <http://www.amazon.com> and <http://www.barnesandnoble.com>.

30. K. Brooker, "Amazon vs Everybody."

31. Insights from B. Leucke, "Hang on for a Wild Ride: The Race for the Moon versus the Race for the Internet," *Vital Speeches for the Day* 65, no. 22 (1999): 682–85.

32. For the seminal work on critical success factors see J. Rockart, "Chief Executives Define Their Own Data Needs," *Harvard Business Review* 57, no. 2 (1979): 81–93.

Chapter 2

1. Our thinking and definitions of business strategy were inspired by and drawn upon the work of Costantinos Markides, Henry Mintzberg, and Michael Porter.

2. Adapted from R. Hall, *Organizations: Structure and Process,* 3rd ed. (Englewood Cliffs, NJ: Prentice Hall, 1982), 53–54.

3. Adapted from G. B. Davis and M. H. Olson, *Management Information Systems: Conceptual Foundations, Structure and Development* (New York: McGraw-Hill, 1985), 333; T. Malone, "The Dawn of the E-Lance Economy," *Harvard Business Review* 76, no. 5 (1998): 144–52.

4. K. Laudon and J. Laudon, *Management Information Systems: Organization and Technology,* 4th ed. (Englewood Cliffs, NJ: Prentice Hall, 1996), 75.

5. T. H. Davenport, *Process Innovation: Reengineering Work Through Information Technology* (Boston: Harvard Business School Press, 1993).

6. M. Porter and V. Millar, "How Information Gives You Competitive Advantage," *Harvard Business Review* 63, no. 4 (1985), 149–61.

7. C. K. Prahalad and G. Hamel, "The Core Competence of the Corporation," *Harvard Business Review* 68, no. 3 (1990): 79–90; see particularly chapter 2 of J. B. Quinn, *Intelligent Enterprise* (New York: Free Press, 1992).

8. To learn more about these developments see T. Berners-Lee and M. Fischetti, *Weaving the Web* (New York: HarperSanFrancisco, 1999), 213.

9. "Creating a Business Model for E-Commerce," *CIO* 12, no. 14 (1999): 3–18.

10. Ibid.

11. For an insightful discussion of evaluating business change projects before implementation, see R. Paul, G. Giaglis, and V. Hlupic, "Simulation of Business Processes," *American Behavioral Scientist* 42, no. 10 (1999): 1551–76. In a very interesting article Henry Mintzberg and Ludo Van Der Heyden propose another way to represent a business: as "organigraphs." See H. Mintzberg and L. Van Der Heyden, "Organigraphs: Drawing How Companies Really Work," *Harvard Business Review* 77, no. 5 (1999): 87–94.

12. Our thinking on business models has been influenced by a number of authors. In particular see P. Timmers, "Business Models for Electronic Markets," *EM—Electronic Markets* 8, no. 2 (1998): 3–8.

13. See Timmers, "Business Models for Electronic Markets," as well as Michael Rappa, "Taxonomies of Business Models on the Web," 19 April 2000, <http://www.ecommerce.ncsu.edu/business_models.html>. Both have provided very useful and quite different taxonomies of business models.

14. Much of the information on AccuWeather is from <http://www.accuweather.com>.

15. V. K. Rangan and M. Bell, "Dell Online," Case 9-598-116 (Boston: Harvard Business School, 1998).

16. M. Dobbie, "Quicken's One Stop Shop," *Personal Investor,* May 1999, 96. Quicken's Web sites are at <http://www.quicken.com> and <http://www.quicken.com.au>.

17. D. Diamond, "Can Intuit Remake Itself for the Net," *Upside* 10, no. 9 (1998): 96–105; D. Cay Johnson, "Jostling of Share for E-Mortgages," *New York Times,* 31 May 1999; S. Hamm, "This Intuit Hunch May Pay Off," *Business Week,* 15 June 1998, 123.

18. For details and source see Yahoo!'s Web site at <http://www.yahoo.com/docs/pr>.

19. For details see <http://www.edgaradvantage.com>; Yahoo! 10-K form filed with the Securities and Exchange Commission (SEC) on 30 March 2000, <http://www.sec.gov/archives>.

Chapter 3

1. H. Mintzberg, *The Structuring of Organizations* (Englewood Cliffs, NJ: Prentice Hall, 1979), 468.

2. These market segment classifications come from a study by the Australian Stock Exchange (ASX), "ASX 1997 Shareowners Segmentation Study," <http://www.asx.com.au>.

3. The phrase "word of mouse" comes from a thought-provoking article by G. Hamel and G. Sampler, "The E-Corp.," *Fortune,* 7 December 1998, 80–92.

4. These market segment classifications come from a study by the ASX, "ASX 1997 Shareowners Segmentation Study."

5. G. J. Hooley, J. A. Saunders, and N. F. Piercy, *Market Strategy and Competitive Positioning,* 2d ed. (London: Prentice Hall, 1998), 201.

6. P. Kotler, *Marketing Management: Analysis, Planning, Implementation and Control,* 6th ed. (Englewood Cliffs, NJ: Prentice Hall, 1988).

7. See P. R. Dickson and J. L. Ginter, "Market Segmentation, Product Differentiation, and Marketing Strategy," *Journal of Marketing* 51, no. 2 (1987): 1–10.

8. L. McPhee and J. Lieb, "Internet Users Top 92 Million in the U.S. and Canada," CommerceNet Research Note #99, 23 June 1999, <http://www.commerce.net>.

9. This information comes from "About 24/7 Media," <http://www.247media.com/corp–info>.

10. Information on Dell's approach to segmentation was taken from V. K. Rangan and M. Bell, "Dell Online," Case 9-598-116 (Boston: Harvard Business School, 1998); and M. Dell and C. Fredman, *Direct from Dell: Strategies That Revolutionized an Industry* (New York: HarperCollins, 1999).

11. For an interesting discussion of viewing the channel as a feature of the product see G. J. Hoeg, "Valuing the Channel," *Best's Review* 100, no. 1 (1999): 82–83.

12. Insights from B. Leucke, "Hang on for a Wild Ride: The Race for the Moon versus the Race for the Internet," *Vital Speeches for the Day* 65, no. 22 (1999): 682–85. This is the transcript of a thought-provoking speech by Leucke delivered to *Business Week*'s E-Customer Forum, San Francisco, CA, 20 July 1999, <http://www.bankone.com> and <http://www.wingspanbank.com>.

13. *IBIS Industry Outlook Reports: K7321 Banks,* October 1999, <http://www.ibis.com.au>.

14. For more details see T. Field, "Trade Secrets," *CIO* 13, no. 8 (2000): 70–76.

15. This work on channels was developed with Richard Speed, a marketing professor at the Melbourne Business School, University of Melbourne, Australia.

16. See "E-commerce Poster Child Grows Up," *Datamation,* B. Roberts, August 1998, <http://www.datamation.com/ecomm/08ecom.html>; and

A. Reinhardt, "Meet Cisco's Mr Internet," *Business Week Online,* 13 September 1999, <http://www.businessweek.com/1999/99_37/b3646001.htm>.

17. For this section we draw heavily on P. Weill and M. Broadbent, *Leveraging the New Infrastructure: How Market Leaders Capitalize on Information Technology* (Boston: Harvard Business School Press, 1998).

18. See J. Barney, "Firm Resources and Sustained Competitive Advantage," *Journal of Management* 17, no. 1 (1991): 99–120.

19. Weill and Broadbent, *Leveraging the New Infrastructure,* 58–62.

20. The authors would like to acknowledge Peter Raisbeck, a senior research fellow at the Melbourne Business School, who worked with us to collect and analyze the data.

21. The starting point was the list of twenty-five infrastructure services in figure 4.2 on page 88 and the eight clusters of infrastructure services in figure 5.3 on page 119 of Weill and Broadbent, *Leveraging the New Infrastructure.* The ninth category of infrastructure services, "e-channel management," was added to include the ability of the firm to support a direct electronic connection to the customer via a variety of channels.

22. As reported in C. V. Callahan and B. Parsternack, "Corporate Strategy in the Digital Age," *Journal of Strategy and Business,* second quarter 1999, <http://www.strategy-business.com/research/00202/page1.html>. Callahan and Parsternack's article summarizes a study by Booz•Allen & Hamilton entitled "Competing in the Digital Age: Will the Internet Change Corporate Strategy?" <http://www.strategy-business.com>. The study involved 525 survey responses, interviews at fifty companies, and two thought leadership panels.

Chapter 4

1. K. Regan, "Q1 E-Commerce Matches Holiday Pace," *E-Commerce Times,* 1 May 2000, <http://www.ecommercetimes.com/news/articles2000/000501-3.shtml>.

2. L. Enos, "Online Shopping Will Top $61 billion in 2000," *E-Commerce Times,* 18 April 2000, <http://www.ecommercetimes.com/news/articles2000/000418-1.shtml>.

3. Sources on Dell include <http://www.dell.com>; V. K. Rangan and M. Bell, "Dell Online," Case 9-598-116 (Boston: Harvard Business School, 1998); M. Dell and C. Fredman, *Direct from Dell: Strategies That Revolutionized an Industry* (New York: HarperCollins, 1999); G. Payne, "DELL Computer: Business to Business Over the Web," Case UVA-C-2144 (Char-

lottesville, VA: Darden Graduate School of Business Administration, University of Virginia, 1999).

4. For more information see <http://www.realnetworks.com/company>.

5. L. Lee, "Clicks and Mortar at Gap.com," *Business Week,* 18 October 1999, 150.

6. "Forrester Research Predicts the Imminent Demise of Most Dot Com Retailers," press release, 11 April 2000, <http://www.forrester.com/ER/Press/Release/0,1769,270,FF.html>.

7. United States Small Business Administration, Office of Advocacy, "The Facts about Small Business 1999," <http://www.sba.gov/advo/stats/facts99.pdf>; and H. Sherman, "Assessing the Intervention Effectiveness of Business Incubation Programs on New Business Start-Ups," *Journal of Business Development* 4, no. 2 (1999): 117–33.

8. As reported in H. Green, "Shakeout e-Tailer in This Brave New World, Only the Profitable Survive," *Business Week,* 15 May 2000, EB102.

9. Reported in R. Hof, H. Green, and D. Brady, "Suddenly Amazon's Books Look Better: The Retailer Is Raking in a Bundle from Other Merchants," *Business Week,* 21 February 2000, 78.

10. For completeness, this chapter should also include "C2B" and "C2C" sites as well, but because consumers tend to have limited product lines, such sites are generally of little interest in the direct-to-customer sense. They will be considered in chapter 7, where we discuss intermediaries.

11. L. Schmidt, "The Retail Kings: Harvey Norman, A Structured Success," *BRW,* 8 October 1999, <http://www.brw.com.au/stories/19991008/3746.htm>.

12. See D. Morrison and K. N. Cukier, "Boo's Blues," *Red Herring,* 4 May 2000, <http://www.redherring.com/vc/2000/0504/vc-boo050400.html>.

13. E. Nussenbaum and A. Lieberman, "Big-Deal E-Tailer Boo Is Through," *New York Post,* 6 May 2000, <http://www.nypost.com/business/3306.htm>.

14. K. Regan and N. Macaluso, "Boo.com Saga Ends with Asset Sale," *E-Commerce Times,* 30 May 2000, <http://www.ecommercetimes.com/news/articles2000/000530-4.shtml>.

15. R. Conlin, "UPS, e-Bay Grab Highest E-Business Honors," *E-Commerce Times,* 13 April 2000, <http://www.ecommercetimes.com/news/articles2000/000413-4.shtml>.

16. The full report makes sober reading: It can be found on the Internet at (www.freeedgar.com) by entering the company name ETOYS and then accessing the 10-Q form filed by the company on February 14, 2000.

17. M. D. Dunn, "Discover the 7 Revenue Streams of Your Web Site," 1998, <http://www.inetdesign.com/7streams.html>.

18. R. Seidman and M. Hurst, "In Search of E-Commerce: Lessons from the Internet's Top Sites," 1999, <http://www.goodreports.com/cgi-bin/Soft Cart.100.exe/info.html?E+scstore>.

19. B. Tedeschi, "CDNOW Struggles to Be Heard," *New York Times,* 24 May 1999, <http://www.qc.edu/Economics/Classpgs/eco383_internet/low_val.htm>.

20. <http://www.cdnow.com/aboutcdnow.html>.

21. P. Patsuris, "CDNOW Burning Out of Cash," *Forbes,* 29 March 2000, <http://www.forbes.com/tool/html/00/mar/0329/MU5.htm>.

22. B. Warner, "That Was CDNOW, This Is Then," *The Standard,* 29 March 2000, <http://www.thestandard.com/article/display/0,1151,13462,00.html>.

23. M. Summers, "CDNOW Faces Unsavory Choices as Cash Runs Short," *ZDNet News,* 31 March 2000, <http://www.zdnet.com/zdnn/stories/news/0,4586,2499138,00.html>.

24. J. Willoughby, "Warning: Internet Companies Are Running Out of Cash . . . Fast!" *Barron's,* 19 March 2000, <http://www.barrons.com>.

25. R. Spector, *Amazon.com: Get Big Fast* (London: Random House Business Books, 2000), 202–3.

26. M. Summers, "CDNOW Faces Unsavory Choices As Cash Runs Short," *ZDNet News,* 31 March 2000, <http://www.zdnet.com/zdnn/stories/news/0,4586,2499138,00.html>.

27. B. Bennett, "Online Retailers Need to Speed Up Delivery," *Australian Financial Review,* 16 May 2000, 44.

28. R. Beck, "Weak Link in Online Shopping/Delivery: Doorstep," *Los Angeles Times,* 5 June 2000.

29. R. Hof, H. Green, and D. Brady, "Suddenly Amazon's Books Look Better: The Retailer Is Raking in a Bundle from Other Merchants," *Business Week,* 21 February 2000, 78.

30. "At Your Service: How Amazon Tries to Keep Its Customers Satisfied," *Wall Street Journal,* 17 May 2000.

31. <http://www.fedex.com/us/marketplace> and <http://www.fedex.com/us/marketplace/premiumstores.html>.

32. N. Hutheesing, "Last Chance," *Forbes*, 15 June 1998, <http://www.forbes.com/forbesglobal/98/0615/0106087a.htm>.

33. L. W. Stern and A. I. El-Ansary, *Marketing Channels* (Englewood Cliffs, NJ: Prentice Hall), 285.

34. A. Gilbert and B. Bacheldor, "The Big Squeeze," *Information Week*, 27 March 2000, <http://www.informationweek.com/779/channel.htm>.

35. W. Andrews, "Brick-and-Mortars in 2000: Payback Time," *Internetworld*, 1 January 2000, <http://www.internetworld.com/2000/01/01/business/20000101-payback.html>.

36. Describing the affiliates program, the Maidenform site says, "If you have a website, you can make money selling ladies' underwear. It's easy and it's free to join." <http://www.maidenform.com/egi-bin/mf/main.jsp>.

37. Some analysts were critical of Levi's reaction. "That's pre-Web mentality, that there's a scarcity of customers out there," said Internet guru Patricia Seybold. "To be successful, companies will ultimately sell merchandise online and offline, both directly and through retailers." A. Stuart, "Clicks & Bricks," *CIO*, 15 March 2000, 77.

38. A. Stuart, "Clicks & Bricks," *CIO*, 15 March 2000, 77.

39. "For example, according to internal [Amazon.com] documents, [the publisher] Scribner paid $10,000 for Stephen King's novel *Bag of Bones* to gain prominent placement on Amazon.com's 'Best-seller' page, along with a profile of the author and a feature in Amazon.com's listing 'Destined for Greatness.'" Spector, *Amazon.com: Get Big Fast*, 234.

40. "Is Rob Glaser for Real?" *Fortune*, 4 September 2000, 216–25.

CHAPTER 5

1. "Products and Services," "Prudential Advisor," <http://www.prusec.com/products_services/pruadvisor.htm>.

2. Customers are not required to do all of their investing through the relationship, but the pricing structure makes it attractive for them to do so.

3. A firm that directly provides *none* of what the customer is buying is an agent or intermediary (see chapter 9), not a full-service provider.

4. "About Us," <http://www.orica-chemnet.com/Business/CHE/CHEMNET/WCHE00003.nsf/webnav2/about+us>.

5. G. Calvin, "America's Most Admired Companies," *Fortune*, 21 February 2000, <http://www.pathfinder.com/fortune/mostadmired/intro.html>.

6. "Company Profile," <http://www.ge.com/supply/profile.html>.

7. The "manufacturer's line card" (the list of manufacturers who produce each item offered by GE Supply) at <http://www.ge.com/supply/line card.html> suggests the degree of overlap in the GE Supply product line between GE-produced items and those made by GE's competitors.

8. "Company Profile," <http://www.ge.com/supply/profile.html>.

Chapter 6

1. For more details see A. Brand, P. Weill, C. Soh, and P. Periasamy, "Citibank—Asia Pacific: Positioning IT As a Strategic Resource," Melbourne Business School, Melbourne, Australia, 1999.

2. <http://www.southcorp.com.au>.

3. This section draws on a case study of the Victorian Government's whole-of-enterprise government model implementation. For more details see P. Richardson and P. Weill, "Multimedia Victoria." Case CL387(Melbourne, Australia: Melbourne Business School, 1999).

4. See <http://www.mmv.vic.gov.au> for more details. "Bill Gates presented with Smart Card for award winning Maxi." News release from the Office of the Treasurer and Minister for Multi-Media, Victoria, Australia, 18 March 1998.

5. Victorian Law Reform Committee, "Technology and Law Report 1999," 1999, <http://www.parliament.vic.gov.au/lawreform/tech/5.html>.

6. "Online Government 2001—from Vision to Reality," Victoria Department of State Development, Multimedia Victoria, <http://www.mmv.vic.gov.au>.

7. G. Jones, "Blair Wants Everyone on the Internet in Five Years," *The Electronic Telegraph*, 8 March 2000, <http://www.telegraph.co.uk>.

8. "Whitehall Drive for E-Government," *BBC News*, 3 April 2000, <http://news2.thls.bbc.co.uk/hi/english/uk%5Fpolitics/newsid%5F699000/699504.stm>.

9. "UK to Offer All Govt. Services Online," *USA Today Tech Report*, 3 April 2000, <http://www.usatoday.com/life/cyber/tech/cth655.htm>.

10. For a more detailed discussion see P. Weill and M. Broadbent, *Leveraging the New Infrastructure: How Market Leaders Capitalize on Information Technology* (Boston: Harvard Business School Press, 1998), 37.

11. For a detailed discussion of techniques to financially evaluate IT infrastructure investment see Weill and Broadbent, *Leveraging the New Infrastructure,* chapter 9.

12. Welcoming message from U.S. President Bill Clinton on the FirstGov Web site, <http://www.firstgov.gov/top_nav/welcome1.html>.

13. P. J. Smedley, "Presentation to the Annual General Meeting of Colonial Limited," 28 April 1998, <http://www.colonial.com.au/download/News/1998_AGM_speeches.pdf>.

14. Colonial Limited, "Colonial Limited Annual Report," 1999, 9.

Chapter 7

1. R. Needleman, "Retail is Toast," *Red Herring*, 2 August 1999, <http://www.redherring.com/cod/080299.html>.

2. For a very insightful discussion of the necessary conditions for successful e-business see A. Kambil, "Doing Business in the Wired World," *IEEE Computer* 30, no. 5 (1997): 56–61.

3. "In 1998, roughly one million people took part in online auctions. That number will grow to 14 million by 2003 according to Forrester Research." J. Berst, "The Plan to Kill eBay (and Why It Won't Work)," *ZDNet Anchor Desk,* 20 September 1999, <http://www.zdnet.com/anchordesk/story/story_3877.html>.

4. According to the Weekly Flash from Media Metrix (www.mediametrix.com), for the week ending January 9, 2000, eBay's daily reach topped 6.5 percent, outpacing Amazon.com, the number two site, by 58 percent, and the number of unique visitors to eBay on an average daily basis set a new Internet record of 1.782 million.

5. <http://pages.ebay.com/help/sellerguide/after-whatnow.html>.

6. eBay initial public offering document, September 1998, <http://www.sec.gov>.

7. "eBay Launches Business Exchange," press release, 15 March 2000, <http://www.shareholder.com/ebay/releases-general.cfm>.

8. <http://www.freemarkets.com/company/default.asp>.

9. Information taken from <http://www.priceline.com/PriceLineASPOurCompany/asp/company.asp>.

10. Description of e-STEEL is from <http://www.e-steel.com/faq.shtml>.

11. <http://www.tpn.com/tpnmark/faq9.htm>.

12. "Europe's 50 Hottest Tech Firms," 19 June 2000, <http://www.time.com/time/europe/specials>.

13. Of course, masterpiece paintings, racehorses, and even used cars are regularly auctioned over the Internet. These cases are different, however, because in an auction there is one seller and many buyers. The seller's identity and reputation are important clues to quality and integrity, and if there

is disagreement about the characteristics of an item, the seller's identity can readily be established. None of this holds true for an electronic marketplace, in which buyers generally bid without knowledge of the seller's identity. A stock exchange is a good example of this sort of marketplace.

14. Stores include Mom and Pop Software, TEKVisions, and A.N.A., which sells computers, TVs, VCRs, home/auto stereo equipment, perfumes/colognes, and jewelry.

15. Excite@Home offers media services through the Excite Network (www.excite.com, www.bluemountain.com, and other properties), and broadband subscription services through @Home (www.home.com) and @Work (www.work.home.net). The company has a worldwide footprint of seventy-two million cable homes under long-term contract.

16. K. Yamada, "Mall Things Considered," *Redherring.com Shop Talk*, 25 April 2000, <http://www.redherring.com>.

17. Ibid.

18. Ibid.

19. Usage data taken from "Yahoo! Reports First Quarter 2000 Financial Results," press release, 5 April 2000, <http://docs.yahoo.com/docs/pr/1q00pr.html>. U.S. audience size reported by Media Metrix (www.mediametrix.com).

20. Nielsen//NetRatings, <http://www.nielsen-netratings.com>. "Neilsen//NetRatings Expands Global Internet Index to 17 Countries-Yahoo!, AOL, MSN retain leadership with global Internet users," press release, 31 October 2000, <http://63.140.238.20/press_releases/pr_001031_global.htm>.

21. Most early portals listed Web sites alphabetically, a major reason cited by Jeff Bezos for calling his new online book business "Amazon."

22. R. Chandrasekaran, "Today's Hot Web Concept Is 'Portals,'" *Washington Post*, 11 October 1998.

23. K. Swisher, *AOL.COM*, updated edition (New York: Times Business Books, 1999), 312.

24. "Yahoo! Reports First Quarter 2000 Financial Results," press release, 5 April 2000, <http://docs.yahoo.com/docs/pr/1q00pr.html>.

25. J. Berst, "Why You'll Never Go to Yahoo Again," *ZDNet AnchorDesk*, 2 June 1999, <http://www.zdnet.com/anchordesk/story/story_3456.html>.

26. K. De Clercq, "The Best Price? Winerobot Rules," *BRW*, 31 March 2000, 79.

27. Ibid.

CHAPTER 8

1. The epigraph is Harold Kutner's comment on the announcement by Ford, General Motors, and DaimlerChrysler of the creation of an integrated B2B supplier exchange through a single global Web site. "Ford, General Motors and DaimlerChrysler Create World's Largest Internet-Based Virtual Market Place," press release, 25 February 2000, <http://www.generalmotors.com>.

2. M. Beefy, "Well-supplied by Artesian," *The Australian Financial Review*, 22–23 January 2000, 11.

3. A. White, "Glassy Trio Mixes Its Drinks Online," *The Weekend Australian*, 22–23 January 2000, 31.

4. K. Needham, "List Barrelled by Wine Venture," *Fairfax IT*, 25 January 2000, <http://www.it.fairfax.com.au/breaking/20000125/A44663-2000Jan25.html>.

5. S. Evans, "UK Turns on Glass Act for BRL," *The Australian Financial Review*, 25 January 2000, 21.

6. W. Brown, "Automakers, Tech Firms Form Alliance to Put Motorists Online," *Washington Post*, 25 January 2000.

7. "Ford, General Motors and DaimlerChrysler Create World's Largest Internet-Based Virtual Market Place."

8. Ibid.

9. <http://www.ams-ix.net/home.html>.

10. The story of the early computer reservation systems is compellingly related in J. L. McKenney, *Waves of Change* (Boston: Harvard Business School Press, 1995), chapter 4.

11. U.S. Department of Transportation, *Study of Airline Computer Reservations Systems*, DOT-P-37-88-2 (Washington, DC: U.S. Department of Transportation, 1988).

12. Current information for this case study is drawn from "Corporate Profiles," <http://www.abacus.com.sg/corporate/profile/index.htm>. Historical information relies heavily on the following excellent case study on ABACUS: Neo Boon Siong, "ABACUS Distribution System: Collaboration to Compete in the Asia-Pacific Skies," in *Exploiting Information Technology for Business Competitiveness: Cases and Insights from Singapore-based Organisation* (Reading, MA: Addison-Wesley Publishing, 1996), 75–95.

13. Ibid.

14. "ABACUS and The SABRE Group Sign a Joint-Venture Establishing the Largest & Most Comprehensive Global Distribution System in the Asia-Pacific," press release, 1 March 1998, <http://www.abacus.com.sg>.

Chapter 9

1. <http://www.tacobell.com> (accessed 19 January 2000). The bulletin board also included several messages from Taco Bell employees, identified by store number, complaining that their managers used drugs at work.

2. A more formal statement of this effect, known as *Metcalfe's Law,* is that the overall value of the community is proportional to the number of members squared.

3. <http://www.ivillage.com/help/privacy.html>.

4. <http://www.planetout.com/pno>.

5. <http://www.fishing.com/privacy.html>.

6. <http://www.ivillage.com/help/tos.html>.

7. <http://www.fool.com/help/FoolsRules.htm>.

8. "Money Now on Electric Minds," *CNET News.com,* 7 April 1997, <http://news.cnet.com/news/0-1005-200-317926.html?tag=st.ne.1005-200-320291>.

9. S. Jarvenpaa, N. Tractinsky, and M. Vitale, "Consumer Trust in an Internet Store," *Information Technology and Management Journal* 1, nos. 1 & 2 (1999): 45–72.

10. R. Hof, S. Browder, and P. Elstrom, "Internet Communities," *Business Week,* 5 May 1997, 40–47. The sites are, respectively, <http://www.planetout.com>, <http://www.momsonline.com>, <http://www.tripod.com>, <http://www.agriculture.com>, and <http://www.gardenescape.com>.

11. "Money Now on Electric Minds."

12. J. Kornblum, "Virtual Community Quizzes Buyer," *CNET News.com,* 7 July 1997, <http://news.cnet.com/news/0-1005-200-320291.html?tag=st.ne.1005-200-320514>.

13. "Money Now on Electric Minds."

14. See, respectively, <http://www.horizons.com.lb/stamps/wwwres.html>, <http://21st-centurymktg.com/soho>, and <http://www.supermancollectors.com>.

15. <http://www.vir-comm.com>.

16. "The Well Background," <http://www.thewell.com/background.html>.

17. J. Schwartz, "Salon to Buy The WELL," *Washington Post,* 8 April 1999, <http://www.washingtonpost.com/wp-srv/business/feed/biztop923570204432.htm>.

18. Research on The WELL is published in H. Rheingold, *The Virtual Community: Homesteading on the Virtual Frontier* (Reading, MA: HarperCollins, 1993); and K. Hafner, "The Epic Saga of The WELL," *Wired Magazine*, 5 May 1997, <http://www.wired.com/wired/archive/5.05/ff_well.html>. As for lamentation, "My Resignation," 1 July 1992, <http://www.jaedworks.com/shoebox/well/resignation.html> contains the resignation letter of a disillusioned member of the Board of The WELL who noted, "The user base and its collective goodwill are the main asset of this business. The Board's actions, its failure to act, its words, and the resultant perceptions over the past year have done much to erode the value of that asset."

Chapter 10

1. The notion of the virtual value chain was introduced by J. Rayport and J. Sviokla, "Exploiting the Virtual Value Chain," *Harvard Business Review* 73, no. 6 (1995): 75–85.

2. R. Gottliebsen, "Coles Myer Plots a Revolution," *BRW* (Australia), 30 March 1998.

3. Much of the details on Seven-Eleven Japan are from the following excellent case study: B. Bensaou, "Seven-Eleven Japan: Managing a Networked Organization," 05/97-4690 (Fontainbleau, France: Insead Euro-Asia Center, 1997). Other sources include: visits to Seven-Eleven stores by the authors; financial statements from <http://japanfinancials.com>; A. Cornell, ". . . And Japan Would . . . If It Only Could," *Australian Financial Review Weekend*, 5–6 February 2000: 23, <http://www.afr.com.au>; <http://quote.yahoo.co.jp>; R. Kunitomo, "Seven-Eleven Is Revolutionalizing Grocery Distribution in Japan," Long Range Planning 30, no. 6 (1997): 877–99.

4. B. Bensaou, "Seven-Eleven Japan: Managing a Networked Organization."

5. Ibid.

6. Ibid.

7. Ibid.

8. P. Leroy, "7dream.com, Futur Amazon Japonais?" *ACTUALITE [E-Commerce]*, 6 January 2000, <http://france.internet.com>.

9. M. Williams, "7-Eleven Japan Embraces E-Commerce," *The Standard*, 6 January 2000, <http://www.thestandard.com/article/display/0,1151,8624,00.html>.

10. These advertisements can be viewed on the company's Web site, www.cisco.com. Much of the material in this section is from B. Roberts,

"E-commerce Poster Child Grows Up," *Datamation,* August 1998, <http://www.datamation.com/ecomm/08ecom.html>; and A. Reinhardt, "Meet Cisco's Mr Internet," *Business Week Online,* 13 September 1999, <http://www.businessweek.com/1999/99_37/b3646001.htm> and <http://www.cisco.com>.

11. A. Reinhardt, "Meet Cisco's Mr Internet."

Chapter 11

1. "America Online and Time Warner will Merge to Create World's Internet-Age Media and Communications Company," press release, 10 January 2000, <http://timewarner.com>.

2. J. LaMartina, "Weathernews to Provide Content to LA Times Syndicate," *MediaCentral,* 2 September 1999, <http://mediacentral.com/channels//newspapers/936311138_492.html>.

3. See, for example, <http://www.wx.com/partnership/wxonmysite.cfm?userid=43>.

4. <http://www.lycos.com/press/juno.html>, 20 July 1998.

5. See <http://www.wx.com/link/wxstickers.cfm>.

6. <http://www.wx.com/legal>.

7. <http://www.morningstar.com>.

8. <http://www.mutualfundwire.com>.

9. Press release, 17 April 2000, <http://www.morningstar.com/press/release>.

10. On September 8, 1999, Quote.com was acquired by Lycos for $78.3 million. The press release, "Lycos Acquires Quote.com for $78.3 million," dated 8 September 1999 contains the information about Quote.com usage. <http:www.lycos.com/press/quote.html>.

11. R. Ganesan, "The Messyware Advantage," *Communications of the ACM* 42, no. 11 (1999): 68–73.

12. See <http://www.springs.com/customerservice/retailstores/index.html> for a full list.

13. See W. F. McFarlan and M. Dailey, "www.springs.com," Case 9-398-091 (Boston: Harvard Business School, 1998), for a more complete description of Springs Industries and its adoption of e-business. Much of the firm's e-business effort has gone into connections with suppliers, which are very important but beyond the scope of this discussion.

14. <http://www.isyndicate.com/company>.

15. See <http://www.isyndicate.com/providers/cplist.html>.

16. <http://www.aboutreuters.com/results/1999-pr/030.asp>, 8 February 2000.

17. Press release, 8 February 2000, <http://www.aboutreuters.com/investormedia/newsreleases>.

18. Ibid.

19. <http://www.aboutreuters.com/products/financial.htm>.

20. <http://www.aboutreuters.com/investormedia/company info/index.asp>, October 2000.

21. FTSE International is one of the world's leading experts in the creation and management of equity indices and is jointly owned by the London Stock Exchange and the *Financial Times*. For information on the joint venture with Microsoft, see "Reuters and Microsoft Announce Joint Internet Initiatives," <http://www.aboutreuters.com/investormedia/news releases/art 22-3-2000 id72.asp>. VentureSource is an Internet-accessible database of comprehensive information on more than ninety-two hundred venture-backed companies, twenty-six thousand financing transactions, and sixty-one thousand key executives in the U.S. venture capital industry. VentureSource is owned by VentureOne (http://www.ventureone.com).

22. See, for example, <http://www.schwab.com>, and the results of any stock quotation requested from that site.

23. See, for example, <http://www.bordersstores.com>.

CHAPTER 12

1. A bivariate correlation analysis between a firm's investment in each of seventy infrastructure services and their use of the eight atomic models was performed using a single-tailed test with a probability of significance (alpha) of 0.1 or smaller, which is suitable for an exploratory analysis. All services listed for each model were statistically significant and positively correlated with the use of the atomic model. Where more than six services are listed they were all statistically significant.

2. eKorp.com was later renamed eKit.com to avoid confusion with eCorp, the online subsidiary of Publishing and Broadcasting, Ltd. The company's Web site address is <http://www.ekit.com>.

3. Bryan Rowe, interview with authors, 20 March 1999.

4. See <http://www.ekno.lonelyplanet.com>.

5. Steve Hibbard, interview with authors, March 2000.

6. Ibid.

7. Ibid.

8. Ibid.

Chapter 13

1. The ten issues were identified via discussions with firms and facilitation of e-business strategies and were influenced by a Giga report, Giga Information Group, Cambridge, MA (www.gigaweb.com), and a Gartner Group presentation. A. Bartels, "Updating Giga's Model for Assessing the Impact of the Internet on an Industry," No. 218192-AB 99, 29 November 1999; "The Serious E-Business Opportunity/Threat Questions," Gartner conference presentation, October 11–15, 1999, Lake Buena Vista, FL, SYM9E-Business 1099Alill, 1999.

2. For more details see B. Roberts, "E-Commerce Poster Child Grows Up," *Datamation,* August 1998, <http://www.datamation.com/ecomm/08ecom.html>.

3. See the writings of G. Hamel and C. K. Prahalad, whose influential work popularized the notion of strategic intent. For example, G. Hamel and C. K. Prahalad, "Strategic Intent," *Harvard Business Review* 67, no. 3 (1989): 63–76.

4. <http://www.racv.com.au> and K. Dery and P. Weill, "Case Vignette of RACV: Information Technology Infrastructure Study" (Melbourne, Australia: Melbourne Business School, 1995).

5. See J. Quinn, J. Baruch, and K. Zien, *Innovation Explosion: Using Intellect and Software to Revolutionize Growth Strategies* (New York: Free Press, 1997), 194–202, for excellent discussions on core competencies.

6. Table 13-2 was compiled by analyzing the correlation matrix of the use of atomic business models in the fifty initiatives studied. Clear conflict represents a strongly significant negative correlation ($\propto < 0.01$). Caution represents a significant negative correlation ($\propto < 0.05$), and clear synergy represents a significant positive correlation between the use of two models ($\propto < 0.05$). Before the analysis we posited four causes for incompatibility: channel, competency, infrastructure, and information conflict. Then we identified significant negative and positive correlations and explained each with one or more of the four causes of incompatibility. In general, the more of the four causes present in the combination of atomic models, the more conflict we found.

7. S. Collett, "Channel Conflicts Push Levi to Halt Web Sales," *Computerworld*, 8 November 1999, 8.

8. The material on channel conflict was developed with Professor Richard Speed, Melbourne Business School, University of Melbourne, Australia, who can be contacted at r.speed@mbs.unimelb.edu.au.

9. The check marks in table 12-5 represent the infrastructure service categories that received the heaviest investment by firms pursuing each atomic business model.

10. For more details on the responsibility of senior management for IT infrastructure see P. Weill and M. Broadbent, *Leveraging the New Infrastructure: How Market Leaders Capitalize on Information Technology* (Boston: Harvard Business School Press, 1998). Of particular relevance is the list of "Top Ten Leadership Principles" for generating business value from IT infrastructure on pp. 244–54.

11. See Weill and Broadbent, *Leveraging the New Infrastructure*, 64.

12. For an excellent discussion of this issue of managing disruptive technologies see C. Christensen, *The Innovator's Dilemma: When New Technologies Cause Great Firms to Fail* (Boston: Harvard Business School Press, 1997).

13. As we said in note 10, our discussion of the responsibilities of senior management for IT ininfrastructure draws on Weill and Broadbent, *Leveraging the New Infrastructure*, particularly the list of "Top Ten Leadership Principles" on pp. 244–54.

14. Weill and Broadbent, *Leveraging the New Infrastructure*, 56.

Appendix

1. For two excellent discussions of IT architecture, see P. G. W. Keen, *Every Manager's Guide to Information Technology*, 2d ed. (Boston: Harvard Business School Press, 1995); and M. J. Earl, *Management Strategies for Information Technology* (London: Prentice Hall, 1989).

Index

ABACUS system, 187, 192–198, 199, 202
AccuWeather, 239
    core competencies of, 35
    critical success factors for, 35
Across Asia on the Cheap (Wheeler and Wheeler), 17
Active Concepts, 65–66
advertising
    customer segments and, 66
    fees, 50
    network model of, 245–246
    permission-based, 66
    in virtual communities, 205
agents
    intelligent, 8, 170–171
aggregators, 164–165
    attention, 218–219
air travel industry, 191–192
    ABACUS, 192–198
allfinanz, 146
Amazon
    business model of, 10, 22–23, 58
    CDs on, 100
    customer base of, 94
    shipping by, 102
    stickiness of, 216

American Airlines, 191–192
American Society of Travel Agents (ASTA), 191
Ameritrade, Quicken and, 46
Amsterdam Internet Exchange (AMS-IX), 189–190, 200
APOLLO system, 191, 192
application service proviser (ASP), 208
applications management, 323
architecture, IT, 79, 330–331, 325
Artesian Innovation, 132, 184–185
asset identification, 310–311
atomic business models, 21–23, 24, 55–59. *See also individual models*
    as building blocks, 56, 258, 318
    combining, 55–56, 58–59
    combining into initiatives, 59–60, 81–83, 257–290
    combining with Lonely Planet case study, 16–20, 278–290
    conflict between, 301–304
    core competencies for, 56–57
    decomposing business models into, 33–35, 258, 318
    definition of, 25, 34–35
    incompatibilities between, 58

atomic business models *(continued)*
  initiatives and, 59–85, 257–290
  lessons from, 259–278
  profitability of, 85
  as pure types, 56, 258, 318
  related to e-business models and initiatives, 59
  synergies between, 58–59, 301–304
  uses of, 56
attention aggregators, 218–219
auctions, 154–161
  building traffic on, 156
  eBay as, 9
  services by, 153
Auctions.com, 158
Australian Stock Exchange, 163
AutoByTel, 246
automotive industry, 188–190
AutoTrader.com, 155–156
AutoWeb, 162

BabyCenter, 98
Bank of Montreal, 16
Bank One
  Retail Group, 23, 67–68
  Wingspan Bank, 45
banks
  personal-banking models, 131
  transaction costs by channel, 14–15
Barnes & Noble, 115–117
Better Business Bureau, 101
big bang implementations, 313
BizRate, 243
Blair, Tony, 138
boo.com, 97, 98
Booz•Allen & Hamilton, 14–15
Boston Consulting Group (BCG), 87, 93, 94, 105
Boston Globe, 96
bots. *See* intelligent search agents

branding, 6
  AccuWeather, 35
  by content providers, 56–57
  for content providers, 254
  in direct-to-customer model, 94, 95
  in full-service provider model, 126, 127
  segmenting by, 307
  for value net integrators, 234
BRL Hardy Limited, 185
Bucksbaum, John, 166–167
building blocks
  atomic models as, 56, 258, 318
  identifying, 300
  investing in, 312–313
BuildOnline, 162–163
bulletin boards, 19–20
business models. *See* atomic business models; *individual models*
  analyzing, 314–315
  characteristics of, 317–318
  combining, 13, 22–23, 24
  combining, effects of, 301–304
  combining place and space in, 12
  customer confusion and, 130–131
  decomposing into atomic, 33–35
  definition of, 25, 34–35
  in dot-coms, 9–10
  in initiative evaluation, 302–304
  ownership in, 50–54
  related to atomic models and initiatives, 59
  schematics, 24, 29–54
  testing, 24
  uses of, 33–35
business-to-business (B2B), 5
  atomic business models and, 57
  auctions, 158
  full-service providers, 117–118
  market makers, 161–162
  revenues in, 8

business-to-consumer (B2C), 5
    atomic business models and, 57
    full-service providers, 115–117
business-to-employees (B2E), 169
Business Week, 215
Butterfield & Butterfield, 155
buyer-driven commerce, 159

call centers, 71
    customer relationships and, 131
    in full-service provider model, 120
    for value net integrators, 232
cannibalization, 96
Cathay Pacific, 192–198
CDNOW, 98–101
channel conflict, 14, 82
    in direct-to-customer model, 96–97
    Lonely Planet and, 287, 289
    managing, 306–307
channels, 297–298
    capacity of, 72–74
    for content providers, 247
    customer segmentation and, 67–70
    definition of, 67
    face-to-face, 69, 71, 72
    in full-service provider model, 120
    information capture by, 73–74
    in initiative evaluation, 305–307
    integrating, 71–72
    interactive voice response (IVR), 14, 69, 72
    intermediaries and, 176
    kiosks, 71, 72
    managing, 67–74, 103–105, 325
    for shared-infrastructure model, 198–199
    strengths and weaknesses of, 69–73

in traditional firms, 68–69
unbiased, 201
for virtual communities, 210
in whole-of-enterprise model, 136–138
Charles Schwab, 69
Chase Manhattan Bank, 133
Chemnet, 117–118
Cisco Systems
    business model of, 11
    configurator, 227–231
    Internet as channel for, 73–74
    as value net integrator, 223, 227–232
Citibank, 131
CityAuction, 156
CitySync, 280–281, 283–284
click-to-talk option, 72
Clinique, 104
Coles Myer, 222–223
Colonial Limited, 146–148
Columbia House, 99
CommerceNet/Nielsen, 65
commissions, 49–50
communication
    network services, 273, 275
    in virtual communities, 205
    for whole-of-enterprise model, 144
communications management, 324
Compaq
    channel conflict of, 15, 96–97
    compared to Dell, 88–89
    intermediaries, 41
comparison shopping–agent intermediary, 8, 10, 170–171. *See also* intelligent search agents
competitive advantage enabled by IT, 319
completeness of service, 152–153
computer reservation systems, 191–192
    ABACUS, 192–198

358 | INDEX

consumer-to-business (C2B) model
    auctions, 159
consumer-to-consumer (C2C), 5
    auctions, 158–159
content, in direct-to-customer model, 109
content providers, 237–256
    branding by, 56–57
    case study, 250–253
    channels for, 247
    Cisco as, 11
    content distribution and, 248
    core competencies for, 255–256
    critical success factors for, 254–255
    customer relationships in, 42
    customer segments for, 247–248
    definition of, 21, 34–35, 238
    financial, 241–243
    future of, 249–250
    information and physical goods and, 248–249
    infrastructure for, 246–247, 278
    Lonely Planet as, 284
    ownership issues for, 240–241
    pricing structure for, 42
    reasons for, 243–246
    Reuters as, 10
    revenue sources for, 254
    schematics for, 240–241
    skills for, 243–244
    strategic objectives for, 253
    value proposition for, 253
convergence, 31–33
core competencies, 24
    for atomic business models, 56–57
    as building blocks, 300
    compared with critical success factors, 102–103
    for content providers, 255–256
    in direct-to-customer model, 109
    in full-service provider model, 127

    identifying, 33
    in initiative evaluation, 302
    in initiatives, 268–272
    for intermediaries, 181–182
    Lonely Planet and, 288
    model conflicts with, 82
    in schematics, 31
    in shared-infrastructure model, 202
    for value net integrators, 234–235
    in virtual communities, 220
    for whole-of-enterprise model, 150
costs
    marketing, 245
    reductions via e-business, 14–15
    in shared-infrastructure model, 190–191
    structure of, 294
    for whole-of-enterprise model, 143–144, 149
COVISINT (COllaboration VISion INTegrity), 188–190
credibility, 126, 254, 255
critical success factors, 24, 33
    compared with core competencies, 102–103
    for content providers, 56–57, 254–255
    in direct-to-customer model, 108
    in full-service provider model, 125–126
    in initiative evaluation, 302
    in initiatives, 268–272
    for intermediaries, 181
    for Jango, 174
    Lonely Planet and, 288
    in shared-infrastructure model, 201
    for value net integrators, 234
    in virtual communities, 219–220
    for whole-of-enterprise model, 149

cross-selling, 39
    CDNOW and, 101
    in full-service provider model, 124
culture, traditional vs. e-business, 13
customer relationships
    in auction model, 156
    channel management and, 71–72
    in content provider model, 240
    in direct-to-customer model, 39,
        40–41, 95–96, 109
    in full-service provider model,
        2–5, 114–115, 124, 126, 128
    initiatives and, 259–264
    for intermediaries, 178
    intermediaries and, 175–176
    intimacy of, 260–261
    leverage of owning, 4
    Lonely Planet and, 288
    ownership of, 51–52, 84–85,
        259–264
    protecting and utilizing,
        315–317
    representing in schematics, 36–37
    in shared-infrastructure model,
        187
    of value net integrators, 222
    in virtual communities, 205, 220
    vs. content, 237–238
    in whole-of-enterprise model, 131
customers
    acquisition costs for, 94
    changing behavior of, 149
    channel conflict and, 104–105
    for content providers, 247–248
    focus on in model analysis, 43
    in full-service provider model, 120
    information about, 53–54
    intermediaries and, 176
    loyalty of, 294
    online base of, 296
    repeat, 94
    segments in initiative evaluation,
        305
    self-service gap, 294–295

    for shared-infrastructure model,
        198–199, 201
    targeting, 59, 61, 64–66, 67–70,
        150
    tracking programs, 65–66
    value proposition and, 67–68
    for virtual communities, 210
    for whole-of-enterprise model,
        150
    in whole-of-enterprise model,
        134, 135–138
customization, 261, 296–297

Dahlsen, Geoff, 178
DaimlerChrysler, 188–189
data management, 324
data mapping, 143–144
data ownership, 52–53, 260
    in atomic models, 84–85, 259,
        260, 261, 262–264
    in content provider model,
        240–241
    in direct-to-customer model,
        95–96
    in full-service provider model, 3,
        124, 126, 128
    in initiatives, 261
    for intermediaries, 177
    protecting and utilizing, 315–317
    in virtual communities, 220
    for whole-of-enterprise model,
        143–144
Data Transmission Network
        Corporation
    Weather Services division, 239,
        244
data warehousing
    customer relationships and, 71
    in full-service provider model,
        118–119
    for value net integrators, 232
Datek, 46
decision costs, 160

delivery problems, 101–103
Dell Computer Corporation, 10–11
    customer segmentation by, 66
    as direct-to-customer business, 40–41, 88–89
demand, intermediaries and forecasting, 41
DIAGEO. *See* United Distillers & Vintners
digital economy, 6
digitally describe or deliver, 293–294
direct-to-customer model, 87–109
    AccuWeather as, 35
    benefits of, 93
    business types for, 92–93
    case study, 98–101
    channel management in, 103–105
    content providers and, 243, 244–245
    core competencies for, 109
    critical success factors for, 108
    definition of, 21
    Dell as, 10–11, 40–41
    E*TRADE, 9
    examples of successful, 88–92
    flows in 39–41
    Hilton.com, 32–33
    information type in, 53–54
    infrastructure for, 106, 273, 275
    logistics challenges in, 101–103
    Lonely Planet as, 286
    profitability of, 93–95, 107, 263
    revenue sources in, 107–108
    schematic for, 95–101
    strategic objective in, 107
    value proposition in, 107
    with virtual communities, 58
disintermediating, 39, 151. *See also* intermediaries
distribution channel conflicts, 96–97
domains
    in full-service provider model, 120–121
    leadership in, 125–126

Donnelly Company, 191
dot-coms
    acquiring, 318–319
    growth in, 9–10
    marketing expenditures of, 245
    selling third-party products, 93, 97
DoubleClick, 245–246
dream-7.com, 226
Drexler, Millard S., 91
Durand Communications, Inc., 215–216
dynamic pricing, 295

eBay, 9, 154–161
    Business Exchange, 155–156
    business model, 154–155, 156–157
    Feedback Forum, 155
    Half.com and, 161
    as intermediary, 151
    profitability of, 154
    services of, 155–156
    stickiness of, 181
    virtual community of, 157
e-business
    characteristics of second wave, 12–13
    convergence in, 31–33
    definition of, 5–6
    effects of, 6, 23–24
    growth in, 7, 9–10
    integration with traditional commerce, 6
    migration frameworks to, 16–20
    motives for moving to, 7–13
    pioneers in, 10–12
    size of economy in, 7–9
    traditional business struggles with, 13–16
e-business implementations, definition of, 26

Eck, Denis, 222–223
Edmunds.com, 203–214
Egghead, 103, 105
eKorp.com, 279–280
Electric Minds, 215–216
electronic crossing networks (ECNs), 164
electronic malls, 165–167
electronic markets, 153, 161–164
enforcement costs, 160
enterprise resource planning systems (ERPs), 15, 140, 273
Ernie, 11, 296
Ernst & Young, 11
e-STEEL, 161–162
Estée Lauder, 104
E-Stock Club proposal, 60–64
E*TRADE, 9
Etzioni, Oren, 173
evenbetter.com, 164
Excite
    iMALL and, 166
    Jango and, 172–174
    walled garden approach, 168–169
extranets, 106

failure rates
    in direct-to-customer model, 93
Federal Express, 102
fees. *See also* revenue sources
    in direct-to-customer model, 95–96
    transaction ownership and, 4
financial content, 241–243
firm of interest, definition of, 36
FirstGov, 145
Fishing.com, 205, 207
    governance of, 211–212
flows, representing in schematics, 39
Ford Motor Company, 132–133, 145–146
    COVISINT and, 188, 189

Forrester Research, 93, 102
Foster's Brewing Group, Ltd., 185
FreeMarkets, 158, 159
fulfillment services, 152
full-service provider model, 111–128
    B2B, 117–118
    B2C, 115–117
    case study, 121–123
    channels in, 120
    core competencies in, 127
    critical success factors in, 125–126
    customer relationships in, 2–5, 51–52
    customer segments in, 120
    data ownership in, 52–53
    definition of, 21, 111–112
    domains for, 120–121
    e-brokerage, 43–46
    examples of, 45
    information types in, 54
    infrastructure for, 118–120, 275
    intimacy of, 260
    ownership issues in, 128
    profitability of, 263–264
    Prudential Advisor as, 112–113
    revenue sources in, 49–51, 125
    schematic of, 113–115
    strategic objective in, 124–125
    transaction ownership in, 52–53
    value proposition in, 124–125
Funnel Web, 65–66
futures exchanges, 163

Gallagher, Ron, 281–282
Gap.com, 90–92
Gartner Group, 170
Gates, Bill, 135
Gateway, 41
gender, buying patterns online by, 65
General Electric (GE), 162
General Growth Properties (GGP), 166

General Motors, 188, 189
  OnStar, 300
General Reinsurance Corporation, 15–16
geographical reach, 295
GE Supply Company, 121–123
government business model, 22, 129–150
  United Kingdom, 129, 138
  Victoria, Australia, 135–138, 142, 144

Half.com, 160–161
Harkness, Jim, 84
Harris Technologies, 14
Harvey Norman, 14, 96–97
Hibbard, Steve, 20, 279, 281, 282–283
Hilton.com, 32–33
hypertext markup language (HTML), 7

IBM, 188
ICI, 117
IDC, 7–8
iMALL, 165–166
incentive systems, 144
i-netmall, 166
influence, 4, 95–96, 262
information
  in direct-to-customer model, 95–96
  fees for, 49
  integration of, 76
  model conflicts with, 82
  type of in different models, 53–54
  for whole-of-enterprise model, 150
information-reporting systems, 187
information systems
  planning, 208, 329

  in whole-of-enterprise model, 133–134
infrastructure, 8–9, 15
  agency-specific, 142
  areas of, 79
  for business processes, 77
  categories of, 323–326
  centralized management of, 120, 140
  as competitive advantage, 77
  for content providers, 246–247
  convergence and, 31–32
  as critical success factor, 24–25
  department, 142
  determining required, 317
  in direct-to-customer model, 106
  elements of, 75, 76
  in full-service provider model, 118–120, 127
  human, 76
  initiative evaluation and, 307–309
  initiative implementation time and, 77
  in initiatives, 59, 61, 63, 64, 74–81, 273–278
  for intermediaries, 177
  internal vs. public, 75
  IT portfolios, 74–75
  measures for, 308
  model conflicts caused by, 82
  services, 77–78, 79–81, 327–332
  shared, 76
  for shared-infrastructure model, 198
  study on, 79–81, 321–332
  for value net integrators, 232
  for virtual communities, 208–210
  for whole-of-enterprise model, 139–143
initiatives, 24
  atomic models and, 56–85
  channels in, 59, 60, 67–74

choosing, 291–320
combining atomic models into, 257–290
compared to atomic and e-business models, 59
customer relationships in, 259–264
customer segments in, 59, 64–66
data ownership in, 261
decomposition of, 56–57, 258
definition of, 25–26
evaluating viability of, 21–23, 302–309
identifying building blocks for, 25
implementation time for, 77
infrastructure capability in, 59, 64, 74–81
leadership and, 309–319
model combinations in, 59–60, 81–83
portfolio of, 74–75, 301, 311–312
sample, 60–64
transaction ownership in, 261
use of business models in, 33–35
viability of, 64, 83
volatility of, 312
insight, 4, 262
Intel, 188
intelligent search agents, 8, 170–171
interactive voice response (IVR), 6, 69, 72
intermediaries, 151–182
    aggregators, 164–165
    auctions, 154–161
    benefits of, 159–160
    case study, 172–174
    channel conflict and, 104–105
    channels for, 176
    comparison of, 152–169
    completeness of service of, 152–153
    content providers as, 239–241
    core competencies for, 181–182
    critical success factors for, 181
    customer segments for, 176
    definition of, 21
    demand forecast and, 41
    electronic malls, 165–167
    future of, 179–180
    impact of, 178–179
    infrastructure for, 177, 276
    intelligent agents, 170–171
    market makers, 161–164
    portals, 167–170
    power of, 297–298
    price transparency, 178
    profitability of, 264
    revenues from, 8
    revenue sources for, 180
    schematics for, 175–176
    strategic objective of, 180
    value proposition for, 180
    vortals, 45–46
Internet
    access to, 7
    commerce estimates, 7–8
    convergence and, 32
    digitized profiling with, 73–74
    marketing costs, 101
    media delivery via, 89–90
    as nonproprietary network, 5–6
    number of customers buying on, 87
    revenues on, 105
    user profile, 65
interoperability, 201
Intuit, 46
InvestmentWires community, 242
iship.com, 164
iSyndicate, 249–250
IT infrastructure. *See* infrastructure
IT management, 324
IT portfolios, 74–75
iVillage, 10, 209–210
    subcommunities, 211
    terms of service, 212

Jango, 151, 172–174
Japan Airlines Company, Ltd. (JAL), 193
Juno Online Services, 239

kiosks, 71, 72
Kiwi Co-Operative Dairies, 117–118
Knowledge Bank, 281–282, 284, 312–313. *See also* Lonely Planet
knowledge economy, 6
knowledge management, 177, 296, 329

Land's End, 106
leadership
    for e-business, 309–310
    traditional vs. e-business, 13
    for whole-of-enterprise model, 143, 150
Leucke, Bruce, 23, 67
leverage, 4, 95–96, 262
Levin, Gerald, 237–238
Levi Strauss & Co., 104, 306
liability identification for e-businesses, 310–311
life events, in whole-of-enterprise model, 136–137, 149
Lion Nathan, 184, 186
List (Liquor Industry Services Technology), 184–185
local area networks, 208
Lonely Planet, 16–20, 278–290
    business model, 22
    eKorp and, 279–280
    Knowledge Bank, 281–282, 312–313
    revenues, 19
    schematic, 283–284
    Thorn Tree virtual community, 19–20
loyalty, customer, 294
Lycos, 239–240

Maher, Peter, 184, 185
Maidenform, 104–105
make-to-order manufacturing, 89
Mallibu.com, 166–167
management
    conflict, 201
    for intermediaries, 177
    panaceas, 29
    for shared-infrastructure model, 201, 202
    tools, 30
    for value net integrators, 234
    in whole-of-enterprise model, 150
Management Review, 98
Manheim Auctions, 158
MapQuest.com, 244
marketing costs, 94
market makers, 161–164
market penetration, 91–92
marketspace, 6, 13
Maxi project, 138
maxmiles.com, 164
McCoy, John, 67
members
    gaining virtual community, 214–215
    privileges of, 207
Merrill Lynch
    information types in, 53–54
    subscription fees, 49
middleware, 71, 327
    for value net integrators, 232
    in whole-of-enterprise model, 134
Mintzberg, Henry, 56
Morgan Stanley Dean Witter, 46
Morningstar, 241–243
The Motley Fool, 205, 206, 207
    features, 208
    governance of, 213–214
    subcommunities, 211
Motorola, 188
MP3, 100, 250, 294
Mr. Cybermall, 166

INDEX | 365

music industry, 250, 294
MutualFundWire.com, 242
MySimon, 171

Napster, 294
NASDAQ, 163
Nasser, Jac, 188–189
National Retail Federation (NRF), 91
Neo, Boon Siong, 193
Netbot, Inc., 173
network effect, 207
network model of advertising, 245–246
newspapers, profitability of online, 16
New York Times Magazine, 19
nonprofit alliances, 268
Northern Light, 115
N2K, 99

one-stop shopping, 11–12
OnStar, 300
opportunity for e-business, 292–298, 301, 310–311
organizational structure, 56
    in schematics, 30
    for whole-of-enterprise model, 150
Organization for Economic Co-operation and Development (OECD), 7
Orica, 117
Orlando Wyndham Group Pty. Ltd., 185
outsourcing
    infrastructure, 80–81, 308–309
    shipping, 102

Parent Soup, 205, 206, 207, 208
    privacy policy, 209–210
    subcommunities, 211

performance ratings content, 242–243
permission-based advertising, 66
place-based firms, 92–93, 309–310
    with space outlets, 105
Planet Out Corporation, 209–210
PolymerSite, 162
portals, 167–170
    B2E commerce, 169
    content providers and, 248
    customer relationship ownership in, 53
    customer relationships in, 52
    customization of, 170
    electronic malls and, 167
    information types in, 54
    intranet, 169
    revenue sources for, 168
    services by, 153
    as walled gardens, 168–169
    Yahoo! as, 9, 46–47
Preview Travel, 10
Priceline, 159
pricing, dynamic, 295
privacy
    in content provider model, 241
    for value net integrators, 232
    in virtual communities, 209–210
processes
    in direct-to-customer model, 109
    IT for, 77
    in schematics, 30–31
product delivery, digital, 293–294
products, segmenting by, 307
profitability
    of atomic models, 85, 263–264
    of direct-to-customer model, 93–95
    in full-service model, 114
    ownership issues and, 262–264
Prudential Insurance Company of America, 118–119
Prudential Advisor, 45, 112–114, 115

publishing
  Lonely Planet, 17–20, 278–290
  model incompatibilities in, 58

Qantas, 192
Quicken
  as one-stop shop, 11–12
  vortals, 45–46
Quote.com, 244

RACV, 299–300
Raisbeck, Peter, 321
RealJukebox, 90
RealNetworks.com, 89–90, 91–92, 108
RealPlayer, 89–90
RealSystem, 90
Red Herring, 151
reengineering, 149
relationship management, 127
relationships, representing in schematics, 36–37, 39. *See also* customer relationships
RemarQ Communities, 58
research and development, IT, 79, 325, 332
reservation services, 32–33, 191–198
retailers, differentiating, 243
Reuters, 10, 250–253
revenue sources, 24, 49–51
  for content providers, 245, 254
  in direct-to-customer model, 107–108
  in full-service provider model, 115, 125
  in initiative evaluation, 302
  for intelligent agents, 171
  for intermediaries, 168, 180
  Lonely Planet and, 289
  in model analysis, 43
  in shared-infrastructure model, 200
  for value net integrators, 233
  for virtual communities, 205–206
  in virtual communities, 219
  for whole-of-enterprise model, 148–149
ReverseAuction, 158
Rheingold, Howard, 214, 215–216
roadside services, 299–300
RoboBid, 158

SABRE system, 191–192, 194
schematics, 26, 29–54
  analyzing, 315
  business strategy in, 30
  content provider, 240–241
  core competencies in, 31
  direct-to-customer model, 95–101
  elements in, 36–42
  full-service model, 113–115
  for intermediaries, 175–176
  Lonely Planet, 283–284
  merging, 259
  organizational structure in, 30
  processes in, 30–31
  Seven-Eleven Japan, 225
  shared-infrastructure model, 186–187
  stockbroking, 42–54
  uses of, 36
  value chain in, 31
  value net integrators, 222
  virtual community, 204–205
  whole-of-enterprise model, 134–135
search costs, 160, 171
search engines, 167
search for extraterrestrial intelligence (SETI), 12
search services, 152
security, 324–325
self-service gap, 294–295

services
　fees for, 49–50, 262
　of intermediaries, 152–153
　for whole-of-enterprise model, 140, 142
SETI (search for extraterrestrial intelligence), 12
Seven-Eleven, 223–226, 231
Seven-Eleven Japan, 223–226, 231
shared infrastructure model, 183–202
　Artesian Innovation as, 184–185, 198–199
　in the auto industry, 188–190
　case study, 192–198
　channels for, 198–199
　core competencies for, 202
　critical success factors in, 201
　customer relationship in, 187
　customer segments for, 198–199
　definition of, 21
　infrastructure for, 198, 276–277
　market makers and, 162
　motivations for, 190–192
　revenue sources in, 200
　schematic for, 186–187
　strategic objectives in, 200, 264, 268
shopping agents
　electronic malls and, 167
　Jango, 172–174
　services by, 153
shopping carts, abandoned, 94–95
Singapore Airlines, 192–198
single point of contact, 131. *See also* whole-of-enterprise model
　shared-infrastructure model and, 199
Singleton, John, 19
skills shortages in e-business, 15, 77–78
Small Business Administration, Office of Advocacy, 93
Smith, John F., Jr., 188

Sold.com.au, 158
Sotheby's, 158
Southcorp, 132, 184, 186
South-East Asia on a Shoestring (Wheeler and Wheeler), 17
space-based firms, 92
Springs Industries, Inc., 249
standards, IT, 325
stickiness, 37, 181, 216
stockbroking
　e-business models for, 42–54
　intermediaries, 45–47
　revenue sources in, 49
　viability of, 47–48
Stockdale, The Honourable Alan, 135
stock exchanges, 190–191
　as market makers, 163–164
stock market valuations, 9–10, 12, 230–231, 291
strategic experiments, 24, 313–314
strategic intent, 298–301
strategic objectives, 24
　for content providers, 253
　in direct-to-customer model, 107
　in full-service provider model, 124–125
　in initiative evaluation, 302
　initiatives and, 264–268
　for intermediaries, 180
　in shared-infrastructure model, 200
　for value net integrators, 233
　in virtual communities, 218–219
　for whole-of-enterprise model, 148
strategic partnerships
　direct-to-customer model and, 109
　intermediaries and, 178–179
strategy, in schematics, 30
The Structuring of Organizations (Mintzberg), 56
surveillance costs, 160, 161

surveillance services, 152
Suzuki, Toshifumi, 223, 224
switching costs, 294
synergy, 23
    in atomic model combinations, 58–59
    in initiative evaluation, 302

Taco Bell, 204
Tahai Airlines, 192
Target Club Wedd, 103–104
TCP/IP, 7
technical convergence, 31–32
technology, 76. *See also* infrastructure
    identifying and testing, 120
    valuing, 77–78
terminology, 25–26
third-party providers
    competition with internal units and, 118
    in full-service provider model, 113, 114–115, 126
Thomas Publishing, 162
Thorn Tree virtual community, 19–20. *See also* Lonely Planet
threats from e-business, 292–298, 301, 310–311
TIAA-CREF, 84
Time Warner, 237–238
TPN Register, 162, 179
training, for use of IT, 208, 326, 332
transaction fees, 49
    in full-service provider model, 124
    for intermediaries, 160
    portals, 169
transaction ownership, 52–53, 259, 260, 261–264
    in atomic models, 84–85
    in auction model, 156–157
    in content provider model, 240–241
    in direct to customer model, 95–96
    fees from, 4
    in full-service provider model, 3, 128
    in initiatives, 261–262
    protecting and utilizing, 315–317
    in virtual communities, 207
Travel & Leisure, 19
travel guides, 17–20
trust, 6, 126
24/7 Media, 66

United Airlines, 191
United Distillers & Vintners (DIAGEO), 184, 186
United Kingdom, 138–139
upselling, 39
urgency to migrate to e-business, 297–298, 311
URLs, 32
used goods markets, 179

value chain
    e-business impact on, 111
    in full-service model, 111
    intermediaries in, 151
    in schematics, 31
    in value net integrators, 221, 222–231
value creation, by aggregators, 164–165
value net integrators, 221–235
    case study, 223–231
    Cisco as, 11
    core competencies for, 234–235
    critical success factors for, 234
    definition of, 22
    as evolved business model, 231–232
    infrastructure for, 232, 277
    ownership in, 235

revenue sources for, 233
schematics for, 222
strategic objectives for, 233
value chain coordination and, 222–231
value proposition for, 233
value proposition
for content providers, 253
customer segment and, 67–70
for customer segments, 65
at Dell, 89
in direct-to-customer model, 107
in full-service provider model, 124–125
for intermediaries, 180
in model analysis, 43
for value net integrators, 233
in virtual communities, 218–219
for whole-of-enterprise model, 148
VerticalNet, 170
Victoria, Australia, 135–138, 142, 144
virtual communities, 203–220
case study, 217–218
channels for, 210
combined with direct-to-customer model, 58
competition and, 203
core competencies for, 220
critical success factors for, 219–220
customer relationships in, 205
customer segments in, 211
definition of, 22
future of, 217
gaining members in, 214–215
governance of, 211–214
infrastructure for, 208–210, 277
iVillage as, 10
links in, 206–207
Lonely Planet as, 284, 286, 287
membership privileges in, 207
ownership issues in, 207, 220

privacy and, 209–210
profitability of, 264
revenue sources for, 205–206, 219
schematic for, 204–205
strategic objectives in, 218–219
sustainability of, 215–216
Thorn Tree virtual community, 19–20
value proposition in, 218–219
variations in, 216
vortals, 169–170. *See also* portals
customer relationship ownership in, 53
customer relationships in, 52
definition of, 45–46
future of, 170
information types in, 54
transaction ownership in, 53

walled gardens, 168–169
weather as content, 238–241
Weathernews Incorporated (WNI), 238–239, 244
Weather Services International, 239, 241, 244
Welch, Jack, 121–123
The Well, 217–218
Wells Fargo Bank, 155
Wheeler, Maureen, 17
Wheeler, Tony, 17, 19
whole-of-enterprise model, 129–150
case study, 146–148
challenges in, 143–144
communication in, 135, 144
core competencies for, 150
critical success factors in, 149
definition of, 22
front-page, 132–133, 135, 148
future of, 144–146
in government, 135–139, 149
infrastructure for, 139–143, 275–276

whole-of-enterprise model
(continued)
  integrated, 133–134, 135, 146, 148
  profitability of, 264
  revenue sources in, 148–149
  schematic of, 134–135
  strategic objectives in, 148
  value proposition, 148
Wine Planet, 185
Winerobot, 171, 178
Wingspan Bank, 133
wireless applications protocol (WAP), 176
Women's Network, 212
women's networks, 10
workflow, 32–33, 273

workstation networks, 177
World Wide Web, 7, 9. *See also* Internet

Yahoo!
  Auctions, 168
  B2B Market place, 169
  CDNOW and, 99
  as portal intermediary, 9, 46–47, 151
  revenue sources, 50
  usage statistics, 167–168
  Weathernews Incorporated (WNI) and, 238–239
Yang, Jerry, 167

About the Authors

PETER WEILL is the Director of the Center for Information Systems Research (CISR) and Senior Research Scientist at the MIT Sloan School. Before joining MIT, Peter was Foundation Chaired Professor of Management and the Director of the Centre for Management of Information Technology (CMIT) at the Melbourne Business School, University of Melbourne. Peter regularly advises corporations and governments on issues of IT investment, e-business models, and aligning the IT portfolio to business strategy. His research focuses on the business value of information technology in organizations. He has published widely including award-winning books, journal articles, and case studies. Peter and Marianne Broadbent are coauthors of *Leveraging the New Infrastructure: How Market Leaders Capitalize on Information Technology,* published by Harvard Business School Press in 1998 and now in its fourth printing.

MICHAEL R. VITALE is the Dean and Director of the Australian Graduate School of Management (AGSM) in Sydney. Before becoming Dean, Michael was a Professor at the Melbourne Business School and the Foundation Professor of Information Systems and Head of the Department of Information

Systems at the University of Melbourne. Michael's professional career in America includes consulting (Ernst & Young), industry (Prudential Insurance Company of America), and academia (Harvard Business School and Skidmore College). Michael is the coauthor, with Harvard Business School professors James Cash, Warren McFarlan, and James McKenney, of *Corporate Information Systems Management: Text and Cases,* published by Irwin (1988). While at Harvard Business School he wrote more than fifty case studies exploring the relationship between information systems and corporate strategy.